Leveraging Brands in Sport Business

This edited text compiles advanced material relating to strategy and marketing in the field of sports business. Featuring contributions from experts across the sports business field, the book approaches strategy from the standpoint of managing and marketing a brand. With in Tel: C d current-day examples highlighting practices and issues, as well as 'real-world video cases, this book is ideal for marketing students and sports business practitioners looking to gain strategic insights into the industry.

Dr. Mark P. Pritchard serves as Professor of Marketing in the College of Business at Central Washington University. Having earned his Ph.D. from the University of Oregon, Dr. Pritchard was the founding Director of the Northwest Center for Sport Business (NWCSB) and has held faculty appointments in marketing in Canada, Australia, Singapore, France, and the United States. His research concentrates on issues in services marketing and specializes in the area of brand loyalty and repeat purchase behavior in the sport and tourism industries. Recent research and instructional interests have focused on the role of personal ethics and social responsibility in shaping a winning brand team.

Dr. Jeffrey L. Stinson is Chair of the Department of Management and Director of the Northwest Center for Sport Business (NWCSB) at Central Washington University. With a Ph.D. in Marketing from the University of Oregon, Dr. Stinson has primarily researched the influence of intercollegiate athletics on athletic and academic fundraising to colleges and universities. Other research interests include donor decision making, nonprofit fundraising, and social marketing in sport.

Leveraging Brands in Sport Business

Edited by
Mark P. Pritchard &
Jeffrey L. Stinson

Routledge
Taylor & Francis Group

NEW YORK AND LONDON

Please visit the companion eResource at
www.routledge.com/textbooks/9780415534857

First published 2014
by Routledge
711 Third Avenue, New York, NY 10017

Simultaneously published in the UK
by Routledge
2 Park Square, Milton Park, Abingdon, Oxon OX14 4RN

Routledge is an imprint of the Taylor & Francis Group, an informa business

Library of Congress Cataloging-in-Publication Data

Leveraging brand in sport business / edited by Mark Pritchard & Jeffrey L. Stinson.
    pages cm
  Includes bibliographical references and index.
  1. Sports—Marketing.   I. Pritchard, Mark.
GV716.L48 2013
796.06'88—dc23   2013006886

ISBN: 978-0-415-53484-0 (hbk)
ISBN: 978-0-415-53485-7 (pbk)
ISBN: 978-0-203-10899-4 (ebk)

Typeset in Minion
by Apex CoVantage, LLC

Contents

Part III: Topical Extensions

Part IV: Sport Business Case presentations (online)

Acknowledgement

In memory of those who led us to believe that we too could run with endurance the race set before us. . . .

Figure A.1 Australian Olympic Hockey Team, Rome 1960

BACK ROW: R. Evans, D. Spackman, L. Hailey, E. Pierce, **P. Pritchard**, J. Pierce, J. McBryde, M. Crossman, G. Wood.

FRONT ROW: E. Bill, G. Pierce, M. Craig, C. Morley, **K. Carton**, D. Currie, B. Malcolm.

Northwest Center for Sport Business (NWCSB) Advisory Council

The Sport Business Advisory Council is composed of industry executives from the private, public, and nonprofit sectors, who provide advice, guidance, and expertise for the continued development of the center.

The efforts behind this book and the annual conferences that contributed to the case materials resulted from the generous support and involvement of the NWCSB Advisory Board members listed below:

Board Members

Figure A.2
Copyright Central Washington University. Used with permission.

- Aaron Artman, President, Tacoma Rainiers
- Jack Bishop, Athletic Director, Central Washington U.
- Bill Chapin, Vice-President, Seattle Sounders/Seahawks
- Kevin Martinez, Vice President, Seattle Mariners
- Darrell Rutter, President, The Management Group
- Jon Spoelstra, Former President, Mandalay Entertainment, Professional Teams
- Liz Wilson, Sales Director, Brooks Running
- K. L. Wombacher, General Manager, Yakima Bears

Foreword by Jon Spoelstra

(Author of *Marketing Outrageously, Ice to Eskimos, and former* President of Mandalay Sport Entertainment's Pro Teams Division, President of the New Jersey Nets, and General Manager for the Portland Trail Blazers.)

Branding Begins and Ends at the Same Place

If you looked on Amazon.com right now for a book on *branding*, you could choose among 4,518 books. If you wait a month, there might be 100 more. I've read six or seven, so I only have 4,512 to go.

To me, the sole purpose of branding is to differentiate your product or company from its competitors. However, many so-called branding efforts cost a fortune. That sorta leaves many folks standing still.

Now don't get me wrong. I think the branding that Nike has done is terrific and fun. Nike has taken gym shoes, spent a few billion dollars in edgy ads, and turned its shoes and clothing into *lifestyle* products.

I think the branding that Budweiser does is fantastic. Think of how much fun it would be to produce the nonsensical thirty-second commercials for Bud Light! Or a cool commercial featuring the Clydesdales tromping through snow. These commercials helped Budweiser achieve a market share of over 50%! So, long live branding.

What about the rest of us who don't have a few extra billion (or millions or even thousands) to spend on branding? What about local sport teams that don't have the budgets that a national or even a global company has?

Well, I've got two laws on branding for folks that don't have billions in an ad budget. Here they are:

1. **Branding begins and ends with your current customer.** *Begins* and *ends* are the operative words. For the moment, forget about your *prospective* customers. For now, *only* think of your current customers. How can your branding sink into their brains?
2. **Get your current customers to say nice things about you.** When I was president of Mandalay Baseball Properties, we would have an annual retreat with each of our teams just thinking about our current customers.

I wrote a book on the cool and unusual things we did on branding sport teams. It's called *Marketing Outrageously Redux*. But, I always snap to attention when I see how some other non-sport company does some unique branding.

How about garbage collection? If you were in that business, how in the world would you brand *garbage*?

Let's look at a garbage company in Oregon. This garbage company's name is Western Oregon Waste. Or W.O.W. That's right, WOW. That's what they have plastered on the sides of their garbage trucks—WOW.

If you lived in WOW's marketing area, the company would collect your garbage every week. If you went to its website, www.westernoregonwaste.com, you could do the traditional things such as paying your bill. But there's also a downloadable comic book that in a clear and fun way describes all of WOW's services. (If you're currently a customer, you received the WOW comic book with one of your billings.)

Here are just a few of the possibilities you'll find in the comic book:

- Order extra garbage pick-up.
- Clean up your garage and you don't lift a finger.
- Have old appliances picked up.
- Have hazardous wastes picked up and disposed of.
- Spread bark dust where you want it on your lawn.

Heck, if you lived in WOW's marketing area and paged through their comic book, you'd see about seven to ten new ways of spending your money with them.

So, WOW is not Nike, it's not McDonald's, it's not a baseball team, *it's a garbage company*. Let's see how they spent their so-called branding budget.

1. **Painted trucks**. They painted WOW and Western Oregon Waste on the sides of their trucks. Wouldn't they have painted their trucks anyway? They just made their trucks *interesting*. WOW!
2. **Website**. They would have had a website anyway, right? They just made it entertaining with their comic book motif. WOW!
3. **Comic books**. They would have done some type of brochure about their services, right? Do you cringe at the thought of a traditional brochure about garbage? It would have been uninteresting, boring, and unread. As a comic book, however, their brochure was actually *fun* to read. It covered everything you would ever need to know about your garbage, and you enjoyed the time you spent becoming so knowledgeable. WOW!

Western Oregon Waste is a fun company. And, they're a garbage company. Does that branding and having nice things said about WOW make any difference? Well, about 10% of a typical waste management company's revenue comes from extra services. At WOW it's twice that amount and growing. That extra 10% is a huge plus, particularly in a bad economy.

How did W.O.W. do in relation to my two laws of branding?

1. **Did W.O.W.'s branding begin and end with their current customer?** Yep, their branding was *all* current customers and it doubled the highly profitable extra services products.
2. **Did W.O.W.'s branding get their current customers to say nice things about them?** If we did some shoe-leather research and walked around McMinnville, Astoria, or Seaside, Oregon, and asked folks about WOW, you'd hear them talk glowingly about their garbage company. Wow.

Branding is essential to the success of any company. If a company has billions of branding dollars, they should spend them as wisely as Nike has. Unfortunately, few companies have the wherewithal to do that. Companies with few branding dollars should spend them just as wisely as W.O.W. has and get their own customers to become *fans* and willing advocates for them.

Part I

Foundations in Sport Business

1

Brand Equity

Management and Measurement in Sport

Jay Gladden
Indiana University Purdue University, Indianapolis

Abstract: The management of sport brands has received significant attention from both industry and the academe over the past 20 years. This chapter provides an overview of branding in the sport industry, including a summary of research on the brand equity development process. This circular process stipulates that antecedents, such as brand attributes, benefits, and attitudes, result in brand equity. Brand equity results in brand loyalty, which provides many benefits to sport brands, such as the ability to charge price premiums and the development of a consistent base of repeat purchasers. Brand equity also helps prevent drastic revenue decreases during the inevitable swings of performance that occur in sport. This chapter offers suggestions on a model for measuring brand equity. This model suggests both quantitative and qualitative methods for assessing various elements of a company's brand-building effort.

Keywords: brand, brand equity, brand loyalty, brand management, brand measurement, sport brands

Introduction

The last 20 years have seen sport-oriented businesses increase their focus on managing brands to increase brand equity. Increasingly, corporations sponsoring sport and events use brand-building and image transfer as justifications for their financial investments. Meanwhile, sport organizations see the strong brand resulting in loyal fans, which protects against the intensified competition for the consumer's leisure dollar. Conversations around branding in sport largely began with a focus on team logos, marks, nicknames, and colors in the early 1990s, but have more recently evolved into a deeper focus on the more strategic elements of brand-building such as customer loyalty, brand image, customer relationship management, and fan development.

Industry provides many examples of this evolution in thinking. For example, SME, a leading brand consultant for sport teams, has evolved significantly during its 20 years of existence. In the 1990s, SME created its corporate brand by providing expertise around logo development and redesign, developing more contemporary marks and color schemes guided by stakeholder insights. The goal of these efforts was to drive popularity for the marks and even the team, resulting in merchandise sales. As the understanding of branding has become more sophisticated, SME evolved into a company that employs a process focused on broadly understanding each brand they serve as a means of providing comprehensive brand-building consulting services.[1]

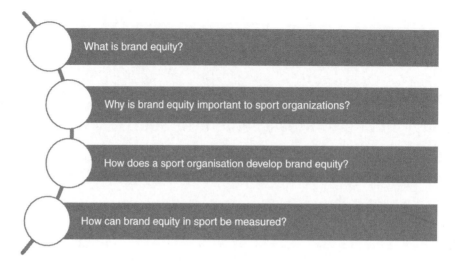

Figure 1.1 Overview of Chapter 1

Logo redesign and development remains a piece of SME's services today, but they are also now heavily involved in defining brand values, and understanding and managing brand image.

As the complexity and depth of approaches have increased over time, an understanding has emerged of what constitutes brand equity, how it is developed, and how it can be measured in the sport setting. One purpose of this chapter is to summarize the understanding of brand equity in sport and provide some actionable frameworks for brand-building activities. Another purpose is to provide tools that can assist in assessing and measuring brand equity so that it can be managed over time. Measurement efforts to date are summarized, followed by a prescription for a comprehensive brand equity measurement program. Figure 1.1 highlights the focus and flow of the chapter.

This chapter focuses on brand management efforts for a sport property (team, league, facility, event, athlete, etc.). It does not focus on the development of brand equity for the sport sponsor for two reasons. First, our existing knowledge on brand equity in sport is confined to two areas: (a) brand equity development by sport properties and (b) brand image matching measurement as it relates to sponsorship. Because there are prescriptions readily available to measure the brand equity of non-sport brands, this chapter focuses on summarizing the existing understanding of brand equity development by sport properties as it can be used to measure and manage brand equity. Second, and perhaps more importantly, when corporations align with a sport property, they are often seeking to modify or reinforce certain brand image–based elements the property possesses. This chapter provides an understanding of the brand image of a sport property that allows for greater sophistication on the part of sponsors. If the sport brand image is understood, then it stands to reason that the image benefits which the corporation seeks to receive will also be understood, and the degree to which matching or enhancement occurs for the corporate sponsor can be measured.

What Is Brand Equity?

Two of the more significant advances to the thinking around brand equity were offered by David Aaker in his book *Managing Brand Equity: Capitalizing on the Value of a Brand Name*[2] and by Kevin Keller, in his 1993 *Journal of Marketing* article entitled "Conceptualizing, Measuring, and Managing Customer-Based Brand Equity."[3] Aaker's definition of brand equity as "a set of brand assets and liabilities linked to a brand, its name and symbol, that add to or subtract from the value provided by a product or service to a firm and/or that firm's customers"[4] provides a useful way of thinking about brand equity. This perspective suggests branding or brand management can be thought of as understanding and coordinating the portfolio of positive *and negative* elements attached to an outsider's view of the brand. Just as a professional tennis event can develop positive associations based on Roger Federer or Maria Sharapova participating, so too can the tournament develop negative associations if none of the top players choose to participate. Aaker suggested that there were five categories of these assets and liabilities: brand loyalty, awareness, perceived quality, brand associations (anything linked to memory in the consumer's mind), and other proprietary assets.

Keller's "customer-based brand equity" advanced the thinking on brand equity by focusing on the customer's knowledge about a brand as the primary driver of brand equity. Keller suggested the knowledge of a brand was built based on brand awareness and brand image.[5] Although measures of awareness, such as the ability to recall a brand when given a product category or to recognize a brand when given a variety of alternatives, are quite pertinent in a variety of business settings, they are at times less relevant when focusing on sport teams and events. Many sport properties have some level of awareness in their respective marketplaces.[6] Arguably more important to sport is an understanding of how brand image is built in the minds of consumers, as this begins to provide specific direction on how to manage a spectator sport entity to build equity.

Brand image can be thought of as the *strength, uniqueness, and favorability* of the associations with the brand.[7] An illustrative example of this would be stadium development in U.S. Major League Baseball over the past 20 years. As new stadia were first developed, these buildings (such as Camden Yards, home of Major League Baseball's Baltimore Orioles) provided a strong, unique, and favorable association due to their unique designs, which attempted to capitalize on both the character of the city and the history of the team. In many ways, these new designs effectively generated nostalgic feelings of a positive nature tied to the history of baseball. However, as these new stadia became more prevalent, it could be argued that the impact of each new stadium in developing brand associations lessened because the association with the facility was less unique.

The Benefits of Loyalty: Why Brand Equity Is Important in Spectator Sport

Keller advanced brand equity thinking by suggesting brand loyalty was a key outcome, rather than a component, of brand equity.[8] As brand equity increases for the sport brand, so too should brand loyalty increase. This thinking justifies the focus on brand equity, as loyalty can be monetized, or translated into revenues. Unlike a mainstream consumer product or even a number of service-oriented products, the spectator sport product's performance cannot be standardized. In fact, the inconsistency and uncertainty related to the spectator sport product is one of its great attractions. However, injuries, transactions, turnover, playing conditions, and competition all create a situation in which it is very difficult for a property to always be the best. We also know that revenues tend to increase after a team experiences a championship (or close to championship) season, and often decrease when a team has a particularly poor season or does not realize performance expectations. If the marketer relies solely on success as a marketing platform, he or she will be at the mercy of the many uncontrollable factors mentioned above. A broader and more strategic view suggests managers should seek loyalty to the product among the customer base, which allows for the property to weather downturns in team, player, or event performance.

The mechanism for achieving this loyalty is brand management. It mandates a more long-term strategic view by suggesting that the development of a strong brand (which evolves over time) results in brand loyalty. This view does not take a year-to-year approach or employ an exclusive focus on winning/success as a means to building loyalty. It assumes there are other strategies and tactics to build a strong brand and that those will be employed to varying degrees. The end result is a larger and more loyal base of supporters, which protects the sport organization from the sometimes violent swings that can result from significant variance in performance.[9] Wouldn't everyone like to have loyal fans like the Chicago Bulls, or the Dallas Cowboys? IndyCar auto racing declined when the sport split into two organizations in 1996. But, because of a well-established brand, and a loyal following, the Indianapolis 500 has still been able to attract hundreds of thousands of fans to its annual race. In all of these cases, there are significant brand drivers, other than current success, which have helped create a loyal fan following.

The development of brand equity is important for another financially compelling reason—it can lead to the realization of higher margins, most often due to premium pricing.[10] This has obvious relevance to teams and events whose revenues are derived from ticket sales, luxury seating sales, sponsorship sales, broadcasting inventory sales, and even concessions sales. Though a winning team or successful event could increase ticket prices or sponsorship prices solely based on the previous year's success, it would be vulnerable to poor performance the next year. As team, event, and facility financial strategies have moved to rely heavily on revenues from premium and luxury seating sold at high price points, it has become even more important for brand loyalty to exist such that this inventory can be sold and renewed. The financial crisis of 2008–2010 introduced new challenges around selling premium seating. The significantly increased unsold inventory caused many entities to explore new strategies such as time sharing of luxury suites to realize revenue targets, thus underscoring the need for brand loyalty development.

How Is Brand Equity Developed for Spectator Sport–Based Organizations?

The understanding of brand equity in sport has built on the work of Aaker and Keller to suggest frameworks for understanding brand equity in the spectator sport setting.[11] This discussion begins by presenting a simplified view of brand-building and progresses to a more granular and complex view. The simplified view is a useful starting point and

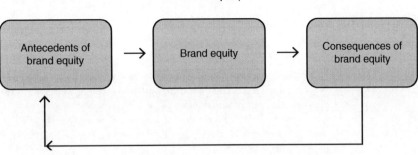

Figure 1.2 Simplified View of Brand Equity Development in Spectator Sport[12]

offers an easy means of explaining how and why brands are managed. The more complex view at the end of this discussion presents much more direction for managers of a sport brand looking to implement brand equity measurement systems and identify strategies to increase brand equity. Figure 1.2 outlines a very basic view of brand equity development based on common elements of the frameworks that have been developed.

This view includes three important considerations as it relates to brand equity management:

- There are antecedents of brand equity derived from a variety of sources, including factors related to the organization, factors related to the marketplace, and factors related to the consumption experience. These antecedents lead to the creation of brand equity.
- The development of brand equity leads to outcomes such as media exposure, corporate sales, ticket sales, and merchandise sales.[12]
- A feedback loop exists whereby the consequences realized can also impact further brand equity creation. The existence of this feedback loop ensures that brands are not static; rather they are continually evolving over time.[13]

Zeroing in on brand equity specifically, research to this point suggests that brand associations may be the most important component of brand equity. Referring back to Keller's conceptualization of customer-based brand equity, he argued that brand awareness and brand image (created by associations) were the two key components of brand knowledge, which shaped brand equity. Where the sport entity has awareness, brand management efforts can focus in on brand associations as the primary tool to realize brand loyalty. Not surprisingly, research on brand equity in sport has identified a wide variety of brand associations in the sport setting. To fully understand brand associations, they need to be thought of in three categories: brand attributes, brand benefits, and brand attitudes.[14]

Brand Attributes

Brand attributes are typically thought of as the features of the brand. With traditional goods, this can include packaging or features of the brand such as color, taste, design, etc. Since such categories of attributes do not exist in the sport setting, a unique set

Table 1.1 Attributes of the Sport Brand[1]

Attribute	Description
Success*	How successful is the property? Won/loss record is not the only proxy for success. Championships are important as well. This attribute also captures the notion of perceived quality.
Head coach*	Particularly relevant when coaches become iconic either due to performance or persona. Relates to both success and personality of the coach.
Players/star players*	Can refer to star players or a collection of players.
Team characteristics	Does the team/event have a unique style of play or a distinct personality?
Rivalry*	Does property have notable rivals or compete in a notoriously difficult or notable conference/division?
Management/personnel*	Management and oversight of the property and its operations. Can also relate to whether or not fans think that the team cares about its fans.
Logo/mark*	The property's nickname, logo, marks, and colors.
Stadium/arena/venue*	Defining characteristics of the facility in which the team plays or event occurs. Whether the stadium has distinctive features and/or is effective at creating community. Concessions offerings, where unique, can also be considered as part of the stadium experience.
Team history/traditions*	Notable traditions of the property, both performance- and nonperformance-based.
Fans*	The existing fan base in the stadium and any characteristics of those fans and the way in which they interact with the game/event.

[1]Developed from analyzing commonalities among work by Gladden & Funk, 2002; Ross, James, & Vargas, 2006; and Bauer, Stokburger-Sauer, & Exler, 2008.

Attributes that may apply beyond teams.

of attributes have been developed and examined. In all cases, these attributes apply to teams, and in some cases the attributes also apply to other sport properties. A summary of some of the brand attributes that have been supported through research to date is presented in Table 1.1.[15]

As some of the attributes are typically controlled by the personnel side of the organization, brand-building activities in the sport context should consider the impact of player/coach acquisition decisions on brand associations if the brand is to be optimally managed. For example, when a sport organization moves toward hiring a coach, it will consider the ability of that coach to build unique, favorable, and strong associations, *in addition* to her/his ability to coach. The University of Kentucky's hiring of John Calipari to coach men's basketball is a good example. Coach Calipari not only has proven his ability to develop successful teams, he also had proven his ability to manage the media, and interact with the fan base, two significant expectations of any Kentucky coach. This logic can also even extend to player personnel decisions. If brand equity represents all of the positive and negative associations with a brand, the negative actions of a player can have a significant impact on how a brand is perceived. This is even more pronounced when a string of cases of player misbehavior occurs, such as happened to the NBA's Portland Trail Blazers between 2000 and 2005.[16]

During this time, there were eight incidents in which Blazers players were arrested for various crimes. Concurrent with these misdeeds, a once very loyal fan base began to erode and Portland's attendance declined for the first time in more than 10 years. The Portland example is a great case of how strong, *negative*, and unique associations can harm a brand.

Beyond the personnel side, appreciating these attributes offers significant guidance to the marketing of a sport entity. For example, unique elements of a stadium or an event's history can be leveraged for brand-building purposes. In fact, an organization's history or heritage often offers strong associations.[17] Old Trafford, the home of the world-popular Manchester United of the English Premier League, is a great example of how history and heritage translate into associations. Old Trafford is referred to as "The Theatre of Dreams" on the United website,[18] thus reminding fans of the incredible scenes and action that have taken and will take place in that venue. Although marketers often do not control the creation of rivalries, the associations with the rivalry can be enhanced through marketing efforts. Such was the case with the Boston Red Sox–New York Yankees rivalry when the Red Sox management referred to the Yankees as the "evil empire." This phrase brilliantly captured the dislike of the Yankees among Red Sox fans and by virtue strengthened a unique association tied to the Red Sox brand, and its intense rivalry with the Yankees.

Brand Benefits

A second type of brand association is benefits, the meanings and value consumers derive from the consumption of the sport product.[19] It drives to the deeper meaning and, at times, motivations a consumer might have to follow a particular sport property. A list of brand benefits that have received significant attention and support from research are presented in Table 1.2 along with each benefit's respective description.

Research has documented that brand attributes result in brand benefits.[20] Although benefits are more difficult for the brand manager to control or impact, they can be managed by focusing on attributes and understanding their relationship to benefits. Returning to Manchester United's Old Trafford, there is also a museum at Old Trafford, which serves to memorialize great players, coaches, and moments of United's past as a means of providing nostalgic benefits. Minor League Baseball in the United States provides another good example of managing this relationship. A common feature to the design of most new minor league parks is an open seating area, often in the outfield on a hill or lawn, where people can sit together in large groups. The incorporation of this feature demonstrates an understanding of both fans as an attribute and its ability to impact socialization as a benefit. Another good example of managing a brand with an eye on the benefits provided is the practice of nurturing brand names and traditions for fan bases as a means of reinforcing the identification a consumer may have with a particular team. The Indianapolis Colts have been successful in this way by creating "Blue Fridays," when Colts fans are encouraged to wear their blue Colts merchandise to work or school on the Friday before Colts games.

Table 1.2 Benefits Provided by the Sport Brand[1]

Benefit	Description
Escape*	The following of a sport property allows the consumer a diversion from the challenges of everyday life.
Nostalgia*	Following the sport property provides a mechanism for the consumer to recall aspects of the past fondly.
Socializing*	The sport entity provides a platform for people to socialize with one another and for friends and family to connect.
Peer-group acceptance*	Becoming a fan of a sport property affords someone acceptance within a peer group or social group.
Entertainment*	The sport entity provides a value entertainment outlet.
Identification	When the sport entity succeeds, the consumer also feels as if they have succeeded. For example, fans often say "we won" when their favorite entity succeeds.
Emotions*	Refers to the variety of emotions that can be elicited from following sport, including exhilaration, happiness, anger, sadness, and others.

*Benefits that may apply beyond teams.
[1]Developed from analyzing commonalities among work by Gladden & Funk, 2002; Ross, James, & Vargas, 2006; and Bauer, Stokburger-Sauer, & Exler, 2008.

Brand Attitudes

Even more difficult to directly impact are attitudes, which represent a consumer's evaluation or judgment of a brand as a whole.[21] As opposed to attributes and benefits, there is less agreement in the research to date as to how to think about brand attitudes. The one point where there is agreement is around measuring consumer feelings about a brand. However, the feelings to measure are less clear. Among the feelings measured related to consumers' perceptions are whether or not the organization is:[22]

- Unique
- Trustworthy
- Positive
- Likeable
- Foolish or wise
- Strong or weak
- Good or bad
- Worthless or beneficial

This list of feelings mostly focuses on whether there is a positive attitude toward the brand or not. A unique exception to this is trustworthiness, and this may be an area that bears detailed examination in the future. As a consumer's attitude toward a sport brand may at least be in part driven by that organization's ability to satisfy the consumer's needs through benefits, and a key attribute for developing associations is the management of the sport entity, the degree to which a consumer trusts a sport organization may be an important predictor of loyalty and thereby an important attitudinal component of brand associations and brand equity. Using the Portland

Trail Blazers example, it could be argued that the numerous arrests eroded the level of trust that fans had toward the Portland organization, thus decreasing brand equity and brand loyalty.

Associations Linked to Loyalty

Significant evidence exists to suggest that brand associations create brand loyalty in the sport context.[23] Several studies have documented that brand associations, as defined by attributes, benefits, and attitudes, lead to brand loyalty. One study takes this understanding a step further and provides the basis for a more complex framework for managing the sport brand. Figure 1.3 depicts the proven links between brand attributes, brand benefits, brand attitudes, and brand loyalty:

Rather than the three types of associations operating somewhat independently of each other, this framework highlights a sequential relationship in which attributes cause benefits and benefits cause attitudes, which ultimately then leads to the creation, maintenance, and enhancement of loyalty. This has significant implications for brand management practice. For example, managers hoping to build a brand must first focus on attributes as a means of generating benefits for consumers and shaping their overall assessment of the sport brand. Lacking immediate success, managers should look at the other attributes to determine which can be enhanced to build associations. However, once equity is established, part of the focus should shift to understanding which attributes are creating strong, unique, and favorable associations and what impact these attributes are having on the benefits provided to the consumer.

One caveat is associated with the framework presented below. Brand loyalty has two components: behavioral loyalty (or propensity to repeatedly purchase a product) and attitudinal loyalty (or holding very favorable attitudes toward a brand over time).[25] The framework documented a link between brand attitudes and behavioral loyalty. It could be that brand attitudes (particularly psychological commitment to the brand) and attitudinal loyalty to the brand are so similar that it is hard to discriminate between the two.[26] Adopting this view, brand attributes lead to brand benefits, which result in attitudinal loyalty and subsequently in behavioral loyalty. The only problem with this thinking is that there are circumstances in which behavioral loyalty is high, but attitudinal loyalty is low. Take a corporate season ticket purchaser as an example. In this case, the tickets could be purchased with business cultivation or hospitality as a primary motivation. High levels of attitudinal loyalty would not necessarily be present in this case. Therefore, when utilizing the above framework, caution is recommended because a more precise understanding is still required.

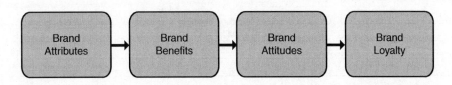

Figure 1.3 How Associations Lead to Loyalty[24]

Prescriptions for Measuring Brand Equity in Sport

When discussing the measurement of brand equity in the sport setting, several reminders are important. First, brand equity is developed over time. As such, any system built to measure brand equity should be implemented with an eye on periodic/longitudinal measurement as opposed to measurement at only one point in time. Second, brands evolve. Brands are formed in the minds of consumers. Therefore, the sport consumer must be engaged on a regular basis to understand brand perceptions. In the ideal setting, the sport entity will implement a brand equity measurement system that serves as a tracking system and can be used to measure the strength of the brand on an annual or semi-annual basis. Of course, this assumes unlimited resources and, as the reader will soon see, the ideal brand equity measurement system could be quite costly to implement. Any direct measurement system needs to establish whether brand awareness exists and whether there are strong, unique, and favorable associations with the brand. There are also a variety of outcomes for which data could be collected as a means of keeping track of the positive impact of brand equity. Syndicated data on sport properties is increasingly available and can provide either supplemental or substitute information for the sport brand manager relating to brand equity measurement.

Figure 1.4 presents an overview of a comprehensive brand equity measurement system that could be employed by a sport entity. This figure presents a detailed system, which uses a mixture of proprietary and syndicated research to gauge brand equity. In both instances it is recommended that, based on their perceived connection to the sport property, the group of people from which data are collected is segmented into several categories. For example, it is vital to understand the strength of the brand in the eyes of season ticket holders, partial season ticket holders, and premium seat/luxury

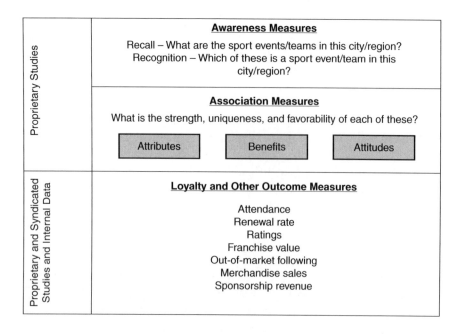

Figure 1.4 Prescription for a Brand Equity Measurement System

suite holders. However, it would also be important to understand the level of brand associations in the eyes of people who might watch the event or team on television, or follow it through the Internet. New media tools have enabled the formulation of worldwide communities of fans and it is this segment that arguably presents the most significant potential for revenue growth.

Does Brand Awareness Exist?

Brand awareness is important because it is quite difficult to have strong, unique, and favorable associations without significant brand awareness. Usually, however, this is less problematic for sport entities, given their prominence in the marketplace. That said, if there is doubt about whether brand has awareness, some very basic measures can be employed. Although recall and recognition measures are both recommended for use in measuring awareness,[27] recall is a more appropriate measure for sport brands for several reasons. Recall measures the top-of-mind awareness of the sport entity using such questions as

- Name all of the sport events in your area
- Name all of the professional sport teams in your area
- Name all of the entertainment options in your area

This last question is an interesting one in that it assumes the consumer will consider sport options as entertainment offerings. Because the respondent is being asked to retrieve what is in their memory regarding a particular product category (i.e., sport events, sport teams, entertainment offerings), it is a more pure assessment of how much awareness the entity has in the minds of the consumer. In contrast, recognition measures offer the consumer a variety of options within each category and simply ask the consumer whether or not they recognize a particular brand as associated with the product category. Considering the number of sport offerings is often low, and these offerings tend to regularly receive significant sport coverage, such measures would most likely yield high results even when recall measures would yield lower results. Data yielded from these measures should be used differently than measures of associations. The first question to be asked is: do the brand recall measures show strong awareness? If these measures show high awareness, it may not be important to continue to measure awareness. However, if recall measures show low to moderate awareness, marketing communications strategies should be employed to generate awareness about the existence of the team.

Measuring Associations: Qualitative Techniques

Both qualitative and quantitative research methods should be utilized to collect data on brand associations with the sport entity. Past research efforts provide a strong foundation on the directions to be employed with respect to quantitative research.[28] However, strategic use of qualitative research can also greatly enhance the understanding of brand associations. Focus groups can be used to identify what brand associations might be the strongest, the most unique, or the most favorable. Focus groups may also help uncover new associations with sport properties not previously understood. Additionally, focus groups can be used to understand *why* a particular brand association is positive or negative, or strong or weak. For this reason, focus groups should be employed less based on a schedule, but more based on where an understanding of quantitative results is needed. In this way, costs associated with focus groups can be kept at a more manageable level.

When conducting focus groups, a variety of techniques can be used to understand the brand associations held by consumers. At a basic level, the facilitator can place a piece of paper in front of the participants and start the focus group by saying "for the next two minutes, write down everything that comes to mind associated with brand A." This method will identify an initial pool of brand associations that exist in the minds of consumers. This represents just a start, though. A strong argument can be made that a person's subconscious also impacts brand associations.[29] For this reason, techniques that require more thought and indirectly elicit brand associations should be used. One such type of technique is referred to as projective technique.[30] Comparison tasks, one form of a projective technique, ask questions such as "if brand b were a car, what kind of a car would it be?" and "if brand c were an animal, what kind of animal would it be?" These questions tend to elicit fairly quick responses from focus group participants, which then provide the substance for discussion as to why the brand was like a particular car or animal. The follow-up discussion often leads to a significant picture regarding the overall character and personality of a brand, and might be useful in identifying and gauging which associations are the strongest. Another method pioneered by Harvard researcher Gerald Zaltman asks focus group participants or individual interview participants to collect pictures that best capture what the brand stands for or means and bring those pictures to the focus group session or interview as a means of starting a conversation about a consumer's associations with a brand.[31]

Measuring Associations: Quantitative Techniques

Thanks to a significant amount of work that has been done on developing measurement tools for the sport setting, significant direction can be offered with respect to how to measure brand associations in the sport setting. The measurement strategy begins with the understanding that associations are composed of attributes, benefits, and attitudes. Additionally, it requires an appreciation that the key to having brand equity is that these associations are strong, unique, and favorable. Incorporating these basic principles results in a strategy that focuses on measuring the associations that are known to exist and assessing the strength, uniqueness, and favorability of these associations (where applicable). Consumer perceptions of the attributes noted earlier in this chapter can be measured by turning the attribute into a scale item, which is then presented to the respondent with a request for judgment on strength, uniqueness, and favorability. Accepted measurement practice would suggest using a minimum of three items for each attribute, but this may not be possible in the interest of presenting a manageable instrument to the respondent. Therefore, when looking at Table 1.3, the brand manager may want to choose one of the items (of the multiple items presented) to measure the attributes, depending on the type of

Table 1.3 Potential Items to Measure Brand Attributes

Attribute	Item
Success	Team success
	Entity success
Head coach	The team's head coach
Players/star players	The team's players
	The player's personality or style of play
	The event's participants
Team characteristics	The team's style of play
Rivalry	Rivalry between the property and other properties
Management/personnel	The management of the property
Logo/mark	The property's logo
Stadium/arena/venue	Stadium of the property
Team history/traditions	History of winning by the team
	History of the event
	History of success by the property
Fans	Fans of the team
	Fans of the event
	Fans of the property

team or event that is being measured. For each of the items selected, three questions should be asked in scale format so that the respondent ranks the attribute in relation to anchors (e.g., "do not associate at all" and "strongly associate" as anchors to measure strength):[32]

1. "How strongly do you associate the following attribute with the team/entity?" (to measure strength)
2. "How do you feel about the following attributes of the team/entity?" (to measure favorability)
3. "In comparison with other teams/entities, how unique are the following attributes of the team/entity?" (to measure uniqueness)[33]

A similar approach can be used with benefits. Table 1.4 presents a list of items that can be used to measure each of the benefits. In contrast to the attributes, though, there is no need to measure the favorability of the benefits given the wording of the items. In essence, given its definition as a benefit, it is positive. Measuring attitudes is a trickier subject. This is in part because there is some confusion as to whether attitudinal loyalty, often measured as psychological commitment, should be considered an attitude or part of loyalty.[34]

In this chapter, attitudinal loyalty is considered strictly as an attitude. Accordingly, it is recommended that knowledge, affect (positive or negative feeling), trustworthiness, and attitudinal loyalty be measured by asking for respondents to rate their agreement on the following items:

- Knowledge: "I know a great deal about the team/event"
- Affect: "I have positive feelings toward the team/event"
- Trustworthiness: "The team/event is trustworthy"
- Attitudinal loyalty: "I am committed to the team/event" and "I would defend the team/event publicly even if it caused problems"

Table 1.4 Items Used to Measure Benefits

Benefit	Description
Escape	Watching, reading, and talking about the property takes me away from life's hassles.
Nostalgia	Thinking of the property brings back good memories.
Socializing	The property provides me with a way to spend time with family and friends.
Peer-group acceptance	I follow the property because my friends and family follow the team.
Entertainment	The property provides an excellent entertainment option.
Identification	It is important that my friends and family recognize me as a fan of the property.
Emotions	The property generates positive emotions.

Measuring Outcomes

A wide variety of outcome measures can be employed to examine the results of branding efforts. As opposed to the measurement of brand associations, the measurement of outcomes can utilize a variety of data collection techniques. The focus of these efforts should be on indicators of loyalty or indicators that present opportunities for revenue gains. Because our thinking on brand equity suggests attitudinal loyalty is accounted for within the attitudes as brand associations, the bulk of the conversation regarding the measurement of outcomes focuses on measures of behavior that could be indicative of loyalty.

Where budgets permit the collection of data through proprietary research, it is advisable to collect data on consumption of the sport entity both presently and in the past to gauge behavioral loyalty. When including behavioral questions into a survey instrument, it is important to collect data on a wide variety of consumption behaviors, including games/sessions/events attended, frequency of consumption on television, frequency of media consumption (all forms including online) about the sport entity, and the amount spent on the merchandise of the sport entity. Gathering multiple years of data on these dimensions could allow for the type of advanced analysis recommended at the end of this section.

Where it is not possible to collect data through proprietary research, a wide variety of measures can be used to examine the outcomes of brand equity. Today's technology affords the sport manager with considerable opportunities to collect data about consumption. Many events and teams have become more systematic and strategic in the maintenance of databases and tools to more optimally manage customer relationships. To examine loyalty among what should be the heavy consumers—season ticket, or full event ticket holders—renewal rates provide an excellent data point indicative of loyalty. The data generated from scanning bar codes on tickets also presents a potential outcome measure. For example, the percent of dates or sessions for which a ticket was utilized on an annual basis could be used as an outcome indicator. The willingness and interest of corporations in sponsoring the sport entity also provides a potential measure of brand loyalty. For this reason, the number of sponsors, the dollars raised through sponsorship, and the dollars saved from sponsorship agreements (i.e., in-kind agreements) should be tracked over time to gauge the loyalty of corporations to the sport brand.

Beyond data collected from proprietary measures and internal data that exists within most organization's information systems, a wide variety of market-based measures could be used in analysis of brand equity outcomes. Annual information on attendance is now available for most sport entities. A consideration with respect to attendance may be the actual size of the facility in which the team plays or the event is held. If the strengths of different sport brands are being compared, it may make more sense to look at attendance as a percentage of capacity as a means of standardizing the comparison. Similarly, television ratings are either readily available or available for a price from the Nielsen company. Tracking these ratings over a season or the duration of the event as well on a year-to-year basis can present an indicator of brand loyalty.

With respect to major professional sport in the United States, *Forbes* magazine publishes estimations of franchise values annually. Although revenue streams are the primary source of information for this measure, the magnitude of the stream has a significant impact on value and for this reason it could be considered as a measure of outcomes. In fact, one study created a brand measure by multiplying franchise value by the percentage of seats sold and then dividing by the team's winning percentage over the past 25 years (to account for the impact of success on brand equity).[35] In doing so, it further demonstrated how market-generated measures can be useful in creating measures for brand equity. Other measures that could be used to assess followings include television ratings and social network followings.

One company has taken the effort to measure brand strength in North American major professional sport one step further. Turnkey Sport and Entertainment utilized its marketing research capabilities to conduct a study of brand strength in every North American market. In sampling sport fans in each of these markets, Turnkey asked a battery of brand-related questions including questions relating to team popularity, team ownership, fan loyalty, and sponsor loyalty. The survey also asked respondents to judge each team in their market on a variety of brand personality attributes such as aggressive, tough, and visionary. The result was the Turnkey Team Brand Index which developed an overarching brand score for each professional team, representing the strength of the team brand in the team's market.[36] This study generated a great deal of interesting and useable data for the sport marketer. However, the overall brand score was limited by the fact that only fans in the team's market were answering questions about the team. Given the length of the survey, it would have been time prohibitive to ask the same questions for every team. The study did, however, ask a question that could be indicative of overall brand strength. Every respondent was asked to indicate which sport teams outside of their market they followed. Combining the responses from all 47 markets yielded an index that allowed for teams to be ranked based on their out-of-market following. Table 1.5 presents the top 10 out-of-market teams from the 2007 study.

Does Table 1.5 represent a North American measure of brand strength? Is the out-of-market following a better measure than the in-market following of brand strength? When looking at the list of teams in the table, one might be able to make an argument that this represents an interesting way to look at brand strength, as it would be hard to argue that these teams do not represent strong sport brands.

Table 1.5 Top 10 Out-of-Market Followings

Team	Index
New York Yankees	499.6
Dallas Cowboys	381.0
Green Bay Packers	376.0
Boston Red Sox	371.3
Chicago Cubs	354.6
Atlanta Braves	288.6
Chicago Bears	272.0
Indianapolis Colts	267.0
San Francisco 49ers	258.8
Los Angeles Lakers	257.0

Making Use of the Data

Assuming the ideal proprietary research system is put in place, a variety of approaches can be used to examine the data that is collected. At a very basic level, it is important to understand the degree to which the associations are unique, favorable, and strong. Each of the attributes, benefits, and attitudes could be evaluated, both in comparison to each other and across consumer market segments (e.g., season ticket holders, viewers, out-of-market followers, etc.). Once identified, associations that are strong, unique, and favorable should be leveraged in marketing communications. Similarly, if the measurement system were employed over time, the impact of marketing communications efforts to create specific associations could be examined. Where the ability exists to employ more complex statistical analysis techniques such as regression analysis or structural equation modeling, sport entities should examine the linkage between associations and loyalty to understand which associations are most likely to predict or create both attitudinal and behavioral loyalty. If certain associations were found to be more predictive of loyalty, then the sport marketer would have even more direction about where to focus marketing resources strategically.

Conclusion

A managerial focus on brand equity in the sport setting is imperative for the long-term health of the sport property, whether it be a team, league, event, facility, or athlete. In all cases, the establishment of a strong brand will provide protection against the drastic swings in revenue that can occur when the performance of the sport brand invariably falters. Though the inconsistency and unpredictability of the sport product creates entertainment, provides drama, and is one of the unique and compelling elements of the sport product, it also presents challenges from the managerial standpoint. Wherever possible, efforts should be made to manage the various attributes of the sport brand such that they provide substantive benefits to sport consumers. Doing so will lead to the creation of strong and favorable attitudes, and accordingly brand equity.

A managerial focus on brand equity also requires periodic measurement and assessment. Sport brands are not static; they evolve over time. Additionally, sport brands are created in the minds of sport consumers. Therefore, measurement of the equity associated with the sport brand requires measurement at different points in time. Measurement efforts should determine the level of awareness for the sport brand and the strength, uniqueness, and favorability of the attributes, benefits, and attitudes associated with the brand. Though quantitative measures are available, the use of qualitative techniques is also important if the depth and meaning of brand associations are to be fully understood. Though the ideal measurement model requires a significant amount of primary data collection, a number of industry measures can serve as proxies for brand equity and loyalty. Measurement allows for a regular understanding of brand strength, trends related to its direction, and an opportunity to employ different strategies depending on the status of the brand.

References

1. SME (Sean Michael Edwards) Branding. Retrieved from http://www.smebranding.com/
2. Aaker, D. A. (1991). *Managing brand equity: Capitalizing on the value of a brand name.* New York: The Free Press.
3. Keller, K. L. (1993, January). Conceptualizing, measuring, and managing customer-based brand equity. *Journal of Marketing,* 57, 1–22.
4. Same as 2, p. 15.
5. Same as 3, p. 2.
6. Gladden, J. (2007). Managing sport brands. In B. J. Mullin, S. H. Hardy, & W. A. Sutton(Eds.), *Sport Marketing.* Champaign, IL: Human Kinetics.
7. Same as 3.
8. Same as 3.
9. Same as 6.
10. Same as 2, p. 18.
11. See Gladden, J. M. & Milne, G. R. (1999). Examining the importance of brand equity in professional sport. *Sport Marketing Quarterly,* 8(1), 21–30; and Ross, S. D. (2006). A conceptual framework for understanding spectator-based brand equity. *Journal of Sport Management,* 20, 22–36.
12. Same as 11. Development based on Gladden & Milne, 1999; and Ross, 2006.
13. Same as 6.
14. Same as 3.
15. See Gladden, J. M., & Funk, D. C. (2002). Developing an understanding of brand associations in team sport: Empirical evidence from consumers of professional sport. *Journal of Sport Management,* 16, 54–81; and Ross, S. D., James, J. D., & Vargas, P. (2006). Development of a scale to measure team brand associations in professional sport. *Journal of Sport Management,* 20, 260–279; and Bauer, H. H., Stokburger-Sauer, N. E., & Exler, S. (2008). Brand image and fan loyalty in professional team sport: A refined model and empirical assessment. *Journal of Sport Management,* 22, 205–226.
16. Same as 6.
17. Aaker, D. A. (2004, Spring). Leveraging the corporate brand. *California Management Review,* 46(3), 6–18.
18. Manchester United Website. Retrieved from http://www.manutd.com.
19. Same as 3.
20. Bauer, H. H., Stokburger-Sauer, N. E., & Exler, S. (2008). Brand image and fan loyalty in professional team sport: A refined model and empirical assessment. *Journal of Sport Management,* 22, 205–226.
21. Same as 3.
22. Derived from Bauer, Stokburger-Sauer, & Exler, 2008 and Gladden, J. M., & Funk, D. C. (2001). Understanding brand loyalty in professional sport: Examining the link between brand associations and brand loyalty. *International Journal of Sport Marketing and Sponsorship,* 3, 67–91.
23. Bauer, Stokburger-Sauer, & Exler, 2008; and Gladden & Funk, 2001.
24. Summarizes key findings of Bauer, Stokburger-Sauer, & Exler, 2008.

25. Day, G. S. (1969). A two-dimensional concept of brand loyalty. *Journal of Advertising Research*, *9*(3), 29–35.
26. Same as 20.
27. Same as 3.
28. See Gladden & Milne, 1999; and Gladden & Funk, 2002; and Ross, James, & Vargas, 2006; and Bauer, Stokburger-Sauer, & Exler, 2008.
29. Zaltman, G. (2003). *How Consumers Think.* Cambridge, MA: Harvard Business School Press.
30. Keller, K. L. (1998). *Strategic brand management: Building, measuring and managing brand equity.* New Jersey: Prentice Hall.
31. Same as 29.
32. Same as 20, p. 225.
33. Adapted from Bauer, Stokburger-Sauer, & Exler, 2008.
34. Same as 20.
35. Gladden, J. M. & Milne, G. R. (1999). Examining the importance of brand equity in professional sport. *Sport Marketing Quarterly*, *8*(1), 21–30.
36. 2007 Turnkey Brand Index. Haddonfield, NJ: Turnkey Sport and Entertainment.

2

Consumer Behavior and Motivation
Why Are Sport Event Consumers So Special?

Dr. Frank Pons
Laval University, Canada

Marilyn Giroux
Concordia University, Canada

Mehdi Mourali
University of Calgary, Canada

Abstract: This chapter focuses on sport event consumers and offers an overview of the uniqueness of sporting events and the mechanisms through which they may fulfill various consumers' needs. It also highlights the importance of using appropriate measures to capture consumers' motives and provides several examples of measurement that can be used in both the academic and managerial world. Finally, it details the role that merchandising may play in fulfilling these consumers' motives and providing a better event experience. Sport marketers may use these results to better target and serve consumers using appropriate merchandising or event strategies.

Keywords: fans, measures, merchandising, motivation, segmentation

Introduction

Figure 2.1 summarizes some of the key questions this chapter will address. Questions like these help us to unravel the motives that bring individuals in front of their TV or to a stadium, and are vital to being an effective sport marketer, a matter of concern for both researchers and practitioners alike.[1, 2, 3] From an economic standpoint, the global sport industry is a significant sector, with an average growth of 4% per year. Global sport revenues should continue to grow in the coming years and are projected to generate more than $145 billion in 2015.[4] From those revenues, gate receipts account for the largest source of income, with 32.60% of the total sport market.[5] This is especially true for North America and Europe, where live events are part of their cultural traditions (e.g., the National Collegiate Athletic Association's March Madness, which began in the United States in 1939, or Europe's Formula One Grand Prix races, which began in 1906). Despite the amount of dollars involved, gate receipts have the slowest growth compared to other types of income sport businesses enjoy. The second largest revenue stream is sponsorship, which records a significant proportion (28.80%) of total income.[5] Sponsorships are one of the more promising factors for sport organizations and

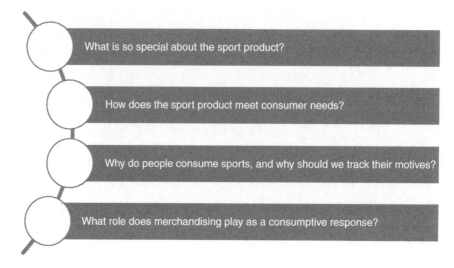

Figure 2.1 Overview of Chapter 2

teams over the next years, with an average increase rate of 5.3%.[5] Media rights account for 24.10% of total revenues, while merchandising constitutes 14.50%.[5] On a global scale, North America represents 71% of all sport merchandising revenues.[5] Merchandising is particularly crucial for sport organizations, because it is an important part of the fans' experience and it can significantly increase the involvement of individuals.

In terms of total attendance, Major League Baseball (MLB) is the most popular sport in the U.S., with a total attendance of more than 73 million spectators in 2011,[6] while the National Football League has the best average attendance.[7] The gate revenues constitute one of the most important parts of the total revenues for the different teams. For example, in 2007, the New York Yankees had $302 million in annual revenues. Of this total, $117 million came from the 4.2 million tickets sold for the games and $27 million for premium seating, while $15 million was from catering and concessions.[8] The remaining income came from TV/radio rights, licensing, sponsorships, and advertising. Those numbers illustrate why it is so important to understand the spectators' motivations to go to sport activities. In addition to contextual motives (scarcity, price, etc.), a spectator at a sporting event is often described as having an inherent predisposition to attend those activities.[3] Several attempts in the services marketing literature[10,11] and in the sport marketing literature[3, 12] have attempted to develop an understanding of what these intrapersonal motives are. Researchers in sport marketing have constructed several different measures to capture intrapersonal fan motivations.[3, 12, 13] As shown in Figure 2.2, this chapter discusses sport event consumption and conducts a motivation assessment that introduces different measures of motivation. These approaches can be used to describe and define segmentation and positioning elements (i.e., motivational benefits desired by the consumer) that will enable the practitioner to build lasting brand relationships with event consumers. An application that describes how consumer motives can enhance merchandising consumption so it reinforces and establishes fan relationships with teams is also presented.

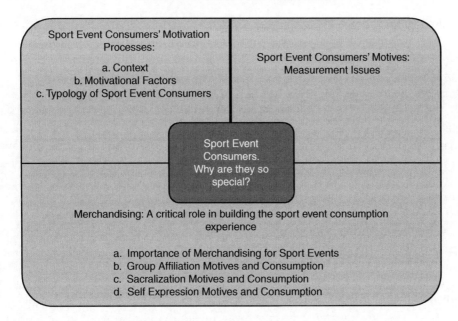

Figure 2.2 Issues and Implications of Tracking Consumer Motivation in Sport

Elements to Consider in Sport Event Consumer Motivation

Context

As the importance of sport in the economic, cultural, and social fields is recognized, it becomes essential to gain useful insights on its nature and in particular which aspects of sport can spark so much passion. Sport participation certainly contributes to spreading specific values and triggering passionate behaviors. But, attending sport events also significantly impacts on individuals in ways that positively contribute to our societies. In fact, sport are often presented as important parts of culture in many countries (e.g.,Superbowl[14]; FIFA World Cup[15]). They represent an important economic stake in terms of television rights.[16] They also carry strong meaning for individuals, and the values and attributes they display allow consumers to express their self-identity and their sense of belonging to peer groups. In addition, the acceleration and the ease of worldwide communications strengthen the importance and prevalence of sporting events.[17]

Finally, sport events also present specific characteristics that make them stand out for consumers. They are intangible, short-lived, unpredictable, and subjective in nature.[18] They are produced and consumed at the same time and they are often paired with a strong emotional display or commitment from consumers.[16] These unique characteristics and their multiple facets can fulfill a wide range of consumers' needs and motivations.

Influencing Factors and the Motivation Process

Most studies dealing with sport event consumers have identified recurrent factors that influence event attendance.[19] These factors include **sport attractiveness** (e.g., league or team competitiveness, team and players performance[20]); **environmental factors** (e.g., free time available, easy access, and appropriate infrastructure[2]); **economic factors** (e.g., ticket prices, promotions[21]) and **socio-demographic factors** (e.g., gender, ethnic origin[22]). The previous factors are often presented as *secondary* factors whereas the *primary* factors are defined as **internal or emotional factors** (e.g., team identification, motivation[22]). Among the previous influencing factors, motivational factors are certainly the most influential ones. They are often described as fundamental determinants in understanding sporting events consumption. In the consumer behavior literature, motivation is defined as an inner drive that reflects goal-directed arousal. Motivation is the process that describes how internal/external forces trigger, direct, and modulate behaviors that consumers adopt to fulfill their needs. When these behaviors are relatively anchored and persisting, motivation is often associated with the concept of orientation. Orientation can be defined as an individual's specific inclination toward adopting a predictable behavior during a particular consumption act.[18] Motivation calls on the ability of the activity or the product toward which the individual is oriented to satisfy his/her particular needs. In the case of sporting events, motivation refers to the event's capacity to meet the specific needs of the individual. Such needs vary greatly and can range from the desire to be a part of some unforgettable moments in sport, to be able to express one's joy (e.g., shouts, applause, etc.), or cognitive or relational motives (e.g., to know and master sport information, share unique sport moments with friends and family).[13]

Sport event attendance motivation has been of interest to researchers in the field for over 15 years. They have identified factors such as pleasure, aestheticism and experience,[23] escape,[24] social interactions,[??] community involvement, identification with the team,[22] eustress or self-esteem enhancement[25] to explain why individuals consume sporting events. Detailed measures of these motives are presented in the next section of this chapter. The following figure (Figure 2.3) describes the role played by these motives and other variables in the sporting event attendance decision process. Several authors also underline the importance of discriminating between sporting events consumers and suggest using a typology of consumers based on their attachment and identification to the sport to better understand their motivation and their intensity.

Typologies of Sport Event Consumers

The most common categorization among events consumers lies in the difference between sport spectator and sport fans. Wann[3] states that "*sport consumers are those individuals that actually witness a sporting event in person or through different media outlets, while sport fans actively follow a team, athlete, or sport*". This distinction between spectators and fans implies a different degree of identification with the event or the team as the fan shows a greater personal attachment and affective involvement than the spectator.[26] In the academic literature, this simplistic typology has paved the way to extensive work on more detailed typologies.[27] A few of them are presented in Figure 2.4. Most of these typologies use motives and/or attitudes and behaviors to classify consumers. Quick[28] developed a model using the five categories identified by Stewart and Smith[29] to show that the level of identification with the event and the performance level sought

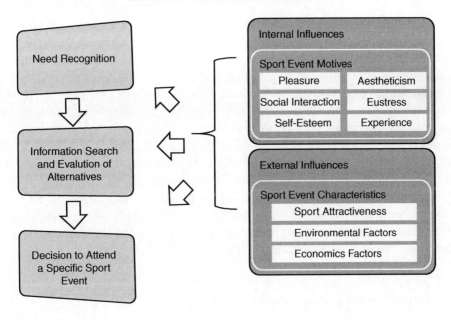

Figure 2.3 Motivation and the Decision Making Process to Attend a Sport Event

	Typologies				
Wann & Branscombe[30]	Fair-weather Fans			Die-hard Fans	
Stewart & Smith[29]	afficionado	theater goer	champ follower	passionate partisan	reclusive partisan
Sutton, McDonald, Milne, & Cimperman[31]	Social Fans		Focused Fans		Vested Fans

Figure 2.4 Examples of Motive-Based Fan Typologies (Adapted from Pierrat[27])

were two key variables that influence the type of consumption experience that each individual seeks during a sport event. In the same line, more recently, researchers suggested more complex typologies that include a mix of motives and contextual sport-related variables (e.g., *sport dichotomies: individual vs. team sport, aggressive vs. non aggressive sport, stylistic vs. non-stylistic sport*).[24]

Spectators and Fans

Regardless of the typology adopted and its conceptual and academic contribution, the distinction between spectators and fans (2 groups) seems to be the one providing more managerial value for sport organizations as strategies can be tailored more easily to these well-defined groups. For instance, Trail, Fink, and Anderson[2] note that "*The distinction between fans and spectators is important to sport marketing practitioners as well. They must recognize that they may have two distinct groups attending games and therefore should consciously attempt to meet their needs and desires".* Campbell, Aiken, and Ketit[32] highlight the importance of this distinction through their contribution to the fan behavior literature with the conceptualization of categories of fans who "Cut Off Reflected Success" (CORS) or "Bask In Reflected Failure" (BIRF). Their findings show that highly identified consumers (**fans**) may have a totally distinct behavior from more traditional consumers (**spectators**), who are more driven by performance and generally "Bask In Reflected Glory" (BIRG) or "Cut Off Reflected Failure" (CORF). Thus, managerial decisions must address fans or spectators differently. Even though fans and spectators are important assets for a sport property, they require tailored product and communication strategies. It is important to notice that more complex typologies are critical for sport organizations; that understanding the distinction between fan and spectator segments in terms of motives should be the baseline or starting point for any strategy implemented by sport marketers.

Measurement Issues in Assessing Event Motivation

As the strategic importance of better segmenting sport event consumers increased, several researchers developed and proposed measurement tools to capture edit to, different consumer motives. The following section of this chapter presents selected pertinent scales that capture different facets behind sport event consumption.

Sport Fan Motivation Scale (SFMS)[3]

Wann[3] was one of the first researchers to propose a measure to capture motives of fans (Sport Fan Motivation Scale). This 23-item scale is structured around eight factors encompassing what consumers look for in sport events. These factors are quickly described hereafter and an example of the scale is presented in Table 2.1.

The ***Group affiliation*** dimension refers to the social nature of events and their ability to fulfill belongingness needs for consumers. Consumers involved in sport events seize the opportunity to affiliate with different social groups and networks such as friends, work friends, or even supporter groups. The ***Aesthetics*** dimension pertains to individuals attracted by the beauty and artistic displays during sport events. This characteristic fulfills an intrinsic motivation for consumers and justifies their attraction to sport events providing this feature. ***Eustress*** represents a very specific appeal. This positive stress refers to the ability of sporting events to provide a mix of arousal, pleasure, and stimulation. According to Wann,[3] event consumers can also fulfill their ***self-esteem*** through the pride they feel in being part of an event or supporting a team. They gain real pleasure from the event when it fulfills their expectation or when their team wins or offers a great performance. The ***Entertainment*** dimension refers to feelings of pleasure and enjoyment that only sport events can offer to certain consumers. Some individuals are inclined to follow sport events mainly for ***Economic*** motives. This dimension pertains to individuals for whom the biggest motivation is to financially benefit from the event itself (mainly gamblers or resellers). Studies clearly show

Table 2.1 Items and factors for the 23-Item Sport Fan Motivation Scale (SFMS)

Eustress
- One of the main reasons that I watch, read, and/or discuss sport is that I get pumped up when I am watching my favorite teams.
- One of the main reasons that I watch, read, and/or discuss sport is that I enjoy being physiologically aroused by the competition.
- I like the stimulation I get from watching sport.

Self Esteem
- One of the main reasons that I watch, read, and/or discuss sport is that doing so makes me feel good when my team wins.
- I enjoy watching sport because it increases my self-esteem.
- To me, my favorite team's successes are my successes and their losses are my losses.

Escape
- One of the main reasons that I watch, read, and/or discuss sport is that doing so gives me the opportunity to temporarily escape life's problems.
- One of the main reasons that I watch, read, and/or discuss sport is that doing so allows me to forget about my problems.
- To me, watching, reading, and/or discussing sport is like daydreaming because it takes me away from life's hassles.

Entertainment
- I enjoy sport because of their entertainment value.
- I enjoy watching, reading, and/or discussing sport simply because it is a good time.
- To me, sport spectating is simply a form of recreation.

Economic
- One of the main reasons that I watch, read, and/or discuss sport is so I can bet on the sporting events.
- Sport are enjoyable only if you can bet on the outcome.
- Making wagers is the most enjoyable aspect of being a sport fan.

Aesthetic
- One of the main reasons that I watch, read, and/or discuss sport is for the artistic value.
- One of the main reasons that I watch, read, or discuss sport is that I enjoy the beauty and grace of sport.
- I enjoy watching sporting events because to me sport are a form of art.

Group Affiliation
- One of the main reasons that I watch, read, and/or discuss sport is because most of my friends are sport fans.
- One of the main reasons that I watch, read, and/or discuss sport is I am the kind of person who likes to be with other people.
- I enjoy watching sport more when I am with a large group of people.

Family
- I like to watch, read, and/or discuss sport because doing so gives me an opportunity to be with my spouse.
- I like to watch, read, and/or discuss sport because doing so gives me an opportunity to be with my family.

*Adapted from Wann (1995).

that these individuals cannot be considered as fans in most occurrences, as they mainly show interest in an economic gain.

Sport events also offer the opportunity for consumers to **Escape** from their daily routine, as they often provide an opportunity to focus for a short period of time (depending on the sport) on an event and put daily difficulties behind them. Finally, closely related to the group affiliation dimension, the **Family** dimension refers to the opportunity provided by sporting events to strengthen family ties and to increase time spent as a family unit. Through sport event consumption, individuals can enhance family cohesion. An adapted version of the scale and its respective items are presented below in Table 2.1. Despite its interesting diagnostic value, this scale has been criticized by some for its limited psychometric properties (internal consistency in

Table 2.2 The Motivation Scale for Sport Consumption (MSSC)

Vicarious Achievement
- I feel a personal sense of achievement when the team does well.
- I feel like I have won when the team wins.
- I feel proud when the team plays well.

Aesthetics
- I appreciate the beauty inherent in the game of basketball.
- I enjoy the natural beauty in the game of basketball.
- I enjoy the gracefulness associated with the game of basketball.

Drama
- I enjoy the drama of close games.
- I prefer watching a close game rather than a one-sided game.
- I enjoy it when the outcome is not decided until the very end.

Escape
- The game provides an escape for me from my day-to-day routine.
- Going to the game is a change of pace from what I regularly do.
- The game provides a diversion from "life's little problems" for me.

Knowledge
- I increase my knowledge about basketball at the game.
- I increase my understanding of basketball strategy by watching the game.
- I can learn about the technical aspects of basketball by watching the game.

Physical Skills
- The athletic skills of the players are something I appreciate.
- I enjoy watching a well-executed athletic performance.
- I enjoy a skillful performance by the team.

Social
- I enjoy interacting with other spectators at the game.
- I enjoy talking with others at the game.
- I enjoy socializing with people sitting near me at the game.

Family
- The game provides an opportunity for me to spend time with my family.
- The game provides an opportunity for me to spend time with my spouse.
- The game provides an opportunity for me to spend time with my children.

*Adapted from Trail & James (2001).

particular).[33] To answer several of these issues over measurement validity, Trail and James[12] proposed the eight-factor Motivation Scale for Sport Consumption (MSSC), shown in Table 2.2.

Motivation Scale for Sport Consumption (MSSC)[12]

This scale offers several additional contributions to the measurement of motives. In particular, the inclusion of a drama dimension introduces the notion that sport events have the ability to provide excitement related to suspense and uncertainty on how events unfold during the sport performance. This is a potentially exciting and rewarding facet for sport events consumers. In addition, the **Knowledge** dimension highlights a component of sporting event experience previously ignored in the Sport Fan Motivation scale.[3] According to the authors, sport event consumers also seek to increase their knowledge and to develop their mastery of the sport they follow. This need to better understand and know technical aspects or actors of the sport may fulfill additional motives such as facilitating group affiliation. Finally, building on the self-esteem dimension introduced in the Sport Fan Motivation scale,[3] Trail and James identified the **vicarious achievement** dimension to capture the sense of achievement a sport event consumer may feel when the event unfolds as he expects or when his favorite team performs well.

In addition to Trail and James,[12] other authors have worked on overcoming concerns expressed about the shortcomings of Wann's initial instrument. Several researchers have focused on developing complex scales to offer a more detailed perspective on motives. Whereas, other researchers have tried to address practitioner requests for valid but shorter instruments that more easily collect data in sport event contexts. Two of these scales are presented in the following material.

The SPEED[34] and OSE[13] Scales

Funk, Filo, Beaton, and Pritchard's work is worth discussing as their SPEED scale (Socialization, Performance, Excitement, Esteem and Diversion) offers excellent performance in explaining attendance and team commitment. The 10-item scale, shown in Table 2.3, presents five potential motives closely related to dimensions previously introduced, but its shorter version is a drastic improvement for professional sport marketers as it has excellent psychometric properties and managerial applications.

Pons, Mourali, and Nyeck's[35] assessment of a consumer's Orientation Toward Sporting Events (OTS) is shown in Table 2.4 and is positioned to answer the dual requirements of both managerial usefulness and validity (i.e., accurate psychometric properties). The measure only has three dimensions of motivation, which allows managers to segment sport events consumers easily on the basis of the level of socialization, sensation, and knowledge they seek. Despite its simplistic categorization of motives, the OTS scale has several benefits: (a) it is relatively short and easy to implement in event research, (b) it demonstrates strong validity across different contexts, sport, and cultures, and (c) it possesses strong reliability with different types of sport event consumers.

Table 2.3 The SPEED Scale

Socialization (SOC)
- The chance to socialize with others.
- The opportunity to interact with other people.

Performance (PER)
- The gracefulness associated with the game.
- The natural elegance of the game.

Excitement (EXC)
- I enjoy the excitement associated with the games.
- I find the games very exciting.

Esteem (EST)
- I feel like I have won when the team wins.
- I get a sense of accomplishment when the team wins.

Diversion (DIV)
- I can get away from the tension in my life.
- It provides me with a break from my daily routine.

---

*Adapted from Funk, Filo, Beaton, & Pritchard (2009).

Merchandising's Role in Augmenting the Consumption Experience

In order to illustrate how sport events consumers live their match day experience and fulfill the different motives highlighted in the first part of this chapter, this section will describe how these motives may lead to additional revenue streams for teams and sport brands that sell sport-related apparel and merchandise. It is critical for sport marketers to understand what kind of fans attend their events and how to segment them, but it is equally important to understand how to market products to these consumers and tap the rationale they follow when deciding to purchase merchandise.

Importance of Merchandising for Sporting Events

Being part of an extremely competitive environment, teams are using different techniques to attract fans and receive a part of their entertainment budgets. One important part of those revenues comes from league-licensed sport merchandise. In 2009, the sport retail industry experienced $11.5 billion in sales, and sport merchandise sales went up by 20% in 2010.[35] With the increasing importance of this type of revenue, sport teams have no other option than to use diverse strategies that build their fan base by fulfilling their motives and increasing identification with their teams. Sport organizations organizations have to be proactive in refining strategies that encourage spectators to consume their different products. Merchandising is one of the principal sources of revenue for the different leagues, and some teams are really capitalizing on their different offerings of apparel. For example, in 2006, the New York Yankees captured 25.4% of all the sales of merchandised products in Major League Baseball.[37]

Some research has investigated the impact of merchandising on supporters. Kwon and Armstrong[38] demonstrated that licensed sport merchandise increased feelings of belongingness to the team, had a significant impact on consumers' social identity, and

Table 2.4 Orientation Toward Sporting Events Scale

Socialization Dimension

1. I am often involved in conversations about sporting events.
2. I like talking about sporting events with people I know.
3. Watching a sporting event on TV is a good opportunity to socialize with one's friends.
4. I generally share my thoughts and feelings about sporting events with others.
5. Attending sporting events is a good opportunity to socialize.

Sensation-Seeking Dimension

6. For me, attending sporting events is a real pleasure.
7. I am always excited when I am going to a sporting event.
8. I am always enthusiastic when I think about attending a sporting event.
9. When I attend a sporting event, I sometimes feel like I am part of the event.
10. I feel really happy when I can attend a sporting event.

Cognition-Seeking Dimension

11. Watching sporting events gives me greater familiarity with the stars of the game.
12. I consider myself a sport expert.
13. I can talk about sport tactics and strategies as well as professional sport reporters.
14. I know very little about sport.
15. I am really interested in any information regarding sport (records, scorers, contracts).

*Adapted from Pons, Mourali & Nyeck (2006).

helped fans classify and separate themselves from other groups of people, especially partisans of rival teams. Also, individuals choose to display and wear more team apparel when their club has been successful.[38] Consumers show a desire to be associated with positive teams that enhance their self-perception. In one study, the authors suggest basking in reflected glory drives some individuals to publicize their association with successful teams. Consumers can experience a personal sense of success through their consumption of products.[40]

In an ethnographic study, Kraszewski[41] investigated the different consumption acts of people in Fort Worth, Texas, and their identification with the Pittsburgh Steelers. With this research, the author found that consumerism helps people to mark themselves as cool rather than as residents of a particular geographic region. In this city, the team's fans are going to the Steelers' bar to perform specific rituals. They asked the owner to carry the Iron City beer and they only drink this beer that captures Pittsburgh's blue-collar identity. Also, fans brought Steelers merchandise with them, but fans don't only want the typical jerseys, they want products sold only in Pennsylvania. The fans established their credibility and authenticity by wearing products that are only sold in the local market. The relationship between sport events consumers and their desire for branded merchandise is detailed below and explained in terms of a fan's motivational makeup.

Group Affiliation Motives and Consumption

The consumption of merchandise related to a specific sport entity can increase the sense of belongingness to the specific team and other similar individuals.[38] A strong motivation for buying such products is that fans enjoy the bonding it creates with other supporters of the team. Supporters often feel an instant connection with the other fans of the team, thinking of them as having a lot in common with themselves, especially sharing related interests and passion. The decision to purchase products is motivated by this factor because people want to show to others what they are, what they represent, and want to be part of this special community. This seems to be a criterion for them to be included in this community of fans. Real and authentic supporters need to have products that identify themselves with the specific team.

Individuals who watch the same game or participate in the same tailgate, even if they don't know each other, view this activity as a mutual experience. People affiliate themselves easily with each other. The group identity is really important in the case of sport. By wearing and consuming merchandise products, people express their love for the team and their identity as part of a group of fans. With the collection of products, individuals want to express their group identity. They also want people around them to show this similar identity. This is especially true when the team is local. Fans are proud to express with their diverse products that they are a fan of the local team and signal their attachment to their team and their city. Organizations can even create this bonding on a more global perspective. One good example is the Red Sox Nation. This expression was first used by a journalist of the *Boston Globe* in 1986, and delineates how the Boston Red Sox are popular all over North America, not just in the Boston region. Since 2004, fans can have an official citizenship and have access to different newsletters and exclusive merchandise items. People from all over America join, and some famous celebrities such as Ben Affleck, Matt Damon, and Jake Gyllenhall are proud to exhibit their preferences for this team.

The affiliation and the support for different causes are also important in fans' choices of products. In sport business, corporate social responsibility has reached an equally significant place such that the vast majority of the organizations in professional leagues are involved in those types of activities.[42] Leagues, teams (i.e., franchises), events (e.g., Olympic Games) and even athletes have initiated programs to support their communities.[43] Organizations and athletes can coordinate different events to raise money for foundations or causes. Nowadays, fans can buy products to encourage their teams and support different causes simultaneously.

Sacred Motives and Consumption

Sport fans often consume products for the sacred meanings related to them. In their article, Belk, Wallendorf, and Sherry[44] mentioned that sacralization processes can lead consumers to a stronger and deeper feeling of attachment and commitment to the brand. These processes include quintessence, inheritance, external sanction, collecting, gift giving, pilgrimage, and ritual.[45]

In this context, sacralization offers a direct connection to the social motives (in particular with the family) as several fans may have been initiated into game-time rituals by people in their immediate social surroundings (e.g., family members, friends, colleagues, boyfriends or girlfriends). For some of them, the team has been a hallowed part of their lives since their childhood. Sacralization by inference occurs when the team holds a revered place in its importance for the social group in question (e.g., the family).[45] Consumers associate different products as being an important part of their family traditions. This forms a nostalgic link that is shared by parents or other family members. For some spectators, they can remember the first time they entered the stadium, their first game, or their first merchandise purchase.

In addition, sport fans and teams are often involved in different types of rituals. A ritual is a behavior that has to "occur the same way every time it is observed" and requires repetition over time.[46] Some rituals are first initiated by the team. In this collective setting, sport teams often ask their fans to wear different products or specific colors during the season or the playoffs. Many devoted fans reported a feeling of urgency and an obligation to participate in those rituals. One good example of collective ceremonies are tailgates. For football fans, tailgating is an important event before the game. Some spectators intensively prepare for it, enjoy the experience and the socialization that they get from this activity.

Also, some fans have their own individual rituals. Those individual artifact rituals often take the form of consumption of products.[46] Consumers use team products as a lucky charm. Other fans decorate their rooms or cars with different objects related to their favorite teams. In this case, the sacred character of those objects increases significantly. Those behaviors help to objectify or animate the team. This animism of object is due to the belief that objects possess souls. Once products and brands are associated with human qualities, people may interact with them in ways that parallel social relationships, where interactions are guided by the norms that govern these relationships. Some people will even paint their cars or homes with the slogan or color of their favorite team or athlete.

Furthermore, supporters like to buy products that are related to special events or memories. Collecting products is a frequent activity among fans.[44] People are collecting the diverse products from different periods, mostly important moments in the history of the team. Devoted fans like to have a variety of products related to their favorite teams. All these processes have been closely linked to the emotional attachment that fans have for their favorite and should be part of a good team's strategy. The sacralization processes can also increase the sense of belonging and devotion to the team in general.[45]

Self-Expression Motives and Consumption

The consumption of sport products can be used to express the identity and the different roles of the individual.[47] The symbolic aspects of sport apparel can be utilized to express a particular part of the identity or a specific role.[48] The consumption of certain products can imbue the self with certain important qualities desired by the consumer.[49] The products that are bought also express what the person perceives herself to be. Consumers are going to use products with different styles for different occasions. People choose carefully the products they decide to buy, so these objects have to represent their identities. Indeed, those products can help the creation of the consumers' identity and can influence the perceptions of others.[50] Teams have to be able to offer both the bonding and sharing of products but also provide opportunities for fans, or facilitate the limited personalization of products, to allow them to express their identity within the realm of the team. Personalized jerseys or t-shirts have been very successful and constitute the basis for innovation for teams. More advanced strategies include technology as a means to personalize team products and merchandising.

Conclusion

In a difficult economic and hyper-competitive environment, sport organizations cannot rely any more on performance and quality only to ensure the development of a strong consumer base. It becomes essential for them to better understand why consumers attend their events and what they are looking for during their consumption experience in order to deliver consistently on the attributes that their consumers favor.

Consistency on tangible and intangible attributes allows sport organizations to establish their brand and increase brand equity. The development of a strong brand is often presented as the solution to instill trust and trigger fan loyalty.[51] In return, this trust and loyalty help the team leverage its brand equity and generate additional revenues through attendance and the sale of merchandise, within and outside the sport arena.[11] It is therefore critical that sport teams' marketers develop a relationship based on reciprocity between the fans' and the team's values and motives.

To implement these branding strategies, sporting events marketers need to be able to assess these motives and values and to use them to better segment their market and know their different groups of consumers. Traditional segmentation of sport event consumers (socio-demographic and behavioral only) have been shown to explain less than 10% of attendance, whereas an instrument measuring motives may explain up to 75% of attendance.[34] This finding underlines the importance of instruments measuring consumers' motives like the ones presented in this chapter. Sport organizations that want to establish coherent branding strategies and financial returns from merchandising and attendance need to adopt appropriate segmentation techniques based on motivation. These approaches deliver content, messages, and scripts that resonate with the most important motives of their consumers.

References

1. King, B. (2004, March). What makes fans tick? *Sport Business Journal*, 25–34.
2. Trail, G., Fink, J., & Anderson, D. (2003). Sport spectator consumption behavior. *Sport Marketing Quarterly*, 12(1), 8–15.
3. Wann, D. L. (1995). Preliminary validation of the sport motivation scale. *Journal of Sport and Social Issues*, 19(1), 377–397.
4. http://www.reportlinker.com/ci02220/Sport.html
5. PricewaterhouseCoopers (2011). *Outlook for the global sport market to 2015*. A report from Pricewaterhouse-Coopers International Limited.
6. MLB Attendance Report—2011. (2011). ESPN.com. Retrieved from http://espn.go.com/mlb/attendance/_/year/2011
7. NFL Attendance—2011. (2011). ESPN. Retrieved from http://espn.go.com/nfl/attendance/_/year/2011
8. http://nymag.com/news/features/2007/profit/32903/
9. Cialdini, R. B. (2000). *Influence: Science and practice* (4th ed.). Boston: Allyn & Bacon.
10. Arnould, E., & Price, L. (1993). River magic: Extraordinary experience and the extended service encounter. *Journal of Consumer Research*, 20(6), 24–45.

11. Unger, L., & Kernan, J. (1983, March). On the meaning of leisure: An investigation of some determinants of the subjective experience. *Journal of Consumer Research*, 9 457–472.

12. Trail, T. J., & James, J. (2001). An analysis of the sport fan motivation scale. *Journal of Sport Behavior*, 12(1), 8–17.

13. Pons, F., Mourali, M., & Nyeck, S. (2006). Consumers' orientation toward sporting events: Scale development and validation. *Journal of Service Research*, 8, 276–287.

14. Shank, M. D. (1999), *Sport marketing: A strategic perspective*, Upper Saddle River, NJ: Prentice Hall.

15. Dietschy, P. (2010). *Histoire du football*, coll. Pour l'histoire, Perrin.

16. Mullin, B. J., Hardy, S., & Sutton, W. A. (2007). *Sport Marketing*, (3rd ed.). Champaign, IL: Human Kinetics.

17. Chalip, L., Green, C., & VanderVelden, L. (2000). The effects of polysemic structures on Olympic viewing. *International Journal of Sport Marketing and Sponsorship*, 2(1), 23–34.

18. Gladden, J. M., & Funk, D. C. (2001). Developing an understanding of brand associations in team sport: Empirical evidence from consumers of professional sport. *Journal of Sport Management*, 16(1), 54–81.

19. Won, J. U., & Kitamura, K. (2007). Comparative analysis of sport consumer motivations between South Korea and Japan. *Sport Marketing Quarterly*, 16(2), 93–105.

20. Zhang, J. J., Pease, D. C., Smith, D. W., Lee, T. J., Lam, T. C., & Jambor, E. A. (1997). Factors affecting the decision making of spectators to attend minor league hockey games. *International Sport Journal*, 7(1), 39–53.

21. Rishe, P., & Mondello, M. (2004). Ticket price determination in professional sport: an empirical analysis of the NBA, NFL, NHL, and Major League Baseball., *Sport Marketing Quarterly*, 13(2), 104–112.

22. Fink, J. S., Trail, G. T., & Anderson, D. F. (2002a). An examination of team identification: Which motives are most salient to its existence? *International Sport Journal/Summer*, 195–207.

23. Pons, F., Laroche, M., et Perreault, S. (2001). Role of sporting events as ethnoculture's emblems: Impact of acculturation and ethnic identity on consumers' orientation toward sporting events. *Sport Marketing Quarterly*, 10(4), 132–146.

24. Wann D. L., Grieve, F., Zapalac, R, and Pease, D. G (2008). Motivational profiles of sport fans of different sport, West Virginia University. *Sport Marketing Quarterly*, 17(1), 6–19.

25. Swanson, S. R., Gwinner, K., Larson, B. V., & Janda, S. (2003). Motivations of college student game attendance and word-of-mouth behavior: the impact of gender differences. *Sport Marketing Quarterly*, 12(3), 151–162.

26. Milne, G. R., & McDonald, M. A. (1999). *Sport marketing: Managing the exchange process*. Sudbury, MA: Jones and Bartlett Publishers.

27. Pierrat, M. (2011). Fans et Ultras; Etude phenomenologique de la relation développée entre une marque et ses consommateurs fidèles dans un club de football. Unpublished hesis, HEC Montreal.

28. Quick S. (2000). Contemporary sport consumers: Some implications of linking fan typology with key spectator variables, University of Technology, Sydney. *Sport Marketing Quarterly*, 9(3), 149–156.

29. Stewart R. K., & Smith, A. C. T. (1997). Sport watching in Australia: A conceptual framework. In D. Shilbury et L. Chalip (Eds.), *Advancing management of Australia and New Zealand sport*, SMAANZ, Deakin University, Australia.

30. Wann, D. L., & Branscombe, N. R. (1993)., Sport fans: Measuring degree of identification with their team. *International Journal of Sport Psychology*, 24(1), 1–17.

31. Sutton, W. A., McDonald, M. A., Milne, G., & Cimperman, J. (1997). Creating and fostering fan identification in professional sport. *Sport Marketing Quarterly*, 6, 15–22.

32. Campbell, R., Aiken, D., & Ketit, A. (2004). Beyond BIRGing and CORFing: Continuing the exploration of fan behavior. *Sport Marketing Quarterly*, 13, 151–157.

33. Mahony, D. F., Nakazawa, M., Funk, D. C., James, J. D., & Gladden, J. M. (2002). Motivational factors influencing the behavior of J-league spectators. *Sport Management Review*, 5, 1–24.

34. Funk, D. C., Filo, K., Beaton, A. A., & Pritchard, M. P. (2009). Measuring the motives of sport event attendance: Bridging the academic-practitioner divide to understanding behavior. *Sport Marketing Quarterly, 18*, p. 126–138.

35. Pons, Mourali, & Nyeck (2006).

36. Retrieved from http://www.businessinsider.com/sport-merchandise-sales-are-strong-heading-into-holiday-season-2010-11

37. Retrieved from http://www.bizofbaseball.com/index.php?option=com_content&task=view&id=980&Itemid=42

38. Kwon, H. H,. & Amstrong, K. L. (2002). Factors influencing impulse buying of sport team licensed merchandise. *Sport Marketing Quarterly*, 11(3), 151–163.

39. Cialdini, R. B., Borden, R. J., Thorne, A., Walker, M. R., Freeman, S., & Sloan, L. R. (1996). Basking in reflected glory: Three (football) field studies. *Journal of Personality and Social Psychology*, 34(3), 366–375.

40. Andrew, Damon P. S., Seungmo, K., O'Neal, N., Greenwell, T. C., & James, J. D. (2009). The relationship between spectator motivations and media and merchandise consumption at a professional mixed martial arts event. *Sport Marketing Quarterly*, 18(4), 199–209.

41. Kraszewski, J. (2008). Fandom, and the management of home Pittsburgh in Fort Worth: Football bars, sport television, sport. *Journal of Sport and Social Issues*, 32(2), 139–157.

42. Walker, M., Kent, A., & Vincent, J. (2010). Communicating socially responsible initiatives: An analysis of U.S. professional teams. *Sport Marketing Quarterly, 19*(4), 187–195.

43. Babiak, K., & Wolfe, R. (2006). More than just a game? Corporate social responsibility and Super Bowl XL. *Sport Marketing Quarterly, 15*(4), 214–222.

44. Belk, R. W., Wallendorf, M., & Sherry, J. F., Jr. (1989). The sacred and the profane in consumer behaviour: Theodicy on the Odyssey. *Journal of Consumer Research, 16*(1), 1–38.

45. Pimentel, R. W., & Reynolds, K. E. (2004). A model for consumer devotion: Affective commitment with proactive sustaining behaviors. *Academy of Marketing Science Review, 5*, 1–45.

46. Rook, D. (1985). The ritual dimension of consumer behavior. *Journal of Consumer Research, 12*(3), 251–264.

47. Dickson, M. A., & Pollack, A. (2000). Clothing and identity among female in-line skaters. *Clothing and Textiles Research Journal, 18*(2), 65–72.

48. Solomon, M. R. (1983). The role of products as social stimuli: A symbolic interactionism perspective. *Journal of Consumer Research, 10*(3), 319–329.

49. Belk, R. W. (1988). Possessions and the extended self. *Journal of Consumer Research, 15*(2), 139–168.

50. Snyder, E. E. (1983). Identity, commitment, and type of sport roles. *Quest, 35*, 97–106.

51. Richelieu, A., & Pons, F. (2009). If brand equity matters, where is the brand strategy? A look at the National Hockey League (NHL). *International Journal of Sport Marketing and Management, 5*(1), 34–45.

3

Sport Consumer Attitudes

Formation, Function, and Effects on Information Processing

Daniel C. Funk
Temple University and Griffith University

Daniel Lock
Griffith University

Abstract: An individual forms his or her attitudes, impressions, and opinions toward a professional sport team based on information provided by a variety of external sources. The consumer socialization process involves external socializing agents, such as mass media, advertising, parents, friends, work colleagues, relatives, teachers and coaches, schools, religious institutions, cultural beliefs, and community-based programs, introducing a sports team to an individual. Among the sources, mass media is an important medium for shaping the attitudes of children as they mature through adolescence and into adulthood. As a result, informational content conveyed through mass media plays a dominant role in shaping attitudes and identities toward professional sport teams.

Keywords: attitude change, attitude formation, categorization, information processing, sport identity

Introduction

Few industries are given as much media exposure as professional sports. Professional sport organizations receive free and contracted publicity in the form of event coverage and news, while the media receives programming and content to augment their product and services. Hence, the potential persuasiveness of media content in shaping the attitudes of a sport organization's various stakeholders (e.g., current consumers, sponsors, politicians, local business owners, community residents) is important for sustainability. This chapter will discuss the form, function, and effect of an individual's attitude to illustrate the cognitive effects of how information embedded in media content is interpreted, framed, and processed. This discussion will draw on theories of attitude, categorization, and social identity to provide insight into how attitudinal and social factors contribute understanding of how message effects are processed.

Professional Sports and the Media

The sport entertainment industry receives considerable media attention and continues to operate as an attractive source for content.[1] Sport content generated from

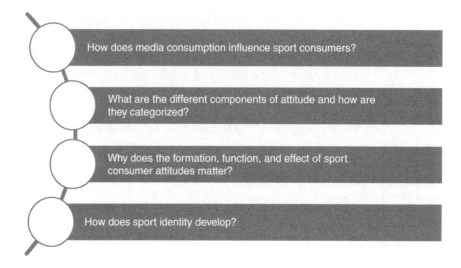

How does media consumption influence sport consumers?

What are the different components of attitude and how are they categorized?

Why does the formation, function, and effect of sport consumer attitudes matter?

How does sport identity develop?

Figure 3.1 An Overview of Chapter 3

professional and collegiate sport contests continues to be a key asset for media organizations to increase ratings, circulation and visits, which ultimately drives advertising and sponsorship revenues. This creates a symbiotic relationship between sports and the media whereby sport organizations receive publicity, promotion, and revenues and the media gains programming, content, and revenue.[2] However, a substitutionary relationship may also exist as spectators may not attend a sports event and instead view related media accounts at home, via the web, or in local pubs.[3] Currently, the relationship between sports and the media is described best as symbiotic and substitutionary because four different patterns of consumption exist:

1. Light consumption; where both live attendance and media use is minimal
2. Media dominant consumption; where media consumption is the primary form
3. Sport event dominant consumption; where live attendance is the primary form
4. Heavy consumption; where both frequent live attendance and media consumption are present.[4]

Regardless of which consumption pattern occurs, the media's communication of sport content plays a fundamental role in shaping public attitudes, impressions, and opinions by providing much of the information individuals think about.[5] As a result, understanding the media's influence on shaping an individual's attitude is important for building and sustaining successful sport brands.

Few business entities demonstrate greater evidence of the development of strong and well-formed attitudes than those in the domain of competitive sports.[6] The level of commitment, passion, anger, and indifference that sports teams and players engender is visible in fan behavior, which explains the considerable attention paid to the domain by sociologists and psychologists alike.[7] Hence, two different perspectives exist to assess the influence of media content on consumers. The first is a psychological perspective, which examines the cognitive effects of individuals' information framing and processing.[8] This perspective highlights that media content in relation to sport events, teams, individual players, and coaches is perceived and processed based on individuals' current level of attitude formation. For example, an individual's prior knowledge and direct experience related to a sport object (such as a team, organization, etc.) provides the basis to evaluate media content concerning that entity.

The second is a sociological perspective, which considers how various societal and environmental factors interact with the consumer during a process of socialization.[9] This perspective focuses on how socializing agents, such as media persons, institutions, or organizations communicate norms, attitudes, and behaviors related to sport entities through a process of social learning.[10] Sociologists suggest that mass media can construct information in such a way that it promotes dominant group interests as normal.[11] Therefore, such information can influence how people think and feel about the social and political environment. Media coverage can influence public opinion by controlling what individuals know about an event in the absence of actual observation or first-hand knowledge.[12] For example, editorials can influence respondents' beliefs about a sports team based on the position advocated by a columnist. Moreover, in sports, positive editorials that support specific sport franchises lead to more favorable team attitudes, whereas negative editorials create less favorable attitudes.[13]

A combination of the psychological and sociological perspectives into a social-psychological framework is particularly relevant for understanding the media's influence on attitude formation and change in the sport industry. This follows the logic that the relative influence of evaluating media content varies depending on whether an individual is a fan, casual spectator, community resident, tourist, or member of the public. Funk and Pritchard found that an individual's level of commitment moderates his/her attitudinal response to reading sports editorials.[14] In other words, team commitment functions to stabilize beliefs and feelings in relation to sporting objects, as well as determining the evaluation of informational stimuli embedded in the message. Hence, social learning from exposure to media appears to be more influential in the less committed, but less impactful for committed individuals. This information is useful for guiding strategies designed to build and maintain relationships with a sports team's fan base. The next section provides a discussion of attitude theory to develop understanding of how an attitude toward a sport object forms and changes in response to external stimuli such as persuasive messages from mass media outlets.

Attitude Theory

The term "attitude" has been the subject of varied conceptualizations and definitions during its extensive history. The term attitude represents a hypothetical construct referring to a general and enduring positive or negative feeling toward, or evaluative response to, some person, object, or issue.[15] Attitudes possess three distinguishing features: they are learned, can be relatively enduring, and they influence behavior.[16] Within the context of sport, this knowledge of attitudes equates to understanding the manner in which a sport consumer evaluates a sports team, including any information related to the team, and the outcome of that evaluation in terms of the effect produced.

Hence, attitudes can be learned and they reflect a predisposition toward an object that expresses some important aspect of an individual's personality.[17]

There has been considerable research devoted to understanding the nature and operation of attitude formation and change. Theoretical and empirical research has followed three major orientations: (a) tripartite, (b) one-dimensional, and (c) structural.[18] Sport consumer behavior research has generally followed these approaches.[19] The tripartite perspective was the first, initially arguing that an attitude consists of three main components: affect, cognition, and conation. This perspective led to different explanations of attitude formation and change due to the three separate components.[20] Hence, an attitude toward a sport object reflects three independent but related components of feelings, thoughts, and behavioral intent. The one-dimensional perspective evolved later, suggesting a causal flow among the attitude components (Beliefs→ Affect→ Intentions). Essentially, this sequence highlights how beliefs about a sports team lead to feelings that influence intentions and commitment, which then guide sport consumer behavior.[21] The structural perspective emerged from studies attempting to verify various discrete strength properties that formed and sustained attitude toward a focal object.[22] These distinct structural properties include extremity, accessibility, importance, intensity, certainty, knowledge, direct experience, affective-cognitive consistency, personal relevance. Each has been used in professional sport research to understand loyalty.[23]

A common theme throughout the literature is that attitudes comprise an evaluative component.[24] In an effort to provide an umbrella definition to guide attitude research, Eagly and Chaiken (p. 585) defined attitude as "a psychological tendency that is expressed by evaluating a particular entity with some degree of favor or disfavor".[25] The authors further suggest that an attitude has three key elements—evaluation, entity, and tendency. See Figure 3.2 for a conceptualization of attitudinal elements. *Evaluation* refers to responses to external stimuli such as social interactions, sport content and information processing with respect to any combination of cognition, affect, or behavior. These evaluative responses manifest in cognitive beliefs, values, and thoughts, affective feelings or emotions, and overt or intentional behaviors regarding the sports team. *Entity* refers to the focal object of the attitude. This can be any distinguishable entity, tangible or intangible, capable of producing an evaluative response. Hence, the attitude object could be a sports team, sporting event, stadium, sponsor, or player as well as any association (i.e., attribute or benefit) linked to the sport object.[26] *Tendency* refers to an attitude as an enduring evaluative response or personal disposition. Individuals can develop a strong tendency to evaluate a sport object consistently in varying contexts, and resist overt and covert attempts to change the attitude.[27] The terms loyal, committed, or die-hard fan represent terms used to describe this enduring tendency.

The conceptualization of an attitude in terms of an evaluative tendency toward an object provides a means to examine attitude formation and change. The notion of formation and change is important to understand consumer attitudes toward products and services such as sports because knowing how consumers think and feel about objects enables the prediction of consumer choice and facilitates the design of strategies to influence behavior.[28] Advertising and particularly media coverage can create and maintain strong and enduring attitudes toward sports teams.[29] Hence, exploring

Figure 3.2 Conceptualization of Sport Team Attitude

how attitude structure and function provides the ability to understand the effects of media and marketing activities on sport consumers. The literature on classification as applied to sport objects provides a good conceptual means to explore the intangibility of attitudes.

Object Classification

The psychological tendency to evaluate media content leads to a process whereby external stimuli is processed and cognitively categorized and linked to existing information in terms of abstraction. Social psychologists have studied the way human cultures categorize stimuli in their social world. Efforts to study classification systems originated in anthropology, where taxonomic hierarchies provided a method of categorizing plants and animals.[30] For example, plants fit classifications at six levels of abstraction, e.g., Plant, Tree, Evergreen Tree, Pine Tree, White Pine Tree, and Western White Pine Tree. This pattern of social-cognitive classification describes a system by which individuals consider perceived similarities between objects in their physical and social world and then construct categories to represent and place such objects. Categorization serves to reduce diversity of objects and events by considering similarities and differences based upon informational factors embedded in stimuli.[31]

Work on categorization predominantly emerged from Elenor Rosch's work. Rosch suggested that humans categorize stimuli at three levels of abstraction.[32] The most abstract level is the superordinate level (e.g., furniture). An example of this category in the sport industry would be spectator sports. The second level of abstraction is the basic level (e.g., table). This category level would equate to the sport of football or basketball in the United States. The least abstract is the subordinate level (e.g., kitchen table). In sports, this represents a professional football league such as the National Football League (NFL) or National Collegiate Athletic Association (NCAA). Within spectator sports, additional subordinate-level categories can emerge, such as the professional sport franchise (e.g., Dallas Cowboys or Ohio State Buckeyes) or a marquee player or coach (e.g., Troy Aiken, Tom Landry). As a result, the structure of the category levels

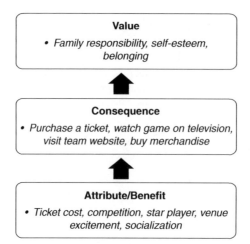

Figure 3.3 Laddering of Team Brand Associations

(breadth and depth of categories) influences the evaluation of media content related to professional sports teams. In other words, the structure of existing knowledge categories would frame the information and influence the individual's ability to interpret, assimilate, or reject information embedded in content. Hence, these categories have both structure and function.

Research in marketing has used the structure and function of categorization to frame associations. This approach is similar to laddering, which can be used to organize mental associations into a vertical sequence based on the perceived connection of an object to self.[33] In other words, an individual's perceptual orientation toward a product or service can be constructed using a vertical chain of associations (i.e., rungs on a stepladder) based on the meaning ascribed to a range of attributes and benefits, consequences and values. The ladder allows associations to be categorized and sequenced, creating distinctions, and these distinctions represent different levels of abstraction. Figure 3.3 provides an example of laddering in a spectator sport context. In Figure 3.3, the first level of abstraction is a range of attributes and benefits associated with a professional sports team. The second level is consequences determined by the meaning placed on the associations that direct individual action. The top and most abstract level is value, which represents the psychological significance placed on the consequences of an action in relation to the self.

The ladder approach provides researchers with the ability to translate into practice how and why individuals evaluate and choose different products and services by describing the structure and function of key associations. One key assumption is that the perceived relevance of the product or service will determine if certain attributes and benefits are linked to personal values.[34] An individual evaluates media content by categorizing product-related information on attributes and benefits into different levels of abstraction in order to help determine the product's psychological significance and value. The categorizing and linking of information to self-concept and values reflects the degree of attitude formation. Self-concept and values are desirable end states that go beyond specific situations and guide decision making, providing a means to gain an understanding of attitudes toward sport objects.[35]

The categorization of external stimuli is useful to conceptualize attitudinal processing and informational framing. Hence, an attitude has both structure and function in sport consumer behavior. The structure of an individual's attitude toward a professional sports team determines how the attitude functions in terms of cognitive processing of external situational and framing informational stimuli. Both the structure and function determine the effect of the external stimuli on behavior. The following section integrates attitude strength theory with categorization to illustrate an attitude in terms of three levels of abstraction: formation, function, and effects.

Attitude Formation, Function, and Effects

A description of an attitude's formation, function, and effect is presented in Table 3.1. This breakdown provides a useful way for understanding how various attitude strength properties bundle together structurally and functionally to evaluate information about a sport object. Conceptualizing various attitude properties within three distinct levels of abstraction provides a richer account of how attitude formation, function, and effects occur. The first level of abstraction, labeled "Attitude Formation" represents the composition of attitude formation toward the entity or focal sport object. The second level of abstraction, labeled "Attitude Function," represents evaluative mechanisms of the attitude in terms of processing external stimuli. The final level of abstraction, "Attitude Effects," represents the response to the external stimuli that produces outcomes. This perspective assumes that the individual can perform three basic functions: judge similarities between stimuli, perceive and process the attributes and benefits of stimuli, and maintain a capacity to learn.

Formation

The attitude formation level represents the attitudinal structure and the first level of abstraction. At this level, attitude properties that contain consistency, complexity, and conviction create a platform for evaluating media content. See Figure 3.4 for attitude characteristics. Consistency represents the degree of affective-cognitive consistency between feeling and beliefs about a team. In other words, evaluation occurs between an

Table 3.1 Attitude Model: Form, Function, and Effect

Level of Abstraction	Attitude Characteristics
Effect Impact & Durability	An attitude's capacity to remain unchanged over time and its effect on information processing
Function Accessibility & Centrality	Evaluative processes determining the immediacy of information retrieval from memory and framing stimuli in relationship to "self."
Formation Complexity, Consistency, & Conviction	Aspects of the attitude determined by the quality and quantity of the internal structure

individual's feelings about the team and his or her beliefs about the team: for example, an individual who likes the Dallas Cowboys but understands that they are horrible [this season] and have no chance of making the playoffs. Complexity represents the formation of properties related to the amount of team-relevant knowledge and direct experience with various team activities derived from an individual's evaluation from memory. For example, an individual may know a great deal about a sports team and have attended or watched a number of games on television but still not have positive feelings or a sense of conviction toward the team. Conviction represents the formation of extremity and certainty properties. A Boston Red Sox fan can hate the New York Yankees with the same level of conviction as a die-hard Yankees fan can love the team. The formation of complexity, consistency, and conviction are critical facets underpinning how individuals construct categories to place informational factors embedded in stimuli.

Function

Attitude function operates at the second level of abstraction and represents the elaboration processes and framing of media content. Message elaboration deals with mental activity, and determines the type of processing that is devoted to the classification of media content. For example, central route processing takes place when individuals are sufficiently motivated (e.g., high involvement) and have the opportunity and ability to process a message's specific arguments.[36] In contrast, peripheral route processing occurs when motivation, ability, or opportunity is low (e.g., low involvement). Individuals typically utilize peripheral cues here instead of message arguments to process the persuasive appeal. Hence, central and peripheral route processing contribute to processes of accessibility and centrality. The functioning of the attitude centrality and accessibility governs the attitude's responsiveness and sensitivity toward new or competing information.

The functional processes of centrality and accessibility determine the attitude's proximity in two different ways; by determining how close to top-of-mind the attitude is, and how available it is as a vehicle for self-representation (propinquity to self). (See Table 3.1.) The probability that an attitude will automatically activate corresponds to its accessibility. The retrieval of highly accessible attitudes occurs effortlessly from memory when the attitude object is encountered, potentially to the point of being subconsciously aroused. Centrality represents an attitude that centrally aligns with salient values and self-concept through properties of importance and personal relevance. Importance is a subjective measure of the psychological significance one ascribes to an attitude, which refers to the level of caring and concern for an attitude object. The more important an attitude object is, the more sensitive consumers become to competing or new information that relates to the object.[37] Personal relevance represents links between an attitude object and aspects of the self, such as values, self-interest, and social/group identification. Overall, an attitude functions more effectively and efficiently when it is salient, readily accessible from memory, and the individual places a great deal of psychological significance and value in the attitude toward an object. The function provides the ability to interpret the stimuli and either assimilate or reject the information embedded in content to create an effect.

Effects

The final level of attitude effects operates at the highest level of abstraction. This level depicts the consequences of a well-formed and fully functioning attitude in terms of its ability to process information. A well-formed attitude is more durable and has a greater capacity for impact through resistance to change and persistence of thought regardless of the introduction of conflicting information.[38] The process of retrieving relevant data from a complex schema to evaluate information provides the ability to assimilate or contrast information.[39] Assimilation occurs when new information is perceived as being closer to the current attitude. In contrast, discrepant information is perceived as being further from the current attitude.

Based on social judgment theory, individuals interpret, arrange, and respond to stimuli along an attitudinal continuum.[40] The new information shifts toward or away from an anchor or reference point (i.e., one's commitment toward the team). For example, individuals may shift or adjust their attitude so that it avoids dissonance (i.e., conflicting information is screened) and selectively focuses on positive elements related to the sport or a team.[41] Funk and Pritchard reported that an individual's commitment toward a sports team determined the number and type of thoughts elicited from an editorial and the ability to recall facts embedded in the editorial.[42] Overall, the response to external stimuli may be influenced by the impact of attitude processing and durability. As a result, the attitude perspective outlined and discussed in Figure 3.3 is useful for understanding the interpretation of message effects at a personal level; however, sport identity provides additional insight into responses and reactions to media content at an intergroup level.

Sport Identity: Form, Function, and Effect

An individual's sport identity reflects a social-psychological position in relation to a group, such as a sporting team.[43] Sport identity represents an additional layer of understanding to decipher consumer responses to media content, as group membership can explain situational reactions underpinned by group norms and socialization, which transcend those attitudes and beliefs that are innately personal.[44] Sport identity is a prime example of social category membership that represents an individual's knowledge that s/he belongs to a specific sporting group. This group membership has emotional value, symbolic meaning, and functional significance.[45] Sport identity occurs when an individual integrates a sports team into his or her sense of self, resulting in the team becoming an integral part of their self-definition.[46]

While the attitudinal evaluation process introduced earlier includes a cognitive, affective, and conative response in relation to specific tangible or intangible objects, social identity operates at an intergroup, not interpersonal, level of abstraction, thus shifting the foci of analysis and the connotations in relation to the interpretation of media content from a personal to a social level.[47] As such, the evaluation process occurs on cognitive (I am part of X), evaluative (Compared with other teams, X is superior), and affective (Being part of X is important to me) levels.[48] When an individual's social identity is active, personal attitudes and innate individual characteristics become less salient as the role of the norms, values, and beliefs that bind members of the sport group influences thought and action.

The transition from intra-individual psychological attitudes and identity shifts across a continuum, from personal to social.[49] Personal identity includes the traits and attitudes that a person already possesses, and social identity reflects self-categories (i.e., chosen by an individual) selected as self-representative reference groups, which influence attitudes and behavior.[50] This is not to say that personal and social identities do not interact—far from it—but that distinguishing each from a theoretical perspective can elaborate understanding of responses to specific situations, such as evaluations of specific media messages.

Previously, Funk and James suggested that group and personal identities can be collapsed into aspects of a single sport identity since the content of each identity reflects similarities between desired personal traits and characteristics and perceived group traits and characteristics.[51] However, distinguishing personal from social identity as two levels of identity abstraction provides additional utility in understanding how consumers respond to media content in relation to sporting groups, because thought processes in relation to sport identities are externally socialized, which influences the construction of the identity content beyond what can be explained by innate personal factors. Evidence suggests that the shift from personal to social levels of identity abstraction occurs when an individual perceives that being associated with a sports team will reflect positively on his or her self-concept (e.g., Basking In Reflected Glory (BIRG).[52] Moreover, the shift toward social identity is activated as the salience and strength of a sport identity increases.[53] Whereas the evaluation of attitudes occurs at a personal level of abstraction, the evaluation of social identity occurs between different social groups. Thus, the perceived status (positive or negative) of an ingroup provides the basis of comparison with relevant outgroups.[54] As individuals are motivated to improve self-esteem through group membership, status is a key variable underpinning this type of behavior.[55] For this reason, intergroup comparison provides a platform framing why social identity theory and self-categorization theory enable a better understanding of responses to media content.

The cognitive effects of sport identity are based on the capacity of group members to frame and process information that relates to the ingroup. Hence, the evaluation of media content reflects, and is influenced by, the extent that it enhances, or damages the status of the ingroup. When the status of a sport identity is threatened, members generally respond in three ways: individual mobility, social creativity, or social competition strategies. In individual mobility, if the status of the sport identity is reduced, individuals have been shown to distance themselves and Cut Off Reflected Failure (CORF), or seek to increase their relative standing within the ingroup.[56] Social creativity arises when group members change the dimension on which the intergroup comparison is made, talk positively about the ingroup, or talk up the team to non-group members to improve the relative status of the ingroup.[57] Group members can also employ social competition strategies and actively seek to reduce the status of outgroups. For example, BLASTing refers to ingroup members actively degrading opposing players, fans, and coaches, thus seeking to improve the ingroup's status by engaging in behaviors to reduce the status of outgroups.[58] Put simply, when the status of a sport identity is threatened, members will respond by leaving, or seeking to improve ingroup status.

The social identity perspective shows that evaluations of media content emanate to the extent that media messages are congruent or incongruent with ingroup norms and values, and evaluated to the extent that content is favorable or unfavorable to the status of the sport identity. This point solidifies why social identity extends on a purely attitudinal focus. Ingroup norms and values form through similarities between ingroup members and a process of uncertainty reduction, which serves to enhance the cohesiveness of the ingroup by depersonalizing members toward agreement on one or more key aspects of "what the ingroup is" (we are all Patriots fans, and the Patriots are our team).[59] Therefore, as this process occurs externally to the individual through a process of self and group negotiation, it occurs beyond what could be solely accounted for by innate, psychological forces.

In a fashion similar to attitudinal research, previous research indicates that as the strength of identification increases (or internalizes), the degree of response to positive or negative editorials is magnified.[60] Therefore, sport identity imbues an evaluation framework on group members driven by key normative features of the ingroup, which members share. If media content contrasts, or is seen as derogatory about key features of the ingroup (player behavior, club traditions, etc.), ingroup members will respond negatively to the news and this response will strengthen as the sport identity becomes more salient. Reactions to media content that negatively influences the status of a sport identity could include actively seeking to discredit the media source to improve ingroup status. Other responses include active boycotts of certain media organizations (e.g., Liverpool Football Club fans boycott of the Sun Newspaper following its coverage of the Hillsborough Stadium tragedy) or consumers actively distancing themselves from the sport identity due to the negative reflection. Conversely, content that increases the status will lead to consumers endorsing and promoting the positive content to maximize the positive reflection of association with the group on his or her self-concept.[61]

Sport identity functions to evaluate media content in relation to the ingroup status, norms, and subcultural values that bind members together and differentiate the ingroup from outgroups. Hence, an external stimulus that reinforces and confirms the status of the sport identity concerning subcultural norms and expectancies is central to the formation and functioning of attitudes that shape, and are shaped by, group membership.[62] Furthermore, because individuals place significant social and psychological significance and value on sport identities, information that provides confirmation and affirmation of the identity represent an important source of self-concept validation in the sportscape. This knowledge provides an explanation for the plethora of sporting teams that now operate organizationally controlled television channels and publications. This functioning produces the ability of the sport identity to endure, influence behavior, and interact with the shaping of personal and social attitudes and identities.

Conclusion

The potential persuasiveness of mass media on professional sport franchises is considerable. The informational stimuli embedded in media content can influence various stakeholders at a personal attitudinal and social level. This chapter provided a discussion of the formation, function, and effects of attitudes and sport identities to help understand how informational content is categorized, processed, and acted upon. Evaluative processes at personal and social levels were outlined as critical in understanding the key forces that shape responses to media content.

References

1. Nichols, W., Moynahan, P., Hall, A., & Taylor, J. (2002). *Media relations in sport*. Morgantown: WV: Fitness Information Technology, Inc.
2. Mason, D. S. (1999). What is the sports product and who buys it? The marketing of professional sports leagues. *European Journal of Marketing, 33*, 402–418.
3. Bambridge, M., Cameron, S., & Dawson, P. (1996). Satellite television and the demand for football: A whole new ball game? *Scottish Journal of Political Economy, 43*, 17–334
4. Pritchard, M. P., & Funk, D. C. (2006). Symbiosis and substitution in spectator sport, *Journal of Sport Management, 20*( )3, 297–320.
5. Entman, R. M. (1989). How the media affect what people think: An information processing approach. *Journal of Politics, 51*, 347–370.
6. Bristow, D., & Sebastian, R. (2001). Holy cow! Wait 'til next year! A closer look at the brand loyalty of Chicago Cubs baseball fans. *Journal of Consumer Marketing, 18*(3), 256–275.
7. Gaunt, R., Sindic, D., & Leyens, J. (2005). Intergroup relations in soccer finals: People's forecasts of the duration of emotional reactions of in-group and out-group soccer fans. *The Journal of Social Psychology, 145*(2), 117–126; and Wann, D., & Schrader, M. (2000). Controllability and stability in the self-serving attributions of sport spectators. *Journal of Social Psychology, 140*(2), 160–168.
8. Drew, D., & Weaver, D. (1990). Media attention, media exposure, and media effects. *Journalism Quarterly, 67*, 740–748.
9. Domke, D. (2001). The press, race relations, and social change. *Journal of Communication, 51*, 317–344.
10. Bush, A. J., Smith, R., & Martin, C. (1999). The influence of consumer socialization variables on attitude toward advertising: A comparison of African-American and Caucasians. *Journal of Advertising, 28*, 13–24; and James, J. D. (2001). The role of cognitive development and socialization in the initial development of team loyalty. *Leisure Sciences, 23*, 233–262.
11. Eitzen, D. S., & Sage, G. H. (2003). *Sociology of North American sport* (7th ed.). New York: McGraw-Hill.
12. Bartels, L. (1993). Messages received: The political impact of media exposure. *American Political Science Review, 87*, 267–285.
13. Funk, D. C., & Pritchard, M. P. (2006). Sport publicity: Commitment's moderation of message effects. *Journal of Business Research, 59*, 613–621.
14. Ibid.
15. Petty, R. E., & Cacioppo, J. T. (1986). The elaboration likelihood model of persuasion. In L. Berkowitz (Ed.), *Advances in experimental social psychology* (Vol. 19, pp. 123–205). San Diego, CA: Academic Press.
16. O'Keefe, D. J. (1990). *Persuasion: Theory and research*. Newbury Park, CA: Sage Publications.
17. Eagly, A. H., & Chaiken, S. (2007, October). The advantages of an inclusive definition of attitude. *Social Cognition, 25*(5), 582–602.
18. Ibid.; and Fazio, R. H. (2007). Attitudes as object-evaluation associations of varying strength. *Social Cognition, 25*(5), 603–637.
19. Cunningham, G. B., & Kwon, H. (2003). The theory of planned behaviour and intentions to attend a sport event. *Sport Management Review, 6*(2), 127–145; and Funk, D. C., Haugtvedt, C. P., & Howard, D. R. (2000). Contemporary attitude theory in sport: Theoretical considerations and implications. *Sport Management Review, 3*, 124–144.
20. Bagozzi, R. P, Tybout, A. M., Craig, C. S, & Sternthal, B. (1979). The construct validity of the tripartite classification of attitudes. *Journal of Marketing Research, 16*, 88–95.
21. Funk, D. C., & Pritchard, M. P. (2006). Sport publicity: Commitment's moderation of message effects. *Journal of Business Research, 59*, 613–621.
22. Bassili, J. N. (1996). Meta-judgments versus operative indexes of psychological attributes: The case of measures of attitude strength. *Journal of Personality and Social Psychology, 71*, 637–653.
23. Funk, D. C., & Pastore, D. L. (2000). Equating attitudes to allegiance: The usefulness of selected attitudinal information in segmenting loyalty to professional sports teams. *Sport Marketing Quarterly, 9*(4), 175–184.

24. Petty, R. E., Briñol, P., & DeMarree, K. G. (2007). The meta-cognitive model (MCM) of attitudes: Implications for attitude measurement, change, and strength. *Social Cognition, 25*(5), 657–686.

25. Eagly, A. H., & Chaiken, S. (2007, October). The advantages of an inclusive definition of attitude. *Social Cognition, 25*(5), 582–602.

26. Gladden, J. M., & Funk, D. C. (2002). Developing and understanding of brand association in team sport: Empirical evidence from professional sport consumers. *Journal of Sport Management, 16,* 54–81.

27. Tormala, Z. L., & Petty, R. E. (2004). Source credibility and attitude certainty: A metacognitive analysis of resistance to persuasion. *Journal of Consumer Psychology, 14*(4), 427–442.

28. Dick, A. S., & Basu, K. (1994). Customer loyalty: Toward an integrated conceptual framework. *Journal of the Academy of Marketing Science, 22,* 99–113.

29. Bristow, D., & Sebastian, R. (2001). Holy cow! Wait 'til next year! A closer look at the brand loyalty of Chicago Cubs baseball fans. *Journal of Consumer Marketing, 18*(3), 256–275.

30. Berlin, B. (1972). Speculations on the growth of ethnobotanical nomenclature. *Language in Society, 1,* 51–86.

31. Rosch, E. (1978). Principles of categorization. In E. Rosch & B. B. Lloyd (Eds.), *Cognition and categorization* (pp.27–48). Hillsdale, NJ: Erlbaum.

32. Ibid.; and Rosch, E., Mervis, C. B., Gray, W. D., Jonson, D. M., & Boyes-Braem, P. (1976). Basic objects in natural categories. *Cognitive Psychology, 8,* 382–439

33. Gutman, J. (1982). A means-end chain model based on consumer categorization processes, *Journal of Marketing 46,* 60–72.

34. Reynolds, T. J., & Gutman, J. (1988). Laddering theory, method, analysis and interpretation. *Journal of Advertising Research 28,* 11–34.

35. Kahle, L., Duncan, M., Dalakas, V., & Aiken, D. (2001). The social values of fans for men's versus women's university basketball. *Sport Marketing Quarterly, 10,* 156–16; and Schwartz, S. H., & Bilsky, W. (1987). Toward a universal psychological structure of human values. *Journal of Personality and Social Psychology, 53*(3), 550–562.

36. Petty, R. E., & Cacioppo, J. T. (1986). The elaboration likelihood model of persuasion. In L. Berkowitz (Ed.), *Advances in experimental social psychology* (Vol. 19, pp. 123–205). San Diego, CA: Academic Press.

37. Petty, R. E., & Cacioppo, J. T. (1986). The elaboration likelihood model of persuasion. In L. Berkowitz (Ed.), *Advances in experimental social psychology* (Vol. 19, pp. 123–205). San Diego, CA: Academic Press.

38. Ahluwalia, R., Burnkrant, R. E., & Unnava, H. R. (2000, May). Consumer response to negative publicity: The moderating role of commitment. *Journal of Marketing Research 37,* 203–214.

39. Hovland, C. I., Campbell, E. II., & Brock, T. C. (1957). The effects of commitment on opinion change following communication. In C. I. Hovland (Ed.), *The Order of Presentation in Persuasion.* (pp. 23-32) New Haven, CT: Yale University Press.

40. Sherif, C. W. (1963, August). Social categorization as a function of latitude of acceptance and series range. *Journal of Abnormal & Social Psychology 67,* 148–156.

41. Festinger, L. (1957). *A theory of cognitive dissonance.* Stanford: Stanford University Press.

42. Funk, D. C., & Pritchard, M. P. (2006). Sport publicity: Commitment's moderation of message effects. *Journal of Business Research, 59,* 613–621.

43. Funk, D. C., & James, J. (2001). The Psychological Continuum Model: A conceptual framework for understanding an individual's psychological connection to sport. *Sport Management Review, 4*(2), 119–150.

44. Tajfel, H. (1972). Experiments in a vacuum. In J. Israel & H. Tajfel (Eds.), *The context of social psychology; a critical assessment* (pp. 69–119). London: published in cooperation with the European Association of Experimental Psychology by Academic Press.

45. Funk, D. C., & James, J. (2006). Consumer loyalty: The meaning of attachment in the development of sport team allegiance. *Journal of Sport Management, 20,* 189–217

46. Kolbe, R. H., & James, J. D. (2003). The internalisation process among team followers: Implications for team loyalty. *International Journal of Sport Management, 4*(1), 25–43.

47. Turner, J. (1985). Social categorization and the self-concept: A social cognitive theory of group behavior. In E. J. Lawler (Ed.), *Advances in Group Processes, 2,* 77–122

48. Tajfel, H. (1982) Social psychology of intergroup relations. *Annual Review of Psychology, 33,* 1–39.

49. Turner, J., & Brown, R. (1978). Social status, cognitive alternatives and intergroup relations. In Henri Tajfel (ed.) *Differentiation between social groups: Studies in the social psychology of intergroup relations.* London, UK: Academic Press, pp. 201–234.

50. Fleming, M. A., & Petty, R. E. (1997). Identity and persuasion: An elaboration likelihood approach. In D. J. Terry, & M. A. Hogg (Eds.), *Attitudes, behaviour, and social context: The role of norms and group membership* (pp. 171–200). Mahwah, NJ: Lawrence Erlbaum Associates; and Turner, J. (1975). Social comparison and social identity: Some prospects for intergroup behaviour. *European Journal of Social Psychology, 5*(1), 1–34.

51. Funk, D. C., & James, J. D. (2004). The Fan Attitude Network (FAN) Model: Propositions for exploring identity and attitude formation among sport consumers. *Sport Management Review, 7,* 1–26.

52. Cialdini, R. B., Thorne, A., Walker, M. R., Freeman, S., & Sloan, L. R. (1976). Basking in reflected glory: Three (football) field studies. *Journal of Personality and Social Psychology, 34*(3), 366–375.

53. Wann, D., & Branscombe, N. (1992). Emotional responses to the sports page. *Journal of Sport & Social Issues, 16*(1), 49–64.

54. Turner, J. (1975). Social comparison and social identity: Some prospects for intergroup behaviour. *European Journal of Social Psychology, 5*(1), 1–34.

55. Abrams, D., & Hogg, M. (1988). Comments on the motivational status of self-esteem in social identity and intergroup discrimination. *European Journal of Social Psychology, 18*(4), 317–334.

56. Snyder, C. R., Lassegard, M. A., & Ford, C. E. (1986). Distancing after group success and failure: Basking in reflected glory and cutting off reflected failure. *Journal of Personality and Social Psychology, 51,* 382–388; and Tajfel, H., & Turner, J. C. (1985) The social identity theory of intergroup behavior. In S. Worchel, and W. G. Austin (Eds.), *Psychology of intergroup relations.* (Vol. 2). Chicago: Nelson Hall.

57. Jones, I. (2000). A model of serious leisure identification: The case of football fandom. *Leisure Studies, 19*(4), 283–298; and Lalonde, R. (1992). The dynamics of group differentiation in the face of defeat. *Personality and Social Psychology Bulletin, 18*(3), 336–342; and Lock, D., Taylor, T., Funk, D., & Darcy, S. (2012). Exploring the development of team identification. *Journal of Sport Management, 26,* 283–294

58. Cialdini, R. B., & Richardson, K. D. (1980). Two indirect tactics of image management: BASKing and BLASTing. *Journal of Personality and Social Psychology, 39*(3), 406–415.

59. Hogg, M. (2000). Subjective uncertainty reduction through self-categorization: A motivational theory of social identity processes. *European Review of Social Psychology, 11*(1), 223–255.

60. Wann, D., & Branscombe, N. (1992). Emotional responses to the sports page. *Journal of Sport & Social Issues, 16*(1), 49–64.

61. Cialdini, R. B., Thorne, A., Walker, M. R., Freeman, S., & Sloan, L. R. (1976). Basking in reflected glory: Three (football) field studies. *Journal of Personality and Social Psychology, 34*(3), 366–375.

62. Hogg, M., & Smith, J. (2007). Attitudes in social context: A social identity perspective. *European Review of Social Psychology, 18*(1), 89–131.

4

Creating Value as Part of Sport Marketing*

Ron McCarville
University of Waterloo

Jeffrey L. Stinson
Central Washington University

Abstract: The sport marketer's job is one of creating value for various client segments. Indeed, value creation is the driving force behind all marketing activity. This chapter explores how our clients think about value and how marketers might mobilize resources to provide it. We assume that our clients calculate value in two ways. First, our clients calculate **acquisition value.**[1] They do so by comparing the benefits they feel they receive to the costs they incur.[2] Second, clients evaluate the "deal" they just received. This is called **transaction value.**[3] They want to be sure that the price they paid is reasonable or fair.

These simple calculations suggest that the marketer's task begins with discovering benefits sought by the client. Specifically, marketers must discover the desires of consumer segments. The challenge then is to mobilize resources to fulfill those desires. The marketer may anticipate desires, respond to desires, or even shape desires, but desire fulfillment is at the heart of marketing effort.[4]

The client's calculation of value suggests that marketers must constantly work to reduce costs for the client. Clients are faced with a variety of costs, ranging from monetary expense to embarrassment. It is the marketer's job to minimize those costs. Finally, the ways in which our clients calculate value emphasize that our clients want to feel that they have been treated with fairness. They want to feel secure in the understanding that our service is worth all they have given up to enjoy it.

Keywords: acquisition, delivery, experience, transaction, value criteria, value proposition

Introduction

Everyone reading this chapter already has an intuitive grasp of what we mean by value. It represents something that we all desire. We all enjoy the sensation that value realization brings. It can be both profound and satisfying. Fortunately, the sport product can be immensely satisfying. Indeed, we sport marketers enjoy a considerable advantage over our more traditional product bound marketing colleagues. It is difficult for marketers of many products to truly engage their intended clients. Think about the challenge of getting consumers excited about a kitchen chair or a flu shot and you begin to see the challenge for marketers of less involving opportunities. Sport marketers, on the other hand, work with a product that can be both engaging and exciting.

---

*This chapter represents an extension of the ideas presented in "Offering More Than Programs: Creating Solutions for Your Clients" in Chapter 37: *Leisure for Canadians* (2nd ed.).

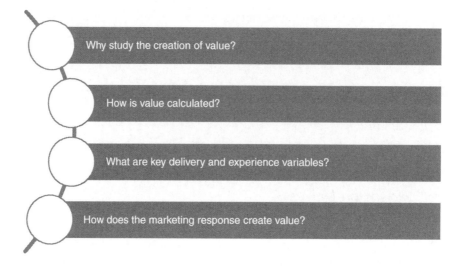

Figure 4.1 Overview to Chapter 4

The psychological and social connections between consumers and sports have been highlighted in other chapters of this text (e.g., involvement, identification, etc.). For many marketers, sports is the holy grail of product offerings.

Our goal for this chapter is primarily one of providing a client-focused perspective on value creation (see Figure 4.1). In our view, value emerges by creating solutions sought by clients (e.g., fans, participants). The key to value creation is being client centered. This is a perspective that will serve any sport marketer well. The goal of all marketing effort should be one of discovering client's desires and fulfilling them. This is where value is found; this is how value is created.

Why Study Value Creation?

The term "value" refers generally to advantage or benefit. Resources that improve benefit/satisfaction or reduce cost/risk are thought to be valuable.[5] Consequently, marketing is largely concerned with value creation. For example, the NFL continues to attempt to add benefit to the in-stadium experience (e.g., adding wi-fi capacity, showing Red Zone in stadium) to counter the value provided by HDTVs in-home.[6] Likewise, teams such as the Golden State Warriors seek to reduce risk by providing on-court performance guarantees to season ticket holders.[7]

In many ways, our lives consist of the ongoing search for value. Without value there would be no reason to follow or play sports. Without value, there would be no interest in sport behavior. Without value, there would be no sport-related industry: no professional leagues, no television coverage of those leagues, no Olympic games, and no community fun runs. We seek out events and people that help us achieve value while avoiding those who do not. As providers, we must pull apart the conditions that enhance value so that we might understand how to create it again and again for our clients.

The sport product offers many sources of value. We know, for example, that sport is a profoundly social activity and clients seek social benefits through their involvement. Such benefits may emerge from the acceptance of significant others, a sense of shared achievement (called BIRGing—Basking In Reflected Glory),[8] a sense of community, and a sense of identity.[9] We are usually introduced to sports by those close to us, and bonds are strengthened as we share the drama that sports offer. We tend to build a sense of identity around our favourite sport activities and share a sense of belonging with those who share that same sense of identity. These characteristics offer a unique and profound sense of value. If we enjoy a sport-related event, we will continue to search for new opportunities to repeat that experience. More than that, we are more likely to tell others about the experience.[10] Indeed, as Petrick reminds us, "perceived value may be a better predictor of repurchase intentions, than either satisfaction or quality" (p. 398). Value is the gift that keeps on giving. Marketers understand that those who provide the greatest value will enjoy a competitive advantage over other providers. That is why many providers build competitive strategy around value creation.[11]

How Is Value Calculated?

Our clients calculate the quality (or value) of the sport product we provide. They compare "the 'give' and 'get' components of a product."[12,13] Consumers compare all they have to sacrifice in order to consume our product. They then compare the costs they incurred to the costs they expected to incur. These two comparisons result in what Chang and Wildt call "perceived value." Figure 4.2 suggests how perceived value is calculated.

As Figure 4–2 suggests, perceived value is a result of both acquisition and transaction value. First, let's consider **acquisition value**. Acquisition value is the "get" in the equation.[14] It emerges through the assessment of both delivery and experience variables.[15] **Delivery** variables are those that minimize various costs for the consumer (such as discomfort or inconvenience). Delivery variables rarely generate personal satisfaction.[16] Instead, their goal is to remove obstacles; to isolate the consumer from setting characteristics they would rather avoid. This separation facilitates the enjoyment of more rewarding tasks. Conversely, **experience** variables focus directly on personal engagement. They are intended to immerse rather than remove the participant from the setting characteristics. For example, sport consumers may seek entertainment, diversion, affiliation, and even a sense of identity.[17] The goal is to help the clients find whatever they seek within the sport experience. In doing so, the marketer enhances acquisition value.

Next the clients calculate what is called **transaction value**. Transaction value is the clients' assessment of the price they are being asked to pay. They are assessing the quality of the "deal."[18,19] They do so by comparing the prices they observe (called "objective prices") to price ranges held in memory (called "reference prices"). Think of reference price as the price clients expect to pay. It may be a function of prices they have paid in the past or of advertising they have seen or heard. They use their own personal experience to establish what price they should expect to pay; what price is fair.[20]

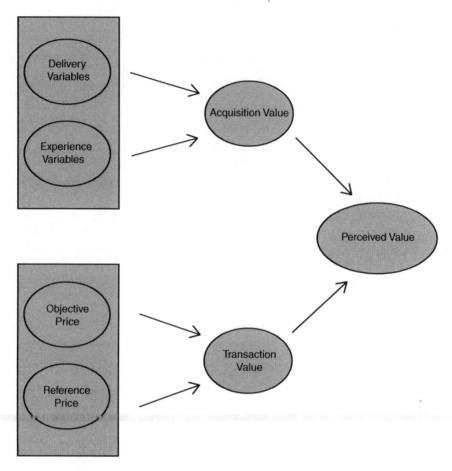

Figure 4.2 A Model for Assessing Perceived Value (Adapted from Chang & Wildt, 1994; Grewal, Montore, & Krishnan, 1989)

There is an extensive pricing literature suggesting the complexity of calculations of transaction value. We know that objective prices that clients classify as "high" typically discourage purchase while prices thought to be low may encourage purchase. However, objective price is rarely considered on its own merits. For example, consumers may expect to pay more for a championship game and less for a regular season offering. In these cases, the same objective ticket price may be considered a bargain in one case and over-priced in another.[21, 22]

That is why marketing professionals typically offer a favorable context when clients assess their prices. The more favorable the context, the more acceptable the price seems. That is why marketers focus so much on benefits before they pass along price information. They cannot assume that the clients are aware of all the benefits that have been provided. As a result, many sports teams provide detailed charts or tables highlighting the benefits a season-ticket holder receives beyond the actual tickets (e.g., newsletters, club access, team store discounts, etc.) Such information can influence price expectations and assessments of transaction value.

As you have no doubt guessed, perceived value is a result of both cognitive and affective/emotional assessments of a sport product.[23] It is cognitive in that our clients are comparing different elements of our offering and are assessing their relative quality. It is affective or emotional in that clients include feelings and sensations as they make this assessment. Motives, commitment levels, meanings, and norms (what Pons et. al label as "orientation") all influence perceptions of quality and value. Further, these perceptions allow consumers to compare products in making decisions, either directly or indirectly. For example, a consumer may weigh the value offered by attending an NFL game in-person vs. the perceived value of watching the game on HDTV at home with friends. Each offers a different set of benefits and costs. Or a consumer may calculate the value of attending an NBA game and compare it with the value of an evening at the theater.

We now explore the perceived value model in detail. Each variable is described below. We wish to stress that we take the view that value is a creation of perception. It is not set in stone. Marketers can and should take an active role in helping clients both understand and assess the value a product or service offers. You will note that our heading titles are action oriented. We use words like influencing, easing, building, creating, and reducing as we describe the role of the marketer.

We also offer leveraging activities to help bring our various suggestions to life. Leveraging is the process of using existing resources to better effect. It amplifies the effects of a given action. Readers can develop their own activities and we encourage you to do so. Through leveraging, the sport marketer turns a game into an event, a building into a sport shrine, and elevates a simple team logo to the status of an icon. The goal is not to offer an exhaustive list of options here but, rather, to suggest various ways to think about leveraging opportunities.

Influencing Key Delivery Variables

Enhancing the Setting

Kotler suggested decades ago that "One of the most important features of the total product is the *place* where it is bought and consumed."[24] Marketers seek to create a space that facilitates delivery of the sport product. The most dominant delivery variable is typically the physical environment (often called the "sportscape"). This variable provides the setting in which the offering can be enjoyed.

The sportscape has several dimensions. In terms of spectator sports, the sportscape is composed of variables such as stadium access, aesthetics and cleanliness, layout, crowding, food service, and fan control.[25] Relevant factors may be general (like availability of parking) or specific (like the comfort of seating) in nature. As noted earlier, teams and leagues now often emphasize stadium enhancements as part of the value provided spectators. From the participants' perspective, the emphasis is more on performance variables such as field conditions and protection from the elements. In some cases, the situation may demand convenient parking and comfortable seats for thousands of spectators. In other cases, clients may seek muddy trails for running, pristine links for golf, or open roads for cycling. The desires of the participant and the spectator will determine the appropriate sportscape. Sportscapes that respond to the desires of the client lead to perceptions of improved service quality and of increased perceptions of value.[26]

Delivery also refers to the actual provision of services to clients. There is a satisfaction literature which tells us that clients come to us with positive expectations. When our actions meet these expectations, clients are satisfied.[27] When we exceed these positive expectations, however, the clients experience what is called the "WOW" factor.

Leveraging Activities

- Look for setting-based ways to ease the burden of participation. Create a setting that anticipates clients' desires and offers convenient solutions. For example, many marathons provide transportation to the start line directly from local hotels, easing the "costs" of participating in the event, both real and psychological.
- Build the look and feel of the sportscape around the experience you wish to create. Localization of the stadium experience has become an increased point of emphasis since the opening of Oriole Park at Camden Yards in Baltimore.[28] Teams also commonly use localized concessions to add value, and to differentiate the sportscape experience. For example, former Seattle Seahawks President Bob Whitsett, in referencing the opening of Century Link Field (formerly Qwest Field), was quoted as saying "We wanted something that was really unique to the Pacific Northwest and fit our culture."[29]
- Identify locations or setting elements that surround key activities and ensure they support clients' experiences (apply appropriate signage, provide food carts, provide shade or shelter as necessary).

Easing Participation Costs

As suggested above, delivery variables are largely concerned with easing participation for customers.[30] Two of the greatest burdens that sport consumers must bear are inconvenience and lines (or queues). The sections below offer ways of dealing with both.

Reducing inconvenience costs—Inconvenience is one of those constraints or costs that clients want to avoid. Unfortunately, service delivery tends to be inherently inconvenient. The service delivery literature tells us that clients must "co-produce" whatever product they hope to enjoy.[31] They help create the moment and produce the event. They must be ready, willing, and able to carry out whatever task is assigned them. Participants must have the requisite skills and fans must be both knowledgeable and "connected" to the sport. If they are unprepared or uncertain, the event can be ruined and its value compromised. The sport marketers' goal, then, is to assist the client in co-producing the service. In this way, convenience is highlighted and value is enhanced.

Leveraging Activities

- Break consumption down into its component parts and consider how each stage challenges the client and how this challenge might be reduced.
- Find ways to simplify each stage of the event. Start with any planning the customer might have to do and end with post-event recollections.
- Help customers with problem solving; tell them what to expect, when to arrive to ensure a good seat, where to park, and what to wear to better enjoy the venue. Answer all their questions so their next step is always obvious.

Another convenience-related issue is that of the queue. People typically hate to wait in line. Meyer referred to queues as a form of captivity.[32] Freedom is limited because the individual has no power to modify the delay. Resulting perceived lack of control may lead to increased levels of stress and dissatisfaction.[33]

Queuing need not always result in dissatisfaction, however. We know now that distractions while in queue may reduce anger and uncertainty, thereby improving moods and increasing satisfaction. Any effort to entertain and distract queued clients will result in a more positive experience. In particular, the very act of viewing distractions while in line may oblige clients to stand side by side during the wait. Focusing on something other than the person ahead will improve the queuing experience. Likewise, many teams have sought a move toward wireless concessions ordering that can reduce or eliminate concessions lines.[34]

Leveraging Activities

- Distract (engage, enlighten, and entertain) clients while they are waiting in queue.
- Use queues as an opportunity to build sense of belonging and community. Encourage fans to interact while in line (perhaps distribute sport/team-related paraphernalia or hold contests to encourage interaction).
- Plan strategic activities around the arrival to the stadium to spread the time of arrival, reducing queues for entrance (e.g., family events, tailgating, etc.).

Influencing Key Experience Variables

Fans and participants alike may seek any variety of experiences in sport settings. The literature tells us that sports can provide personal relevance, escape, excitement, and entertainment.[35,36] All emerge from the drama that sports can provide. Participants in marathons weep with joy as they cross the finish line. Members of winning teams can recall in vivid detail all the events surrounding their win. These events can be just as emotional for observers. Imagine the celebrations that surround a world championship or an Olympic gold medal performance and you might begin to appreciate the emotional outpouring that can accompany a sport-related event. Crowds rush the field, flood the streets, hug strangers, and shout at their televisions in an emotional outburst that can rival that of their wedding day or even the birth of their children.

Table 4.1 Leveraging Activities

- Build celebrations around your product (for example, arrange an athletes' dinner before a tournament)
- Find moments and events to celebrate (post pictures of winning plays, teams, or individuals)
- Build tradition around noteworthy events
- Build associations between brand elements and already held beliefs and preferences
- Build emotional connections between your product and clients
- Help clients identify with various brand elements (Mascots help clients identify with a team)
- Reinforce team traditions

Emotional intensity is largely a function of commitment. Commitment involves some form of emotional or affective attachment. This attachment may exist along a continuum.[37] Low levels of commitment are often associated with motivators that are unrelated to the sport itself. These motivators are called side-bets. For example, a fan might regularly attend games because he purchased a season's pass and doesn't want to waste the money he invested. His interest is more monetary than emotional. Indeed, he may never truly commit to the game and may discontinue attendance once the pass can no longer be used. Stronger commitment levels at the other end of the continuum tend to involve a deeper emotional connection with the sport.

The challenge is that the sport marketer cannot build commitment through victory on the field of play. Such victory may not be forthcoming. Success is not preordained, nor is comfort, pleasure, or even satisfaction from a given sports encounter. As a result, the sport marketer must learn that, many times, sport-related value comes from unexpected sources. Yes, it may come from the performance of a performer/athlete or team but, more often than not, it will come from connections we create between the client and the overall sport experience.[38] This is a theme that will emerge throughout this chapter. The sport marketer's job is to help build connections between the client and the sport product. From connections come satisfaction; from satisfaction comes value. The sport marketer must continually seek opportunities to create and support this connection (see examples in Table 4.1).

Assessing Objective Prices

Objective prices are the price levels to which your clients are exposed. We know that these prices are of interest to everyone. They tend to be the first rather than the last piece of information sought. Our clients may even ignore other bits of relevant information in favor of price information. For many of our clients, price levels represent a sort of threshold. If the price level is acceptable, they will cross the threshold and seek more information about the offering. If the price is too high, they will look elsewhere for solutions to their particular problems.

For decades, marketers have understood that our clients tend to view objective prices in consistent ways. For example, they tend to underestimate prices ending in an odd number.[39] By way of example, they tend to view a price ending in 5 or 9 (e.g., $5.99) more favorably than one ending in 0 (e.g., $6.00). This is why providers engage in a practice called "odd pricing," in which they set prices ending in odd numbers. We know too that demand is higher than expected for a variety of products when prices are set at odd rather than even amounts.[40]

Sport marketers in the public sector should also remember that small fees, even those unlikely to displace potential users, may still generate public outcry. This is due to fees' often symbolic nature. Fees for public events and services (sports leagues, facility rentals, etc.), in particular, carry a great deal of symbolic baggage. Many clients believe they have already paid for these services through their tax dollars. They may feel that these fees are denying them access to their natural birthright. Outrage over fees often results. Research suggests that such outrage may be moderated or even eliminated through concerted efforts to manage impressions around fees. This same research suggests that visitors are typically open to fees once the reasons for the fees have been made clear. The key to gaining acceptance of fees is a clear and compelling statement of value. We offer more on that topic below.

Influencing Reference Price Levels

Recall that reference prices become the standard against which your objective prices are compared. Social judgement theory suggests that regions of acceptance are established around reference prices. Objective prices that fall within these ranges are generally considered acceptable. As price levels deviate from the expected levels, the individual is less likely to find the new price as acceptable. Prices thought less than the expected price are typically considered a better value.

Fortunately, reference prices are not set in stone. They change with new information; especially information about the appropriateness of an objective price level. This is one of the reasons so much advertising is devoted to extolling the virtues of a product or service offering. These advertisers know that the greater the perceived benefit from purchase, the higher the potential reference price. They are attempting to establish a context in which the expected price is high and the objective price benefits from the comparison. In this way, they elevate transaction value.[41]

Sport organizations have increasingly tried to advantage themselves through dynamic ticket pricing, allowing ticket prices to vary with demand for a given contest. Spurred by the growth of the secondary market (e.g., StubHub, Ticket Exchange) and technological advancement, varying the price of tickets throughout the season with changes in demand factors is now becoming the norm in professional sports.[42] Now, rather than needing to anticipate demand before the season, teams can adjust ticket prices as demand fluctuates, increasing price for high-demand games and decreasing price for lower-demand games (to protect season ticket holders, many teams and leagues institute price floors for tickets).[43] Supporters of dynamic ticket pricing regularly point to increased revenues as a prime reason to adopt, and one study reporting on MLB teams who implemented the strategy noted average revenue gains of $900,000.[44]

Client knowledge is also an important variable in establishing transaction value. Those with little experience in paying for your services may have very large regions of acceptance around their reference prices. After all, they have little experience in knowing what your tickets might cost. In that case, it might be difficult to violate their price expectations. They may believe that many price levels are fair and appropriate. However, those with greater knowledge of your pricing structure may have very specific

Table 4.2 Leveraging Tactics

- Focus on benefits rather than costs.
- The notion of a "deal" increases transaction value, so if you are offering a discount provide "was-is" information. "The regular price was . . . but the price this week is . . ." The regular price information provides a reference point for comparison.
- If prices rise, focus on additional benefits (to your clients) that necessitate the increase.
- Use bundles to maximize benefits and minimize costs.

price expectations. The price last paid, in particular, may provide users with a simple straightforward indicator for developing a personal reference price.[45] Consistent with the notion of reference price, new prices that are incompatible with the level of price last paid may meet with disapproval. Such unfavorable evaluations may have profound consequences. McCarville, Reiling, and While[46] found that users who had traditionally enjoyed access to recreational services free of charge (and presumably adopted a reference point of $0) were most likely to reject any new pricing initiatives. They thought of any price as poor value because they expected to receive the service for free.

Taken together, these insights suggest that sport marketers must provide a context in which objective price levels are assessed. By doing so, marketers increase the transaction value enjoyed by consumers (see tactics in Table 4.2). The better the context, the greater the transaction value enjoyed by the client. In this way, reference prices are more likely to compare favorably with objective price information.

Thinking Strategically About Creating Value

Up to this point we have discussed the various ways in which perceived value might be enhanced. We have focused on creating and enhancing acquisition and transaction value. Though these are necessary components of any value creation initiative, we should also note the importance of a comprehensive vision regarding value creation. In the sections below we offer a broadened view of how the marketer might plan for value creation. We focus here on (a) establishing clients' value criteria, (b) creating a value proposition, and (c) building connections with clients. These are the building blocks of value creation.

Establishing Value Criteria

Involvement in sport may range from simple awareness to allegiance.[47] The roots of this involvement are often cultural in nature. First, sports tend to rely on the application of things very much valued by society (skill, strength, knowledge, and so on) in overcoming an obstacle. This obstacle may be natural (like gravity in the high jump), contrived (triathlon comes to mind . . . participants are forced to swim, bike, then run in order to cover a given distance), and may involve overcoming the efforts of opponents. The struggle to do so is very much prized in our society. Against this cultural backdrop, sport involvement also emerges from personal interest. This interest has been discussed in terms of commitment, orientation,[48] and connection.[49]

Combine these social and personal priorities with the unique characteristics of sports (challenge, uncertainty, goal achievement) and sport involvement can be immensely satisfying. In sports, goals are clear and agreed upon by all those who take part. The participant hopes to get to the top of the hill, to place the ball through the hoop, to pin the opponent. There is a sense of closure achieved when such goals are fulfilled. More than that, these goals are very much valued by those involved. Participants and fans must place importance on the outcome that is being sought. It is better to win than to lose, it is better to dominate than to be dominated. There is prestige and celebration associated with one outcome and not the other.

The sport marketer can create value by using these insights. We know that value is something sought by the client. This search begins with the client's own desires and motives. Remember that benefit and cost-related variables play very different roles in our consumer's decision making processes. Clients become involved because of the benefits the product has to offer. They are compelled by all that the product promises. But not all benefits appeal to all individuals in all settings.

As a result, sport marketers must begin by establishing their various client segments' **value criteria**. Value criteria are those things individual consumers seek as they pursue their sport interests. When value criteria are fulfilled, a variety of positive things happen. In particular, clients are more likely to be satisfied[50] and will be less likely to consider switching to other providers.[51,52]

The challenge for the sport marketer is to discover those criteria within the diversity found in various consumer groups. For example, primary consumers for sport marketers are participants, spectators, and volunteers. All these consumer groups will differ both in their behavioral and emotional connections with the sport products we offer. In other words, their value criteria may vary dramatically. Participants may be taking part on the field of play or in their basement through a video game.[53] They may express only a passing interest or conversely they may be rabid, face painting and tailgating fans. They may be attending events simply to spend time with a loved one or they may live and breathe a sport and all that goes with it.

Creating a Value Proposition

Modern marketers typically create strategy using the **value proposition**. The value proposition details how you plan to fulfill your consumers' desires. And to be clear, these desires can be both wide ranging and profound. When creating the value proposition, the goal is to create a "detailed description of what is to be done for the customer (what needs and wishes are to be satisfied), and how this is to be achieved."[54] This concept needs to be both clear and compelling. Every decision you make, every policy you generate, and every event you promote must be assessed against that proposition. Once the proposition is clarified, the actual solutions you create can be planned accordingly.

One of the ways that sport marketers can deliver on the promise of the value proposition is through the development of product bundles. A product bundle is a package that offers both benefits and cost reductions to consumer groups. The goal of the product bundle is to maximize benefits but also to reduce various costs to customers. For example, in the spectator sports context, many teams now offer all-inclusive ticket packages, including ticket, food, and beverages throughout the game. This approach deals directly with the variables outlined in Figure 4.2. As the model suggests, marketers must help consumers find a good reason to take part, and then discover ways to minimize constraints to doing so.[55]

It might help to think of the bundle as a solution. The best solutions maximize benefit **and** minimize costs that irritate and constrain customers. Begin by maximizing benefits. After all, they make clear the reason to get involved. Sport marketers must be relentless in providing those experiences and products sought by their clients.

Building Connections with Clients

One of the keys to successful sport marketing is building connections between the client and the sport product. Such connections are enhanced when we build personal commitment and emotional involvement. These connections have been linked to positive self-esteem and increased social ties[56, 57] as well as reduced price sensitivity and a reduced emphasis on performance/outcomes.

The stronger the connection made by the individual, the greater becomes the feeling of personal success when a desired outcome is realized; conversely, the greater becomes the disappointment when failure occurs.[58] In such cases, value emerges not from a win/loss record, but rather from the degree to which the fan identifies with the activity, team, or sport. For these fans, it is the connection that sustains them. It builds their personal sense of identity and in doing so their emotional well-being.[59]

By leveraging personal involvement levels, the marketer can gain access to deep-seated values and beliefs. The challenge for the sport marketer is to build connections between brand elements and existing beliefs and preferences. The creation of value is very much tied up in making these connections. It is the connections that create value, and value helps strengthen the connection. It is the connections that enhance the experience for the consumer. It is the connections that can influence behavior over the lifetime of the individual. As a result, building this connection is at the heart of the sport marketing enterprise.

Conclusion

The chapter offers four primary insights. The first relates to how the marketer thinks about value. The world of sport marketing is diverse and competitive. Those who believe in the importance of value, those who believe in the centrality of the customer, who live and breathe the value proposition, will be most successful in the long term.

Second, the chapter provides a basic model of value creation. As the model suggests, clients compare the benefits they feel they gained to the costs they believe they endured. This comparison has elements that relate to both acquisition and transaction value. Sport marketers must understand the dynamics behind both acquisition and transaction value if they are to create value through their own offerings. This is perhaps the greatest insight a marketer can have when dealing with value.

Third, much of sport's success relies on its ability to delivery memorable experience. Such experiences, in turn, create emotional attachment to an intended product. Such attachment often emerges from social interactions and resulting feelings of belonging. As these feelings grow, the participant may feel increasing dedication to the norms, values, and convictions of other participants in this activity. In other words, the participant begins to feel a sense of community with others who are involved in that sport. These social worlds can be a source of great meaning and create a profound sense of belonging. It is these more profound and personal feelings that help build value for the participant.

Finally, value is created only with constant and deliberate effort on the part of the marketer. The sport marketer must continually ask, "How does this initiative (or policy) build value?" The value proposition must remain central to any marketing effort. By doing so, sport marketers will delight clients and gain competitive advantage as a result.

References

1. Al-Sabbahy, H., Ekinci, Y., & Riley, M. (2004). An investigation of perceived value dimensions: Implications for hospitality research. *Journal of Travel Research, 42*, 226–234.
2. Zeithaml, V. A. (1988, July). Consumer perceptions of price, quality, and value: A means-end model and synthesis of evidence. *Journal of Marketing, 52*, 2–22.
3. Thaler, R. (1985). Mental accounting and consumer choice. *Marketing Science, 4* (3), 199–214.
4. Kotler, P. (1999). *Kotler on marketing.* New York: The Free Press.
5. Bowman, C., & Ambrosini. (2000). Value creation versus value capture: Towards a coherent definition of value in strategy. *British Journal of Management, 11*, 1–15.
6. Madkour, A. (2012). NFL in strong position but plenty of issues to watch. *Sport Business Journal.* Retrieved from http://www.sportsbusinessdaily.com/Journal/Issues/2012/09/03/Opinion/From-the-Executive-Editor. aspx?hl=stadium%20experience&sc=0
7. Lombardo, J. (2011). Warriors ownership sets benchmarks for team as part of season-ticket renewal effort. *Sport Business Journal.* Retrieved from http://www.sportsbusinessdaily.com/Journal/Issues/2011/03/Mar-14/ Franchises/Warriors.aspx?hl=ticket%20playoff%20guarantee&sc=0
8. Funk, D. C., & James, J. D. (2006). Consumer loyalty: The meaning of attachment in the development of sport team allegiance. *Journal of Sport Management, 20*, 189–217.
9. Green, C., & Jones, I. (2005). Serious leisure, social identity and sport tourism. *Sport in Society, 8*(2), 164–181.
10. Petrick, J. F. (2004). The roles of quality, value, and satisfaction in predicting cruise passengers' behavioral intentions. *Journal of Travel Research, 42*, 397–407.
11. Walters, D., & Lancaster, G. (1999). Value and information-concepts and issues for management. *Management Decision, 37*(8), 643–656.
12. Chang, T. Z., & Wildt, A. R. (1994). Price, product, and purchase intention: An empirical study. *Journal of the Academy of Marketing Science, 22*(1), 16–27.
13. Grewal, D., Monrow, K. B., & Krishnan, R. (1998). The effects of price-comparison advertising on buyers' perceptions of acquisition value, transaction value, and behavioral intentions. *Journal of Marketing, 62*(2), 46–59.
14. Al-Sabbahy, H., Ekinci, Y., & Riley, M. (2004). An investigation of perceived value dimensions: Implications for hospitality research. *Journal of Travel Research, 42*, 226–234.
15. Shonk, D. J., & Chelladurai, P. (2008). Service quality, satisfaction, and intent to return in event sport tourism. *Journal of Sport Management, 22*, 587–602.
16. Rossman, J. R., & Ellis, G. D. (2012). Thoughts on experience: Introduction to the special issue. *Journal of Park & Recreation Administration, 30*(3), 1–6.
17. Walters, D., & Lancaster, G. (2000). Implementing value strategy through the value chain. *Management Decision, 38*(3/4), 160–178.

18. Grewal, D., Monrow, K. B., & Krishnan, R. (1998). The effects of price-comparison advertising on buyers' perceptions of acquisition value, transaction value, and behavioral intentions. *Journal of Marketing, 62*(2), 46–59.

19. Thaler, R. (1985). Mental accounting and consumer choice. *Marketing Science, 4*(3), 199–214.

20. Mazumdar, T., Raj, S. P., & Sinha, I. (2005). Reference price research: Review and propositions. *Journal of Marketing, 69*(4), 84–102.

21. Niedrich, R. W., Sharma, S., & Wedell, D. H. (2001). Reference price and price perceptions: A comparison of alternative models. *Journal of Consumer Research, 28*, 339–354.

22. Mazumdar, T., Raj, S. P., & Sinha, I. (2005). Reference price research: Review and propositions. *Journal of Marketing, 69*(4), 84–102.

23. Pons, F., Mourali, M., & Nyeck, S.(2006). Consumer orientation toward sporting events: Scale development and validation. *Journal of Service Research, 8*(3), 276–287.

24. Kotler, P. (1999). *Kotler on marketing*, New York: The Free Press.

25. Chelladurai, P., & Chang, K. (2000). Targets and standards of quality in sports services. *Sport Management Review, 3*, 1–22.

26. Hightower, R., Brady, M. K., & Baket, T. L. (2002). Investigating the role of the physical environment in hedonic service consumption: an exploratory study of sporting events. *Journal of Business Research, 55*, 697–707.

27. McDougall, G. H. G., & Levesque, T. J. (2000). Customer satisfaction with services: Putting perceived value in the equation. *Journal of Services Marketing, 14*, 392–409.

28. Howard, D. R., & Crompton, J. L. (1980). *Financing, managing and marketing recreation and park resources*. Dubuque, IA: Brown.

29. Retrieved from http://www.sportsbusinessdaily.com/Journal/Issues/2012/08/06/In-Depth/Opening-day-reviews.aspx?hl=concessions&sc=0

30. Pritchard, M. P., Funk, D. C., & Alexandris, K. (2009). Barriers to repeat patronage: The impact of spectator constraints. *European Journal of Marketing, 43*(1/2): 169–187.

31. Prahalad, C. K., & Ramaswamy, V. (2004). Co-creation experiences: The next practice in value creation. *Journal of Interactive Marketing, 30*(2), 1–9.

32. Meyer, T. (1995). Subjective importance of goal and reactions to waiting in line. *The Journal of Social Psychology, 134*(6), 819–827.

33. Coleman, J, McCarville, R. E., & Colenutt, C. E. (1999/2000). Queues and the leisure experience: The consequences of waiting for leisure. *Leisure/Loisir, 24*(3/4), 207–232.

34. Anonymous. (2012). Tales from the high-tech venue: 'The only certainty is that bandwidth is no longer an amenity'. *Sport Business Journal*. Retrieved from http://www.sportsbusinessdaily.com/Journal/Issues/2012/11/12/Facilities/Bob-Jordan.aspx?hl=wireless%20concessions&sc=0

35. Funk, D. C., & James, J. (2006). Consumer loyalty: the meaning of attachment in the development of sport team allegiance. *Journal of Sport Management, 20*, 189–217.

36. Funk, D., Filo, K., Beaton, A., & Pritchard, M. P. (2009). Measuring the motives of sport event attendance: Bridging the academic-practitioner divide to understanding behavior. *Sport Marketing Quarterly, 18*, 126–148.

37. Funk, D. C., & James, J. (2006). Consumer loyalty: the meaning of attachment in the development of sport team allegiance. *Journal of Sport Management, 20*, 189–217.

38. Funk, D., Filo, K., Beaton, A., & Pritchard, M. P. (2009). Measuring the motives of sport event attendance: Bridging the academic-practitioner divide to understanding behavior. *Sport Marketing Quarterly, 18*, 126–148.

39. Schindler, R. M., & Wiman, A. R. (1989). Effects of odd pricing on price recall. *Journal of Business Research, 19*(3), 165–177.

40. Gendall, P., Holdershaw, J., & Garland, R. (1997). The effect of odd pricing on demand. *European Journal of Marketing, 31*(11/12), 799—813.

41. McCarville, R., Crompton, J. L., & Sell, J. A. (1993). The influence of outcome messages on reference prices. *Leisure Sciences, 15*, 115–130.

42. Howard, D. R., & Crompton, J. L. (1980). *Financing, managing and marketing recreation and park resources*. Dubuque, IA: Brown.

43. Fisher, E. (2012). StubHub, MLBAM renew deal. *Sport Business Journal*. Retrieved from http://www.sportsbusinessdaily.com/Journal/Issues/2012/12/10/Leagues-and-Governing-Bodies/StubHub.aspx?hl=StubHub&sc=0

44. Howard, D. R., & Crompton, J. L. (1980). *Financing, managing and marketing recreation and park resources*. Dubuque, IA: Brown.

45. McCarville, R., Reiling, S., & White, C. (1996). The role of fairness in users' assessments of first-time fees for a public recreation service. *Leisure Sciences, 18*, 61–76.

46. McCarville, R., Reiling, S., & White, C. (1996). The role of fairness in users' assessments of first-time fees for a public recreation service. *Leisure Sciences, 18*, 61–76.

47. Funk, D. C., & James, J. (2001). The psychological continuum model: A conceptual framework for understanding an individual's psychological connection to sport. *Sport Management Review 4*, 119–150.

48. Pons, F., Mourali, M., & Nyeck, S.(2006). Consumer orientation toward sporting events: Scale development and validation. *Journal of Service Research, 8*(3), 276–287.

49. Funk, D. C., & James, J. (2001). The psychological continuum model: A conceptual framework for understanding an individual's psychological connection to sport. *Sport Management Review 4,* 119–150.

50. Petrick, J. F. (2004). The roles of quality, value, and satisfaction in predicting cruise passengers' behavioral intentions. *Journal of Travel Research, 42,* 397–407.

51. Petrick, J. F., Backman, S. J., & Bixler, R. (1999). An investigation of selected factors' impact on golfer satisfaction and perceived value. *Journal of Park and Recreation Administration, 17*(1), 40–59.

52. McDougall, G. H., & Levesque, T. (2000). Customer satisfaction with services: putting perceived value into the equation. *Journal of Services Marketing, 14*(5), 392–410.

53. Oates, T. P. (2009). New media and repackaging of NFL fandom. *Sociology of Sport Journal, 26,* 31–49.

54. Edvardsson, B., & Olsson, J. (1996). Key concepts for new service development, *The Service Industries Journal, 16,* 140–164.

55. Pritchard, M. P., Funk, D. C., & Alexandris, K. (2009). Barriers to repeat patronage: The impact of spectator constraints. *European Journal of Marketing, 43*(1/2), 169–187.

56. Johnson, B., Groothuis, P., & Whitehead, J. (2001). The value of public goods generated by a major league sports team: The CVM approach. *Journal of Sports Economics, 2,* 6–21.

57. Branscombe, N., & Wann, D. (1991). The positive social and self-concept consequences of sports team identification. *Journal of Sport and Social Issues, 15,* 115–127.

58. Funk, D. C., & James, J. D. (2001). Consumer loyalty: The meaning of attachment in the development of sport team allegiance. *Journal of Sport Management, 20,* 189–217.

59. Branscombe, N., & Wann, D. (1991). The positive social and self-concept consequences of sports team identification. *Journal of Sport and Social Issues, 15,* 115–127.

5

Ethical Decision Making in Sport and Business

Mark P. Pritchard
Central Washington University

Abstract: Few social institutions are as visible or constitute such a large part of our lives today as sports. Whether on or off the field, ethical miscues or individual breaches have become much more prominent today than they were in the past. With unparalleled media exposure we see our heroes and the organizations they represent in living color, the good, the bad, and the ugly, replete with noble deeds and shameful failures. But why is this much overlooked topic important and why should we care? This chapter takes up the challenge of discussing the nature of ethical decision making, and places a call before the readers to step up their game in the business of sports today.

Keywords: decision making, ethics, personal worldview, systems theory, values

Goodness is easier to recognize than define . . .	W. H. Auden
A man's action is only a picture book of his creed . . .	Ralph Waldo Emerson
If anyone competes as an athlete,	Paul of Tarsus
He does not receive the victor's crown unless he competes according to the rules . . .	

Introduction

Have you ever wondered why we recognize athletic perfection, acknowledge academic excellence, and yet all too often leave ethical aspiration on the floor of our personal workshop? Aristotle observed that virtue and good conduct arise from habits acquired by repeated action and correction.[1] Francis Bacon took a similar stance when he noted that *our abilities were like natural plants that need pruning by study*. Despite our gifts, character left untended and untried has left a wake of ethical failures dotting today's social landscape. With many perceiving widespread decline in ethical standards, educators are scrambling for a remedy. But is there one? Aristotle's pronouncement of practice appears to make ethics intensely practical, a lot like how we refine or improve athletic or intellectual skills. However, another philosopher thinks there is more to it and likens the malady of a lack of moral knowledge to an incident several years ago when a fighter pilot executing a stunt failed to determine which way was up or down.[2] Gravity, the usual reference point, was nullified by the speed of the performance, and coming out of an inverted roll the pilot promptly turned the nose of the jet straight down, hurtling into the ground and a fiery end to the show.

Ethical issues in sports appear to suffer from a similar lack of knowledge over up or down, what to do and what not to. Take the recent example of a court case

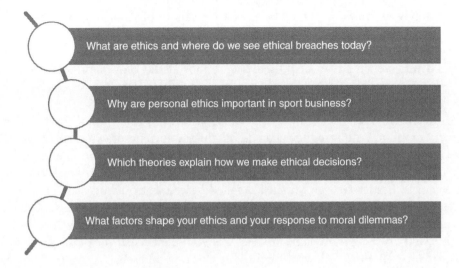

Figure 5.1 An Overview of Chapter 5

about sanctions the National Collegiate Athletic Association (NCAA) applied to the University of Southern California (USC) over support that Reggie Bush's parents received from an agent. According to the most recent court judgment, the case made by the body against an assistant coach, and thereby the school, had no proof and relied on unsubstantiated comments of one agent against USC's coaching staff. Zealous yet misguided work by investigators (aka the "good guys") to censure wrongdoing led to a ruling of malicious conduct against those same enforcement officials.[3] Although we are not privy to all the information, it appears doing the right thing became complicated for the NCAA when they lost their bearings and forgot an ancient rule: *bear no false witness against your neighbor*. According to one commentator, moral knowledge of how to act, knowing the "goods" we ought to pursue, has largely been removed from any serious consideration in our places of learning.[4] Such a discussion is the focus of the current chapter, which tackles questions about what constitutes up or down, right or wrong, moral and ethical virtue in sport business today (see Figure 5.1).

Ethics are judgments about whether human behavior is right or wrong. Some distinguish ethics from morals by delineating ethics as the study of principles of right or wrong, versus morals,[5] which are viewed as specific standards of right or wrong (e.g., "I cannot tell a lie; I cut the tree.").[6] In the sport industry, errors in ethical judgment by players, coaches, and leaders appear repeatedly in the press, impacting on sports fans, organizations, and businesses alike. For example:

- Lance Armstrong's doping decision cost him his titles, sponsors, and a charity role.[7]
- Tiger Woods' deception "let his family down" and distanced fans and sponsors.[8]
- Jerry Sandusky's sexual abuse and the failures in Penn. State's chain of command resulted in jail, litigation, and sanctions.[9]

- Bobby Petrino's breach of trust as a University of Arkansas coach led to his dismissal.[10]
- George O'Leary and Sandy Baldwin were asked to resign after using false academic credentials to help them secure jobs at the University of Notre Dame (UND) and the United States Olympic Committee (USOC).[11]

Although ethical breaches in sports vary considerably, they're not limited to one country or culture, nor are they taken lightly by the societies in which they occur. In the United States, nothing less than a congressional hearing was convened to discuss one sport's rampant use of steroids. A December 2007 report prepared by former Senate Majority Leader George Mitchell detailed baseball's troubling drug culture and named 85 current and former players linked to performance-enhancing substances. Included were heroes of the game Roger Clemens, Barry Bonds, Miguel Tejada, Andy Pettitte, and Eric Gagne, to name but a few. Government censuring of drug-enhanced performance activities followed, forcing Major League Baseball to confront its past and rethink its future with player testing.[12] Doping scandals have plagued other sports and are considered a major challenge for the profession.[13] Armstrong's recent fall is one of many over the last 15 years for the Tour de France, which is regularly plagued with doping controversies.[14] Thousands of years earlier, other European administrators tried to avoid claims of performance-enhancing substances by sequestering Roman athletes at games for months on a strict diet. Recurring storms such as these appear to support one ancient observer's view on human nature, that there really is nothing new under the sun, that "what has been will be again, what has been done will be done again."[15]

Graft is another malady that historically plagues sports. For instance, India and Pakistan regularly face gambling and corruption scandals in their national pastime. Cricket's biggest match-fixing scandal was unearthed in 2000, when one star admitted he had accepted money to throw matches. Players from other countries were soon implicated. Since then, allegations of fixing regularly crop up, as bookmakers and the underworld actively try to influence cricket results.[16] Another classic example of gambling shaking the legitimacy of an industry occurred during Major League Baseball's infancy. In an account published in the *New York Times*, Chicago White Sox pitcher Eddie Cicotte admitted that in a scheme hatched by a pair of professional gamblers he and several teammates had agreed to throw the 1919 World Series in exchange for cash. The eight players indicted in the "Black Sox" scandal were found innocent in court, but banned for life by baseball's first commissioner, Kenesaw Mountain Landis. Seventy years later, Cincinnati Reds manager and former star player Pete Rose, baseball's career hit leader, was banned from the sport for life for betting on his own team. Although Rose steadfastly denied the gambling allegations until 2004,[17] a late apology for the breach hasn't moved him closer to Baseball's Hall of Fame.[18]

The variety, severity, and potential for ethical misconduct in sport business are perplexing and go well beyond athletes and coaches. Those wanting to work in the profession would do well to keep this in mind. As Burton and his colleagues remark, any new developing area of marketing and business, as is the case with sports, faces challenges for those setting a course for "right" practice.[19] Poor professional judgments can occur at various parts of the sports marketing mix (e.g., product, price, promotion), but in an industry with a sales-intensive culture[20] the ethical "full-court press" thrown at sales personnel is particularly worrisome. For instance, results from a survey of 200 sales managers describe some of the ethical tensions sales reps face when trying to close business:[21]

- 49% of surveyed managers say their reps have lied on a sales call.
- 34% say they've heard reps make unrealistic promises on a sales call.
- 22% say their reps have sold products their customers didn't need.
- 30% say customers have demanded a kickback for buying their product or service.
- 54% say the drive to meet sales goals does a disservice to customers.
- 27% say they have caught employees cheating on an expense report.

But why should we care if people, regardless of their job title, fudge on principles? What's the big deal? It's a dog-eat-dog world, isn't it? And, *after all, the chief business of the [American] people is busines,s,*[22] right? To answer this I would like us to consider a few factors that underscore why ethical conduct in sport business is of paramount importance.

The Importance of Personal Ethics in Sport

Good Organizations Need Good Employees

Four reasons are offered below to explain why personal ethics are of critical importance to those working in the business of sports. First, let's step back from the notion that businesses are only "better at doing good" in a top-down manner.[23] Yes ethical leadership helps,[24] but good organizations are very much dependent on securing "good" employees. The reverse idea that "good organizations can make people good" may be a time-intensive liability for management, as the personal ethics of "untrained" employees may color the organization's ethical initiatives. Thus to some degree, the ship may only be as good as her crew. This explains why HR professionals often act as ethical matchmakers, testing applicants to see if potential new hires fit and believe in the ethical culture of an organization. Ranked in *Fortune* magazine's "100 Best Companies to Work For," Seattle-based REI (Recreation Equipment Inc.) is a good example of this. The company explicitly communicates the ethics of their culture and then recruits those who identify with this (see website statements below).[25]

> **Company Statement**: REI's culture, the heart of our work environment, is one that supports our values as well as our business goals. It's one of the primary reasons why people come to work for us. They want to be part of the special place known as REI.
> **Employee Comment**: I tell my friends that working at REI is a lifestyle. It's about what you believe in and what the company stands for—service, adventure, community, integrity and balance. I love my job, and I'll be younger because of it.

Another approach to determining ethical fit is noted in Table 5.1. This presents several questions a global HR firm actually uses to examine the ethical fit of sales applicants.[26] Recruiting, however, isn't the only place personal ethics are in the

Table 5.1 Ethical Sales Test Questions

1. While speaking with a sales manager at a competitor's trade show booth, you spot hard copy from the competitor's database listing 100 qualified leads from the show. You can slip it into your briefcase easily, and no one will see. What do you do?	1. You're on a sales call and a key customer from a Fortune 500 company says she won't buy from you unless you match a competitor's offer. The competitor's offer includes a 10-day trip to Hawaii for her and her husband. What do you do?
2. A few months after joining the company your colleagues tell you about a diner's club card that gives 20% cash refunds at certain restaurants. Easy money—especially if you're just beginning to establish a territory. Since the company encourages entertaining, the salespeople reason, why not take clients to those restaurants and pocket the refunds? It won't cost the company any money. Do you join in?	2. After meeting with a customer you discover a competitor has lowballed your offer by 15%. This competitor has a reputation for offering products at the lowest possible price, but failing to provide an acceptable level of service. Do you warn the customer, attempting to move him toward your offer, or walk away from the business, hoping he'll find out for himself and choose your company in the future?

spotlight. Sport businesses also monitor the actions of current employees and in some cases hold zero-tolerance policies for certain ethical breaches.

A well-known example of this occurred in the NBA with the transfer of Jason Kidd from the Phoenix Suns to the New Jersey Nets. The move followed the day after a domestic violence response at the player's home, and reflected an ethical commitment by Suns management to overcoming what the franchise believes is a "societal problem".[27] Hiring the "right" people is one way organizations can avoid some unexpected bombshells and the negative PR that ends up tarnishing the brand. Some believe the Salt Lake City bribery allegation against the USOC, a 'once pure' Olympic movement, tarnished that organization with "fallout that was less about athlete greed and more about influence, power and perks."[28]

High Credence Services and Social Expectations

Have you ever wondered why such strong emotional responses arise from its stake-holders when ethical breaches occur in sports? For many patrons and sponsors it's a betrayal of trust. Expert service providers such as doctors, lawyers, accountants, and to some degree sport business professionals are subject to high-credence expectations from their stakeholders. Credence means trust, and services high in this usually are difficult to evaluate, contain a level of uncertainty or risk, and have high expectations over the nature of the specialized performance being rendered.[29] Parasuraman and his colleagues found services with high expectations for credibility involved stakeholder hopes of trustworthiness, believability, and honesty in their service provider. The bulk of these qualities drew largely from customer perceptions of behavior by the firm's personnel.[30] This means that if stakeholders feel connected with sport businesses they will have high credibility expectations, and that ethical breaches by the organization's personnel will often result in disconfirmation of those expectations and a strong emotional response. An example of this type of response occurred in one corruption scandal, when survey findings by a nonprofit sport organization's official sponsors indicated that 20% of consumers had not only lost faith in the organization but in the companies affiliated with it. Public disappointment with the failure fueled emotional responses in stakeholders where non-purchasing of sponsors' products was used to voice dissatisfaction.[31]

In addition to administrators, other sport professionals such as athletes have earned 'credentials' or performance track records that often inspire us to trust that they will do right by the brand/product (team or sport). Usually that performance is judged on the field of play (i.e., the core product). But because many feel a kinship to the activity itself, there is also a strong expectation that performers and the service organization itself will represent "the brand" well off-field. Professional athletes both embrace and dismiss the idea of being trusted representatives or role models. Featured in a Nike commercial, Charles Barkley's now famous comment *"I'm not paid to be a role model. I'm paid to wreak havoc on the basketball court,"* still stirs considerable debate over what could be expected and questions whether our on-field heroes should also serve as ethical role models off the field. Fellow league MVP Karl Malone disagreed with Barkley and Nike's view on this, commenting *"I don't think it's your decision to make. We don't choose to be role models, we are chosen. Our only choice is whether to be a good role model or a bad one."*[32] For better or worse the golf industry is another sport, replete with "elder statesmen" and "spokesmen," that seems prone to holding its heroes to a broader expectation of them serving as role models. This to some degree explains the strong emotional response many had about Tiger Woods' fall, that his breach of trust failed more than just his family.[33]

Civic Benefits and the Public Trust

The social benefits of sports are further cause for some stakeholders to respond, as many hold a strong desire to defend the integrity of the games we play and object loudly when ethical failures occur. In this sense sports can be a highly valued force that serves as a type of public trust, where breaches threaten the institution's impact as a proving ground for younger generations, a vehicle for physical and mental health, or as the means for building bridges with other countries or peoples (i.e., Track Two Diplomacy).[34] Several historic movements reflect a serious concern for the "right" use of sports; from Chicago's Playground Movement in the 1900s,[35] that sought to preserve the health and moral fiber of inner-city children through sport, to Muscular Christianity in the Victorian era, which connected physical health and training with Christian ideals of service and the common good. More recently, athletic teams and professional leagues (e.g., NBA Cares program) have taken a renewed interest in funding playgrounds to promote physical fitness,[36] while popular athletes such as Tim Tebow, Jeremy Lin, Mariano Rivera, and Brazilian soccer superstar Kaka have reignited discussions on faith, moral fortitude, and fitness.[37] Another example of sports acting as a vehicle for character development is The First Tee, whose core values (Honesty,

Integrity, Sportsmanship, Respect, Confidence, Responsibility, Perseverance, Courtesy, Judgment) and mission[38] as a nonprofit sport organization explicitly note the character traits they hope to develop in inner city youth from their exposure to golf.

> **First Tee's Mission Statement:** To impact the lives of young people around the world by creating affordable and accessible golf facilities to primarily serve those who have not previously had exposure to the game and its positive values.

Significant Meaning, Inspiration, and Involvement

A final reason behind why strong emotional responses may occur after an ethical failure is that many people ascribe extraordinary meaning to the leisure experiences they have connected to a sport.[39] Whether they are running rivers[40] or going to games with grandparents,[41] sports enthusiasts can develop great attachment to sport-related products and brands.[42] Some believe that participants connect themselves (become ego-involved) with entities they feel strongly about,[43] and that this symbolic attachment prompts a strong emotional response or defense (CORFing: cutting-off-reflected-failure).[44] If we're involved in this manner,[45] our commitment prompts us to deflect or distance ourselves from the negative information entailed in ethical breaches; whether they're committed by employees, athletes, or those acting as representatives of the sport.[46] Equally significant is the transcendent meaning we can draw from sports when at times we witness remarkable events on the field of play that lift our sense of humanity up, beyond ourselves. Novak provides a compelling account of Jackie Robinson, who broke baseball's color line as the first African-American to play in the major leagues with the Brooklyn Dodgers. Novak describes Robinson stealing home in the late 1950s, where in a single instant his athletic feat catapulted the whole stadium to their feet as this young man inspired all, regardless of creed, color, or club.[47]

Another more recent example of sport's ability to inspire occurred on a softball field in 2008 when a crippling knee injury left a University of Western Oregon player stranded, unable to round the bases under her own power after a home run. Faced with playoff elimination, two Central Washington teammates, Mallorie Holtman and Liz Wallace, carried their opponent, Sara Tucholsky, the rest of the way. Witnessed by perhaps a hundred people, this image of sportsmanship went viral across the country.[48] Later that year all three were accorded national acclaim for the event and honored with a "Best Moments in Sports" ESPY award. However, perhaps the most compelling testimony that day was the response from Central's head coach. He wept. With the season on the line, his players acted selflessly. On the stage of high-pressure performance how much brighter does the light of a good deed shine? It is the larger sense of sport, its wonder, anxieties, heights, and depths that has us willing to say that's not "*how you play the game.*" The issue of conduct is important to us and prompts a response.[49] Rice, a famous sports writer, relates a sentiment key to the endeavor, the ethic of "fair play": [50]

> For when the One Great Scorer comes to write against your name,
> He marks not that you won or lost but how you played the game.

The Nature of Personal Ethics

How Do Ethics Develop?

When faced with questions on how ethical standards develop, one way to think about it is by comparing the matter to the development of athletic skills. For instance, Dan O'Brien, one of the most successful decathletes in the world, had a particular approach to training that serves as a useful analogy. O'Brien won Olympic gold in the event during the summer of 1996 in Atlanta, and followed that with three consecutive World Championship titles. In a recent interview, O'Brien described the training mind-set needed to build a complex set of skills in ten different areas: (a) a range of preparation strategies, (b) the role of feedback (from a coach or mentor), and (c) the importance of consistency and perseverance in training.[51] To excel, decathletes need a lot of repetition, heaps of skill training, and a willingness to push to the limit. According to O'Brien, tough competition and large audiences are daunting but success comes when you truly embrace the challenge and give all you have to running the course through.

Virtue ethics (VE) offer an interesting parallel to athletic training and preparation inasmuch as self-discipline and moral action are also within our power to perform or avoid, and that we can be held accountable for success or the consequences of our failure on the field of play. Plato and Aristotle support the link arguing ethics were virtues of character and dispositions to act in certain ways. Their philosophy was that good conduct resulted from habits acquired by repeated action and correction. Other writers on ethics offer competing views to this, asserting that simple rules or approaches to what is right are misleading, for while *"some people believe there are fundamentally simple approaches to hard moral choices such as: let the market decide, search one's heart and be true to one's values, do what is best for the shareholders, take care of the people in the company 'family', do what is right for all of a company's stakeholders. These ways of resolving the moral dilemmas of management are beguilingly clear, simple, praiseworthy— and misleading. The search for a grand unifying principle of management morality leads to frustration and often cynicism."*[52] Some of the pessimism expressed here leans on Jean-Paul Sartre's work, who also believed "pure" courses of action were open only to naïve idealists.[53] But is it true? Are noble, right, pure, or praiseworthy ways open to us? Can there be simple approaches to ethical dilemmas? Is it possible to build virtues that help us weather the storms we face personally or professionally? A healthy contingent of philosophers would say yes, that higher principles of navigation can be drawn from a "morality of aspiration"[54] and that ethics like these have the potential to infuse our lives with greater meaning and purpose.[55]

To this point, two well-known camps exist on the nature of ethics. Deontological ethics (DE) maintain that moral standards about the right or wrong of an action depend on its intrinsic qualities, not on the nature of its consequences. This means that some acts are viewed as morally wrong in themselves (e.g., lying, breaking a promise, murder) and the rightness of an action is often determined by its conformity to moral rules such as "do not steal" or "do not cheat or lie." Diametrically opposed to DE's focus on means, teleological ethics (TE) derive ethical duty from what is valuable as an end. For example, one theory, utilitarianism, holds that the right ends consist in what is best for all concerned (e.g., that one might die for the many).[56] Other TE theories seek different ends as a goal, such as survival, power, or freedom, as in existentialism. According to some marketers, virtue ethics constitutes a third major approach in normative ethics, falling somewhat outside the traditional TE/DE dichotomy. In VE the right or wrong of our action (or inaction) rests on its connection to an end with intrinsic value. However, the qualities of morally right action also constitute an end in itself and cannot simply serve as a means to that end.[57] Concerned with character traits moreso than the enumeration of duties, the concept of virtue is something that makes its possessor good.[58] VE is defined as a kind of moral excellence that focuses on key virtues and in which every activity has a good at which it aims (e.g., patience, chastity, courage, valor).[59] But as there cannot be an infinite regress of merely extrinsic goods, Aristotle argued that there must be a highest good or virtue we could shoot for. The target for ethical response was said to be a virtuous midpoint on a continuum between the vices of excess and deficiency. This meant that with:

- danger, courage was the mean between rashness and cowardice.
- enjoyment of pleasure, moderation was sought between temperance and intemperance.
- money, generosity was the mean between wastefulness and stinginess.
- strangers, being friendly was the mean between being ingratiating and surly.
- self-esteem, magnanimity was the mean between vanity and pusillanimity.

Perhaps the best-known theory on how ethical principles develop in people comes from work by Lawrence Kohlberg. A developmental psychologist in moral education, Kohlberg used support from several studies to explain how people progressed in their moral reasoning (i.e., the basis they used for ethical behavior) through a series of stages. Tied to Piaget's work, the theory describes six sequential stages that are navigated as people progress through three levels of moral thinking (Figure 5.2).[60]

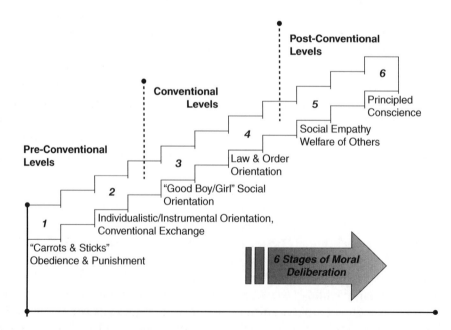

Figure 5.2 Kohlberg's Levels of Moral Development[61]

The first level of moral thinking usually operates at an elementary school level. Here ethical behavior follows socially accepted norms enforced by an authority figure that uses threat of punishment as a primary means to compel compliance. Stage 2 varies somewhat, for instead of avoiding punishment, right behavior is undertaken in order to secure one's own best interests. The second level characterizes stages that are conventionally found in society. In stage 3, right action is prompted by a desire to do what will gain the approval of others. Moral thinking in stage 4 looks to abide by the law and feels obliged to respond out of a sense of duty. According to Kohlberg, the final level is one that the bulk of people do not reach. Stage 5 focuses on acting out of a sense of social empathy and a genuine interest in the welfare of others. Stage 6 stresses action out of respect for principle and conscience. Few individuals are believed to qualify for this level, which makes it difficult to define with examples.

The theory holds that progress in moral thinking is restricted to sequential movement through each stage. People cannot skip stages, as they are limited to comprehending the reason behind an action's morality to the stage immediately above. This underscores using moral dilemmas for discussion as a way for helping people to see and embrace a more reasonable option of a higher stage.[62] Some researchers question the validity of Kohlberg's theory. Concerns vary over whether moral reasoning (what we say) and moral behavior (what we do) are consistent, if stage classifications are reliable a few days later (test-retest), and whether the theory accommodates differences in how women and men approach moral decision making. For instance, women may be more prone to base their moral rationale on concepts like caring or personal relationships (level 2 reasoning) whereas men may be predisposed to use arguments of justice and equity to evaluate a moral dilemma (reasoning from level 3's stages).[63]

Quite a bit of research has been done on how the theory applies to business. Some studies observe that relying on rewards and punishments, "sticks or carrots," for ethical conduct ends up leading employees to operate at Kohlberg's lowest level of moral reasoning.[64] This means reasoning at stages 1 and 2, where we pay taxes or adhere to rules only because we fear the consequences of getting caught not doing so. Some companies use moral imperatives to "do the right thing" or explicit guidelines, such as codes of conduct with complex rules and regulations. Cabela's is a giant outdoor sporting goods retailer whose sales in 2011 from their 37 U.S. stores topped $2.5 billion.[65] For many, the integrity of the Cabela's brand, their consistency and attention to detail, mark them as a top performer in several ways. Taken from an annual report to shareholders, Table 5.2 outlines the five core values that have shaped the company since its inception and guides their code of ethics today on how to treat people both within and outside the firm.[66]

> To live up to these hallmarks, we must dedicate ourselves to high ethical and legal compliance standards in our daily performance—every day, in every action we take. Our success is dependent on the actions of our employees, all employees. We must act with integrity and honesty, just as our Core Values state . . .

Stated expectations of how companies want to operate are essential documents for sport organizations to include when training and guiding their employees. For instance, take the importance Nike's CEO ascribes on how to play the game "Inside the Lines," the company's code of ethics:[67]

Table 5.2 Adapted Version of Cabela's Code of Conduct and Ethics

---

Cabela's success is a result of our dedication to our Core Values

- **Superior Customer Service.** *Our customers are our reason for being – the center of everything we do. We listen to our customers to provide personalized service that is focused on their needs . . .*
- **Quality Products and Services.** *Cabela's is committed to providing high-quality products and services at an exceptional value. Our focus on high quality guides us in all the decisions we make . . .*
- **Integrity and Honesty.** *Integrity and honesty are the soundness of our moral character. We believe in doing what is right even when no one is watching. Integrity and honesty are fundamental in how we deal with others and operate our business. Cabela's insists on uncompromised integrity and honesty from everyone in all their duties . . .*
- **Respect for Individuals.** *Cabela's most valuable asset is its employees. Cabela's respects the uniqueness of every individual by honoring differences and placing value on diversity, while maintaining a spirit of teamwork . . .*
- **Excellence in Performance.** *Cabela's strives for efficiency & excellence in performance in every aspect of our business. We provide a creative atmosphere in which employees are encouraged to be innovative and far thinking . . . .*

A Message from Phil

At NIKE, we are on the offense, always. We play hard, we play to win, & we play by the rules of the game. This Code of Ethics is vitally important. It contains the rules of the game for NIKE, the rules we live by & what we stand for. Please read it. And if you've read it before, read it again. Then take some time to think about what it says & make a commitment to play by it. Defining the NIKE playing field ensures no matter how dynamic & challenging NIKE may be, our actions & decisions fit with our shared values.

Regrettably, research suggests that firms cannot rely solely on written statements to shape how people act. Other strategies beyond admonishments to do the right thing or play by a rule book are needed to spark cognitive moral development in employees.[68] This might call for mentors or leaders within the organization to serve as positive role models (servant leaders) for junior employees operating at Stages 3 and 4, as their ethical decisions tend to be swayed by the conventions of those around them. Understanding the nature of informal leadership within the culture of the organization and whether one casts *light or shadow* on the ethics of those around you is both challenging and needed.[69] No doubt this is why franchises and sport businesses like to build their roster of employees around strong, ethical team leaders (e.g., "franchise players," who'll best represent the values of the organization). Take for instance the description of the character ideals the NFL Seahawks desire to cultivate in their organization (DNA of the Seahawk's Brand Essence = Passion+Character+12th Man+Excellence):[70]

Character describes the inherent set of qualities and features that determine the team's moral and ethical actions and reactions; its moral and ethical strength; its good reputation. It is internal as well as external. It distinguishes the Seahawks from its competition. Character comes from players who have "football character," meaning they love the game, they love to play, and they give everything they have.

Obviously character matters and a small group encouraging the wrong traits can influence the ethical decisions of others in the organization, sometimes in disastrous ways. Take the missteps of the NFL Vikings' team leader in 2005, when he and three Minnesota teammates drew national attention for participating in a bawdy boat party.[71] Or, the bounty scandal in which players' became involved and suspended for participating in an alleged pay-to-injure program at the NFL New Orleans' Saints.[72] Unfortunately, organizations are vulnerable to being tarnished by the immoral actions and influence of a few employees. According to some, one solution is to conduct ethics education, where training interventions can be used to improve employee awareness and decision making at this particular level of moral development.[73]

According to Kohlberg, fewer people make decisions at the higher post-conventional level. Moral decisions here are more autonomous, as they are based on a set of universal ethical principles that enable the individual to determine what is right. This means employees at stages 5 or 6 may ignore "sticks and carrots" or the conventions of the group (organization) in order to follow an ethical principle through because it is right to do so.[74] For instance, even though it was not conventional (the social or league norm) to recruit black athletes from the Negro Leagues, a basic principle of equality justifies the Brooklyn Dodgers' decision to recruit Jackie Robinson. Another more current example of operating at this level occurred when a Walker Cup team member, Blayne Barber, disqualified himself for an infraction during the first stage of the PGA's Tour Qualifying School. Although his caddie said he never saw the leaf move, Barber still applied the penalty stroke to his score but later realized the correct penalty was 2 shots. His comments about his decision to DQ suggest a higher ethic at work. "I just did not have any peace about it," Barber told the magazine. "I knew I needed to do the right thing. I knew it was going to be disqualification."[75] Whistle blowing is a response in which people call attention to an ethical breach by others within an organization. However, Barber's decision to blow the whistle on his own actions reflects an act of conscience that is laudable. Imagine if our actions in other sports and in business carried the same ethic.

Classifying Ethical Dilemmas

One way to view and understand ethical dilemmas when they arise is to classify them by considering the tension between two dimensions.[76] This questions if the action fits with social expectations (Kohlberg's Conventional Level in Figure 5.2) and "universal ethical principles"[77] of conscience (Kohlberg' Post-Conventional Level). The Social Convention dimension evaluates if the response meets the expectations embodied by different social groups a person identifies with (company rules, legal obligations, social mores and values, etc.). Some argue the other dimension of conscience uses principles of *natural law* to dictate values to what is right or wrong. These offer a set of moral norms that are "not merely the products or creations of subjective viewpoints"[78] but act as an objective set of natural dispositions which serve a deep internal conscience or moral regulator for telling right from wrong.[79] Using the dimensions of Social Convention and Principled Conscience, Figure 5.3 shows four potential ethical scenarios that might occur. Two of the outcomes, Ethical Failure and Ethical Leadership, reflect consistency between both dimensions. The other two responses reflect conflict, where either social expectation or principled conscience is sacrificed, omitted, or commissioned, in order to justify the action taken.[80]

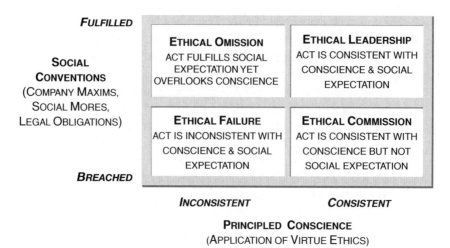

Figure 5.3 Classifying Ethical Responses

Examples of what these responses might look like can be drawn from previous discussions. For instance, the Lance Armstrong doping scandal or Sandusky and the response from Penn State University administrators would qualify as examples of ethical failure.[81] Instances of ethical leadership and principled conscience are evident in the actions taken by Barber in his willingness to disqualify himself during an event, or by the Central Washington softball players helping an injured opponent around the bases.[82] Issues of whether ethical dilemmas constitute conflict and inconsistency between social expectation and principled conscience are more difficult to ascertain due to the intrinsic nature of whether one engages their conscience or not. An honest confession is needed. Perhaps some of the NFL players or coaches associated with the Vikings or the Saints and their "bawdy boat" or "bounty" scandals could be considered as examples of omission[83] to the degree that they went along with others and the action despite conscience, knowing deep down it was not "good" or "right."

Dilemmas of commission, where the individual acts on conscience despite the fact that the response will breach social expectation, are not necessarily wrong. For instance, stands of principle by the Brooklyn Dodgers and Jackie Robinson in breaking baseball's color barrier can serve as examples of doing what's right despite running contrary to social expectations of the day. Potential conflicts can also occur when social expectations of a group are breached primarily in order to commission a principle of greater good. Whistle blowers on poor organizational practices might qualify as cases of this. Other dilemmas of ethical commission in sport business can result from religious adherents being unable to comply with social expectations due to their personal beliefs (e.g., participation or work conflicts with religious observance). A classic example of this was captured in the film "Chariots of Fire" when national athletic hero, Eric Liddle the *flying Scotsman*, refused on the basis of personal conscience and conviction to run on the Sabbath for the Prince of Wales and the British Olympic Team at the 1924 Paris Olympics.[84]

What Influences and Shapes Our Ethics?

Several social and personal factors can shape how our ethics develop. How we are raised (i.e., nurture) is the first influence many people think of, where the ethical values of our parents become our own. Of course other social groups impact on what is important when framing our decisions (friends, co-workers, relatives, etc.). Kohlberg's theory noted this in his conventional phase. However, he also suggested that moral development paralleled cognitive maturation. But a quick look around tells us that intellectual progress doesn't necessarily coincide with moral fortitude. Aristotle and the VE camp would say this is because moral strength is another capacity like the mind or the body that needs a good workout in order to develop.

Another important area that shapes both our principles (ethics) and our standards (morals) of right or wrong is how we view the world. All of us have a personal philosophy about how the world operates. Personal worldview describes the fundamental presuppositions people make about the nature of things, and then use to order their lives. It can also be thought of as a framework of ideas and beliefs individuals, groups, or cultures use to interpret the world and interact with it. The term *Weltanschauung* (*Welt*, world & *Anschauung*, view or outlook) was first coined by German philosophers Kant and Hegel to refer to philosophies, ideologies, cultural or religious perspectives people have about the world. According to Apostel and others, a worldview is an ontology (descriptive model of the world) that is composed of six elements:[85]

- An explanation of the world or reality as we see it.
- A futurology, answering the question "Where are we heading?"
- An axiology, values and answers to ethical questions: "What is right or wrong?"
- A praxeology, methodology, or theory of action: "How should we attain our goals?"
- An epistemology or theory of knowledge: "What is true and false?"
- An etiology: A constructed worldview should contain an account of its own "building blocks" (origin and construction).

The value of trying to understand a person's worldview is that it helps the observer appreciate where the other person is coming from, so that we can track the priorities and understandings operating in the background of a particular ethical choice or decision (see Figure 5.4). For instance some of the six worldview questions listed above could be used to shed light on Barber's decision to DQ, or Rice's poem on *how to play the game*. However, perhaps one of the larger problems here is the range and variation of worldviews that people use to make decisions.

Systems theory offers general tools (e.g., state-space approach) and concepts such as system, communication, and feedback, to help simplify the explanation of complex phenomenon, their interactions, and how they potentially overlap one another.[86] The approach has been used in many disciplines (physics, chemistry, biology, psychology, sociology, etc.), but has a proven track record in engineering, where it is still widely used. There are applications of systems theory in the fields of business[87] and ethics,[88] but the concept is yet to be used to simplify our understanding of different worldview systems. One key characteristic in systems theory is that it looks at the nature of how different elements in seemingly separate fields communicate, engage, or overlap. When

Figure 5.4 Ethics and Decision Making

it comes to worldviews one focal distinguishing feature is how each view explains the nature of the world we live in. Is the physical realm all there is, or is there something larger (i.e., a metaphysical reality, that some may call a spiritual domain)? The question is a popular topic, for instance a survey reported 80% of 114,000 university freshman believed there was a God and expressed a strong interest in spiritual things.[89]

Three well-known worldviews or personal philosophies about the nature of reality (atheistic, agnostic, and theistic perspectives) make different distinctions here, describing whether the world consists only of a physical dimension or has a metaphysical backdrop. In each case worldview can determine how we draw meaning from our actions, and has the potential to influence our answers to ethical questions and sway the conviction with which we hold to them.[90] It is important to note that people with dissimilar worldviews can arrive at the same ethical decision, yet will do so for different reasons. For instance, VE's cardinal or classical virtues (e.g., justice, prudence, temperance, courage) are sustained without necessarily ascribing to one particular worldview or another, whereas other types of virtues such as charity, forgiveness, patience, hope, or self-sacrifice are, more often than not, justified by certain open-system worldviews. Figure 5.5 uses some of the underlying principles of systems theory to describe how these three different worldviews operate in terms of (a) their depiction of reality (whether a metaphysical realm exists beyond the physical), and (b) an assessment of potential interaction/communication between systems.

Worldview labels of closed and open refer primarily to whether adherents in each case believe there is a capacity for interaction or exchange between the physical or metaphysical system. An Open System worldview holds exchange between physical-metaphysical systems is both possible and probable. Some religious persuasions might refer to these Open System exchanges as divine inspiration or prayer (bidirectional). In contrast to this, one Closed System view holds the physical realm to be the full sum of reality. This by definition is "closed," as it does not believe there is a metaphysical realm to engage. Another type of Closed System can be identified when there is recognition of both systems, yet there is no engagement between these two realities; that one sees evidence of something greater (e.g., 25% of American believe in a greater yet impersonal metaphysical force) yet purport there is no personal interaction or communication possible.[91] Further ontological and epistemological contrasts between Open and Closed Systems are offered in Table 5.3. These provide some perspective on how characteristics of a person's worldview might influence their ethical decision making and their conviction in following a particular course of action.[92] For instance, take the first characteristic of system control. The open-system adherent would contend that there is the potential for a larger 'hand' at work in the circumstances they face, whereas their closed-system colleague would contend that they are the prime decision maker and author of the path traveled. The implications of this when facing difficult

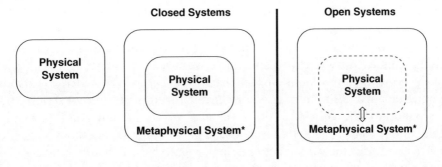

Figure 5.5 Closed and Open Worldview Systems

*Metaphysical Systems include ontological and epistemological assertions of what transcends the physical. Bidirectional arrow represents a capacity for system interaction and exchange.

Table 5.3 Ontological and Epistemological Contrasts of Open and Closed Systems

System Characteristics	Open Systems	Closed Systems
1. System Control	Have a capacity for metaphysical interaction	Physical processes dominate, mitigated within system only
2. Approach to Knowing	Revealed and discovered	Discovery only
3. Personal Meaning & Significance	Derived from both systems	Derived from physical system
4. Ultimate Authority on Good	Sourced from metaphysical system	Physical system, draws from the law & self-determination
5. Personal Conscience	Draws from physical system yet open to metaphysical	Draws only from physical system
6. Personal Moral Accountability	Metaphysical & physical system accountability (social, self, spiritual)	Physical system accountability (social, self-evaluation)

(ethical) dilemmas is that the "open" adherent may ask for metaphysical help in order to know what to do (e.g., 75% of the U.S. population pray weekly for help or guidance), whereas "closed" adherents would believe that insight can only be gleaned from within the physical system (e.g., wise counsel from friends).[93] A disclaimer is needed here as there are many other contrasts that could be offered between the two systems. In fact Table 5.3's contrasts on different worldviews are more illustrative than exhaustive, as they offer the reader an entree to more complex discussions of what people believe about right and wrong.

Conclusions

The social and economic costs of ethical failures in sports and society cannot be ignored.[94] They compel serious consideration about what can be done to remedy "a widespread decline in ethical standards".[95] Though some contend fixes can be found in greater oversight by governments and governing bodies,[96] this does not get to the heart of the matter. What is the role of individual accountability and personal conscience in how we live? Some argue answers can be gleaned from approaches that promise a "morality of aspiration"[97] and virtues of a greater good. Logical premises for doing right here mean first accepting that we have yet to arrive, or have developed ethically to the level we should. But the matter also suggests that there are standards of "good" we can and should aspire to when navigating our course of action.[98] These hopes stand in stark contrast to other views, skeptical that any grand principles of morality are possible.[99] Despite bleak assertions by some skeptics, our society continues to clamor for the very qualities it doubts exist. Nations want and expect virtue in their citizens but struggle against a cultural mind set which denies the very things we're hunger for, "we mock truthfulness as naïve yet are amazed to find deceit; we laugh at honor and are shocked to find traitors in our midst."[100] Despite the difficulty of working out what is good, the labor and heavy lifting is essential. Aristotle and his contemporaries would have us train as we would with any intellectual or athletic pursuit. Traditionally, sports have been the preparatory vehicle we engage to train our youth, but it would appear that even this proving ground has done little to stem the decline. To sum up, this chapter has touched on personal ethics and provided some points of reflection over the different ways people think about the dilemmas they face in sport and business. By design the material hopes to renew discussion over what it means to be and do good, personally and professionally; and consider whether Jiminy Cricket's advice to *give a little whistle* is a feasible solution when conscience is left untrained and unkempt.

References

1. Williams, O., & Murphy, P. (1990). The ethics of virtue: A moral theory of marketing. *Journal of Macromarketing, 10*(1), 19–29.
2. Willard, D. (2004, March). The University's responsibility for moral guidance. *The Real Issue,* 1(March), 1–3.
3. Nocera, J. (2012, December 3). The next tobacco? *The New York Times.* Retrieved from www.nytimes.com/2012/12/04/opinion/nocera-the-next-tobacco.html?nl=todaysheadlines&emc=edit_th_20121204&_r=1&
4. Willard, D. (2006). Moral rights, moral responsibility, and the contemporary failure of moral knowledge. In C. Butler (Ed.), *Guantanamo Bay and the judicial-moral treatment of the other* (pp. 161-178). Purdue, IN: Purdue University Press.
5. Johnson, C. (2009). *Meeting the ethical challenges of leadership: Casting light or shadow.* Thousand Oaks, CA: Sage Publications.
6. Weems, M. (1918). *A history of the life and death, virtues and exploits of General George Washington.* Philadelphia, PA: J.B. Lippincott Co.
7. Carr, D. (2012, October 28). Chasing Armstrong with truth. *The New York Times.* Retrieved from www.nytimes.com/2012/10/29/business/media/chasing-lance-armstrongs-misdeeds-from-the-sidelines.html?pagewanted=all&_r=0; and Pearson, M. (2012, October 22). Doping scandal costs Lance Armstrong sponsors, charity role. *CNN, US Edition,.* Retrieved from http://www.cnn.com/2012/10/17/us/lance-armstrong-doping/index.html
8. Weber, E. (2010, January 4). Tiger Woods, virtue ethics, and corporate sponsorship. *Everyday Ethics: Ethics for Real People and Real Issues.* Retrieved from http://everyday-ethics.org/2010/01/tiger-woods-virtue-ethics-and-corporate-sponsorship/; and Anonymous. (2010, December 5). Tiger Woods ethics, part I: Betrayal's not for heroes. *Ethics Alarms.* Retrieved from http://ethicsalarms.com/2009/12/05/tiger-woods-ethics-part-i-betrayals-not-for-heroes/
9. Perez-Pena, R. (2012, July 12). Failures throughout Penn State. *New York Times.* Retrieved from http://www.nytimes.com/2012/07/13/sports/ncaafootball/in-freeh-report-on-sandusky-failures-throughout-penn-state.html?pagewanted=all; and Johnson, K., & Stanglin, D. (2012, November 1). Ex-Penn State president charged

in Sandusky case. *USA Today*. Retrieved from http://www.usatoday.com/story/news/nation/2012/11/01/penn-state-president-graham-spanier-charges-jerry-sandusky/1674037/

10. Epstein, D., & McCann, M. (2012, April 13). How Bobby Petrino gamed system by hiring mistress. SI.com. Retrieved from http://sportsillustrated.cnn.com/2012/football/ncaa/04/13/arkansas.records/index.html

11. Marquet International. (2012, October 29). Resume Liars Club. *Marquet International: Managing Business Risks Through Strategic Intelligence*. Retrieved from http://www.marquetinternational.com/liars.htm.

12. Sheinin, D. (2005, March 18). Baseball has a day of reckoning in Congress: McGwire remains evasive during steroid testimony. *Washington Post*. Retrieved from http://www.washingtonpost.com/wp-dyn/articles/A43422-2005Mar17.html; and Associated Press. (2007). From gambling to drugs to ugly labor disputes, baseball's history is dotted with dark days. Retrieved from http://usatoday30.usatoday.com/sports/baseball/2007-12-13-1148572516_x.htm

13. Back, T., Blatter, P., & Bughin, J. (2004, July). Playing to win in the business of sports. *McKinsey Quarterly*. Retrieved from https://www.mckinseyquarterly.com/Playing_to_win_in_the_business_of_sports_1454

14. Patrick, A., & Esterl, M. (2007, July 26). Tour de France sponsors may pull out: Doping allegations force marketers to rethink risk of association with race. *Wall Street Journal*, Eastern Ed. B.2; and CBC News (2012, October 25). Doping scandals plague Tour de France history: Several controversies taint top finishes over past 15 years. Canadian Broadcasting Commission. Retrieved from http://www.cbc.ca/news/interactives/tour-de-france/

15. Ecclesiastes 1:9. Holy Bible, New International Version, 2011.

16. Gupta, G. (2012, May 16). Six major match-fixing scandals. *The Times of India*. Retrieved from http://articles.timesofindia.indiatimes.com/2012-05-16/top-stories/31725742_1_life-ban-indian-bookie-hansie-cronje

17. Associated Press. (2007). From gambling to drugs to ugly labor disputes, baseball's history is dotted with dark days. *USA Today*. Retrieved from http://usatoday30.usatoday.com/sports/baseball/2007-12-13-1148572516_x.htm

18. Daugherty, P. (2011, April 15). Why Rose should be in Hall of Fame and drug cheats should not. *Sports Illustrated*. Retrieved from http://sportsillustrated.cnn.com/2011/writers/paul_daugherty/04/15/rose.ramirez.hall/index.html

19. Laczniak, G., Burton, R., & Murphy, P. (1999). Sports marketing ethics in today's marketplace. *Sport Marketing Quarterly*, 8(4), 43–53.

20. Spoelstra, J. (1997). *Ice to Eskimos: How to market a product nobody wants*. New York: Harper Business.

21. Marchetti, M. (1997, December 1). Whatever it takes: In the battle to win sales in today's ferocious marketplace, ethical behavior is the first casualty. *Sales & Marketing Management*, 149, 170.

22. President Calvin Coolidge. In *The Webster's Pocket Quotation Dictionary*. Sydney, Australia: Trident Press Int'l.

23. Bhattacharya, C., & Sen, S. (2004). Doing better at doing good: When, why, and how consumers respond to corporate social initiatives. *California Management Review*, 47(1), 9–24.

24. Johnson, C. (2009). *Meeting the ethical challenges of leadership: Casting light or shadow*. Thousand Oaks, CA: Sage Publications.

25. REI.com website, (2012). Retrieved October 30, 2012 from http://www.rei.com/jobs/culture-values.html

26. Gupta, G. (2012, May 16). Six major match-fixing scandals. *The Times of India*. Retrieved from http://articles.timesofindia.indiatimes.com/2012-05-16/top-stories/31725742_1_life-ban-indian-bookie-hansie-cronje

27. NBA.com (2001). Colangelo/Kidd speak. Retrieved from www.nba.com/suns/news/kidd_colangelo_010119.html; and Associated Press. (2007). Kidd files for divorce from wife Joumana of 10 years. Retrieved from http://sports.espn.go.com/nba/news/story?id=2725524

28. Burton, R., & Howard, D. (2000). Recovery strategies for sports. *Marketing Management*, Spring, 42–49.

29. Mitra, K., Reiss, M., & Capella, L. (1999). An examination of perceived risk, information search and behavioral intentions in search, experience and credence services. *Journal of Services Marketing*, 13(3), 208–228; and Eisingerich, A., & Bell, S. (2007). Maintaining customer relationships in high credence services. *Journal of Services Marketing*, 21(4), 253–262.

30. Parasuraman, A., Zeithaml, V., & Berry, L. (1985). A conceptual model of service quality and its implications for future research. *Journal of Marketing*, 49(4), 41–50.

31. Burton, R., & Howard, D. (2000). Recovery strategies for sports. *Marketing Management*, Spring, 42–49.

32. Newsweek Magazine (1993, June 27). I'm not paid to be a role model. Retrieved from http://www.thedailybeast.com/newsweek/1993/06/27/i-m-not-a-role-model.html

33. Carr, D. (2012, October 28). Chasing Armstrong with truth. *The New York Times*. Retrieved from www.nytimes.com/2012/10/29/business/media/chasing-lance-armstrongs-misdeeds-from-the-sidelines.html?pagewanted=all&_r=0; and Pearson, M. (2012, October 22). Doping scandal costs Lance Armstrong sponsors, charity role. *CNN, US Edition*,. Retrieved from http://www.cnn.com/2012/10/17/us/lance-armstrong-doping/index.html

34. McDonald, J. (1991). Further exploration of Track Two Diplomacy. In L. Kriesberg & S. Thorson (Eds.), *Timing the de-escalation of international conflicts* (pp. 201-220)., Syracuse, NY: Syracuse University Press.

35.   McArthur, B. (1975). The Chicago playground movement: A neglected feature of social justice. *Social Service Review*, *49*(3), 376–395.

36.   Lombardo, J. (2010, October 18). NBA Cares evolving after 5 years of service. *Street & Smith's Sport Business Journal*, 9. Retrieved from http://www.sportsbusinessdaily.com/Journal/Issues/2010/10/20101018/Leagues-and-Governing-Bodies/NBA-Cares.aspx

37.   Christianity Today. (2012). Jeremy Lin, Tim Tebow, Josh Hamilton: Muscular Christianity's newest heroes. *Christianity Today*, *56*(4), 11. Retrieved from http://www.christianitytoday.com/ct/content/pdf/120401spot_athletesmuscular.pdf

38.   First Tee Website. (n.d.). Retrieved from http://www.thefirsttee.org on November 1, 2012.

39.   Gibson, H., Willming, C., & Holdnak, A. (2002). We're Gators . . . not just Gator fans: Serious leisure and University of Florida football. *Journal of Leisure Research, 34*, 397–425; and Stebbins, R. A. (2005). Choice and experiential definitions of leisure. *Leisure Sciences, 27*, 349–352.

40.   Arnould, E., & Price, L. (1993). River magic: Extraordinary experience and the extended service encounter. *Journal of Consumer Research, 20*, 24–45.

41.   James, J. D. (2001). The role of cognitive development and socialization in the initial development of team loyalty. *Leisure Sciences, 23*, 233–262.

42.   Bristow, D. N., & Sebastian, R. J. (2001). Holy cow! Wait 'til next year! A closer look at the brand loyalty of Chicago Cubs baseball fans. *Journal of Consumer Marketing, 18*(3), 256–275.

43.   Cialdini, R., & De Nicholas, M. (1989). Self-presentation by association. *Journal of Personality and Social Psychology, 57*(4), 626–631.

44.   Snyder, C., Lassegard, M., & Ford, C. (1986). Distancing after group success and failure: Basking in reflected glory and cutting off reflected failure. *Journal of Personality and Social Psychology, 51*, 382–388.

45.   Cialdini, R., Borden, R., Thorne, A., Walker, M., Freeman, S., & Sloan, L. (1976). Basking in reflected glory: Three (Football) field studies. *Journal of Personality and Social Psychology, 34*, 366–375.

46.   Funk, D., & Pritchard, M. P. (2006). Sport publicity: Commitment's moderation of message effects. *Journal of Business Research, 59*(5), 613–621.

47.   Novak, M. (1994). *The joy of sports: End zones, bases, baskets, balls, and the consecration of the American spirit*. Lanham, MD: Rowman & Littlefield Publishing Group.

48.   Hays, G. (2012, May 31). Holtman carried home to Central Washington. ESPN-W. Retrieved from http://espn.go.com/espnw/college-sports/7990054/espnw-mallory-holtman-carried-home-central-washington

49.   Burton, S., & Netemeyer, R. (1992). The effect of enduring, situational, and response involvement on preference stability in the context of voting behavior. *Psychology & Marketing, 9*(2), 143–156.

50.   Rice, G. (1941). Alumnus football. *Only the Brave and Other Poems*. New York: S. Barnes & Company.

51.   Webb, A. (2012, August). In the long run, consistency always wins out: An interview with Olympic decathlon champion Dan O'Brien. *McKinsey Quarterly*, 1–7.

52.   Badaracco, J. (1992). Business ethics: Four spheres of executive responsibility. *California Management Review*, Spring, 64–79

53.   Able, L. (1989). Jean-Paul Sartre, "Dirty Hands". In *No Exit and Three other Plays*. New York: Vintage International.

54.   Willard, D. (2006). Why it matters whether there is a higher law or not. *Pepperdine Law Review, 36* (Special Issue on Is There a 'Higher Law'? Does it Matter?), 661–665; and Fuller, L. (1969). *The Morality of Law*. New Haven, CT: Yale University Press.

55.   Novak, M. (1996). *Business as a calling: Work and the examined life*. New York: The Free Press.

56.   Fletcher, J. (1966). *Situational ethics: The new morality*. Philadelphia, PA: The Westminster Press.

57.   Williams, O., & Murphy, P. (1990). The ethics of virtue: A moral theory of marketing. *Journal of Macromarketing, 10*(1), 19–29.

58.   Hursthouse, R. (2012). Virtue ethics. In E. Zalta (Ed.), *The Stanford Encyclopedia of Philosophy* (Summer 2012 Edition). Retrieved from http://plato.stanford.edu/archives/sum2012/entries/ethics-virtue/,

59.   Hursthouse, R. (1999). *On virtue ethics*. Oxford, England: Oxford University Press.

60.   Kohlberg, L. (1971). Stages of moral development as a basis of moral education. In C. Beck, B. Crittenden, & E. Sullivan (Eds.), *Moral Education: Interdisciplinary Approaches*. New York: Newman Press.

61.   Barger, R. (2000). *A summary of Lawrence Kohlberg's Stages of Moral Development*. Notre Dame, IN: University of Notre Dame. Adapted from www.library.spscc.ctc.edu/electronicreserve/swanson/SummaryofLawrenceKohlberg.pdf

62.   Ibid.

63.   Woolfolk, A. (1993). *Educational psychology* (5th ed.). Boston, MA: Allyn & Bacon.

64.   Baucus, M., & Beck-Dudley, C. (2005). Designing ethical organizations: Avoiding the long-term negative effects of rewards and punishments. *Journal of Business Ethics, 56*, 355–370.

65.   Wenk, A. (2012, April 6). Cabela's plans expansion into Southeast. *Atlanta Business Chronicle*. Retrieved from http://www.bizjournals.com/atlanta/print-edition/2012/04/06/cabelas-plans-expansion-into-southeast.html?page=all

66. Cabela's Inc. (2004). *Annual Report to Shareholders*. Retrieved from Cabela's Investor Relations Annual Reports at http://phx.corporate-ir.net/phoenix.zhtml?c=177739&p=irol-reports

67. Nike Inc. (2011). Inside the lines: The Nike Code of Ethics. Retrieved from http://www.nikeresponsibility.com/report/uploads/files/NIKE_INC_Inside_the_Lines_Nov_2011.pdf

68. Izzo, G. (2000). Compulsory ethics education and the cognitive moral development of salespeople: A quasi-experimental assessment. *Journal of Business Ethics, 28*, 223–241.

69. Johnson, C. (2009). *Meeting the ethical challenges of leadership: Casting light or shadow*. Thousand Oaks, CA: Sage Publications.

70. Seattle Seahawks. (2008). Brand Essence. In *Seattle Seahawks Style Guide*. Seattle, WA.

71. Campbell, D. (2005, December 15). Four Vikings charged in boat party scandal. Associated Press News Wire. Retrieved from http://sports.espn.go.com/espn/wire?section=nfl&id=2260018, November 1, 2012.

72. Marvez, A. (2012, May 3). 4 players suspended in bounty scandal. Fox Sports News. Retrieved from http://msn.foxsports.com/nfl/story/jonathan-vilma-scott-fujita-anthony-hargrove-will-smith-suspended-in-new-orleans-saints-bounty-scandal-050212

73. Falkenberg, A. (2004). When in Rome: Moral maturity and ethics for international economic organizations. *Journal of Business Ethics, 54*, 17–32.

74. Ibid.

75. ESPN.com. (2012, November 6). Blayne Barber disqualifies self. ESPN News Service. Retrieved from http://espn.go.com/golf/story/_/id/8599746/blayne-barber-disqualifies-pga-tour-q-school-six-days-later

76. Henderson, V. (1982). The ethical side of enterprise. *Sloan Management Review, 23*(3), 37–47.

77. Falkenberg, A. (2004). When in Rome: Moral maturity and ethics for international economic organizations. *Journal of Business Ethics, 54*, 17–32.

78. Maciejewski, J. (2005). Reason as a nexus of natural law and rhetoric. *Journal of Business Ethics, 59*, 247–257.

79. Budziszewski, J. (2003). *What we can't not know: A guide*. Dallas, TX: Spence Publishing.

80. Pritchard, M. P. (2006, October). *The Role of Conscience & Conflict in Ethical Decision-Making*. Paper presented at the Sports Marketing Association Conference, Denver CO; and Pritchard, M. P. (2004, June). *Seeking the Good: A Framework for Moral Decision-Making in Sports Management*. Paper presented in the Business & Economics Track, National Faculty Leadership Conference, Washington, DC.

81. Carr, D. (2012, October 28). Chasing Armstrong with truth. *The New York Times*. Retrieved from www.nytimes.com/2012/10/29/business/media/chasing-lance-armstrongs-misdeeds-from-the-sidelines.html?pagewanted=all&_r=0, and Pearson, M. (2012, October 22). Doping scandal costs Lance Armstrong sponsors, charity role. *CNN, US Edition,*. Retrieved from http://www.cnn.com/2012/10/17/us/lance-armstrong-doping/index.html; and Perez-Pena, R. (2012, July 12). Failures throughout Penn State. *New York Times*. Retrieved from http://www.nytimes.com/2012/07/13/sports/ncaafootball/in-freeh-report-on-sandusky-failures-throughout-penn-state.html?pagewanted=all; and Johnson, K., & Stanglin, D. (2012, November 1). Ex-Penn State president charged in Sandusky case. *USA Today*. Retrieved from http://www.usatoday.com/story/news/nation/2012/11/01/penn-state-president-graham-spanier-charges-jerry-sandusky/1674037/

82. Hays, G. (2012, May 31). Holtman carried home to Central Washington. ESPN-W. Retrieved from http://espn.go.com/espnw/college-sports/7990054/espnw-mallory-holtman-carried-home-central-washington; and ESPN.com. (2012, November 6). Blayne Barber disqualifies self. ESPN News Service. Retrieved from http://espn.go.com/golf/story/_/id/8599746/blayne-barber-disqualifies-pga-tour-q-school-six-days-later

83. Campbell, D. (2005, December 15). Four Vikings charged in boat party scandal. Associated Press News Wire. Retrieved from http://sports.espn.go.com/espn/wire?section=nfl&id=2260018; and Marvez, A. (2012, May 3). 4 players suspended in bounty scandal. Fox Sports News. Retrieved from http://msn.foxsports.com/nfl/story/jonathan-vilma-scott-fujita-anthony-hargrove-will-smith-suspended-in-new-orleans-saints-bounty-scandal-050212

84. McCasland, D. (2001). *Eric Liddell: Pure gold*. Grand Rapids, MI: Discovery House Publishers.

85. Vidal, C. (2008). What is a worldview? In H. Van Belle, & J. Van der Veken (Eds.), *Nieuwheid denken. De wetenschappen en het creatieve aspect van de werkelijkheid*, in press. Acco, Leuven. Retrieved from http://cogprints.org/6094/2/Vidal_2008-what-is-a-worldview.pdf. Also Aerts, D., Apostel, L., De Moor, B., Hellemans, S., Maex, E., Van Belle, H. and Van der Veken, J. (1994). *World Views. From Fragmentation to Integration*. Brussels: VUB Press. Retrieved from http://www.vub.ac.be/CLEA/pub/books/worldviews.pdf

86. von Bertalanffy, L. (1968). *General systems theory*. New York: Braziller.

87. Boulding, K. E. (1956). General systems theory: The skeleton of science. *Management Science, 2*(3), 197–208.

88. Dallmann, H. (1998). Niklas Luhmann's systems theory as a challenge for ethics Ethical theory and moral practice, *1*(1), 85–102; and Harter, N., & Evanecky, D. J. (1985). Ethical perspectives of systems thinking. Retrieved from http://aa.utpb.edu/media/leadership-journal-files/2007archives/Ethical%20Perspectives%20of%20Systems-%20Thinking.pdf

89. Finder, A. (2007, May 2). Religion gets an 'A' at US colleges. *New York Times*. Retrieved from http://www.iht.com/articles/2007/05/02/news/college.php

90. Conroy, S., & Emerson, T. (2004). Business ethics and religion: Religiosity as a predictor of ethical awareness among students. *Journal of Business Ethics, 50*, 383–396.

91. Pew Research Center. (2007). *Pew Forum on Religion & Public Life: 2007 U.S. Religious Landscape Survey*. Retrieved from http://religions.pewforum.org/pdf/report2religious-landscape-study-key-findings.pdf

92. Dallmann, H. (1998). Niklas Luhmann's systems theory as a challenge for ethics Ethical theory and moral practice, *1*(1), 85–102; and Harter, N., & Evanecky, D. J. (1985). Ethical perspectives of systems thinking. Retrieved from http://aa.utpb.edu/media/leadership-journal-files/2007archives/Ethical%20Perspectives%20 of%20Systems-%20Thinking.pdf

93. Pew Research Center. (2007). *Pew Forum on Religion & Public Life: 2007 U.S. Religious Landscape Survey*. Retrieved from http://religions.pewforum.org/pdf/report2religious-landscape-study-key-findings.pdf

94. Hughes, S. & Shank, M. (2005). Defining scandal in sports: Media and corporate sponsor perspectives. *Sport Marketing Quarterly, 14*, 207–216.

95. Willard, D. (2004, March). The University's responsibility for moral guidance. *The Real Issue*, 1(March), 1–3.

96. Laczniak, G., Burton, R., & Murphy, P. (1999). Sports marketing ethics in today's marketplace. *Sport Marketing Quarterly, 8*(4), 43–53.

97. Fuller, L. (1969). *The Morality of Law*. New Haven, CT: Yale University Press.

98. Pritchard, M. P. (2008, June) *Aspirational Ethics in Business: A Call for Clarity*. Paper presented in the Business & Economics Track, National Faculty Leadership Conference, Washington, DC.

99. Same as 52.

100. Lewis, C. (1944). *The abolition of man*. New York: Harper Collins.

Part II

Applications in Sport Business

6

Undertaking Successful Brand Design in Sport

Keven Malkewitz
Western Oregon University

Colleen Bee
Oregon State University

Abstract: We define the undertaking of brand design in sports as the activities conducted and effort put forth to design the brand elements of a sport entity (e.g., a firm, team, or event). Three important factors have been found to influence the success of activities and efforts undertaken in designing sport brands: (a) adherence to *basic design principles*, (b) managing the *design and development process*, and (c) maintaining a consistent focus on the *brand's identity*. The factors are important because basic design principles are utilized to convey the perceptual and conceptual content of the brand, the design and development process produces the commercially viable products and artifacts required to build brand equity, and a consistent focus on the brand's identity allows the successful long-term positioning of the brand. We then discuss how these three factors influence several frequently occurring and important brand management issues: brand re-positioning, brand image consistency, the improper use of brand elements, and sustainability. A summary then presents the salient points of the chapter.

Keywords: aesthetics, corporate identity, design, new product development

Introduction

In any sporting event or activity, there are multiple examples of design's influence on the perceptions, recollection, and satisfaction of product and service experiences. For example, on a "retro" day at a baseball park or a "throwback" day at a football stadium, old-fashioned uniforms and headwear might evoke positive emotional memories of a visit to a ballpark or stadium decades ago. Design can also be used to signify membership in a brand or consumptive community (wearing FC Bayern München team colors) or to signal socioeconomic status (expensive active outerwear used in a leisure rather than active environment). The business of building and maintaining a brand, and of capitalizing on a brand by designing appropriate products and images providing value to consumers, is big business indeed. In 2011 the market for licensed professional and collegiate products was $17.1 billion, or 13.5% of *all* licensed product sold in the United States (Miller & Washington, 2013). Although the bulk of these sales (approximately 65%) is licensed apparel sales, the use of brand and team elements is an integral part of marketing products and services as varied as toothbrushes, baby mobiles, cuff links, sandwich presses, financial institutions, and cabinetry knobs.

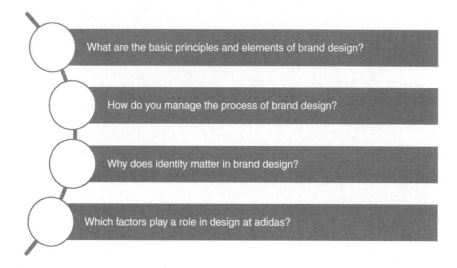

Figure 6.1 Overview of Chapter 6

Taken as a whole, design influences the branding process due to: (a) the utilization of basic design principles (e.g., color, shape, symmetry, etc.) in sports-related artifacts, (b) the use of design in the new product development process that generates brand artifacts, and (c) the use of design to develop a successfully integrated brand identity. In short, great design is needed to build successful brands in sports, and has been shown to have a tremendously powerful and broad influence on consumers. Among the most robust and important of these influences is the ability of design to influence the perception of brand artifacts and brand impressions (Bloch, 1995; Henderson, Giese, & Cote, 2004; Orth & Malkewitz, 2008), to influence consumer choice (Creusen & Schoormans, 2005), and to help construct and communicate a brand's personality (Aaker, 1997) and identity (Underwood, 2003; Underwood & Klein, 2002).

The purpose of this chapter is to provide insight into the manner in which brand design is undertaken in the sports industry, and how sport brands can benefit from the application of effective design principles to appropriately position their brands. It begins with a brief overview of brand design issues, then proceeds to outline the perceptual and conceptual principles of design, the importance of design in the NPD process, and the use of design in establishing and maintaining brand identity. The chapter finishes with a discussion of the managerial implications of design in four important and frequently occurring brand management issues: (a) brand re-positioning, (b) brand image consistency, (c) the improper use of brand elements, and (d) in sustainability or "green design." The intention of this chapter is to provide sport brand managers and academics with a better understanding of design, of design's utilization in the NPD process, and of design's use in building a consistent and powerful brand identity.

Overview of Brand Design Issues

Although in many cases the design and branding of sports and sport artifacts are similar to basic branding principles in general, the nature of sport events and sport products presents challenges and affords opportunities not present in other arenas. Because brands are the sum of impressions formed from all artifacts associated with the brand (i.e., a team's uniforms, the stadium environment in which they play, advertisements and promotions for the team, and the team's logos and brand identity), from this point on we will refer to the pool of artifacts capable of influencing brand impressions as *brand artifacts*.

Brand artifacts carry meaning, and convey this meaning with varying levels of success. Whether the brand artifact is an old-English "D" on the jersey chest or cap of a Detroit Tigers home uniform, a bolt of lightning flashing down the crown and side of the San Diego Chargers football helmet, or a "new-retro" stadium such as Cleveland's Jacobs Field or Oriole Park at Camden Yards in Baltimore, sport products and environments are composed using design elements and basic design principles. These principles influence both the *perceptual* nature of design elements (the ease, speed, and accuracy with which design elements can be realized) and the *conceptual* nature of design elements (the "learned" meaning in the design elements). The perceptual and conceptual content determines the "visual fluency" of artifacts and environments (Reber, Schwarz, & Winkielman, 2004). For example, although Detroit's "D" in Old English font on Tigers' caps is readily perceived because of the strong image/ground contrast provided by the dark-navy letterform on the white background of the uniform, the multiple serifs and design elements incorporated in the letter-form preclude it from being easily and quickly recognized as a letter. In addition, the meaning of the letter-form has to be "learned" by consumers and fans of the Tigers; with increased knowledge over time, fans "learn" that the letter-form represents the Tigers, and for the more involved fan it harkens back to earlier times and greats such as Ty Cobb, Al Kaline, and Kirk Gibson playing in the old Briggs Stadium. This meaning and content assigned to the letter form by fans is referred to as *conceptual design* content. The image/ground contrast clarity and the intricate design of the "D" are *perceptual* design elements, influencing the "legibility" of the letter D.

Regardless of which perceptual and conceptual design elements are utilized in brand design, design also influences the process with which artifacts and environments are developed. Earlier research on the new product development (NPD) process has shown that there are thirteen steps in the process, and that there is a great deal of variance in the frequency, degree, and importance to which these steps are utilized (Cooper & Kleinschmidt, 1986). The level of technology uncertainty is relatively low in the vast majority of design and development work in sport products; although we are occasionally faced with technically challenging development such as Nike's Air midsole or Karsten Solheim's perimeter-weighted Ping golf clubs, most products developed in the sport industry have a high probability that they will function appropriately due to knowledge gained from similar products that were previously developed and sold. For example, Nike is currently on the 28th iteration of their Air Pegasus running shoe, and the need for design and consumer information, rather than information related to the functional "will this work or not?" question, is of more importance in the product's eventual success. More recent work suggests that for incremental innovation and design, knowledge of the symbolic meaning in artifacts and environments, and of the "product language" used in design, is of extreme importance in the NPD process (Dell'Era & Verganti, 2007; Verganti, 2008). This suggests successful brand design needs to look at all brand artifacts (products, logos, environments, retail settings) and *all* attributes imbued within them, not just functional attributes.

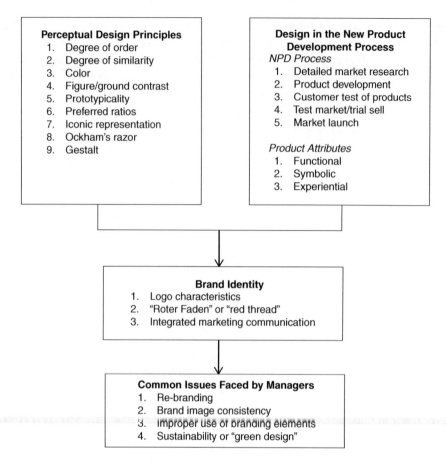

Figure 6.2 Overview of Brand Design Issues Addressed in *Successful Brand Design in Sports*

Both the NPD process and the design elements need to be utilized in a systematic and effective manner to create an impactful brand. This use of design creates a clear brand identity, allowing fans to better understand and remember a brand. Design is utilized in the creation of brand identity to establish similarities in a firm's logo and trademark, in the products and environments a brand offers, and in the promotional and advertising efforts a brand undertakes. This attention to brand identity design builds the bottom line by creating consistent fan impressions. A summary of the perceptual design features, of design in the NPD process, and of the brand identity features addressed in this chapter are presented in Figure 6–2.

Principles of Design

The word design is often used in two very different ways. First, as a noun, *design* is used to describe the sum of the physical characteristics of the product. For example, the design elements of the San Diego Chargers helmet are the three-color lightning-bolt graphics on the sides of the helmet, the exterior white (home) or navy (away) shell, the interior of the helmet with protective bladders for impact attenuation, and multiple styles of facemasks and chinstraps depending on a player's protective needs and preferences. Taken together, these elements comprise the helmet's design. Design in this sense is frequently utilized in two-dimensional settings (such as graphic design, logo design, and trademark design) as well as three-dimensional settings such as product design and the design of environments such as stadiums and retail locations. In a second respect, as a verb, the use of *design* addresses the process of creating the physical characteristics of the product during the product development process. For example, both a graphic designer and an industrial designer would very likely be involved in the process of designing the helmet. In this chapter, to differentiate between the two uses of the word "design," we will refer to the former (design as a noun) as *design* and the latter (design as a verb) as the *design process*.

Perceptual Design Principles

When discussing brand design, a multitude of principles influence the ability of a fan to perceive and remember brand artifacts, leading to brand preference. A recent publication identifies 100 principles, which "should not be interpreted to mean that there are only 100 relevant principles of design—there are obviously many more" (Lidwell, Holden, & Butler, 2003). Following is a brief primer of nine of the most important and often-used perceptual design principles in brand design in sports.

   1. Degree of Order: Design operates on a continuum from complete chaos to perfect order. Extensive research has shown that people prefer order to chaos, and usually exhibit increased positive affect with increased order. Design principles that move artifacts along this "order" continuum are symmetry, balance, and harmony. Symmetry can be found in the reflection, rotation, or translation of design elements (Lidwell, Holden, & Butler, 2003). Reflective symmetry consists of "mirrored" repetition of a design element around a line, rotational symmetry is repetition around a point, and translational symmetry consists of repetition of a design element in another space (i.e., "moved" or translated into another space). Balance ties into symmetry in that it refers to the appropriate location of design elements. For example, an artifact can be balanced by having reflective symmetry, but it can also be balanced and asymmetric: for example, it could have one larger design element on one side of an axis of symmetry "balanced" by two smaller objects on the other side taking up the same "visual space" as the single larger object. Harmony is considered to be a balance of "similar" design elements (referred to as unity) with "dissimilar" design elements, creating appropriate design-element variety. For example, a running shoe designed for outdoor trail running will often have an overall dark, earthen or grey-tone coloration (resulting in "unity"), but the shoe usually has a few "pops" of a bright and aggressive color, providing appropriate design-element variety. The overall product is balanced and harmonious because of the unity given by the product's predominant color, which receives a touch of variety due to the color pops.

   2. Degree of Similarity: The degree to which design elements are similar has a pronounced effect on the perception of their relatedness. For example, in a classic "ringer" t-shirt, the body is of one color, while the collar and the sleeve bands are of a second color. This color similarity of the collar and sleeve bands "ties them together" and is useful in attaining an overall balance, as mentioned previously in the trail running shoe. Making elements similar on a regular basis will lead to consistency; in essence, the repetition of the design element makes it more familiar to consumers, which leads to increased processing fluency, positive affect, and a greater likelihood of both prompted and unprompted recall. Related to similarity is the principle of uniform connectedness, where elements that have some visual connection are more readily grouped together. Unlike the ringer example, in which the color elements are connected by both color and by a similar ribbed texture, a solid-colored t-shirt's collar and sleeve bands are also "tied together" by the ribbed texture.

3. Color: Perhaps the most useful and certainly the most ubiquitous of design elements, color can be used for a number of desired design outcomes. Several of the previous examples have shown the usefulness of color (to highlight, attract attention, balance, etc.). In addition, there is also often a communicative element to color; just as "Old Gold" has grown to communicate Georgia Tech and "Tennessee Orange" communicates the University of Tennessee, color often signifies firm, brand, or category membership. Colors selected for use together are often analogous (located next to each other on the color wheel), complementary (across from one another on the color wheel), or triadic (three colors 120° apart from one another on the color wheel) or quadratic (four colors 90° apart). Colors are also utilized based on their location on the three continua of hue (the specific tone of a color), saturation (the purity or intensity of a color, which is decreased by adding grey and increased by subtracting grey), and brightness (how much white or black is in a color).[1] Some tones receive more attention than others, and the brighter or more saturated a color is, the more visual attention it receives. Although at first glance it may seem that a brand would always desire a saturated and bright color to attract attention, there are several reasons (balance, sophistication requiring understatement, existing brand or product knowledge tied into a nonsaturated or cooler color) why a more appropriate design would often utilize less saturated and less bright colors.

4. Figure/Ground Relationship: Often, multiple design elements are utilized in brand artifacts. Figure/ground contrast is a design principle important in highlighting certain elements more than others. A figure can be an element of a brand artifact or logo. That figure can be made to stand out more if it is placed on a background ("ground") that varies significantly in color (or saturation or brightness). One good example of this is the logo used by the Masters, which clearly demonstrates the value of figure/ground contrast, and at the same time problems that often occur when utilizing image/ground contrast. On the majority of backgrounds, the Masters' name stands out due to its well-known green color, the map of the contiguous 48 states of the United States stands out due to its yellow coloration, and the red flag stands out as well. However, a problem becomes apparent when the logo is placed on the Masters green background: the name and flagstick "disappear," so an additional white color is required to provide the needed figure-ground contrast. To avoid this, a single-color white logo is utilized when the logo and/or name is placed against a green background (e.g., backdrop for press conferences, etc.). However, this is a sub-optimal solution, as the three-color logo is not consistently repeated, reducing the number of consistent impressions consumers form when viewing the logo.

5. Prototypicality: Prototypicality refers to the degree to which a brand artifact conforms to a fan's expectation (Veryzer & Hutchinson, 1998). The sports industry is replete with examples of difficulties due to lack of consumer acceptance of brand artifacts that are too different or unusual compared to existing design. Aluminum baseball bats, metal heads for fairway woods and drivers in golf, and oversize racquets are all examples of products that had longer introduction and growth stages of their product life cycle due to their extensive product form and technology jump from existing artifacts. Another example would be the Tampa Bay Rays' 2007 redesign of brand artifacts such as team uniforms and logos. The previous color scheme of green and black had limited appeal for licensed apparel sales and the redesigned navy blue/light blue with a bright yellow sunburst had a much broader appeal to fans. Finding the right amount of similarity and difference with consumer expectations and preferences is referred to as the "inverted U," where brand artifacts that are too similar to existing designs are not appealing because they are not different enough, and brand artifacts that are extensively different from existing designs are not appealing because they are too different. Consumers prefer "moderately different" designs because they offer the right degree of novelty, yet allow the consumer to easily and clearly understand what he or she is buying (Berlyne, 1971).

6. Preferred Ratios: Extensive evidence indicates that forms that possess certain ratios are preferred over other forms that do not possess these ratios. Perhaps the most common examples among these "preferred" ratios are forms possessing the golden ratio or the golden section. A golden section rectangle is one in which the ratio of the rectangle's width to length ($W/L = 0.618$) is exactly the same as the ratio of the rectangle's length to the sum of the rectangle's length and width ($L/[L+W] = 0.618$). The use of this ratio in lines, rectangles, and spiral forms is commonly found in both nature (the average length from elbow to fingertip is 61.8% of arm length, the elbow-to-shoulder 38.2%) and in manmade artifacts such as buildings (the height of the rectangle forming the lower portion of the Parthenon's facade is 61.8% of its width) and consumer electronics (from the bottom of the iPod screen, the distance to the top of the iPod is 38.2% of the entire length, and it is 61.8% to the bottom). Just a few of the many brand logos and marks used in sports that utilize the "golden ratio" include the Boston Red Sox "B" logo, the Green Bay Packers "G" logo, and the Los Angeles Lakers purple-and-yellow word mark with a basketball background logo. Of course not all brand artifacts or logos consist of the golden ratio; the iPhone has approximately a 1:2 ratio of width to length, and the Nike swoosh has a 1:1.5 width to length ratio. The intention here is not so much prescriptive ("use the golden ratio in your designs") as it is suggestive ("be aware of and select the ratios you use for specific and appropriate reasons").

7. Iconic Representation: Iconic representation refers to the use of logos and symbols that have been imbued with a widely understood meaning. Classic examples are the Olympic sport pictograms utilized to identify the games' different sports, the Jordan Brand "Jumpman" logo, the international signs for radioactivity (a black circle with three black ray-like "blades" emanating from the circle on a black background) and poison (skull-and-crossbones). Iconic representation is important, because often brand artifacts or logos that are anchored so deeply into fans' semantic memory networks allow for brand extension and proliferation opportunities, based on their widely understood meaning.

8. Ockham's Razor: Simply put, Ockham's razor states that when equivalent choices are available, the simpler of the two possibilities should be chosen. Ockham's razor applies to both two-dimensional designed artifacts such as logos and three-dimensional artifacts such as products or designed environments. This principle is discussed at length in Edward Tufte's *The Visual Display of Quantitative Information* (Tufte, 1983). Unnecessary elements in a logo or brand mark can hinder recognition and memory; brand artifacts can have more attention directed to processing more important value-providing attribute information if unneeded or sub-optimal attributes are not occupying processing capacity. This is not to say that there are no complicated designs, only that the design elements and information needed in the brand artifact are there, and unnecessary elements and attributes are removed or downplayed.

9. Gestalt: Most of the perceptual design elements described so far have been examined as individual and discrete design elements. The gestalt of a brand artifact is the sum total of all its design elements and their interactions, requiring a "holistic" view of the artifact. Perhaps the greatest challenge in designing a new artifact is to examine both individual elements and the perceived whole simultaneously; the ringer T is not only about the collar and sleeve bands, but also the silhouette or pattern of the t-shirt (cut for tight-against-the-skin wear or for baggy casual comfort), the weight and content of the fabric utilized in the t-shirt, the texture or "hand" of the material, and any screening, printing, or applications on the t-shirt. Great design finds a way to achieve the balance, harmony, and function of all of these design elements into a brand artifact that maximizes fan value.

Conceptual Design Principles

Until now, we have been discussing perceptual design principles. Conceptual design elements, on the other hand, are those elements capable of conveying meaning, and they may be presented using an almost infinite variety of perceptual design elements. For example, the perceptual design information in the following illustration (see Figure 6.3) consists of simple lines used in the illustrations of trees.

Although the perceptual elements of the drawings of the trees are very similar, the conceptual meaning most people associate with each form causes the drawings to significantly differ in their appropriateness for use with various sport entities. Consider the design execution of trees in the following logos, and how the use of specific tree types conveys appropriate conceptual meaning.

Figure 6.3 Line Illustrations of Trees (Image from http://www.treesaregood.com/treecare/ images/tree_selection.jpg. Copyright International Society of Arboriculture.)

Figure 6.4 Sport Logos with Trees (Courtesy of the Fort Myers Miracle and Stanford University.)

Similar to the line drawings of the trees, the logos with trees (see Figure 6.4) also contain similar perceptual elements. Conceptually, however, the Fort Meyers palm tree illustration facilitates fan recall of "meaning" associated with beaches, the ocean, warm weather and sun, while the conceptual content of the "El Palo Alto" Coast Redwood tree in the Stanford logo evokes a very different recollection of a forest symbolizing the strength, independence, and history of the university.[7]

1. Meaning and Symbolism: What we have referred to as "appropriateness" above is actually the conceptual meaning and symbolism associated with a specific design. The knowledge and information required to select appropriate symbols is fairly easy in some cases (where brands or teams have an extensive history with a specific geographic location or name), and extremely difficult in other situations (a new team or an effort to significantly alter the brand meaning and perceptions associated with a current name or image). One challenge faced in design is incorporating the correct information in artifacts. In several situations, new designs were implemented and fan opinion provided strong evidence that the meaning and symbolism contained in the new design were not consistent with the meaning and symbolism associated with the previous design. For example, when the University of Oregon attempted to replace their much-loved "Disney-based Duck" mascot with a "Robo-Duck" mascot, it was not positively received by University of Oregon Ducks fans due to the firmly embedded culture association of the "Disney-based Duck" mascot that had been associated with the University's athletic teams since the late 1940s. Just as it is often a challenge to get technology developed and functioning in a manner that provides appropriate value to a brand artifact, so is it a challenge to get appropriate meaning and information into an artifact in order for it to provide value. This has been referred to as fluency in the "design language" required to appropriately design artifacts (Dell'Era & Verganti, 2007).

2. Interpretation: Naturally, meaning and associated symbolism do not occur in a vacuum. In order for an artifact's symbolism and meaning to have an effect, a common meaning for the symbol must exist and that meaning must be accurately interpreted by consumers and fans. In dyadic situations (where one person is trying to empathize with another and determine what he/she is feeling), people often vary greatly in how accurate they are in their estimations (Ickes, 2003). Recent research has found that some designs are more effective in accurately communicating an intended symbol or message than others (Orth & Malkewitz, 2012). This lack of agreement among stakeholders in what a symbol conveys is the source of many design mistakes, such as the Robo-Duck example mentioned earlier. Greater familiarity and knowledge increase empathy. In the context of design, this means those stakeholders who both know more about and are more familiar with their fans are more capable of designing appealing brand artifacts.

3. *Culture:* The meaning and interpretation of brand artifacts differs significantly across cultures. Artifacts that are appropriate in one country or setting are often inappropriate in others. For design to have a broader appeal, selection of design elements with conceptual meaning that has little variance between countries is most appropriate. One of the major appeals of constructed design elements like the Nike swoosh is that it possessed no meaning prior to its creation by Carol Davidson in 1971. This allowed the "tabula rasa" or blank slate form to be imbued with the meaning desired by Nike, rather than having to overcome prior associations that would have necessitated fan re-learning. This approach has particular appeal with artifacts intended for use with multiple cultures; design elements with "history" in cultures often present hurdles in their acceptance, or evoke fan knowledge inappropriate for the brand.

Design in the New Product Development Process

The above design principles need some method of getting into artifacts that are being designed and developed by brands. This is done through the new product development process (NPD), in which the design principles are utilized to place the desired attributes into the product. In this section we discuss five important steps in the NPD process and the different types of attributes that are imbued into artifacts in these steps.

The NPD Process. The NPD process is an iterative process in which brand artifacts are created with the intent of providing value to users, fans, and customers. Prior research and NPD best-practices observation provide evidence that there are multiple steps in the process; one of the most often-cited articles (Cooper & Kleinschmidt, 1986) suggests there are 13 steps.[3] Researchers and practitioners agree that many of the 13 steps are often skipped in sport brand NPD, due to the incremental nature of the majority of developments. For example, although preliminary technical assessment (one of the 13 steps) was at one time a necessary step for Nike when they were first developing their Nike Air Midsole, the need for a "preliminary technical assessment" step is greatly reduced when Nike has produced millions of shoes utilizing this technology. Although design is important in all of these steps (e.g., a design is fatally flawed if it is extremely difficult to produce), certain steps among the 13 aid the design process and are capable of adding value to artifacts contributing to brand success. Chief among these value-adding steps are the following five steps: (a) detailed market study/market research, (b) product development, (c) customer tests of products, (d) test market/trial sell, and (e) market launch.

1. Market Study and Research. The benefit of detailed market study and market research provides the designer with high-quality information required to understand the needs, preferences, and demands of the target customer. A variety of methods can be used to collect information from target customers: interviews, focus groups, observation, and surveys. Additionally, secondary information such as sales data, retail reports, and archived customer comments can also be used. Another important consideration is who to collect information from. Should designers solicit feedback from average consumers, heavy users, or a broad range of customers? Although focusing on the large number of average users is important, a problem with this group is that when evaluating novel or new designs, these users will sometimes confuse unfamiliarity with disliking. In order to avoid this confusion, designers should also solicit feedback from lead users. Lead users are heavy users of a product and often discover needs prior to the average customer. They are also less susceptible to disliking a product because of unfamiliarity. Designers use these results to guide development and brand identity integration in successive stages.

2. Product Development. The product development stage involves integrating the results from market study and research into the product and brand design. The product development phase consists of developing one or more prototypes of the product or brand design. It is important to keep in mind that design can be used not only to develop products that are more preferred by customers (leading to increased sales), but can also provide benefit to the firm in at least two other ways: (a) design can be used in the process of "value-engineering" products (i.e., making changes that decrease the cost of the product, but that have minimal impact on product quality), and (b) designs can be managed in such a manner that they provide the "red thread" that allows consumers and fans to form "multiple" integrated impressions, resulting in a more memorable and preferred overall brand impression.

3. Customer Tests of Products. When designing products, stakeholders that put forth substantial effort to determine the preferences of customers will be more likely to achieve product success. The usual manner in which this takes place can be wear tests (for function and quality) and preference tests (to determine customer preference among multiple design options) consisting of customer feedback on prototypes and focus groups examining product concepts. Interestingly, recent evidence has suggested that in at least some cases, stakeholders should develop products based on their understanding of product languages, materials characteristics, and possibilities not previously known to customers, rather than giving customers "what they want." Perhaps more clearly stated, sometimes firms must be "ahead" of where customers "are" and allow customers to discover and interpret the firm's new product offerings, which were based on the stakeholder's understanding of what the customer wants rather than product tests. This does not mean that customer perceptions should not be considered, but rather that the tests consisted of the manager's considered opinion of what the customer will (or will not) prefer.

4. Test Market/Trial Sell. These tests provide stakeholders in the development process with additional information needed to optimize developments. These tests and trials are at various times conducted with retailers, end-users, retail buyers, and athletes, depending on the development's requirements. Design is instrumental in this process, because often the information and input from those being questioned needs to be "interpreted" and given to designers who can generate the requested product improvements. For example, if a prototype were taken to a retail buyer and the information obtained by the salesperson is that the product "looked too heavy," the designer *might* be able to improve the product. If, however, the designer were to receive better information (i.e., "the buyer thinks the toe box seems too bulky and thick, and the darker-colored reinforcement encircling the toe box accentuates the bulkiness"), the designer would have a much better idea of how the perceived heaviness might be ameliorated.

5. *Market Launch.* When launching a new product, marketers must consider their target market, as well as when and how they will launch the product. The marketer will initially target lead users, early adopters, and heavy users of their product during the market launch stage. Marketers must also consider the costs and benefits of being first to market or attaining "first mover advantage." As a first mover, brands can gain consumer and distributor loyalty, however, disadvantages include not understanding and thus not meeting customer needs, as well as higher initial market entry costs than late movers. Market launch activities should also consider communication materials such as catalogs, POS and collateral materials, and sales tools.

When the brand artifact is finalized, the process begins again for the next development process (i.e., for those brand artifacts that will be introduced subsequent to the current brand artifacts). It is not only possible but probable that much of the time a designer is concerned with products in various stages of the product life cycle: he or she will be getting information and feedback from products currently being offered for retail sale, will be receiving feedback from the advance selling process (i.e., products being sold to retailers but not yet on retail shelves), and will be in the initial stages of designing the subsequent product range.

Given the above, three areas could improve the contribution of design in the NPD process. Primary among these is the manner and type of information given to the designers to begin the iterative design process. Very little is known about what type of information is most useful and helpful to designers, and what information can enable them to do their best work. Second, information received in the testing process could be more efficiently worked into the development process. Because of the hectic nature of development induced by the large number of products developed in short periods of time, often information obtained in the testing process cannot be worked into the development. Third, often market launch materials are not developed until the product is finalized; concurrent development could focus the development of both product and marketing materials in a more integrated and effective manner.

Product Attributes in the NPD Process. A number of different types of attributes necessitate design attention. Deciding on which attributes to focus design attention on is a difficult decision due to significant variance in consumers' attribute perceptions, depending on the degree of involvement and expertise of the consumer or fan (Alba & Hutchinson, 1987; Zaichkowsky, 1985). Although several typologies and categorizations of product attributes exist, one of the most commonly used and often-cited attribute categorizations plans consists of (a) functional attributes, (b) symbolic attributes, and (c) experiential attributes (Park, Jaworski, & MacInnis, 1986). These three types of attributes and their influence in design are examined next.

Functional attributes are the affordances designed into a product or environment. For example, the functional nature of design in a basketball shoe requires that it provide sufficient shock attenuation to protect the player from impact, enough support in the forefoot for sharp and forceful lateral movements (requiring a shell sole and materials relatively resistant to stretching, precluding the nylon often used in running shoes), and often an upper (the "top part" of the shoe) that provides additional ankle support to protect the wearer's ankle from the ubiquitous and problematic ankle sprains present as an occupational hazard to basketball players.

Symbolic attributes are those attributes that are capable of communicating information about the user to others. Continuing with the basketball shoe example, several basketball shoes of varying prices provide the functional attributes described above; there is however, only one basketball shoe capable of saying to others "I am a huge Michael Jordan fan." In some cases this may be value derived from an interest in and admiration for Michael Jordan, but there may also be value to the wearer of the Air Jordan in being associated with the Nike brand, and the ability of a Nike Air Jordan shoe to communicate this to others provides symbolic value to the owner of the Air Jordan product.

The third type of attribute is experiential attributes, those attributes that provide value due to sensory perception of the wearer or fan. The soft leather or light weight of a shoe would be experiential attributes, as would be the close-yet-comfortable fit of the product. Likewise, attending a game in a facility with great lines-of-sight, easy egress, and comfortable seats would also be experiential attributes providing a positive brand experience.

Brand Identity

Once design principles are understood and incorporated into the new product development process, an important part of successful branding is a firm's ability to manage and present their products and brand to their customer in an appealing and consistent manner. The result of managing this process determines the brand identity a company achieves. Following we discuss the use of brand artifacts and marketing materials and how they contribute to an integrated message to the fan (integrated marketing communication), building and clarifying the brand's identity.

Previous research suggests logos are often best remembered if they are natural, harmonious, and elaborate (Henderson & Cote, 1998). Several of the perceptual and conceptual design principles mentioned earlier should be considered and implemented (i.e., awareness of figure/ground contrast, use of symmetry, appropriate ratios). Symbolism and iconic representation provide an opportunity to leverage existing visual schemas in semantic memory networks to improve affective responses and logo retention. A clear and rigorous process should be implemented to ensure consistency in the manner in which brand logos are presented. This means when in doubt, managers should be consistent. As with any rule, exceptions should be few. It is clear at times there *are* good strategic and/or tactical reasons for brand artifacts not to be consistent. In these cases, attention to be gained or emotional appeals addressing issues important to target consumers are often the reason for the inconsistency.

For example, Google used Spain's win in the European championship to deviate from their "normal" logo; this shows users in Spain that Google understands the importance of the win, and shares Spaniards' pride and honor associated with the team, thereby increasing user loyalty. In the NFL and WNBA examples, the deviation of "normal" on-the-field brand artifacts such as uniforms and footwear has been made to show awareness and support for a cure for breast cancer; this shows NFL and WNBA fans and consumers that the leagues understand and share their concern, thereby increasing user loyalty and at the same time providing fans with the opportunity to show their support by buying "pink" licensed brand artifacts.

In German, the term "Roter Faden" (a "red thread") is used to indicate a common recurring theme. For example, when Nike decides that they want to utilize a new concept such as visible Air, Zoom Air, or the "Free" minimal footwear concept, they take care to instill a "red thread" into the various products developed in the different categories (e.g., running, basketball, etc.). Red threads ensuring visual relatedness and continuity within the brand are important in the auto industry, due to the long lead times and massive tooling costs required to produce automobiles. In many cases BMW and other car companies obtain information regarding possible "red thread" direction by developing concept cars, which present information to stakeholders on a possible direction the company is considering for new brand artifacts that are significantly different from the existing line. Concept cars can be received by stakeholders with varying degree of enthusiasm; some, such as Volkswagen's Concept 1 "New Beetle," introduced at the 1994 North American International Auto Show, have been raced into production (meaning it hit auto dealers' floors *four years* later!), while other Volkswagen concept cars such as a modern version of the VW bus (introduced at the 2001 auto show) were eventually quietly canned. This "concept-process" is often mimicked in the sport industry; brand artifacts such as "concept shoes" are shown to buyers from large retail chains, focus groups are exposed to potential brand and logo re-designs to obtain information about fan and consumer responses, and "virtual reality" tours of stadiums and exhibits are constructed to examine the potential experiences fans might have. When discussing brand artifacts and the impact design has on the artifacts, a consistent "red thread" used to enhance desired strategic and tactical brand direction is one of the largest contributions design can make.

When brand artifacts are appropriately "red-threaded," marketing communication can more effectively do its job of making fans and consumers aware of artifacts, and increasing their understanding of the brand's value propositions enough to ensure the purchase and use of the brand's products. Design's largest contribution in this area is to provide the brand with the marketing materials required to meet the needs of existing customers. For example, if a brand competing in the Running category were to design marketing materials for a new product, the brand would require substantially different marketing materials for large national accounts such as Footlocker than it would for specialty running stores. POS materials for store windows tied into back-to-school ad campaigns might be appropriate for Footlocker, whereas technical information and product sheets (to inform a specialty running store's on-the-floor employees) and race banners (to promote the brand and the product at 10k races) would be more appropriate for the specialty store. End-users might be persuaded by *Runner's World* reviews (requiring design input and experience to "sell" the product to those involved in the product review process) and by a "red thread" that would tie the current product offering to the earlier versions of the same product (e.g., Nike Pegasus, ASICS Gel-Lyte, or the Brooks Adrenaline). Designers excel at problem solving; design's task in the above situation is to find novel and effective ways to inform and persuade fans and consumers, given the marketing requirements of the product.

Current Issues in Brand Design

The three important design factors that have been addressed in this chapter (the use of design principles, the design and development process, and consistency in brand identity) are essential in addressing many of the day-to-day issues currently facing brand managers. In this section, we examine how these factors could be used to address four important issues: (a) the re-positioning of a brand, (b) maintaining brand presentation consistency, (c) preventing improper use of brand elements, and (d) the utilization of sustainability in a firm's branding efforts.

Re-Branding. By definition, re-branding consists of previous efforts that have been taken to position a brand, and current efforts to attempt to position the brand in a different manner. Following, we detail one such re-branding effort (adidas Equipment) and explain how this re-branding incorporates design principles, the NPD process, and brand identity.

In 1990, adidas was having an extremely difficult time worldwide fighting their competitors, but especially so in the U.S. market. Years of attempting to hit aggressive sales goals had led adidas USA to develop an ad hoc product process where their product range was no longer easily recognized, and the ratio of make-up products (specific products designed for customers that were not part of the company's core product line) to in-line products was significantly higher than it had been in previous years, suggesting that adidas products were not effectively meeting the needs of their retailers and end-users. The company had drifted away from much of the on-the-field product focus that had made them successful in years past, and had recently spent significant time and effort in several markets developing leisure products (e.g., jeans, jackets, dress shirts) to hit their sales numbers. This movement into a more fashion-focused direction was in part a reaction to increased leisure wear of colorful and aggressive products offered by Nike such as the "outlawed in the NBA" white, black, and red Air Jordan line, and the wildly, brightly neon-colored Andre Agassi challenge court Tennis line.

In this environment, Rob Strasser and Peter Moore, consultants who as former Nike executives had been instrumental in helping Nike overcome adidas in global sales volume, proposed a project to adidas AG. The project they proposed, which was to become known as the Equipment brand (EQT) suggested that adidas strategically re-focus on functional athletic products, a core competency not easily replicated by other competitors. Adidas bought off on the proposal and created a small team of employees who would work on the project. The members of the team were selected because of their strong ties to adidas and their expertise and knowledge in the on-field use of sports products. They would operate a skunk works[4] over the next four months to deliver a new brand.

Over those four months, the team designed and developed adidas products intended for use on the field, pitch, or track. Unlike in-line adidas products and adidas competitors, who regularly checked the prototypes of the products they were developing with key accounts to ensure that they were "right" for the accounts, the team relied on extensive knowledge with the team to determine the functional and aesthetic direction of the products. To ensure the products were developed with an appropriate red thread, the entire team was co-located (at the time not the adidas norm) and the EQT design, development, and marketing team members were all involved on a daily basis in the design direction of the EQT logo, product, and marketing materials. Several perceptual design principles highlighted earlier in the chapter were utilized. The products were designed with a form-follows-function orientation (Ockham's razor), were very simple and "clean" at a time when the industry was going the other way (simplicity), had strong logo and branding identification due to the color used (figure-ground contrast), and would achieve the "iconic representation" by having a new-yet-familiar logo containing the three stripes and the adidas Equipment word mark. The products underwent extensive testing in the NPD process, capitalizing on an underutilized adidas resource of extensive contacts in the world of sport. Within 12 months of the inception of the EQT project, prototypes had been tested with top-caliber athletes in soccer, rugby, tennis, basketball, and long-distance running. Feedback from the athletes was incorporated into the design of the products. This close face-to-face contact with athletes led to information about the functional, symbolic, and experiential attributes being incorporated into the design process.

To ensure the red thread of the logo, the products, and the marketing materials, any artifact that was going to be seen outside of adidas was required to pass by the eyes of Peter Moore. While several people were involved in the design and development process, the close contact and the common understanding of those involved resulted in a consistent and integrated range. Common colors, shapes, lines, and materials ensured that the adidas EQT products were easily recognized as a family (thereby drawing more attention and share-of-mind with consumers and retailers), the EQT logo tied together POS materials and marketing collateral materials such as catalogs, brochures, advertisements, posters, sales materials, and "slogo" (slogan-logo) t-shirts telling the adidas EQT story and motto. The red line became a powerful sales tool, in part because of the previously mentioned advantages, but also because the red thread signaled to many customers that the EQT range was a new "business NOT as usual" design and functional product orientation at adidas.

The EQT range had its intended consequences, and was credited with "turning the adidas brand around worldwide." The products were a hit with end-users, although the simple and effective on-the-field designs initially received mixed reviews from adidas sister companies and from retailers. Interestingly, adidas EQT also had unintended consequences: the power of a design orientation to the NPD process showed the organization the value of design in brand-building, and the organization as a whole shifted significantly toward a design-centric NPD process.

Consistency of Brand Presentation. The Equipment range was extremely consistent in its presentation, due to the small number of people involved in decision making and the clear direction provided by the project. However, it is virtually impossible for a firm to be consistent in its branding presentation if the firm does not have a clear understanding of the firm's branding strategy. Although not required, such an understanding is often codified in a "style guide," a "graphics identity" or "graphics style" manual, or a "logo and color standards" document. When not so codified (often in smaller firms utilizing more tacit knowledge), managers need to spend considerable effort to ensure all employees involved in branding and NPD issues have a clear understanding of what the firm is trying to accomplish. Topics requiring clarity are the type(s) of logo(s) utilized by the firm, color specifications, usage situations (for example, several schools have "academic" and "athletic" logos), appropriate fonts and proportions to be utilized, etc.

However, the best brand strategy and the most detailed style guide are useless if they are not properly executed in the firm's corporate identity and in the product and services associated with the brand. Such execution usually requires systems and processes be put into place to ensure there is little difference between the intended and realized strategy of firms. Activities such as having a specific manager "sign off" on all brand artifacts that might influence the brand's image, having the issue of brand consistency for products be addressed in the NPD product review processes, and ensuring all promotional activities and artifacts are reviewed for brand consistency during the creative process are all ways that an intended brand strategy can be more accurately realized in the marketplace.

Improper Use of Brand Elements. Up to this point, we have discussed activities that are conducted by the firm in the development and execution of their branding efforts. However, often there are both approved and "unapproved" utilization of branding elements by others. An "approved" use could be a sponsorship partner of the firm using a brand's logo to promote a sponsored event, whereas an "unapproved" use could be the offering of a product not endorsed by the firm, in an illicit attempt to benefit from the brand's strength without compensating the firm. Although in many cases the "right" course of action for the firm is apparent (e.g., a "black market" vendor can be issued a cease-and-desist order if they are making counterfeit goods), in many cases the appropriate course of action is not so clear (e.g., should a firm's rebranding be executed immediately and completely at the expense of destroying or eliminating existing brand artifacts?).

In such cases where improper elements are utilized, three pieces of information are required before decisions on tactical issues can be reached. The first such piece is the *severity* of the branding infraction: Is the infraction a not-quite-spot-on execution of a particular color (a fairly common occurrence in this age of geographically distributed design and development systems), or is the infraction instead the program cover of a high-profile sponsored event where a valued promotional partner has replicated a firm's logo in "their" firm's color scheme? The second piece of information is the *extent or degree* to which the improper element(s) are utilized (e.g., an internationally utilized brand campaign would be much more deleterious to a brand's corporate identity than would a regional or local execution of the same campaign). It is important to note that this information would also need to include the duration over which the "infraction" would be utilized. A one-and-done TV commercial would potentially be less injurious to a brand than would be a three-month commitment to an ad painted on a high-profile wall in a busy downtown intersection. Third and last, the brand decision maker would also benefit from knowledge of the *cost* required to correct the infraction: A fairly easy and inexpensive fix (a wrong logo color on a website) would be more likely to occur than would a more expensive fix such as correcting a logo color or size issue on a product or a point-of-sale item that has already been prepared for distribution.

Sustainability. A firm's decision to utilize sustainability in their products and processes can also be implemented into their brand design process. Several other industries, most noticeably the construction and the power-generation industries, have already made significant developments in going green and in communicating this orientation to their stakeholders (see the City of Scottsdale's Green Design Principles website[5] and the National Building Museum's Green House Exhibition on the Principles of Sustainable Design[6] and the EPA's Green Power Partnership Top 50 list[7]). To this point in the sports industry, interest in sustainable products and processes has focused on two areas: (a) on utilizing recycled materials for consumer products and use (see Patagonia's *Change Your Clothes for Good* recycling program[8] and Nike's *Nikegrind* sports field surfacing product[9]), and (b) implementing processes that reduce and minimize the footprint of manufacturing products (see Lizard Skin's award for green manufacturing of bike handlebar grips[10] and Keen's recently introduced footwear made in the United States, which reduces the carbon footprint of product provision to U.S. customers[11]).

Conclusion

The following are what we consider to be the important lessons in this chapter that are critical to undertaking the use of design in successfully building a brand. By following these lessons, successful brands can be built and developed, leading to sustainable competitive advantage based on design.

- Utilize perceptual design principles (e.g., symmetry, color, figure/ground contrast) and conceptual design principles (e.g., meaning, symbolism) in an iterative design process.
- Use design in the NPD process in a way that takes full advantage of what design offers, by providing design stakeholders the information they require to do their job (product briefs, feedback in the design and development process).
- Design for *all* attributes, making informed design decisions about functional, symbolic, and experiential attributes.
- Ensure strong brand identity by designing your "red thread" into your logos, products, and marketing materials, building an integrated brand and marketing approach. Utilize the design principles and the NPD process to generate an entire range of artifacts displaying a powerful and consistent brand identity.
- Build design-conscious teams with authority and ability to make design and brand artifact decisions.
- Use stakeholders to create a competitive advantage, leveraging the extensive network of designers, athletes, retailers, and production facilities to generate products. Such networks are a competitive advantage as they are not easily imitable; they are developed over many years and require the commitment of substantial resources.
- The use of the NPD steps mentioned earlier (i.e., product development and product testing, for example) can become part of the "story" utilized to communicate the artifacts and the range to internal audiences (e.g., salespeople, marketing executives from the various sister companies, distributors) as well as external stakeholders such as retailers and media outlets.

References

1. Aaker, J. L. (1997, August). Dimensions of brand personality. *Journal of Marketing Research, 34*, 347–356.
2. Alba, J. W., & Hutchinson, W. J. (1987). Dimensions of consumer expertise. *Journal of Consumer Research, 13*(4), 411–454.
3. Berlyne, D. E. (1971). *Aesthetics and psychobiology*. New York: Appleton-Century-Crofts.
4. Bloch, P. H. (1995, July). Seeking the ideal form: Product design and consumer response. *Journal of Marketing, 59*, 16–29.
5. Cooper, R. G., & Kleinschmidt, E. J. (1986). An investigation into the new product process: Steps, deficiencies, and impact. *Journal of Product Innovation Management, 3*, 71–85.
6. Creusen, M. E. H., & Schoormans, J. P. L. (2005). The different roles of product appearance in consumer choice. *Journal of Product Innovation Management, 22*, 63–81.
7. Dell'Era, C., & Verganti, R. (2007). Strategies of innovation and imitation of product languages. *Journal of Product Innovation Management, 24*, 580–599.
8. Henderson, P. W., & Cote, J. A. (1998, April). Guidelines for selecting or modifying logos. *Journal of Marketing, 62*, 14–30.
9. Henderson, P W., Giese, J. L., & Cote, J. A. (2004, October). Impression management using typeface design. *Journal of Marketing, 68*, 60–72.
10. Ickes, W. (2003). *Everyday mind reading: Understanding what other people think and feel*. Amherst, NY: Prometheus Books.
11. Lidwell, W., Holden, K., & Butler, J. (2003). *Universal principles of design*. Gloucester, MA: Rockport Publishers.
12. Miller, R. K., & Washington, K. (2013). *Sports marketing 2013*. Loganville, GA: Richard K. Miller & Associates.
13. Orth, U. R., & Malkewitz, K. (2012). The accuracy of design-based judgments: A constructivist approach. *Journal of Retailing, 88*(3), 421–436. doi:10.1016/j.retai.2011.11.004.
14. Orth, U. R., & Malkewitz, K. (2008). Holistic package design and consumer brand impressions. *Journal of Marketing, 72*, 64–81.
15. Park, C. W., Jaworski, B. J., & MacInnis, D. J. (1986). Strategic brand concept-image management. *Journal of Marketing, 50*, 35–45.
16. Reber, R., Schwarz, N., & Winkielman, P. (2004). Processing fluency and aesthetic pleasure: Is beauty in the perceiver's processing experience? *Personality and Social Psychology Review, 8*(4), 364–382.
17. Tufte, E. R. (1983). *The visual display of quantitative information*. Cheshire, CT: Graphics Press.
18. Underwood, R. L. (2003). The communicative power of product packaging: Creating brand identity via lived and mediated experience. *Journal of Marketing Theory and Practice, 9*(Winter), 62–76.
19. Underwood, R. L., & Klein, N. M. (2002). Packaging as brand communication: Effects of product pictures on consumer responses to the package and brand. *Journal of Marketing Theory and Practice, 10*(4), 58–68.
20. Verganti, R. (2008). Design, meanings, and radical innovation: A metamodel and a research agenda. *Journal of Product Innovation Management, 25*, 436–456.
21. Veryzer, R. W., & Hutchinson, J. W. (1998, March). The influence of unity and prototypicality on aesthetic responses to new product designs. *Journal of Consumer Research, 24*, 374–94.
22. Zaichkowsky, J. L. (1985). Measuring the involvement construct. *Journal of Consumer Research, 12*(3), 341–352.

Notes

1. For excellent examples that visually clarify these three continua, please see designingfortheweb.co.uk/book/part4/part4_chapter17.php
2. Stanford University has not reviewed or endorsed content related to the Stanford logo.
3. Initial screening, preliminary market assessment, preliminary technical assessment, detailed market study/market research, business/financial analysis, product development, in-house product testing, customer tests of products, test market/trial sell, trial production, pre-commercialization business analysis, production start up, and market launch.
4. "Skunk Works" is the unofficial name of Lockheed Martin's Advanced Development Programs (ADP) founded by Kelly Johnson in 1943, which originated the development of top-secret defense projects through the use of co-located employees and concurrent product engineering, rather than the sequential product development that was the norm. This allowed the Skunk Works to develop products faster and more efficiently. Over the last seven decades, many of the most innovative and effective aircraft have been developed by the Skunk Works (e.g., the U-2 and the SR-71 reconnaissance aircraft, and the F-117 Stealth Fighter).
5. http://www.scottsdaleaz.gov/greenbuilding/designprinc

6. http://www.nbm.org/exhibitions-collections/exhibitions/the-green-house/principles.html
7. http://www.epa.gov/greenpower/toplists/top50.htm
8. http://www.patagonia.com/us/popup/common_threads/faqs.jsp
9. http://www.nikereuseashoe.com/using-nike-grind
10. http://www.heraldextra.com/news/local/lizard-skins-of-orem-honored-for-green-manufacturing/article_07fb954d-48e5-5fd0-a565-63a9f91d479a.html
11. http://www.treehugger.com/sustainable-fashion/keen-on-home-grown-us-footwear-production.html

7

Developing Brand Identity in Sport: Lions, and Tigers, and Bears Oh My

Vassilis Dalakas
California State University San Marcos

Gregory Rose
University of Washington, Tacoma

Abstract: This chapter highlights key factors pertaining to development of brand identity for sports teams. It specifically discusses issues regarding team name, team logo, team colors, rituals, people associated with the team, and the city associated with the team. A branding identity has important implications in terms of a team's image as a competitive team and also in terms of marketing success.

Keywords: brand identity, brand name, brand personality, fan identification, logo, positioning

Introduction

Developing a brand identity is important to sports teams. Multiple factors contribute to a team's perceived identity and personality: the image evoked by the team's branding, like its name and logo, the personality of the people associated with the team (primarily players but also coaches and owners), and the personality of the city in which the team plays. Although a team's name usually remains unchanged over long periods of time, other factors may change more frequently, which suggests that the team's identity would change accordingly. Moreover, from a marketing standpoint, teams have significantly more control over the branding elements than they do over the image of their personnel or the image of their city or region. Within the context of sports teams, branding elements mainly include the team's name, colors and uniforms, mascot, and rituals or traditions (e.g., The Ohio State band forming the word Ohio on the field during football games, or Oregon fans forming the letter O with their hands, or the Lambeau Leap for the Green Bay Packers). This chapter provides an overview of the branding elements and how they influence brand identity, along with key guidelines for developing and managing a brand's identity.

Team Name

The primary branding element for sports teams is their name. This is primarily about the nickname portion of the name rather than the geographic part that usually comes first. In most cases, teams use their city's name as the geographic part of the name

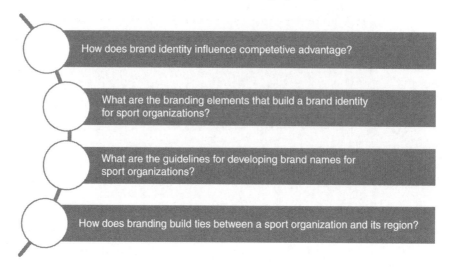

How does brand identity influence competetive advantage?

What are the branding elements that build a brand identity for sport organizations?

What are the guidelines for developing brand names for sport organizations?

How does branding build ties between a sport organization and its region?

Figure 7.1 An Overview of Chapter 7

(e.g., Boston Celtics, Chicago Bears, or Seattle Mariners). Sometimes, the geographic part is the state rather than the city, usually in an effort by the team to make itself embraced by the entire state and be perceived as being that state's team instead of just the city's (e.g., Carolina Panthers, Tennessee Titans, Arizona Cardinals, Indiana Pacers, Utah Jazz, Minnesota Twins, Texas Rangers). Occasionally, the geographic name may be presented in a less obvious manner, as is the case with the NBA's Golden State Warriors, or reflect a broader geographic area than just one state, like the New England Patriots in the NFL, which again makes it easier for a wider population to identify with that team as their own.

In general, selection of how to identify the location of the team is mostly a marketing decision. However, in some cases, there may be legal requirements or pressures associated with stadium lease provisions that stipulate that a city's name be included in the official team name. A case that received much publicity along those lines involved the Angels in Major League Baseball. As part of their deal with the city of Anaheim, they became the Anaheim Angels. However, the team owner wanted to define the team as a Los Angeles team and thus changed the name to the Los Angeles Angels. In order to fulfill the letter of the law that required Anaheim to be part of the name, the official name of the team is the Los Angeles Angels of Anaheim. More recently, when the Miami-Dade County commissioners and the city of Miami agreed to fund a new stadium for the Florida Marlins in Major League Baseball, the team's name changed to the Miami Marlins.

In regard to the nickname, teams obviously have more options to consider, and selecting a name can be quite challenging. The implications of name selection are significantly more important for minor league teams and teams in less popular major professional leagues than for the established major professional leagues. In the case of major professional leagues, a team name is still important but fan interest in the team is typically going to be relatively high regardless of the name; using branding through a name may be essential only in serious cases where the team is losing public support and needs to find ways to reconnect with its fans. For teams in the minor leagues or less popular sports, winning fans through team quality, player recognition, or sport popularity is more difficult; therefore, good branding can help the team establish a desirable identity and make fans more likely to follow the team.

Typically, names in the major professional leagues are fairly standard. Traditionally, the use of cute and creative names is relatively limited, especially in the NFL, although there are a few exceptions, such as the Dolphins in the NFL, the Magic and Wizards in the NBA, and the Penguins in the NHL. In general, major professional leagues are unlikely to endorse overly creative or cute team names because they may undermine a league's credibility and overall image (it is not surprising that we do not see names like Ladybugs or Butterflies in these leagues). These leagues have the right to veto a name for any reason if they so desire. The NBA, for example, discouraged Memphis from naming its newly acquired franchise (relocating from Vancouver) the Memphis Express, given the corporate connection to FedEx, which is also based in Memphis, and the team retained its original nickname and became the Memphis Grizzlies. Of course, one could wonder why this was not an issue for the Orlando franchise being named the Magic, given the strong connection to Disney World and the Magic Kingdom.

As mentioned earlier, another reason that teams in the major leagues of established sports use more conventional names is that teams expect to attract fans primarily because of the strong popularity and tradition of the sport/league rather than because of creative branding. However, this is not the case for the less popular sports or minor leagues. It is no accident that minor league teams in baseball are known for unusual and creative names (e.g., Sand Gnats, Mud Hens, Flying Squirrels, or Isotopes) as a way to create an identity. A memorable name (and/or other branding elements) can be helpful to any team, though, independent of its sport or level, in terms of gaining awareness and familiarity with a broader base, especially away from its own city or region.

It is fairly normal for teams to involve their fans in selecting the team's name by either getting name suggestions from the fans or even actually letting the fans pick through voting. For example, more than one-fourth of the teams that compete in the NFL today have a name that was suggested by fans (Bills, Broncos, Buccaneers, Chargers, Colts, Dolphins, Falcons, Ravens, and Seahawks), and some have in fact kept names that were suggested by fans in the team's original market (e.g., the Colts keeping the name while moving from Baltimore to Indianapolis). Interestingly, the Oakland Raiders also used a fan contest to select a name and the winner was Señors, but team ownership changed it to Raiders, which was another one of the submitted entries. Having fans suggest and select the team's name is especially likely to happen for a new franchise as a way to build fan involvement and excitement for the new team and even a sense of ownership. However, it involves some risk in the sense that the team name selected by the fans may not necessarily fulfill appropriate marketing criteria for branding. Specific guidelines have been recommended in the marketing literature about criteria for a good brand name[1]. Those criteria include the following.

The Name Should Be Easy to Say

This is especially relevant for sports because it needs to be easy for the fans to chant a team's name and cheer during the course of a game. Names that are one or two syllables long are easier to say and, therefore, easier for fans to chant during a game.

The names of most professional sports teams fit this criterion quite well, with numerous team names being one syllable and easy to chant (e.g., Jets, Colts, Chiefs, Rams, Bears). Of the 30 NBA teams, 25 have names that are one or two syllables. Interestingly, the five teams with longer names all have shorter versions that facilitate chanting (Cavaliers are the Cavs, Mavericks are the Mavs, Timberwolves are the Wolves, Trailblazers are the Blazers, and the Knickerbockers are the Knicks). In the case of the Knicks, the nickname has become more established than the original name and the team is now known by that name. The case of shortening the team's official name along those lines can be found in the other leagues as well: the NFL's New England Patriots are often referred to as the Pats, the San Francisco Forty-Niners as the Niners, the Tampa Bay Buccaneers as the Bucs, and the MLB's Arizona Diamondbacks as the D-backs.

In addition to being easy to say and pronounceable, the name should also be relatively easy to spell.[2] From a practical standpoint, this issue relates to licensing partnerships and minimizing the chance of licensed merchandise with spelling errors. It also makes it easier for the fans to identify with a team that they have no difficulty remembering how to spell. Some of the hard-to-say names are also difficult to spell, like the Tampa Bay Buccaneers in the NFL and the West Virginia Mountaineers in the NCAA.

The Name Should Be Tangible

Tangible names are easier to learn and remember.[3] Concrete names that evoke a visual image are especially relevant for less-established leagues and for targeting young children. Tangibility enables the teams to use mascots that children can associate with and support; it is also facilitates licensed merchandising. When the professional women's soccer league WUSA was introduced in the late 1990s, it identified families with children as one of its primary target audiences. The league's teams were introduced with names that conveyed great virtues such as Courage, Freedom, Spirit, and Power. However, although they were communicating noble ideas, those names were very hard to convert to tangible images and relevant mascots to which children, a key target for the league, could relate.

Tangibility is also relevant when focusing on adults. Tangible names support the use of a concrete symbol,[4] such as a lion, a wizard, or a bear. Names that evoke tangible images also allow teams to more easily form traditions and activities for fan participation. Such activities usually increase enjoyment of the game experience and are likely to increase fan identification.[5] A team's name does not necessarily have to be something tangible for rituals to develop; however, tangible names create opportunities and possibilities for such rituals and activities. For example, several college teams named after animals bring live mascots to their football games in ceremonial ways that increase fan anticipation, enjoyment, and excitement. It is much easier to engage in these activities with a bulldog (like Uga for the Georgia Bulldogs), a longhorn (like Bevo for the Texas Longhorns), or a buffalo (like Ralphie for the Colorado Buffaloes), than for a Hoosier (for the Indiana Hoosiers).

The Name Should Help the Team's Positioning

Positioning through a sports team's name usually occurs in one of two key ways: using a name that has a connection to the region the team is from (positioning the team as a local team) and/or using a name that conveys strength and power (positioning the team as a fierce competitor). In some instances, the name may accomplish both (e.g., the Dallas Cowboys). Names should suggest desired associations and excitement.[6] Interestingly, the New York Giants may have successfully evoked powerful imagery even though the original reasoning for the name was not along these lines; for example, one theory about the origin of the Giants nickname for the New York baseball and football teams is that it was originally inspired by the giant buildings in the area rather than the mythical figures.[7]

Fans seek positive identification with teams that embody positive associations, such as strength and virility. Team identification is predicated on organizational affinity (a match between a team's image and a fan's perceived or desired self-image) and organizational affiliation (a match between a fan's values and the teams' values). Self-team congruence, moreover, strengthens fan identification, which drives attendance, increases fan loyalty, reduces price sensitivity, and fosters resistance to negative press.[8] Carefully selecting team names that embody important, desired attributes, such as power (e.g., the Predators), ruggedness (e.g., the Cowboys), and excitement (e.g., the Storm), provides a means of centering subsequent marketing activities around these themes. Successful teams, such as the Seattle Sounders, further facilitate fan identification by promoting local events and junior sports leagues that strengthen the connection between the team, its fans, and its community, and successfully promote the idea of the team as a club where its fans are its members.[9]

The connection to the local region, its self-image, and/or its history (the Nebraska Corn Huskers, the Oklahoma [Boomer] Sooners) is a clever marketing practice as it can create more potential interest and affinity from the local fan base, helping them to perceive and embrace a team as their own. Also, it helps make the name more memorable to people outside the home market by establishing a connection between the city and the team in the other fans' minds. One could argue that the fans in Houston would have loved and embraced their new NFL franchise under most possible name options, but it's easier for the rest of the country to connect Houston to a team named the Texans rather than the Tigers.

Connecting a team to its city or region can be accomplished in various ways. In some cases the connection can be obvious to everyone, whereas in other cases it is less evident. Teams may select a name referring to people that have some relevance to the area (e.g., Steelers in Pittsburgh, Cowboys in Dallas, Forty-Niners in San Francisco) or to natural phenomena with a logical connection to the area (e.g., Avalanche in Colorado, Heat in Miami, Earthquakes in San Jose) or any other connection that makes sense for the area (e.g., Rockets and Astros in Houston due to the connection with NASA, Rockies in Colorado).

Should a team change a name that is relevant to a specific region if it changes locations and leaves its original region? Some have done that; when the Oilers left Houston for Tennessee they soon changed their name to the Titans, given that Oilers seemed to be a poor fit for Nashville. There are other cases where a team did not change its name and it did not seem to be much of an issue. For example, few people would argue that the Lakers are not embraced by the fans of Los Angeles, despite the fact that their name, which made perfect sense when they were in Minneapolis, has no connection to Los Angeles or southern California. Similarly, the Jazz have been embraced and loved by the Utah fans even though their name, which was a great fit for the team in New Orleans, seems out of place in Salt Lake City. One can argue that, even though those teams have been successful in attracting local support despite their name, they probably would have been able to do even better had they changed their name to disassociate themselves from their previous city and facilitate their connection to their new city when moving. In a fairly unique situation, the NBA's Charlotte Bobcats used branding as a way of disassociating themselves, but not from a city. Being the team that was replacing the previous Hornets who had left Charlotte to move to New Orleans and had created a lot of ill will among the fans in Charlotte, the new team intentionally tried to choose branding elements that were different from the Hornets, including both their name and their color schemes of orange compared to the Hornets' teal; it was their way of trying to communicate to the Charlotte fans that they were nothing like the team that hurt them, and that fans should view them as their team.[10]

Sports teams also use names that convey aggression, strength, and power as a way to position themselves as fierce competitors. Going through the names of teams in the major leagues, it appears this is probably the most common characteristic of sports team names. It is expressed through a selection of daunting animals with desirable characteristics such as vigor, speed, and strength (e.g., Broncos, Lions, Jaguars, Panthers) or birds with similar traits (e.g., Eagles, Falcons, Hawks, Ravens) or aggressive people (e.g., Warriors, Pirates, Raiders, Vikings) or dangerous natural phenomena or natural disasters (e.g., Avalanche, Earthquakes, Hurricanes, Thunder). Of course, the characteristics conveyed by a team's name do not necessarily reflect the team's abilities and actual performance. Let us not forget that the worst team ever in NFL history was the Detroit Lions, who went winless in a 16-game season in 2008 despite their fearsome name and all of the powerful traits associated with a lion; a case of overpromising by the team name and under-delivering by the team performance.

Occasionally teams pick names of non-aggressive animals that are more memorable by being unique (given most of the names are ones of fierce animals). There are advantages to such names for marketing purposes in that they are distinctive,[11] especially for otherwise unknown teams. Distinctive names can promote awareness for those teams and potentially increase their sales of licensed merchandise; for example, the University of California Santa Cruz teams are the Banana Slugs and the nickname for Columbia College in South Carolina is the Fighting Koalas (even though it is easy to argue there is a contradiction in using the words fighting and koala together). However, a team should be careful that selecting a "cute" animal as its name does not compromise the image of the team on a competitive level. Tufts University uses the name Jumbos and has an elephant as its mascot/logo, which may hurt its positioning as an athletic and competitive team, inhibit its recruiting of talented student athletes, and make the team an easy target for mockery by competitors and their fans.

An interesting way to use team names for positioning was employed by Major League Soccer (MLS) teams. In an effort to influence perceptions of American soccer fans of MLS as a high-quality league with high-level competition, many of the team names are similar to names used by established and storied teams in Europe.

*In the fall of 2014, the Charlotte team will re-brand back to the Hornets following the release of the Hornets name by the now New Orleans Pelicans.

For example, DC United is similar to Manchester United (one of the most popular franchises in the English Premier League), Real Salt Lake is patterned after Real Madrid, a celebrated Spanish team, Houston Dynamo adopts a name common among strong Russian teams such as Dynamo Kiev and Dynamo Moscow, and Sporting Kansas City mirrors one of Portugal's most successful teams, Sporting Lisbon. Moreover, some MLS teams are incorporating the initials FC (for Football Club, e.g., FC Dallas, Sounders FC, and Toronto FC) as part of their name. This convention is commonly utilized by European teams; the very fact that the word football is used for soccer (consistent with how non-Americans refer to the sport) communicates an effort to position the teams as similar to their famous and successful European counterparts.

The Name Should Have a Positive Connotation

It is generally recommended to avoid names that may be controversial or offensive. The use of Native American names was relatively common in the past, and several teams, professional and collegiate alike, have had such names. The NCAA has required schools to change names of that nature unless there is explicit approval by the tribe whose name is used. Based on this condition, certain teams had to change their names while others, like the Florida State Seminoles and the Utah Utes, were able to maintain them. The University of Illinois was allowed by the NCAA to continue using the name Illini given its similarity to the name of the state, but the university had to stop using Chief Illiniwek as its mascot. Despite the controversy, professional teams with such names have continued to use them. One could argue that the strong tradition of some of those teams (e.g., Washington Redskins) makes it harder to proceed with a change.

In other cases a name's negative connotation became an issue. The name Bullets became a liability for the NBA's formerly named Washington Bullets, given the high rate of homicides in the Washington, DC, area. They changed their name to a nonviolent one, the Washington Wizards. Also, before becoming the Houston Dynamo, the MLS franchise in Houston had proposed to use the name Houston 1836, patterned after European soccer teams that include a year as part of their name (e.g., Hanover 96, Munich 1860, or FC Schalke 04). However, many Hispanic fans of Mexican origin in Houston protested the name choice because of the connection of 1836 to the Texas independence war. Given that they constituted a substantial component of the team's target market, the team changed the name before beginning competition in the MLS.

There are also cases where team names potentially carry negative connotations but the teams have not received much negative publicity for them. Many of those names may be seen as negative in a context outside of sports. For example, some names are associated with people with negative image (e.g., Pirates or Buccaneers) or with negative religious images (e.g., Devils or Blue Devils or Sun Devils) or with natural disasters that can be devastating (e.g., Hurricanes or Earthquakes), but fans do not seem to mind them within sports. However, in a rather amusing twist on this issue, when Tampa's MLB franchise shortened its name from Devil Rays to just Rays many people joked about how dropping Devil from their name may have helped them turn from being one of the worst franchises in baseball to going to the World Series within a year![12]

Team Logo

A team's logo is part of its identity, both in terms of marketing and in terms of team pride. Team logos provide symbols that are central to positioning, merchandising, and differentiating a team and building its equity.[13] Occasionally, players from opposing teams have engaged in altercations because of perceived disrespect regarding one of the team's symbols. A high-profile example involves the NFL game between the Dallas Cowboys and San Francisco 49ers in 2000. After scoring a touchdown, Terrell Owens, then with San Francisco, ran from the endzone to midfield and celebrated on the blue star that is the Cowboys logo. Moments later, when Dallas scored, Cowboy star Emmitt Smith also ran to the center of the field and "reclaimed" the star, only to have Terrell Owens score another touchdown later and engage in the same behavior. That time, though, George Teague, a Cowboys player, ran after Owens and hit him as Owens was celebrating on the star, much to the delight of the Cowboys fans.

A sport organization must strive for balance between keeping its logo fresh and current but not compromising tradition. Typically, teams tend to be relatively conservative with logo changes, both in terms of frequency of change and intensity of change. This tendency is especially true for a team with a longer history and tradition. For example, the Green Bay Packers, one of the most storied NFL franchises, have been using their current logo since 1980. This logo is very slightly changed (adding the gold outline around the G) compared to the previous version that was used from 1960, essentially meaning they have had their logo for about 50 years. Similarly, the Pittsburgh Steelers have had their current logo without any changes since 1963. In baseball, the current primary logo of the New York Yankees was introduced in 1933, whereas, on the other hand, the Seattle Mariners, a team with significantly less tradition, has had four different primary logos and five different cap logos since just 1977. Occasionally teams proceed with redesigned logos as part of rebranding efforts. It is not unusual for such efforts to elicit protest from the team's core fan base that normally tends to be against any changes. In early 2010, Michigan State University, in collaboration with Nike, tried to make slight changes to its Spartan logo, causing a fury of protests by fans, which eventually led the university to reconsider and abandon pursuit of a new logo.

Team Colors

Another branding element that contributes greatly to establishing an identity involves the team's colors. Colors can be so significant that, in some cases, the color name is defined based on its connection to the team (e.g., Carolina blue). In some cases, it may not be the colors per se that give the team a special identity but frequent and unusual combinations of the colors in the team's uniforms. The University of Oregon Ducks football team has received much publicity nationwide for their many uniform combinations, several of which are non-ordinary.

Sometimes, the colors make sense in the context of the team's name (e.g., the colors for the Patriots are red and blue, for the Bengals orange and black, while the Cardinals use red and the Syracuse Orange have orange), but most of the time they seem independent of the name, especially if the name does not necessarily lend itself to a specific color. For example, Tigers is a rather popular name in the NCAA used by several for college teams; however, the Missouri Tigers are gold and black but the Auburn Tigers are orange and blue, the Clemson Tigers are orange, the Memphis Tigers are blue, and the Louisiana State (LSU) Tigers are purple and gold. Similarly, the Northwestern Wildcats are purple while the Kentucky Wildcats are blue and the Arizona Wildcats are red and blue. In some cases, lack of a connection between the name and any colors allows a team to change its colors; the Arizona Diamondbacks used purple as their original color but changed to red a few years later. However, in general, teams have the same approach to color changes as they do to logo changes, preferring infrequent and not very drastic changes. Overall, for major leagues the colors tend to be fairly traditional just like the names do, with the most common primary colors being blue, red, and black while some of the more recent teams have less traditional colors such as purple or teal.

Other Branding Elements

Teams can reinforce their branding identity through several other tools above and beyond their name and colors. Specific examples of what has been branded by sports teams and become part of their identity are listed below.

Rituals

Development of rituals, activities that become traditions, has been a great way for sports teams to create and reinforce an identity while also evoking strong fan involvement and participation, which strengthens fan identification.[14] In some cases, such activities originate from the team itself, while in other cases they may get started by the fans and cultivated by the team. As discussed earlier, the team's name often lends itself to specific rituals that make sense within that context.

Some of those rituals may establish such a strong identity that they have their own name or are associated with products or images with their own nickname. For example, a big part of the NFL Pittsburgh Steelers identity involves the waving of the Terrible Towels, while the Anaheim Angels in MLB capitalized on their Rally Monkey, even though for a much shorter period. Other rituals can include specific songs sung by the fans (e.g., fans of Liverpool FC in the English Premier League sing You'll Never Walk Alone before each game while Boston Red Sox fans sing Neil Diamond's Sweet Caroline in the eighth inning) or chants from songs (like the quite similar Who Dat for the New Orleans Saints and Who Dey for the Cincinnati Bengals).

People Associated with the Team

A team's identity is influenced by the image of the people associated with the team, primarily the players, but also coaches, fans, and sometimes very visible owners. Fans of a team can be branded in the sense that they may have a specific image that reflects on the team's identity or even their own well-known nickname. For example, for many NFL fans, one of the first things that comes to mind when thinking of the Oakland

Raiders is the image of Raider fans in their intimidating outfits. The Raiders' fan base even has its own identity in terms of a nickname, being known as the Black Hole. Other teams with fans that are easily recognizable in terms of looks, behavior, and nickname include the Cheeseheads for the Green Bay Packers, the Dawg Pound for the Cleveland Browns, the Cameron Crazies for Duke basketball, the 12th Man for Texas A&M University as well as the Seattle Seahawks in the NFL, the Timbers Army for the Portland Timbers in MLS, and the Hogettes for the Washington Redskins.

Players' personalities can have a strong impact on how a team is perceived. Obviously, teams have to cope with situations when players' behaviors create a damaging image and identity for the team. For example, the Spygate scandal colored many fans' perceptions of the New England Patriots, and the many legal problems of the NBA Portland Trail Blazers a few years ago earned them the unofficial damaging nickname of Jail Blazers. Poor behavior by athletes may reduce fan identification. The Portland Trail Blazers consciously began incorporating character and community involvement into the selection of athletes, in an effort to reduce potential problems and reposition their franchise as a team with a constructive presence in its community.[15] Some athletes, such as Drew Brees, positively project an image that strengthens organization affiliation (a sense that the team embodies positive values) among team fans, which increases identification.[16] Underdogs and hard working athletes are also frequently embraced by fans. In these cases, where athletes' personalities or performances garner positive attention and promote positive values, teams potentially benefit from consciously incorporating them in their own branding.

It is not uncommon for individual players or groups of players within a team to earn a nickname from the media or the fans, and teams can use players with such an identity to promote broader branding efforts for team. Some nicknames for groups of players in a team or an entire team include the Nasty Boys for the bullpen of the Cincinnati Reds in 1990, the Detroit Pistons Bad Boys in the late 1980s, the Big Red Machine for the Cincinnati Reds in the 1970s, Phi Slamma Jamma for the Houston Cougars basketball team from 1982 to 1984, and Gang Green for the Oregon Ducks defense during the 1994–1995 football season. Similarly, teams have shaped their identity and marketed themselves around individual stars and their well-known nicknames such as The Bus (NFL star Jerome Bettis), Dr. J (NBA great Julius Irving), The Mailman (NBA star Karl Malone), The Big Papi (MLB star David Ortiz), The Big Unit (MLB pitcher Randy Johnson), and Prime Time (NFL and MLB star Deion Sanders). In some cases, teams even capitalize on the identity of other elements besides people associated with the team, including their facilities, like the Green Monster for the Red Sox and the Frozen Tundra (Lambeau Field) of the Green Bay Packers in the NFL.

Representing and Symbolizing a City or Region

Ideally, a team's brand identity should match, enhance, and build on a city or region's self-image. Each city has its own unique sense of history, current set of challenges, and present series of hopes and dreams. Successful teams represent a collective ideal self, which often connects the past to the present. The Dallas Cowboys, for example, incorporate both the mythic past of the city (along with the state of Texas and the west) and the sophistication and confidence of modern Dallas (embodied in the new stadium). The Pittsburgh Steelers evoke the blue-collar, industrial origins of the city but also reflect the hope, achievement, and diversity of modern Pittsburgh.

Successful teams can provide a sense of respect for a city and its fans. Philadelphia, for example, may be seen as the Rodney Dangerfield of cities—it just can't "get no respect." The close attachment of Eagles' fans to their team and their strong emphasis on winning may be a means of achieving respect. Fielding a losing and/or prima donna team is not tolerated in Philly (although it is never appreciated anywhere). A prima donna team just doesn't fit the no-nonsense image of Philly and its fans. Baltimore, Buffalo, and Cleveland provide similar examples of historically blue-collar, no-nonsense towns.

New York is the "Big Apple." Its teams are expected to be competitive and to win. Losing is just not tolerated in a city with the resources and collective personality of New York. Its fans and media are notoriously hard on a losing team and its players.

Teams can also reflect the optimism and growth of a city. Teams such as the Tennessee Titans, the Carolina Panthers, and the Jacksonville Jaguars represent the rise and growth of their communities and provide a sense of esteem. Initial excitement about the awarding of a franchise, however, must be followed by an integration of a team, its players, and its symbols into the community.

Thus, successful sports franchises integrate and tie a team to its community. Evoking a romantic and mythical past is one means of facilitating this connection (the San Francisco Forty-Niners, the New England Patriots, the Portland Trail Blazers in Oregon provide examples). Although not all teams evoke the past, all successful teams do actively symbolize and reflect a community's present and future, its hopes, aspirations, and desires. The successful launch of the Seattle Sounders MLS typifies many of these characteristics. They actively promoted a community partnership with the Seattle Seahawks, which leveraged existing equity from that team; they engaged the fans in naming the Sounders; they facilitated the promotion of rituals, such as the waving of green scarves; and they actively promoted close connections between the team, its players, its fans, and its community.[17] In short, successful teams are actively engaged in the community, practice good citizenship (although each city may vary regarding its tolerance for bad behavior to an extent dictated by its perceived self-image and emphasis on winning), and symbolize the victories and dreams of their fans.

Future Research

Future research should empirically test the effects of brand identity on tangible outcomes, such as fan loyalty and following a team, and the purchase of team-licensed merchandise. The concept of following a team includes many interesting possibilities. The most obvious is a team's ticket sales and game attendance in its home games with its home fans. However, additional variables of interest include how a team's identity affects the interest of opposing fans, either to watch the game in person (e.g., road attendance) or to follow the game through the media (e.g., ratings and scheduling decisions). Along these lines, it is reasonable to expect that internalized fans will purchase licensed merchandise more than other fans.[18] A team's licensed merchandise should also sell better when the team is winning, as fans try to "bask in the reflected glory"[19] of the victories, and a team's strongest market should be the local market with the local fans. However, it is important to examine how a team's identity (including all the different aspects discussed in this chapter) may have an effect on sales among people who are not the "natural" fans of a team.

A good starting point was provided by Carlson, Donavan, and Cumiskey,[20] who found that several dimensions of a team's brand personality affect fan identification with the team and, subsequently, retail spending. However, they used a student sample who were asked about their own university's basketball team. It is logical to assume that the sample was already highly identified with that team, independent of brand personality aspects.[21] Therefore, it is not surprising that they will associate positive personality traits with their favorite team. Conceptually, when it comes to one's most favorite teams, it is easier to argue that it is strong identification that creates positive brand personality associations rather than positive brand personality traits that increase identification. A better way to test the relationship between the brand personality of the team and fan team identification would be to examine teams outside a fan's region, which would normally mean teams that fans are less likely to have as their favorite.

Our understanding of branding identity in sports will also benefit from empirical studies that assess the relative effect of the different branding elements on the perceived identity of a team, both within and outside the local fan base. As we discussed in this chapter, many factors can impact how a team's identity is shaped; however, it is important to study whether some of them are more influential than others. Answering this question can provide valuable insight to teams regarding what to focus their efforts on when making branding decisions.

Conclusion—The Effects of Brand Identity on Competitive Advantage

Branding can enhance a team's identity and tie it to the local community. Although branding generally does not replace winning, there are examples of long-suffering, loyal fans, such as Chicago Cubs fans, whose identities remain tied to the club despite a poor win-loss record and lack of championships. Strong branding can enhance a winning club's ticket sales, merchandising sales, and licensing opportunities, and promote and maintain interest in a losing club or lesser-known franchise or league. Thus, the importance and role of branding will vary depending on the prominence, success, and length of tenure of a particular sports franchise.

Brand equity consists of unique, favorable, and strong associations.[22] Branding can facilitate these associations by enhancing fan involvement, creating unique and memorable symbols, and promoting fan traditions and rituals. Although many of the specific rituals associated with a club will be fan created, astute marketing can promote and facilitate these rituals. Unique associations in Keller's framework generally mean different or differentiated from competitors. Although this is also important in sports, uniqueness is more local in sports and is tied directly to the community. The 12th man, as previously mentioned, is used by both the Seattle Seahawks and the Texas A&M Aggies; thus, it is not unique per se but it is connected to both communities, their traditions, and their rituals (e.g., the raising of the 12th man flag in Seattle). Similarly, though multiple teams may use the name Tigers, each of them has specific traditions and rituals associated with the name in each community, which subsequently build brand equity.

Branding also helps maintain favorable associations. The reality of modern sports is that players move and coaches leave. Branding can help to maintain consistent symbols and ties in an age of free agency. Community involvement at the team level is key. The New Orleans Saints and Drew Brees provide an excellent example of how community involvement can promote a long-term bond between the team and the community. Although specific players, such as Drew Brees, eventually leave or retire, fostering community involvement at the team level will ensure that another player and community leader will emerge. Thus, public relations and community involvement are essential to building long-term, unique, favorable, and strong associations between a team and its community that will ensure the support of the community even in the face of adversity (as was the case with the Saints and the bounty scandal).

Understanding a city (and/or region) and its fans is also essential. Each city has its own history, unique culture, collective set of values, and challenges. Regularly collecting demographic and psychographic data and monitoring fan attitudes is essential. Understanding the symbolic meaning(s) that a team has for its fans, the perceived connection between the team and its community, and the current state of perceptions about the team, provides the foundation for successful branding.

The nature and role of successful branding will vary depending on the specific profile of a team's fans. Kahle, Kambara, and Rose[23] describe three types of fans based on their strength of attitude. The lowest level of commitment is described as camaraderie. Fans who attend for camaraderie are less interested in the game and attend primarily for peripheral reasons, such as tailgating, eating or drinking, and being with friends and family. Creative promotions, entertainment, and events such as fireworks, celebrity meet and greets, themed events, and concerts are essential in attracting this type of fan. Successful branding can help to promote a consistent set of the activities, associations (such as songs played at the stadium), and rituals that increase a fan's commitment to the team. Minor league sports and lesser professional leagues consist of a high proportion of fans who attend for camaraderie, where branding and promotions dominate.

The second level of fan commitment is identification. Identified fans attend primarily to be associated with a winner. Winning teams by definition have a strong opportunity to sell licensed and branded goods to fans that seek to identify themselves with the team. The primary challenge for teams in this enviable position is to maintain consistency in their position and branding. Dependence on identified fans, however, is only as good as a team's win-loss record. Fair-weather fans who attend primarily for identification will abandon a losing team as quickly as they jumped on the bandwagon of a winning team.

The third level of fan commitment is internalization. Internalized fans are deeply committed to a team and will maintain their loyalty to a losing team. Internalized fans are connected to a team and the city that it represents. Thus, one of the most important roles of branding is to promote internalization. Community connections, rituals, public relations, and consistency in branding and behaviors are essential. Internalized fans perceive the team as an inherent symbol and part of the community. Good branding facilitates and enhances this connection and promotes fan internalization.

Lastly, branding can have important implications regarding a team's positioning and appeal to potential sponsors. In many cases, companies pursue specific teams that share similar characteristics with them as a way to capitalize on image transfer principles and reinforce their own image.[24] Therefore, developing an identity as smooth and elegant will attract certain companies with that image but make less sense for others. Depending on the potential sponsorship prospects, the team's market, and the desired image, teams will need to keep branding issues in mind in order to promote sponsorship opportunities, facilitate co-branding, and encourage fan identification.

References

1. Keller, K. L. (2008). *Strategic brand management* (3rd ed.). Upper Saddle River, NJ: Prentice-Hall.
2. Aaker, D. (1991). *Managing brand equity.* New York: Free Press.
3. Aaker, D. (1991). *Managing brand equity.* New York: Free Press.
4. Aaker, D. (1991). *Managing brand equity.* New York: Free Press.
5. Dionisio, P., Leal, C., & Moutinho, L. (2008). Fandom affiliation and tribal behaviour: A sports marketing application. *Qualitative Market Research, 11*, 17–39.
6. Aaker, D. (1991). *Managing brand equity.* New York: Free Press.
7. Anonymous (n.d.). History of NFL Team Names. Retrieved from: http://www.footballhappenings.com/teamnames.htm
8. Pritchard, M. P., Stinson, J., & Patton, E. (2010). Affinity and affiliation: The dual carriage way to team identification. *Sport Marketing Quarterly, 19*, 67–77.
9. Pritchard, M. P., Stinson, J., & Patton, E. (2010). Affinity and affiliation: The dual carriage way to team identification. *Sport Marketing Quarterly, 19*, 67–77.
10. Lombardo, J. (2003). NBA club found its identity in logo design. *Sports Business Journal* (On-line). Retrieved from http://www.sportsbusinessdaily.com/Journal/Issues/2003/06/20030616/This Weeks Issue/NBA Club Found-Its-Identity-In-Logo-Design.aspx?hl=bobcats%20%20lombardo&sc=0
11. Aaker, D. (1991). *Managing brand equity.* New York: Free Press.
12. Keri, J. (2011). *The extra 2%: How Wall Street strategies took a Major League Baseball team from worst to first.* New York: Ballantine Books; ESPN Books.
13. Aaker, D. (1991). *Managing brand equity.* New York: Free Press.
14. Drenten, J., Peters, C., Leigh, T., & Hollenbeck, C. (2009). Not just a party in the parking lot: An exploratory investigation of the motives underlying the ritual commitment of football tailgaters. *Sport Marketing Quarterly, 18*, 92–106.
15. Pritchard, M. P., Stinson, J., & Patton, E. (2010). Affinity and affiliation: The dual carriage way to team identification. *Sport Marketing Quarterly, 19*, 67–77.
16. Pritchard, M. P., Stinson, J., & Patton, E. (2010). Affinity and affiliation: The dual carriage way to team identification. *Sport Marketing Quarterly, 19*, 67–77.
17. Mayers, J. (2010, October 23). Sounders FC's success resonates globally. *Seattle Times.* Retrieved from: http://www.footballhappenings.com/teamnames.htm.
18. Bristow, D. N., & Sebastian, R. J. (2001). Holy cow! Wait 'til next year! A closer look at the brand loyalty of Chicago Cubs baseball fans. *Journal of Consumer Marketing, 18*, 256–275.
19. Dalakas, V., Madrigal, R., & Anderson, K. L. (2004). "We are number one!" The phenomenon of Basking-in-Reflected-Glory and its implications for sports marketing. In L. R. Kahle & C. Riley (Eds.), *Sports marketing and the psychology of marketing communication* (pp. 67–79). Mahwah, NJ: Lawrence Erlbaum Associates.
20. Carlson, B. D., Donavan, D. T., & Cumiskey, K. J. (2009). Consumer-brand relationships in sport: brand personality and identification. *International Journal of Retail and Distribution Management, 37*, 370–384.
21. Madrigal, R., & Dalakas, V. (2008). Consumer psychology of sport: More than just a game. In C. P. Haugtvedt, P. M. Herr, & F. R. Kardes (Eds.), *Handbook of consumer psychology* (pp. 857–876). New York: Taylor & Francis Group.
22. Keller, K. L. (2008). *Strategic brand management* (3rd ed.). Upper Saddle River, NJ: Prentice-Hall.
23. Kahle, L. R., Kambara, K. M., & Rose, G. M. (1996). A functional model of fan attendance motivations for college football. *Sport Marketing Quarterly, 5*, 51–60.
24. Gwinner, K., & Eaton, J. (1999). Building brand image through event sponsorship: The role of image transfer. *Journal of Advertising, 28*, 47–58.

8

Building Loyal Consumers in Sport Business

Mark P. Pritchard
Central Washington University

Abstract: No matter whether you're running a sport league, a franchise, or a sports retail or manufacturing business, few things signal the health of your organization like the number of customers who purchase repeatedly. However, in today's competitive marketplace many managers are forced to look more carefully at what drives these numbers. Why are people buying, or in this case, rebuying? This chapter deals with what some argue constitutes one of the most important parts of marketing effort, repeat purchase behavior (RPB) and the loyal attachment patrons or fans display toward a brand. Insights about why people continue to repurchase, or renew their tickets, enable marketers to become far more effective in deciding how best to build strong, stable, ongoing relationships with their customers. Strategies and tactics that focus on developing loyal "fans-of-the-brand"[1] are believed by many to be critical to in-market success and the long-run financial health of organizations.

Keywords: customer relationships, loyalty, repeat purchase behavior, segmentation

Introduction

Experts on brand loyalty believe that much of the marketing effort can be boiled down to two simple goals, *acquisition and retention*, the getting and keeping of customers.[2] This chapter focuses on the latter goal, more specifically brand loyalty and how sport properties can develop and retain a loyal following in the marketplace. Some commonalities covered here might be relevant for those trying to understand loyalty in sponsors or employees. However, the primary goal of this discussion is to first unpack the heart of why consumers enter into ongoing purchase relationships with sport brands, and then explain how firms cultivate this connection.

In marketing, the most widely held account of what loyalty looks like in your customers is that they are (a) strongly committed to your brand[3] and (b) willing to consistently rebuy despite situational effects (e.g., losing season, negative PR, price increases) or attractive alternatives (e.g., competitive promotions, discounts).[4] Developing a loyal customer base is viewed as having important financial implications for an organization. Research tells us that having a steady base of committed patrons who repeatedly purchase can:

- Boost profits, where 5% increases in retention can realize profit gains of 25–90%.[5]
- Increase positive word-of-mouth, with loyal patrons serving as brand advocates.[6]

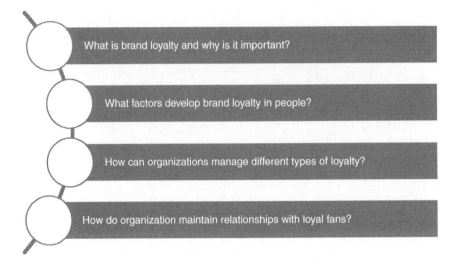

What is brand loyalty and why is it important?

What factors develop brand loyalty in people?

How can organizations manage different types of loyalty?

How do organization maintain relationships with loyal fans?

Figure 8.1 An Overview of Chapter 8

- Reduce promotion costs, in that retention can be six times cheaper than acquisition.[7]
- Stabilize market share against new and existing competition.[8]
- Diminish substitution,[9] brand switching behavior,[10] and churn in customers.[11]
- Minimize the effects of poor product performance.[12]
- And, lessen the impact of negative publicity.[13]

The benefit of having a loyal customer base has attracted a lot of attention over the last 50 years. In fact, the current two-dimensional (attitude & behavior) description of what constitutes a loyal patron has emerged only after quite a bit of research on the construct. Researchers were initially interested in assessing brand loyalty and the consumption of retail goods with one dimension, repeat purchase behavior. Various approaches ensured tracking the sequence (order) of brand purchases (e.g., brand A-B-A-A-A), the frequency (intensity) of repeat purchase over a given timeframe, or the proportion of times a patron purchased a particular brand relative to their overall consumption.[14] However, just focusing on behavior alone can generate errant classifications. People can still purchase a lot and not be truly "brand loyal."[15] Behavior needs to be qualified, and so the case was made for considering attitudinal assessments. In spectator sports, this resulted in complex attitude scales being developed to capture a variety of correlates such as one's willingness to publicly defend a team, use media to follow team games, and patronize teams despite poor performances or the loss of star players.[16] Although these large sets of items capture aspects of being loyal, redundancy and predictive ability make a case for practitioners' keeping it simple and using only one or two attitude statements in customer surveys. With this advice in mind, accurately gauging loyalty in your patrons means assessing behavior along with attitude. Day's equation, which follows, represents loyalty in this manner, as a function of loyal attitude (A) and behavior (B).[17]

L   = P[B] / A, where

L   = the level of patron loyalty for brand (e.g., San Francisco 49ers)

P[B]   = the proportion of total purchases of a service (e.g., football games attended) that buyers devoted to the brand (e.g., NFL team-specific attendance) over a set period of time (e.g., 2012 season)

A   = the mean attitude toward brand (e.g., San Francisco 49ers).

Loyal Patronage

Following the Numbers

Managers still need to track purchase behavior in their customer base, as these numbers provide critical comparative benchmarks for marketing effort. As you can see in Figure 8.2, attendance numbers for U.S. Major League Soccer clubs place the Seattle Sounders FC at the top of the league in ticket sales. These same numbers also underscore the franchise's ability to draw fans relative to other top clubs in Europe. However, with sport brands we do need to look a little more closely at these numbers. For example, attendance/unit sales should be considered relative to the city/market served and capacity (e.g., stadium's seating). Hotels, for instance, view their sales like this, as a percentage sold of the total available (i.e., occupancy rates). Comparative numbers like this can spell out how healthy an organization or an industry is relative to competitors or past performance (seasons).[18] Revenue per unit sold is another performance metric, which if calculated for a sport franchise like the Sounders would entail multiplying the club's average daily ticket rate per seat (ADR) by its occupancy rate. Although this estimate does not include other in-park per capita revenues such as concessions or merchandise sales,[19] it does show a rate of return for numbers sold (tickets purchased) and addresses whether franchises are "buying" occupancy or able to command premium prices from their customers. Another metric, used in the sport industry to calculate repeat purchase behavior (RPB) and efficiencies in existing business, is the ticket renewal rate (i.e., % of ticket holders who renew their purchase relationship the following season).

For example, in 2011 the NHL reported 20 of 29 clubs improved their renewal rate from the previous season to generate a league average of 90.3%. Growing renewal rates by 2.5% in the NHL resulted in stronger sales as season tickets sold that year were up by 4%.[21] The NFL also uses renewal rates to interpret their attendance data. For example, despite declining attendance across the league (2011's per game average of 64,698 fans being the lowest in a dozen years), the league reported positive signs for the 2012 season on the basis of a 90.6% average renewal rate in season ticket holders (STH), a 1.3% increase over the prior year.[22]

"Churn" rates are the corresponding metric for nonrenewal (i.e., the percentage of season-ticket-holders or heavy users who discontinue or defect).[23] Industry experts agree churn rates in STHs and other important repeat customer segments above 20% don't bode well, as few businesses can sustain turning over their primary customer base every 4–5 years. Rates that quantify patron behavior are definitely key. However,

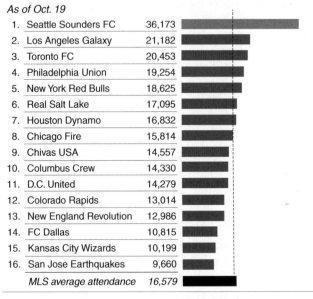

Resounding support

Sounders FC leads Major League Soccer in attendance, and would rank in the top 50 worldwide. Here are the MLS rankings:

As of Oct. 19

1.	Seattle Sounders FC	36,173
2.	Los Angeles Galaxy	21,182
3.	Toronto FC	20,453
4.	Philadelphia Union	19,254
5.	New York Red Bulls	18,625
6.	Real Salt Lake	17,095
7.	Houston Dynamo	16,832
8.	Chicago Fire	15,814
9.	Chivas USA	14,557
10.	Columbus Crew	14,330
11.	D.C. United	14,279
12.	Colorado Rapids	13,014
13.	New England Revolution	12,986
14.	FC Dallas	10,815
15.	Kansas City Wizards	10,199
16.	San Jose Earthquakes	9,660
	MLS average attendance	*16,579*

Where Sounders FC average attendance would rank in the top European leagues:

ENGLAND (20 teams)

1. Manchester United	75,191
2. Arsenal	60,000
3. Manchester City	46,150
4. Newcastle United	44,868
5. Liverpool	43,174
6. Chelsea	41,527
7. Sunderland	39,414
8. Everton	38,003
9. Aston Villa	36,526
10. Seattle Sounders FC	**36,173**

GERMANY (18)

1. Borussia Dortmund	74,855
2. Bayern Munich	69,000
3. Schalke 04	60,853
4. Hamburg SV	54,582
5. FC Cologne	48,550
6. Kaiserslautern	45,983
7. Eintracht Frankfurt	45,066
8. Hannover 96	42,547
9. Borussia Monchengladbach	42,235
10. Nurnberg	40,706
11. VfB Stuttgart	39,625
12. Seattle Sounders FC	**36,173**

FRANCE (20)

1. Marseille	54,677
2. Seattle Sounders FC	**36,173**

SPAIN (20)

1. Barcelona	73,000
2. Real Madrid	70,000
3. Atletico Madrid	45,000
4. Valencia	40,798
5. Seattle Sounders FC	**36,173**

ITALY (20)

1. Inter Milan	53,333
2. AC Milan	40,078
3. Seattle Sounders FC	**36,173**

Source: ESPN Soccernet   **MARK NOWLIN / THE SEATTLE TIMES**

Figure 8.2 Attendance as a Yardstick for Performance[20]

practitioners want to know why repeat business is coming to their door so that they can do a better job of managing returning customers. According to Mullin and others, correctly identifying the strength or intensity of a customer's RPB on the "sport consumer escalator" is a necessary first step (see Figure 8.3). An adaptation of their model shows sport consumers climbing an escalator of behavioral involvement (i.e., increased attendance or consumption).[24] Strong levels of team allegiance (i.e., loyalty) and brand identification in heavy user groups help to diminish churn and make them less likely to defect. Often managers using an escalator approach prioritize one RPB segment over another and invest more effort nurturing a particular customer group. This is primarily because some consumer groups may be worth more to the organization that others.

Four levels of RPB (light-moderate-frequent-heavy consumption) are shown on the escalator. An example of numbers for an NBA franchise attendance mix is also shown, detailing percentage of the fan base and their respective frequency of consumption over the course of the season.[25] This breakdown allows management to assign different $values to each RPB segment. For instance, if average ticket prices were $50 and the arena accommodated 10,000 customers, marketers could answer who the organization's primary customer is by calculating the $value of each segment to the organization. When segments are prioritized by revenues, some organizations use a proportion of sales approach to generate a promotional budget. This enables company resources used to be consistent with a segment's potential worth.

Understanding the value of repeat business over time is at the heart of another diagnostic, customer lifetime value (LTV). However, LTV changes the focus from the

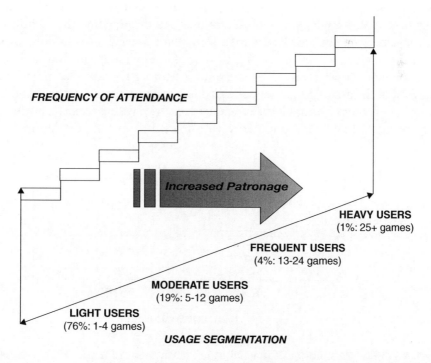

Figure 8.3 Sport Consumer Escalator Model (Adapted from Sutton, McDonald, & Milne, 1997)

value of a segment to the value of an individual consumer over the course of their purchase relationship with the brand. Often an individual's buying power is not taken into account by firms, but using duration and frequency LTV estimates the value of each consumer's RPB. Using estimates from the NBA below, researchers report the value of single fans (STHs) in these terms:[26]

- TP Average season ticket price, $47.07
- SP Average number of seats purchased per customer, 3.23 seats
- GP Number of games in a full-season ticket plan, 43 games
- YR Average number of years a customer remains a STH, 9 years

Adjusting for inflation, TP * SP * GP * YR = average season ticket holder LTV ($83,573.45).

Understanding Brand Loyal Attitude

There is some criticism of the escalator model's usefulness inasmuch as it focuses on behavior and doesn't explain customer thinking behind that purchase behavior: why fans might progress at different rates, drop down the escalator or discontinue (churn).[27] Day's inclusion of a statement of loyalty was one of the first times brand researchers began to qualify patron behavior by whether they were genuinely attached to the brand or not.[28] The advantage of this is that some patrons, although being heavy consumers of the brand, really do so for spurious reasons (it's the cheapest available or the only brand available) or habit, rather than from a willingness to identify themselves as loyal patrons.[29] Incorporating brand attitude along with a customer's degree of patronage (RPB) results in a two-dimensional specification and the identification of four loyalty segments (see Figure 8.4). Here, the *truly loyal* patron purchases the brand frequently and possesses a strong attitude of loyalty toward the brand (i.e., they resist changing their preference).[30] *Latent loyalty* defines a type of customer who feels strongly about the brand yet to that point had not begun to patronize the brand heavily. Identifying types of brand loyal consumers this way, with a dualistic attitude/behavior approach, has gained popularity with marketers in different leisure-related

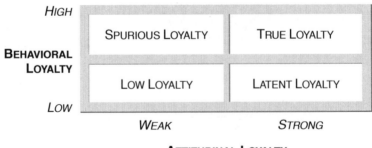

Figure 8.4 Loyalty Classifications (Adapted from Backman & Crompton, 1991; Pritchard & Howard, 1997)[31]

service industries (golf, hotels, municipal recreation etc.),[31] but has more recently been applied to professional sports to describe brand loyalty toward different NFL teams.[32] This attention is primarily due to the typology's usefulness in prescribing differentiated tactical responses, elevating or reinforcing a loyalty segment's attitude or behavior relative to the brand.[33] More will be said on strategies for influencing a customer's level of loyalty later in the chapter.

Although Figure 8.4 is a useful way to think of things, subsequent work has progressively tried to add more detail to what constitutes loyal attitude; that is the "why" behind brand attachment.[34] This specifically unpacks the type of antecedents that develop strong attitudes of loyalty in people and escalate the propensity to repeatedly buy the brand. Some have used a three-component framework (cognitive, affective, conative structure) of attitude to explain how different phases lead up to being loyal (i.e., that positive information, liking, and intentions prompt the attitude).[35] Below are a range of reasons researchers have offered on what helps to develop brand or team loyalty:

- Social factors such as family involvement or experiences as a child.[36]
- Strong emotional reactions to the team, more knowledge about the team, and greater symbolic value associated with the team.[37]
- Strong involvement with the product category, positive brand perceptions and experiences, and a symbolic attachment to the brand.[38]
- Identification with and self-esteem response to the brand, product experience based mood.[39]
- Commitment, supported by positive direct experience with the product and symbolic association and identification with the values and images that represent the brand.[40]

Symbolic attachment to the brand as a means for self-representation appears to be one of the consistent themes across much of the work on loyal attachment.[41] This involves brands being purchased or patronized not so much for functional reasons, but for what it means for a patron to align with the brand. Other attitudes such as satisfaction with the product experience are still important, yet not essential for developing loyalty in fans.[42] For example, "die-hard" loyal Chicago Cubs baseball fans may be dissatisfied with their team's on-field performance or the amenities of the stadium, yet still remain loyal and continue their patronage.[43] Service experience and performance features are usually much more important to those who are only moderately engaged and less loyal to the brand. Involvement with the product (sports activity itself) is also viewed as another key feature behind consumers becoming committed to one brand or another (e.g., I'm a football enthusiast and a loyal fan of the Packers).[44] Yet again, while it may be true for some fans, loyal attachment does not necessarily have to rest on the importance of the sport or one's history of involvement with it.

Other models have been developed to explain how loyal attitude develops and escalates. Funk and James (2001) originally presented the Psychological Continuum Model (PCM) to explain how people became more involved with sport entities.[45] Their stage-based approach was similar to the escalator model but different in that it offered a way to understand how people progress up a continuum through various psychological stages (i.e., Awareness, Attraction, Attachment, and Allegiance to team). Used to characterize customer attachment to professional sports teams or recreation activity,[46] the framework depicts consumers moving through stronger phases of brand attitude: Awareness (e.g., I know about FC Barcelona), Attraction (e.g., I like FC Barcelona), Attachment (e.g., I am a fan of FC Barcelona), or Allegiance (e.g., I live for FC Barcelona). Figure 8.5 illustrates how attitudinal engagement progresses from weak to strong, while behavioral engagement follows from simple to complex. Attitudinal engagement represents the degree of attitude formation that occurs toward the object/ activity. Similar to the escalator in Figure 8.3, behavioral engagement displays various qualities as it becomes more complex (e.g., Trial & Exploratory, Infrequent & Evaluative, Frequent & Expressive, and Consistent & Enduring). The breadth and depth (complexity) of behaviors continues to increase through to Allegiance. There are both pros and cons to viewing loyalty with these four stages.

One disadvantage rests in thinking the PCM's four stages reflect a full complement of customer segments. There are situations where loyal attitude and behavior may end up being inconsistent in some customers and require a targeted response (see spurious and latent loyalty in Figure 8.4). An advantage of the PCM's depiction of loyal engagement in Figure 8.5 is that it considers a range of behaviors (i.e., behavioral engagement becomes increasingly complex). This moves the marketer's thinking beyond a transaction mindset (purchase frequency alone) to considering other relationally oriented behaviors (e.g., word-of-mouth, blogging and participating in online brand communities, wearing team merchandise, information search/ sharing, media use). The nature and degree to which customers become engaged

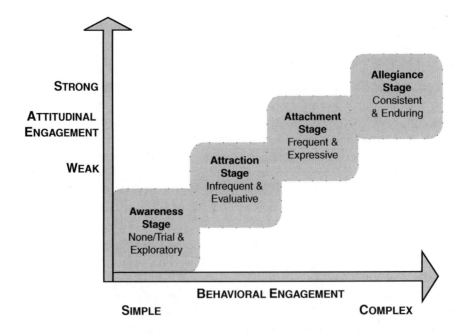

Figure 8.5 Stages of Engagement in the PCM (Adapted from Funk, Beaton & Pritchard, 2011)

with brands has become an increasingly popular topic among service marketers (i.e., the nature, form/modality, scope, and valence of CEB, Customer Engagement Behavior).[47] This is primarily due to technology enabling us to interact with brands online and in ways never before possible (e.g., blogging, tweeting, facebooking, e-WOM, e-valuations).

Understanding Barriers to Continuance

Although the previous section discussed why patrons become loyal and continue to purchase/renew their patronage, the other half of the question is "Why do people stop buying?" Both Assael and Oliver believed that despite being strongly disposed, consumer decisions to continue could be terminated because of outside constraints or obstacles that hindered intentions from ending in repurchase.[48] Although we have discussed attitudinal antecedents that facilitate loyal repeat purchase behavior, constraints can prevent or dampen the frequency of consumptions. Work by economists on spectators observed externalities such as the weather, ticket pricing, and the nature of the competition (close game, rival team etc.) having the potential to influence attendance at U.S. football games. External factors such as league expansion, competitive schedule, player quality, and rain on match day can also act as disincentives to fans attending professional rugby games in Australia and New Zealand.[49]

Some sport marketers argue that conducting an evaluation of the negative factors that cause customers to switch brands or discontinue patronage can offer distinct strategic insights. Several investigators identified the tactical implications of considering five types of barriers to RPB: (a) Marketing Constraints, the type of barrier most easily controlled, which reflects a failed fit between product and consumer, (b) Cultural Constraints operating in prevailing cultural norms and values that curtail patronage, (c) Social Constraints and the dampening influence that reference groups and social expectations have on action, (d) Personal Constraints that develop from lifestyle, and finally (e) Structural Constraints that reduce patronage as a result of physical, temporal, or spatial barriers.[50]

Marketing constraints usually mean considering a range of service failures that can turn customer RPB away from your brand. Keaveney found that 58% of people terminate patronage due to poor service experiences.[51] However, subsequent work reported fewer (15%) stop due to poor performance. In this case the majority (58%), though satisfied, discontinued for other reasons.[52] This signifies cessation may more often rest on factors other than performance (e.g., wins/losses). Research on constraints in sport or leisure services classifies half a dozen reasons sport enthusiasts give behind limited participation (e.g., financial, work obligations, physical health, personal/family priorities, and transportation).[53] A similar set of factors has been found to limit consumption in sports spectators. Results from a mail survey in Table 8.1 report a breakdown of constraints that typically curtail repeat patronage in Major League Baseball spectators. Randomly drawn to represent a franchise's loyalty program of 40,000 members, respondent constraint counts were drawn from open-ended comments made by 308 fans. The count shown qualifies whether members observed internal or external factors limiting their consumption. External factors, such as a time conflict with

Table 8.1 Spectator Constraints to Repeat Patronage (Adapted from Pritchard,
             Funk, & Alexandris, 2009)

Constraints to Attendance	Constraint %	Spectator Count (%)
Internal Constraints		78(25)
Low Priority (personal/other family priorities)	23.1	
Physical (tired, health)	5.9	
External Constraints		190(62)
Financial (cost of tickets, concessions, etc.)	15.2	
Schedule Conflict (work, social obligations)	23.5	
Limited Access (to tickets, good seats)	8.2	
Travel (parking, transportation to ballpark)	20.1	
Diminished Appeal (weather, visiting team)	3.7	
No Constraints		40(13)

a patron's work schedule, constituted the most frequent barrier preventing fans from coming to games 62% of the time.[54] However, a much smaller group, akin to the "die-hard fans" of the Chicago Cubs, announced that nothing would limit or prevent their attendance.[55] Extreme loyalty like this means your consumers are willing to expend a great deal of effort overcoming obstacles to purchase,[56] a very attractive reward for those brands able to elicit such allegiance.

Strategies for Negotiating Loyal Patronage

Strategies can be introduced by sport brands to help their customers overcome some barriers to RPB. For example, overcoming accessibility issues means franchises should stress convenience, and make game times fit work schedules or enable easy event access via mass transit. Economic barriers can also be negotiated. This might mean providing affordable inventory on nonpeak days, or offering cost-saving strategies (e.g., price promotions or flexible concession rules on bringing food/drink to games). Such examples are team-based strategies,[57] but another level of discussion centers on overcoming negatives at an industry or league level. Back and his colleagues believed leagues should constantly be looking for new modes of distribution to increase fan engagement via media technology (e.g., sports programming for mobile phones, online podcasts of events).[58] Ticket prices (e.g., $ increases of 30% for some NFL football teams) can act as another barrier to major league attendance, and induce some to switch their loyalty to second-tier substitutes. Consumer strategies that overcome negatives and prompt consumption usually adopt an "integrated view." This is an efficient way to segment and generate tactical responses as it promotes points of attraction while helping patrons negotiate constraints to behavior.[59]

Adapted from previous work, an X-Y strategy mix appears in Figure 8.6.[60] Based on the loyalty segments identified in Figure 8.4, this underscores which strategies best help patrons adjust their attitude or behavior.[61] For example, the truly loyal (i.e., strong attitude/behavior) segment represents ideal candidates for *Retention Strategies* that reinforce and reward patronage. On the other hand, *latently loyal* patrons need help negotiating barriers to increased attendance. This can use *Inducement Strategies* such as promotional offers (e.g., economic incentives) that underscore the benefits of attending. *Spuriously loyal* spectators with low attachment to the brand offer a particular challenge. However, *Rationalization Strategies* that target attitude change can be employed. Tactics here aim at provoking a level of excitement around the brand, usually with persuasive appeals or colorful information to set the scene and frame upcoming contests in an attractive way. *Confrontation Strategies* represent a greater two-fold test for the marketer, as they aim to influence those with weak attachment to the brand and significant purchase constraints. Confronting weak attachment here could focus on using cost-effective tools that build online media use.

Approaching engagement like this should focus on adding value for the group and beginning to change their involvement (i.e., escalate their awareness, knowledge, and ultimately preference for the brand). Mahony and his colleagues offered a similar array of suggestions for marketing to the four loyalty segments (their tactics are listed in Table 8.2).[62] In essence, the material shown in both the table and Figure 8.6 help practitioners envision ways to escalate loyal engagement, both attitudinally and behaviorally.

Table 8.2 Additional Suggestions for Marketing to the Loyalty Segments (Adapted from Mahony, Madrigal & Howard, 2000)

Suggestions	Segment
Marketers should use a reinforcement strategy that includes strengthening behavioral loyalty through economic incentives and attitudinal loyalty through personalized encouragement. This strategy is designed to increase the yield and avoid losing this segment.	Truly Loyal
Marketers should focus on increasing the fan's psychological commitment through the use of a rationalization strategy. This can be done by promoting the positive attributes of the product or service, getting fans to articulate why they support the team, and/or coupling attendance with support of a relevant social cause.	Spuriously Loyal
Marketers should focus on increasing the positive behaviors of the latently loyal fan by using a market inducement strategy. This can be done by removing significant barriers to behavior and by offering economic incentives to engage in certain behaviors.	Latently Loyal
Although some might suggest marketers use a confrontation strategy, which requires a direct attack on the fan's existing attitudes, others believe this may only lead to strengthening the fan's low level of commitment. Many strategists instead recommend focusing on using either a rationalization strategy to increase commitment or an inducement strategy to increase behavior as a first step toward a stronger display of loyalty.	Low Loyalty

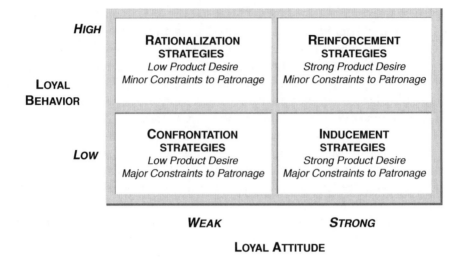

Figure 8.6 Loyalty Tactics and Strategies (Adapted from Pritchard, Funk, & Alexandris, 2009)

Customer Relationship Marketing (CRM)

A CRM is an information-enabled approach to customers whose primary goal is to build retention and satisfaction in patrons through direct response marketing campaigns. Loyalty programs on the other hand constitute part of this marketing effort, but typically are more focused marketing promotions that seek to reward frequent attendance. Many of the tactics and approaches used in CRM these days are fueled and supported by information technology. The idea of CRM has been around for a long time, but three technological developments have given it a great boost: (a) database technology: computers, data warehousing, and data mining. (b) interactivity: websites, call centers, email, phones, fax, etc., (c) mass customization technology: modular production.

Developing sophisticated databases from a variety of touch points has enabled marketers to store and process a considerable amount of customer information. This enables practitioners to develop data-driven insights about a customer's relative value and what customized promotions might be effective. In professional sports, databases often develop around season ticket holders, mapping their participation and expenditure patterns, and in college sports, tracking charitable involvement/giving. Fully understanding the value of a heavy user repeat segment's LTV to an organization enables marketing effort to become more efficient (i.e., budget resources are committed toward satisfying the most valuable patrons).[63] Ways in which databases can be used to aid marketing effort include the following: (a) identifying best prospects, (b) encouraging more product use, (c) supporting greater cross-selling of products, (d) aiding in upselling (sale of upgrades), (e) customizing offerings and messages, and (f) enabling sales and service to develop deeper customer relationships.[64]

In service industries, many loyalty programs attempt to encourage loyal behavior.[65] An early example in sports occurred in the 1980s when the Del Mar Thoroughbred Club decided to reward racing patrons for their attendance. Since then loyalty programs have been adopted by a range of sport franchises (e.g., NBA San Antonio

Spurs, MLB San Diego Padres, MLS Los Angeles Galaxy) and for many, spectators have become a regular fixture in their game-day experience.[66] Loyalty programs typically track the frequency of member-company interactions, or purchases, on a membership card. When enough purchase activity "points" have been earned, members can redeem prizes, or receive benefits and privileges. Programs fit into one of five structural types.[67] Table 8.3 shows some of the different promotional objectives that guide these types of programs. Reward, Rebate, Appreciation, Partnership, and Affinity Programs primarily differ by the choices they offer, the brand connection they seek to foster, and the way they use incentives to reward patrons.

Research on brand loyalty programs has investigated how the different types of reward schemes influence the perceived value of the program. The goal for many program managers is that customers would see the value of the program and that this in turn would build both program and brand loyalty (see Figure 8.7).[68] In a recent franchise expansion by MLB, the Arizona Diamondbacks were pondering how to build a connection with their fan base. The idea of developing a loyalty program in this particular instance focused on how they could 'add value' through rewards and move the attendance dial just a fraction in their STH's, who then have one additional reason to come to games.[69] The bottom line of any program's reward system is whether or not it builds loyalty in the customers it serves; that is, do the rewards build "spurious loyalty" or genuine attachment to the brand ("true loyalty")? Depending on how involved customers are in the sport activity, rewards can be used in different ways to build loyalty to the brand. Highly involved consumers (who love the sport) are willing to delay and wait for direct rewards, whereas low-involvement fans are content with indirect or direct rewards but want them immediately. So, timing and type of rewards can be used differentially to prompt attachment.[70]

Table 8.3 Types of Loyalty Programs (Adapted from Pritchard & Negro, 2001)

Program	Aim	Structure
Reward Programs	To develop borrowed interest in membership and patronage.	Compensates customer purchase behavior with merchandise rewards that are unrelated to the brand.
Rebate Programs	To develop value exchanges that which encourage heavy usage.	The more you spend, the more redemptive points you earn to win more of the same product.
Appreciation Programs	To acknowledge, thank & reward past patronage.	Rewards are determined by the business-customer relationship and are given as an in-kind gift.
Partnership Programs	To appeal to a broader cross-section of market, share promotional cost.	Rewards customer purchases with partner's product.
Affinity Programs	To increase customer lifetime value by building strong affinity with the brand.	Value is added to relationship without rewards via information-intensive communication. Depends on strong involvement with the product category.

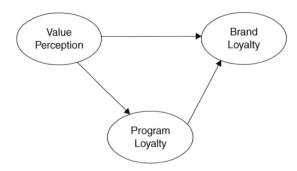

Figure 8.7 Goals of a Loyalty Program

Other research with baseball fans and their preference for different parts of a loyalty program identified additional tactics. The first priority for many customers is often whether the program's promotional offerings are worthwhile or not. Small discounts of 10–20% off did not build perceived value. Another factor for members was whether the program gave them special recognition and unique access to information or areas around the ground (see tactical suggestions in Table 8.4).[71]

When it comes to CRM, Butler identified a significant turning point in the world of college athletics in 2012 when funding needs drove many to embrace and adapt sport business concepts from the professional ranks. This shift uses technology and innovation to increase revenue, and build CRM systems within college athletics departments to inform ticket sales, fundraising, and marketing about their key segments. Incorporating sophisticated CRM platforms can offer entire management teams immediate access to data, ultimately leading to better managed fan and donor relationships.[72] The strategy relies on developing a one-on-one approach to marketing. Peppers and Rogers were some of the first marketers talking about how to nurture relationships with customers. Their recommendations on a firm's line of attack to achieve this goal followed four points:[73]

- Identify your target customers.
- Differentiate your customers by their needs and their value to your company.
- Interact with your customers to form a learning relationship.
- Customize your products, services, and messages.

These steps are at the heart of many CRM systems. The lure of boosting attendance and building connections with fans lies behind recent loyalty initiatives at several well-known universities (e.g., Michigan State, Colorado). The University of Southern California (USC) unveiled its Trojan Fever Loyalty Program in hopes it can spark the same passion for football into other SC sports. The program uses a points-and-prizes system to lift attendance and pack the seats across different offerings.[74] However, not all on campus agree with the approach, arguing that offering incentives for attendance to the student body is not the best solution. Kotler believed loyalty programs and CRM systems may not be the answer for everyone; that businesses with low CLV, high churn, huge numbers buying minor items, and no direct seller/buyer contact, needed to think carefully before investing.[75] Loyalty programs and promotional incentives may seem

Table 8.4 Potential Tactics for Loyalty Programs (Adapted from Pritchard & Negro, 2001)

Program Components	Tactics
Sponsorships	
1. Build sponsors into the program.	Have a program title sponsor andaffiliated day-of-game sponsors.
Service Experience	
2. Increase entertainment value when swiping card.	Reinforce tradition (i.e. mystic of the game). Memorable Moment video runs when swiping. History can increase value by eliciting positive emotions.
Rewards and Prizes	
3. Meaningful coupons.	Two for one coupons most effective. Meaningful fan acknowledgement/ benefits needed.
4. Increase game involvement through choice.	(i) Bonus point option. Extra points given to member if they correctly select/predict game related outcomes.
	(ii) Choice of rewards. Select from a variety of rewards.
Accessibility/Convenience	
5. Access to information.	Team Newsletter. Newsletter emailing of the latest team information. E-mail a copy of upcoming match program.
6. Access to team/players.	Allow fans to meet the players. Autograph signing, member post-game meetings, online chat rooms.

unnecessary when demand is extremely strong (i.e., standing-room-only). However, programs can do more than reward. They also act as a form of two-way communication that enables brands to quickly disseminate information (game-time information, security efforts, franchise response to a PR crisis, etc.).[76] For instance, in the WNBA the Los Angeles Sparks team isn't just serving up points on the basketball court any more, they also look at how to engage fans. Their loyalty program Home Court Advantage, which debuted in May 2006, goes beyond just letting game attendees earn points and redeem rewards. Yes, patronage is important, with rewards for attending home games or back-to-back games. But the program also promotes friend referral (WOM recommendations), information sharing (online survey feedback), and interest in Sparks community events (CSR). These activities often satisfy CRM goals for greater efficiencies and deeper connections with patrons.

A new CRM system launched at USC supports integrated ticketing, marketing, and fundraising efforts there via database management. Arizona State University (ASU) also has a fully integrated CRM system that optimizes sales efforts. Tracking ticketing, fundraising, and consumer trends with a data warehouse solution can allow customer initiatives to be a data-driven decision. Competition was the main reason behind ASU's move to develop a CRM strategy, which had seven primary goals: (a) identify profitable customers, (b) understand online/offline customer behavior, (c) increase sales and affinity through one-to-one marketing, (d) help retain the "right" customers, (e) help increase fan loyalty and affinity, (f) maximize overall revenue generated per customer through all channels, (g) target and increase value for sponsors through data mining. The university's CRM strategy primarily centered on a web portal, the Devil's Domain, accessed through the athletic department's website.[77] The program collects basic information from fans, including birthdays, ticket purchasing preferences, and favorite ASU sports. In exchange for this information members received free access to the Devils Domain portal, ticket and merchandise discounts, newsletters, and exclusive video highlights. Essentially, the online portal had five dynamic elements to add value to the relationship it wanted to establish with loyal members:

- Devil's Insider, a newsletter that provides an exclusive inside look into ASU athletics.
- Devil's Screensaver, delivers daily action photographs, news ticker, game schedules, etc.
- Devil's Informer, keeps members updated with the latest happenings (roster, strategy, tickets).
- Sun Devil Minute, a weekly video retrospective produced by Fox Sports. Emailed to members, the link provides insider analysis and student-athlete features.
- Devil's Advantage, offers members special offers on tickets, concessions, and merchandise.

Conclusions

Building brand loyalty remains one of the key issues for marketers. The discussion throughout this chapter has primarily explained who or what constituted loyalty and how important it was to an organization. Attitudinal and behavioral distinctions were made to provide practitioners with some hands-on advice for developing an environment conducive to developing customer engagement. This included some discussion of barriers to patronage (negatives) and what can be done to remove or minimize their effects. Lastly, the final section talks about how marketing relationships with customers can be monitored and nurtured. This unpacks CRM and loyalty programs as tools for connecting with and adding value to a fan's engagement with the brand.

References

1. Benedikt, J., & Kunz, W. (2012). How to transform consumers into fans of your brand. *Journal of Service Management, 23*(3), 344–361.
2. Jacoby, J., & Chesnut, R. (1978). *Brand loyalty measurement and management.* New York: John Wiley and Sons.
3. Mahony, D. F., Madrigal, R., & Howard, D. R. (2000). Using the psychological commitment to team (PCT) scale to segment sport consumers based on loyalty. *Sport Marketing Quarterly, 9*(1), 15–25.
4. Oliver, R. L. (1999). Whence consumer loyalty? *Journal of Marketing, 63*(3), 33–44.
5. Reichheld, F. F. (1996). *The loyalty effect.* Boston, MA: Harvard Business School Press.
6. Russell-Bennett, R., McColl-Kennedy, J. R., & Coote, L. (2007). Involvement, satisfaction, and brand loyalty in a small business services setting. *Journal of Business Research, 60*, 1253–1260.
7. Pritchard, M. P., & Negro, C. (2001). Sport loyalty programs and their impact on fan relationships. *International Journal of Sports Marketing & Sponsorship, 3*(3), 317–338; and McDonald, M. A., & Milne, G. R. (1997). A conceptual framework for evaluating marketing relationships in professional sport franchises. *Sport Marketing Quarterly, 9*(2), 27–32.

8. Kraft, P. & Lee, J. W. (2009). Protecting the house of Under Armour. *Sport Marketing Quarterly, 18*(2), 112–116; and Jarvis, L. P., & Mayo, E. J. (1986, November). Winning the market-share game. *Cornell Hotel Restaurant Administration Quarterly, 27*, 73–79.

9. Pritchard, M. P. & Funk, D. C. (2006). Symbiosis and substitution in spectator sport. *Journal of Sport Management, 20*, 297–320.

10. Keaveney, S. M. (1995). Customer switching behavior in service industries: An exploratory study. *Journal of Marketing, 59*(2), 71–82.

11. McDonald, H. (2010). The factors influencing churn rates among season ticket holders: An empirical analysis. *Journal of Sport Management, 24*(6), 676–701.

12. Bristow, D. N., & Sebastian, R. J. (2001). Holy cow! Wait 'til next year! A closer look at the brand loyalty of Chicago Cubs baseball fans. *Journal of Consumer Marketing, 18*(3), 256–275.

13. Funk, D. C., & Pritchard, M. P. (2006). Sport publicity: Commitment's moderation of message effects. *Journal of Business Research, 59*(5), 613–621.

14. Pritchard, M. P., Howard, D. R., & Havitz, M. E. (1992). Loyalty measurement: A critical examination and theoretical extension. *Leisure Sciences, 14*, 155–164.

15. Mahony, D. F., Madrigal, R., & Howard, D. R. (2000). Using the psychological commitment to team (PCT) scale to segment sport consumers based on loyalty. *Sport Marketing Quarterly, 9*(1), 15–25.

16. Heere, B., & Dickson, G. (2008). Measuring attitudinal loyalty: Separating the terms of affective commitment and attitudinal loyalty. *Journal of Sport Management, 22*, 227–239.

17. Day, G. S. (1969, September). A two-dimensional concept of brand Loyalty. *Journal of Advertising Research 9*, 29–35.

18. Roush, M. (2012, September 3). Michigan hotel occupancy rates at all-time high. CBSNews Detroit. Retrieved from http://detroit.cbslocal.com/2012/09/03/2012-michigan-hotel-occupancy-rates-at-all-time-high/

19. Muret, D. (2011, February 7). Super Bowl sets per cap record of $89 at Cowboys Stadium. *Sport Business Daily*. Retrieved from www.sportsbusinessdaily.com/Daily/Closing-Bell/2011/02/07/SB-percap.aspx

20. Mayer, J. (2010, October 23). Sounders FC's success resonates globally. *Seattle Times*. Retrieved from http://seattletimes.nwsource.com/ABPub/2010/10/24/2013243638.pdf

21. Anonymous. (2011). NHL season-ticket renewal rate more than 90% in '11-'12. *Sport Business Journal*. Retrieved from www.sportsbusinessdaily.com/Daily/Issues/2011/10/06/NHL-Season-Preview/Season-Tickets. aspx?hl=NHL%20Season-Ticket%20Renewal%20Rate%20More%20Than%2090%25&sc=0

22. Anonymous (2012, August 20). NFL sees promise with attendance as season-ticket renewals are up. *Sport Business Journal*. Retrieved from www.sportsbusinessdaily.com/Daily/Issues/2012/08/20/Leagues-and-Governing-Bodies/NFL-Tickets.aspx

23. McDonald, H. (2010). The factors influencing churn rates among season ticket holders: An empirical analysis. *Journal of Sport Management, 24*(6), 676–701; McDonald, H., & Stavros, C. (2007). A defection analysis of lapsed season ticket holders: A consumer and organizational study. *Sport Marketing Quarterly. 16*(4), 218–229.

24. Mullin, B. J., Hardy, S., & Sutton, W. A. (2000). Sport marketing (2nd ed.). Champaign, IL: Human Kinetics; Sutton, W. A., McDonald, M., & Milne, G. (1997, March). Escalating your fan base. Athletic Management, 4–6.

25. Mullin, B. J., Hardy, S., & Sutton, W. A. (2000). Sport marketing (2nd ed.). Champaign, IL: Human Kinetics; Sutton, W. A., McDonald, M., & Milne, G. (1997, March). Escalating your fan base. Athletic Management, 4–6.

26. Lachowetz, T., McDonald, M., Sutton, W., & Clark, J. (2001). The National Basketball Association: Application of customer lifetime value. *Sport Marketing Quarterly, 10*(3), 57–59.

27. Funk, D. C., & James, J. D. (2001). The Psychological Continuum Model (PCM). A conceptual framework for understanding an individual's psychological connection to sport. *Sport Management Review, 4*, 119–150.

28. Day, G. S. (1969, September). A two-dimensional concept of brand Loyalty. *Journal of Advertising Research 9*, 29–35.

29. Pritchard, M. P., Howard, D. R., & Havitz, M. E. (1992). Loyalty measurement: A critical examination and theoretical extension. *Leisure Sciences, 14*, 155–164.

30. Pritchard, M. P., Havitz, M. E., & Howard, D. R. (1999). Analyzing the commitment-loyalty link in service contexts. *Journal of the Academy of Marketing Science, 27*(3), 333–348.

31. Backman, S. J., & Crompton, J. L. (1991). Using a loyalty matrix to differentiate between high, spurious, latent and low loyalty participants in two leisure services. *Journal of Park and Recreation Administration, 9*(2), 1–17; and Pritchard, M. P., & Howard, D. R. (1997). The loyal traveler: Examining a typology of service patronage. *Journal of Travel Research, 35*(4), 2–11.

32. Mahony, D. F., Madrigal, R., & Howard, D. R. (2000). Using the psychological commitment to team (PCT) scale to segment sport consumers based on loyalty. *Sport Marketing Quarterly, 9*(1), 15–25.

33. Stewart, B., Smith, A., & Nicholson, M. (2003). Sport consumer typologies: A critical review. *Sport Marketing Quarterly, 12*(4), 206–216.

34. Heere, B., & Dickson, G. (2008). Measuring attitudinal loyalty: Separating the terms of affective commitment and attitudinal loyalty. *Journal of Sport Management, 22*, 227–239.

35. Dick, A., & Basu, K. (1994). Customer loyalty: Toward an integrated conceptual framework. *Journal of the Academy of Marketing Science, 22*(Spring), 99–113; and Oliver, R. L. (1999). Whence consumer loyalty? *Journal of Marketing, 63*(3), 33–44.

36. James, J. D. (2001). The role of cognitive development and socialization in the initial development of team loyalty. *Leisure Sciences, 23*, 233–262.

37. Funk, D. C., & James, J. D. (2006). Consumer loyalty: The meaning of attachment in the development of sport team allegiance. *Journal of Sport Management, 20*, 189–217.

38. Pritchard, M. P., & Howard, D. R. (1997). The loyal traveler: Examining a typology of service patronage. *Journal of Travel Research, 35*(4), 2–11.

39. Trail, G. T., Anderson, D. F. & Fink, J. S. (2005). Consumer satisfaction and identity theory: A model of sport spectator conative loyalty. *Sport Marketing Quarterly, 14*(2), 98–111.

40. Pritchard, M. P., Havitz, M. E., & Howard, D. R. (1999). Analyzing the commitment-loyalty link in service contexts. *Journal of the Academy of Marketing Science, 27*(3), 333–348.

41. Funk, D. C., & James, J. D. (2006). Consumer loyalty: The meaning of attachment in the development of sport team allegiance. *Journal of Sport Management, 20*, 189–217; Pritchard, M. P., Stinson, J., & Patton, E. (2010). Affinity and affiliation: A dual carriage-way to team identification. *Sport Marketing Quarterly. 19*(2), 67–77.

42. Oliver, R. L. (1999). Whence consumer loyalty? *Journal of Marketing, 63*(3), 33–44.

43. Bristow, D. N., & Sebastian, R. J. (2001). Holy cow! Wait 'til next year! A closer look at the brand loyalty of Chicago Cubs baseball fans. *Journal of Consumer Marketing, 18*(3), 256–275; Wakefield, K. L., & Sloan, H. J. (1995). The effects of team loyalty and selected stadium factors on spectator attendance. *Journal of Sport Management, 9*, 153–172.

44. Pritchard, M. P., & Funk, D. (2010). The formation and effect of attitude importance in professional sport. *European Journal of Marketing, 44* (7/8), 1017–1036.; and Olsen, S. O. (2007). Repurchase loyalty: The role of involvement and satisfaction. *Psychology & Marketing, 24*(4), 315–341; and Beatty, S., Kahle, L,. & Homer, P. (1988, March). The involvement-commitment model: Theory and Implications. *Journal of Business Research, 16* 149–167.

45. Funk, D. C., & James, J. D. (2001). The Psychological Continuum Model (PCM). A conceptual framework for understanding an individual's psychological connection to sport. *Sport Management Review, 4*, 119–150.

46. Funk, D., Beaton, A., & Pritchard, M. P. (2011). The stage-based development of physically active leisure: A recreational golf perspective. *Journal of Leisure Research, 43*(2): 268–289; and Funk, D. C., & James, J. D. (2006). Consumer loyalty: The meaning of attachment in the development of sport team allegiance. *Journal of Sport Management, 20*, 189–217.

47. Van Doorn, J., Lemon, K. N., Mittal, V., Nass, S., Pick, D., Pirner, P., & Verhoef, P. C. (2010). Customer engagement behavior: Theoretical foundations and research directions. *Journal of Service Research, 13*(3), 253–266.

48. Assael, H. (1995). *Consumer behavior and marketing action*, (5th Ed.). Cincinnati, OH: South-Western College Publishing; and Oliver, R. L. (1999). Whence consumer loyalty? *Journal of Marketing, 63*(3), 33–44.

49. Owen, P., & Weatherston, C. (2004). Uncertainty of outcome, player quality and attendance at national provincial championship rugby union matches: An evaluation in light of the competition review. *Economic Papers, 23*, 301–324.

50. Lepisto, L., & Hannaford, W. (1980). Purchase constraint analysis: An alternative perspective for marketers. *Journal of the Academy of Marketing Science, 8*(1), 12–25.

51. Keaveney, S. M. (1995). Customer switching behavior in service industries: An exploratory study. *Journal of Marketing, 59*(2), 71–82.; and Hightower, R., Brady, M., & Baker, T. (2002). Investigating the role of the physical environment in hedonic service consumption: An exploratory study of sporting events. *Journal of Business Research, 55*, 697–707.

52. Ganesh, J., Arnold, M., & Reynolds, K. (2000). Understanding the customer base of service providers: An examination of the differences between switchers and stayers. *Journal of Marketing, 64*(3), 65–87.

53. Alexandris, K., Funk, D., & Pritchard, M. P. (2011). The impact of constraints on motivation, activity attachment and skier intentions to continue. *Journal of Leisure Research, 43*(1), 56–79; and Alexandris, K., & Carrol, B. (1999). Constraints on recreational sport participation in adults in Greece: Implications for providing and managing sport services. *Journal of Sport Management, 13*(2), 317–332.

54. Pritchard, M. P., Funk, D., & Alexandris, K. (2009). Barriers to repeat patronage: The impact of spectator constraints. *European Journal of Marketing, 43*(1/2): 169–187.

55. Bristow, D. N., & Sebastian, R. J. (2001). Holy cow! Wait 'til next year! A closer look at the brand loyalty of Chicago Cubs baseball fans. *Journal of Consumer Marketing, 18*(3), 256–275.

56. Jackson, E., Crawford, D., & Godbey, G. (1993). Negotiation of leisure constraints. *Leisure Sciences, 15*(1), 1–11.

57. Bauer, H., & Sauer, N. (2005). Customer-based brand equity in the sport team industry. *European Journal of Marketing, 39*(3/4), 496–513; and Bristow, D. N., & Sebastian, R. J. (2001). Holy cow! Wait 'til next year! A closer look at the brand loyalty of Chicago Cubs baseball fans. *Journal of Consumer Marketing, 18*(3), 256–275; Wakefield, K. L., & Sloan, H. J. (1995). The effects of team loyalty and selected stadium factors on spectator attendance. *Journal of Sport Management, 9*, 153–172.

58. Back, T., Blatter, P., & Bughin, J. (2004, July). Playing to win in the business of sports. *McKinsey Quarterly*. Retrieved from http://www.mckinseyquarterly.com/article_page.aspx?ar=1454&l2=16&l3=20&srid=7&gp=1

59. Tian, S., Crompton, J., & Witt, P. (1996). Integrating constraints and benefits to identify responsive target markets for museum attractions. *Journal of Travel Research*, 35(2), 34–45.

60. Pritchard, M. P., Funk, D., & Alexandris, K. (2009). Barriers to repeat patronage: The impact of spectator constraints. *European Journal of Marketing, 43*(1/2): 169–187.

61. Sheth, J., & Frazier, G. (1982). A model of strategy mix choice for planned social change. *Journal of Marketing, 46*(1), 15–26.

62. Mahony, D. F., Madrigal, R., & Howard, D. R. (2000). Using the psychological commitment to team (PCT) scale to segment sport consumers based on loyalty. *Sport Marketing Quarterly, 9*(1), 15–25.

63. McDonald, M. A., & Milne, G. R. (1997). A conceptual framework for evaluating marketing relationships in professional sport franchises. *Sport Marketing Quarterly, 9*(2), 27–32.

64. Kotler, P. (2002, May 30). *When to Use CRM and When to Forget It*. Presentation given at The Academy of Marketing Science Conference, Fort Myers, Florida.

65. Sharp, B., & Sharp, A. (1997). Loyalty programs and their impact on repeat purchase loyalty patterns. *International Journal of Research in Marketing, 14*(5), 473–486.

66. Darko, K. (1999, September). Batter up! Loyalty programs give sport teams much-needed demographic information about their fans. *American Demographics*, 39–41.

67. Johnson, K. (1999). Making loyalty programs more rewarding. *Direct Marketing, 61*(11), 24–27.

68. Yi, Y., & Jeon, H. (2003). Effects of loyalty programs on value perception, program loyalty, and brand loyalty. *Journal of the Academy of Marketing Science, 31*(3), 229–240.

69. Pritchard, M. P., & Negro, C. (2001). Sport loyalty programs and their impact on fan relationships. *International Journal of Sports Marketing & Sponsorship, 3*(3), 317–338.

70. Yi, Y., & Jeon, H. (2003). Effects of loyalty programs on value perception, program loyalty, and brand loyalty. *Journal of the Academy of Marketing Science, 31*(3), 229–240.

71. Pritchard, M. P., & Negro, C. (2001). Sport loyalty programs and their impact on fan relationships. *International Journal of Sports Marketing & Sponsorship, 3*(3), 317–338.

72. Butler, D. (2012, June 4). How colleges are adopting pro concepts in ticketing, CRM. *Sport Business Journal*. Retrieved from http://m.sportsbusinessdaily.com/Journal/Issues/2012/06/04/Opinion/DaveButler.aspx?hl=IMG&sc=0

73. Peppers, D. & Rogers, M. (1996). *The one to one future*. New York: Crown Business Publishing Group.

74. Leyland, M. (2011, November 18). Loyalty program aims to draw students to other sports. Retrieved from http://www.atvn.org/news/2011/11/trojan-fever-loyalty-program

75. Kotler, P. (2002, May 30). *When to Use CRM and When to Forget It*. Presentation given at The Academy of Marketing Science Conference, Fort Myers, Florida.

76. Pritchard, M. P., & Negro, C. (2001). Sport loyalty programs and their impact on fan relationships. *International Journal of Sports Marketing & Sponsorship*, 3(3), 317–338; and McDonald, M. A., & Milne, G. R. (1997). A conceptual framework for evaluating marketing relationships in professional sport franchises. *Sport Marketing Quarterly, 9*(2), 27–32.

77. Anonymous. (2003, July 15). Arizona State to launch Devil's Domain: Free program allows fans an inside look at Sun Devil athletics. Retrieved from http://www.thesundevils.com/genrel/071503aaa.html

9

Leveraging Sport Brands with the Servicescape

Roscoe Hightower, Jr., Ph.D.
Professor of Marketing
Marketing & Management Department
School of Business and Industry
Florida A&M University

Abstract: This chapter uses the current services marketing literature regarding the built environment (i.e., servicescape) and discusses using the sport organization's servicescape to leverage its corporate brand. This "leveraging" can lead to the creation of a sustainable competitive advantage for the firm, which can have a positive influence on the firm's triple bottom line. The professional baseball industry is used to provide examples of how this can be accomplished.

Keywords: branding, built environment, corporate brand, professional baseball, servicescape, sports

Introduction

The servicescape, or service setting, plays a critical role in shaping customer expectations, differentiating service firms, facilitating customer and employee goals, and influencing the nature of customer experiences. The servicescape can influence critical customer relationship goals from the initial attraction of the customer through to retention and even enhancements of the relationship.[1]

For the foreseeable future, the services industry will provide the majority of new jobs to developed countries' economies. As such, more focus should be placed on truly understanding the services industry as a whole. With respect to this chapter, the service industry includes, but is not limited to, the following economic activities: trade; transport; communications; government, financial and business services; personal, social, and community services. Services, for the purposes of this chapter, are defined as any deed, act, or performance. Marketing is defined as a simple exchange that results in value being obtained by all participants in the exchange. That value is suggested to be the resultant of a "gets" minus "gives" calculation in the consumer's mind, where the "get" variable component can be anything and the "gives" variable component refers to things that may be sacrificed (i.e., money, which is a direct cost, along with non-pecuniary costs such as time, effort, and risk associated with the purchase) by the consumer. The services marketing literature started around the mid to late 1960s, and it has progressed steadily to the beginning of the second decade of the 21st century.

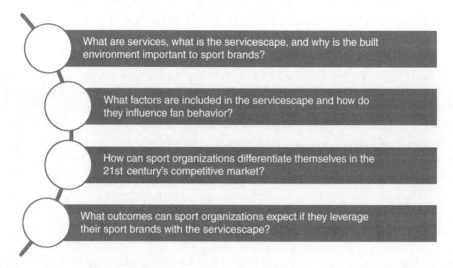

Figure 9.1 An Overview of Chapter 9

This chapter is about the services marketing term "servicescape." Mary Jo Bitner first used the term in a 1992 conceptual article in the *Journal of Marketing*. As she described in her research, the term had come from an older marketing term known as "atmospherics." That term can be traced back to the environmental psychology literature's "ergonomics," and even further back to "man's proximate environment" in the 1960s and earlier. This chapter explains the current and future servicescape directions as they relate to corporate branding.[2] The author utilizes examples from the professional baseball industry in order to demonstrate several concepts within the chapter based on the model in Figure 9.2.

Figure 9.2 is adapted from Hightower, Brady, and Baker's 2002 depiction of the servicescape's relationship with several key items in the professional sports industry. As titled, the figure suggests that the servicescape can be used to leverage positive brand-related outcomes such as consumer loyalty for the sport organization. When the servicescape is correctly leveraged to enhance the sport brand, a sustainable competitive advantage can result for the firm that will significantly contribute to the entity's triple bottom line. (Triple bottom line for the purposes of this chapter refers

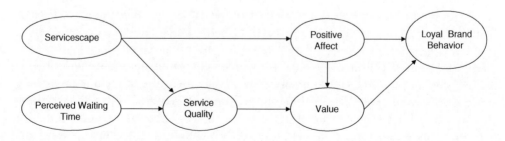

Figure 9.2 The Role of the Servicescape in Brand Research (Adapted from Hightower, Brady, and Baker, 2002)

to the current business practice of focusing not only on the firm's financial profitability, but also on the firm's social and environmental performance as well.) The triple bottom line firm takes a more holistic approach to operating the business than do its traditional "profit only" competitors, and should have a long-term advantage (i.e., respective to the traditionalists) due to the unsustainable nature of utilizing a "profit only" business model in the 21st century. The main message provided by Figure 9.2 is that the physical environment plays a similar role to a physical good's package in that it communicates an image of what is included in the service experience to the market segment for which the service is intended and to differentiate a service firm from its competitors.

Servicescape Background

Work on the servicescape is multidisciplinary and comes from research conducted by several different scholars.[3] The servicescape consists of three levels in a hierarchical factor structure: (a) an overall, (b) a dimension, and (c) a sub-dimension level. These three servicescape levels can be found in the services marketing as well as the facilities management literatures, as indicated by a forthcoming article on innovation entitled "Investigating the Green Leadership in Energy and Environmental Design (LEED) Servicescape Scale in Brazil." This work was done with Brazilian consumers in the context of several service industries associated with futbol in Maracanna Stadium.

Although the researchers have slightly different views regarding the servicescape definition, the common core shared by them is the general feeling that the physical environment has a direct relationship with customer behavior. The definition of servicescape employed in this chapter is explored in greater detail in the next several paragraphs.

So, what is encompassed in the servicescape? The servicescape is defined as everything that is physically present about an individual during the service encounter. Bitner defined the servicescape as the "built environment."[4] This definition has been interpreted to include man-made, physical surroundings as opposed to the natural or social environment. In contrast, Kotler defined the buying environment as the effort to produce specific emotional effects in buyers in order to enhance purchase probabilities.[5] Baker and her colleagues also include the "non-built" environment in their definition of the store environment as consisting of three sets of factors: (a) store ambient factors, (b) store functional/aesthetic design factors, and (c) store social factors.[6]

The definition of the servicescape is not restricted to the "built" environment, if "built" is used to imply physical construction. Rather, the marketing exchange environment appears more appropriately defined as conceptualized by such environmental psychologists as Sommer.[7] Termed "proximate" environments, store environments are conceptualized in the environmental psychology literature to include everything that is physically present.[8] That is, the store environment is considered to be everything that is observable by the consumer when he or she is present at a specific purchase location. This is said to include (a) biotic and (b) physical environments. The former refers to the world of living things, whereas the later includes entities created by humans; respectively, "non-built" and "built" environments.

The servicescape properly represents both the animate and inanimate stimuli to which a consumer is exposed during a service encounter. More specifically, both the marketing and environmental psychology literatures lend support to the proposition that during service encounters consumers may be affected by any, or all of, three sets of stimuli; (a) ambient factors, (b) design factors, and (c) social factors. These three factors form the basis of the servicescape conceptualization used in this chapter, and each is discussed next.

Ambient Factors

Ambient factors are defined as nonvisual, background conditions in the service environment. The ambient factor contains those factors that tend to impact the subconscious. Ambient factors generally exist below the level of customers' immediate awareness, so customers may be less than totally aware of these conditions in the environment. Some examples of ambient environmental conditions are lighting, temperature, music, scent, and cleanliness. Consumers expect a certain level of ambient environmental conditions to exist and may be unaware of these background factors unless the factors are absent or are unfavorable.

The environmental psychology literature suggests that, consistent with the Stimulus-Organism-Response (S-O-R) paradigm, ambient factors may act as stimuli (S) that contain cues that affect consumers' internal evaluations (O), which in turn create approach/avoidance responses (R). The (S-O-R) paradigm acts as a foundation for integrating a sport organization's corporate brand with its servicescape. Specifically, in this chapter, the link is supported based on the Stimulus-Organism-Response (S-O-R) paradigm, where physical or social stimuli (i.e., corporate sport brand) directly affect the emotional state of a person, which in turn influences their behavior.

Design Factors

Design factors are environmental elements that are more visual in nature than are ambient factors. The design factors include stimuli (i.e., things) that are salient or, in other words, visual cues that make one think verbally of what is seen. The design component has two sub-dimensions: functional and aesthetic. The sub-dimensions for the purposes of this chapter can be thought of as two separate but related groups of design factors. The functional sub-dimension includes components such as layout, comfort, privacy, ingress ability, and egress ability. The aesthetic sub-dimension includes architecture, color, style, materials, and fixtures. In general, aesthetic factors are more tangible than ambient factors and may have a stronger impact on the servicescape, on purchase behavior, and on the corporate brand's potential impact.

Social Factors

Social factors are those stimuli (i.e., things) related to people that are present within the environment during a service encounter. It is acknowledged that the physical presence of other persons (i.e., employees, customers, media, and/or protesters, etc.) is a critical environmental element. The number, type, ethnicity, behavior of customers, and employees in the environment are relevant social factor elements. However, it is important to remember that social factors *can* include multiple items for human behaviors similar to the items offered in Figure 9.3 for corporate brand, potential impact, and challenges.

The social factor can also be thought of as the people component of the sport organization's environment. The social factor has two sub-dimensions (or groups): service employees and other patrons in the environment. The sport service employees' appearance, behavior, and accessibility (i.e., number) can affect the way a consumer perceives the sports firm. The number of other patrons (i.e., crowding), dress code, and behavior of other patrons affects the way a consumer perceives the sport service firm as well. The social factor also supports the (S-O-R) paradigm. Studies indicate that such social factors as crowding, the number of employees, and the appearance of employees can act as stimuli (S) that influence consumers' inferences about their service encounters (O) and thereby their decision to approach or avoid a specific service provider (R), as depicted by the steady professional baseball attendance figures that indicate consumers are attending more games despite the difficult economic times experienced in the United States since 2009.[9]

Why is the Servicescape Important?

Marketing hedonic services (i.e., more specifically, sports activities) has become big business around the world. Each of the four major U.S. professional sports leagues (NBA, NFL, MLB, and NHL) has registered high attendance levels during the past few years, and the number of people attending college sporting events continues to increase. Recent data indicated MLS may potentially surpass the NBA in attendance. According to Forbes[10] the average major league baseball (MLB) team's value rose 16% in 2011 to an all-time high total of $18.15 billion for the league or roughly $605 million average for each of the 30 teams. It should be noted here that each team has its own market value, ranging from a high of $1.85 billion to a low of $321 million. Revenue was on average $212 million per team after payments to cover stadium debt, or about $6.36 billion for the entire league. Operating income fell 13% to an average of $14 million per team or $420 million in aggregate for the league. A total of 73,425,568 people attended 2011 regular season games.

The servicescape will be discussed in such a way that readers can develop a solid understanding of the topic, which enables them to be able to develop a sustainable competitive advantage for the sports firm, and to potentially prepare themselves for managerial oversight in this area. The chapter should also help readers to understand the servicescape's contribution to the brand's triple bottom line. Recent empirical research demonstrates sport organizations can improve the probability of positive customer behavioral intentions by enhancing the perceptions of value and positive affect as well as increasing the arousal level of the sport consumer by manipulating the servicescape.

On the surface, the attendance increase identified above appears to bode well for sport marketers. However, at the same time, the cost of attending these sporting events has increased dramatically. This price increase phenomenon places tremendous financial pressure on competing sport organizations, especially from a local marketing perspective. Professional baseball organizations, entities, and stadiums will be used for demonstration purposes in this chapter, but the ideas provided applies to virtually every professional sports league and team in the world.

There is an affinity for professional baseball for any number of reasons. Number one in particular is the family value provided to its fans, as opposed to other professional sports leagues in the U.S. marketplace. As an example, in 2011 U.S. dollars, a family of four (two adults and two children) could enjoy a minor league baseball game for $59.77 or a Major League Baseball game for $197.35. However, the same family of four would pay $287.85 to attend an NHL game, $326.45 for an NBA game, and a whopping $427.42 for one NFL game. Also, minor league baseball (MiLB) has approximately 160 teams, which translates into actual presence in 43 states and one Canadian province, meaning they are almost everywhere in the United States. Third, 2011 saw 41,252,053 people attend MiLB games.[11] And last but not least, minor league baseball as a business is removed from dealing with player personnel issues based on MiLB's contractual relationship with Major League Baseball, Inc. With the personnel issues removed from the basic business analysis, focus can be placed on investigating other key variables of interest such as the team's stadium or the organization's triple bottom line.

MiLB's business model at the individual organization level can be simplified to the following, according to Pat O'Conner, President and CEO of MiLB: ". . . minor league baseball's business model is dependent on three things: 1) cold beverages, 2) hot hotdogs, and 3) good fun."[12] One might ask, "How is attendance going to continue to grow into the foreseeable future given the current competitive environment described in brief previously?" The answer is depicted in Figure 9.2 via leveraging the sport organizations' corporate brand with the servicescape. In order to continue to increase attendance, marketers will have to improve efforts to market their services to those fans who are less knowledgeable about the sporting event itself, but who are attracted by peripheral aspects of the sports event such as the environment in which the event is held. The Master's at historic Augusta National, center court at the All-England Club's Wimbledon grand–slam tournament, the winner's circle at Derby Downs during the Kentucky Derby, or Oriole Park at Camden Yards are just a few examples of venues with this type of corporate brand potential impact.

Servicescape Discussion

For the purposes of this chapter, Hightower and Shariat's[13] definition of the servicescape as everything that is physically surrounding an individual at any given moment during the service encounter is utilized. The physical environment affects and shapes cognitive and emotional responses as well as behavior. The consumers' behaviors may mirror their respective opinion of the corporate sport brand, the potential impact, and the challenges associated with the organization.

The servicescape can cause a consumer to respond cognitively, emotionally, and/or physiologically. These responses are what shape a consumer's behavior. The servicescape can also be thought of as a form of nonverbal communication (i.e., of the sport brand, etc.)

that creates meaning through environmental cues. Some empirical findings suggest that sport consumers rely on environmental cues like those found in a stadium in much the same way that they rely on packaging to categorize and form their initial beliefs about consumer goods. In addition, the more recent literature suggests that consumers may seek tangible cues (i.e., servicescape) to predict what the sports team will actually provide to the ticket purchasers.[14]

It is suggested that the importance of the service provider's physical facility to consumers depends on the nature of the service work and the service consumption experience. It is also suggested that the physical environment is capable of performing several different roles at once. The literature suggests that the physical environment can take on the role of a package, a facilitator, a socializing agent, and/or a differentiator, especially when utilized to leverage the firm's corporate brand.

It is further proposed that the servicescape plays a role similar to a physical good's package, in that it basically communicates an image of what is included in the service. The facilitator role is demonstrated when the servicescape increases or restricts the efficient flow of activities during the service encounter. The socializing role of the servicescape appears when it communicates various roles, behaviors, and relationships to employees and consumers. It is suggested that a sport organization or any service firm can use its servicescape to signal the market segment for which the service is intended and to differentiate the service firm from its competitors.

Shortcomings of Sportscape

Sportscape is another term loosely used in the literatures to attempt to capture the essence of a sport organization's physical environment. Sportscape is partially based on the Mehrabian-Russell model, with the authors substituting their "sportscape" factors for the two major environmental stimuli topics focused on by the Mehrabian-Russell model: (a) the environmental impact of physical stimuli, and (b) the effect of physical stimuli on a variety of behaviors such as work performance or social interaction. They used a Stimulus-Organism-Response (S-O-R) paradigm to offer a description of environments, intervening variables, and behavior relevant to the consumer. They theorized that physical or social stimuli in the environment directly affect the emotional state of a person, which in turn influences their behaviors. In other words, they suggest that the physical environment (i.e., servicescape) affects a consumer's shopping behavior (i.e., fan loyalty in professional baseball's case). Mehrabian and Russell also suggest that three emotional response variables (i.e., pleasure, arousal, and dominance, or the PAD model) summarize the emotion-eliciting qualities of environments and can be seen as having a positive effect on the consumer (see Figure 9.3). This PAD is suggested to serve as a mediator in determining a variety of approach-avoidance behaviors such as physical approach, work performance, exploration, and social interaction that are also synonymous with the relationships depicted in Figure 9.3.

Wakefield, Blodgett, and Sloan do not include arousal in their sportscape model.[15] They review Bitner's framework and suggest that her three environmental components can be reduced to two components, ambient conditions and interior layout and

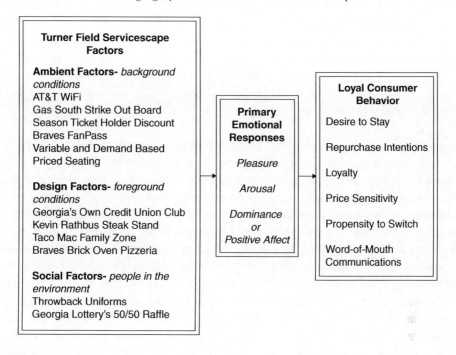

Figure 9.3 The Impact of Turner Field Servicescape Factors on Consumer Responses (Adapted from Mehrabian and Russell, 1974)

design.[16] Wakefield, Blodgett, and Sloan define "sportscape" as the fixed elements in the environment.[17] They do not focus on the ambient conditions because they are considered transient and difficult to control by stadium management. Note here that simply because some items of interest may be more or less controllable by management is not clearance to remove these items from consideration in the overall research process. These and several other conceptual shortcomings point to sportscape's inability to reliably and validly depict the physical environment of multiple service venues across industries and countries. This has led some to lean on the more robust concept of the servicescape.

SERVQUAL Fallacy Note

It should be noted that the servicescape as defined herein is distinct from SERVQUAL. From a historical perspective, the SERVQUAL scale was originally composed of two, 22-item Likert scales (i.e., total of 44 survey questions) that assessed customer's expectations and perception of service quality. The scale accomplished this by measuring the difference between perceptions (P) of service performance and service expectations (E). Some academicians, practitioners, and the media suggest that a consumer's service quality perceptions are synonymous with the SERVQUAL scale. However, numerous empirical studies have been conducted with respect to this, and for the record, the weight of the evidence supports the use of direct performance measures to represent service quality (rather than the P-E difference score SERVQUAL suggests). It is important to note that many marketing scholars continue to move away from issues over fine-tuning service quality measures to investigate more comprehensive explanations of how consumers respond to different situations and effects (e.g., as per Figure 9.2).

Corporate Brand Background

The corporate brand, also known as the organizational brand, defines what the firm is and does with respect to products, services, and customers. Branding has been discussed in great detail in other chapters in this book and the extant literature. However, the following discussion of MiLB's Project Brand will help explain the significant importance of sports entities, organizations, leagues, etc. leveraging the servicescape in order to elicit certain consumer behavior as it relates to the respective brand.

Project Brand, announced at the 2012 Winter Baseball Meetings in Nashville, Tennessee, is a new national marketing program that will leverage the collective brand equity of all 160 minor league teams and deliver the MiLB brand to the consumer more efficiently, emotionally, and in more impactful ways.[18] The key point here is the focus on emotion. As shown in Figure 9.3, emotions help shape / significantly influence fan behavior. The servicescape signals, creates, and sparks emotional responses from the consumer. Research has shown that the more arousal the servicescape creates in the consumer, the more likely the consumer will engage in loyal customer behaviors such as positive word-of-mouth communications.

Project Brand enables MiLB clubs to leverage the servicescape to engage the customer to visit the ball park and participate with the club via in-game branded trivia contests at certain locations or certain key events.[19] Another example could be the use of the electronic scoreboard to show entertaining videos, ads, etc. specifically designed to spur emotional responses in the fans while at the stadium. This in-stadium brand-building can accomplish many things, such as strengthening brand associations using the servicescape. Likewise, once almost forgotten simple techniques like sampling can be taken to a new level by using them in the right context, including the built environment, to provide the customers that come on the special night an opportunity to sample brands that they may not be aware of or have previously used.

Project Brand enables MiLB to be more flexible in its approach to obtaining sponsors and advertisers. This increased flexibility enables the league to leverage its built environment. MiLB is practically everywhere in North America. Facilities of all sizes, ages, and styles, numbering 160, across a continent equally as diverse and reflective of the consumers that have disposable income is a key factor to exploiting MiLB's investment in its real estate. It appears that these facilities' value to the overall business model is being increased through leveraging the servicescape by proactively and strategically planning for the future (i.e., programs like Project Brand). Another way to view servicescape's impact on sport entities that use their facilities to leverage the brand is to think in terms of a "game changer." In this sense, game changer means anything significantly changing the way the game is played once introduced. According to a MiLB 2012 Baseball Winter Meetings statement, "Project Brand, . . . is a transformational, quantum leap beyond past efforts that encompasses branding and marketing in their broadest definitions."[20] The servicescape used to leverage sport branding is a "game changer."

One of the main points of this chapter is to explain the business benefit of using the servicescape to leverage sport brands that can be associated with improving the organization's triple bottom line. The recent research demonstrates that firms that understand what the servicescape is and more importantly use it in combination with a branding strategy are more profitable than those entities that do not leverage the relationship between the brand and the servicescape. Let's use a middle of the pack "value ranked MLB team" by *Forbes Magazine* in 2012, the Atlanta Braves (i.e., ranked 15th of 30 in a 3/21/12 story) as an example.

Braves President John Schuerholz said, "We feel it's important to keep upgrading and improving Turner Field year after year. Our fans are looking for a fun night out that includes an exciting game, great service and great atmosphere and that is our goal each and every season."[21] That statement was not solicited from Mr. Schuerholz for the purposes of this textbook chapter; it was included in a 4/12/12 Atlanta Braves press release offered by the organization itself to inform their potential customers about the changes to Turner Field for the 2012 season. Meaning that as the 21st-century marketplace becomes increasingly more competitive for businesses (i.e., especially sport organizations with well-known established and mature corporate brands), the market leaders are looking for ways to further differentiate themselves from the competition by using their servicescape as a means to strengthen the corporate brand, garner positive potential impact, and address the challenges regularly associated with corporate branding.

There are at least nine benefits that a sport organization can obtain from leveraging its corporate brand with the servicescape. These are discussed in the next section. Keep in mind that the Atlanta Braves introduced 11 new things at Turner Field for the 2012 season that are directly part of the Turner Field servicescape and the Atlanta Braves corporate brand.

These additions to the Braves' corporate brand consist of multiple other brand usages in order to achieve things such as, but not limited to, the following: (a) using corporate programs as branded energizers, i.e., by introducing "AT&T WiFi" with more than 330 access points in the stadium for fans to stay connected to internal Braves marketing programs and to the World Wide Web while at the game, (b) establishing a Kevin Rathbun Steak concession stand by a local award-winning well-known Atlanta chef in Turner Field section 203, and (c) introducing the Gas South Strikeout Board that provides unique information about the pitcher and his stats.

Another heritage aspect of branding is Saturday and Sunday games reserved for the "throwback uniforms" such that the current Atlanta Braves organization can tie itself back to the 1966 and 1967 seasons. Even with these heritage uniforms the Braves are also moving forward by adding their new "crossed tomahawk logo" to the throwback uniform's sleeve, thereby leveraging and supporting internal brand-building, while at the same time making an effort to introduce a new Braves logo. The Braves organization is addressing some common brand challenges with the 2012 servicescape changes mentioned above by Mr. Schuerholz, such as creating value positions by featuring the 50/50 Raffle presented by the Georgia Lottery during the game at Turner Field. This is not just a simple "50/50" game; the winner gets his or her "50" but the other "50" goes to the Atlanta Braves Foundation that addresses things such as corporate citizenship as well as performance. Not to mention that a case can be made to show that the Georgia

Lottery 50/50 Raffle also addresses things like corporate values/priorities along with credibility for the Braves corporate brand.

Starting with the 2012 season, the Turner Field concession stands provide a Braves season ticket holders' price versus a non-season ticket holders' price for items purchased at every cash register. This drives the 33% discount or value position for all fans to observe and for season ticket holders to benefit from. All fans receive the value positions created by the Braves organization for the 2012 season ticket holders by simply noticing the price difference at the register. Each Turner Field visitor that uses the concession stands can start determining the "value" of being a season ticket holder for him or herself.

Prior research also shows us that the servicescape is mediated by cognitive responses. The objective here is to build on this knowledge base to consider these factors that influence the consumer behavioral intentions. In the concluding section, nine benefits of leveraging sport brands with the servicescape are proposed for consideration by the reader.

Benefits of Leveraging Sport Brands with the Servicescape

In addition to the conceptual work advanced in services marketing, other disciplines have contributed to unpacking the nature of the relationship between the physical environment and various consumer-related outcomes (i.e., firm performance, buying intentions, consumer pleasure and arousal). An example is found in the environmental psychology literature that first linked the physical environment to service firm success several decades ago. This connection is based on the Stimulus-Organism-Response (S-O-R) paradigm, where physical or social stimuli (i.e., corporate sport brands or the sportscape) directly affect the emotional state of a person, which in turn influences their behaviors. A later study in the retailing literature provided empirical evidence that the pleasure, arousal, and dominance derived from the physical environment influence retail outcomes such as:

1. the enjoyment of shopping in the store, the time spent browsing the store's environment,
2. the willingness to talk to employees, the tendency to spend more money than originally planned, and
3. the likelihood of returning to the store.[22]

Research has shown that the store environment plays a role in customers' willingness to buy, and for the purposes of this chapter, stadiums are suggested to be similar to the stores mentioned in 1-3 above.

Based on a review of the servicescape literature, the following benefits are suggested to exist for sport organizations or individuals that have developed an appreciation for and understanding of the servicescape as it relates to leveraging the corporate brand:

Benefit 1. Sport organizations that strategically plan their corporate brand make better decisions regarding the servicescape than sports firms that do not.

Benefit 2. Sport organizations that effectively brand their servicescape are more profitable than those organizations that do not. Some organizations may take the business position as briefly mentioned earlier when thinking about leveraging the firm's brand with the servicescape. For example, according to Dave Whinham, President and CEO of Revolution Enterprises, LLC, in a 2008 interview, "... the teams stick to what they can control, the stadium atmosphere and nightly promotions. You've got to really work to make sure the event is worth paying to see, that's not only your patrons' time but their money."[23]

Benefit 3. Sport organizations that leverage the corporate brand with the servicescape satisfy the customers moreso than those service providers who fail to effectively link the brand with its servicescape.

Benefit 4. The servicescape can have various levels of influence on the sport branding process. Some consumers form service opinions by means other than direct physical contact during part/all of the service encounter; others attend events for different reasons and form different perceptions as a result of those motivational benefits. The physical environment, when leveraged appropriately with the brand, can help the consumers form positive opinions about the services being offered and the brand itself. Reasons behind consumer approaching, avoiding, remaining in, or valuing the servicescape vary much as individual consumer emotional responses (pleasure, arousal, and dominance) result from a retail store experience. For instance, Sports Fan 1 may come to the game because of promotion price. Sports Fan 2 may come to the game because of the social networking opportunities/benefits. Sports Fan 3 may come to the game because of the environmental positioning of the team. As you can see from these three different fan possibilities, a sport organization has limitless ways to use the servicescape to enhance and/or leverage the corporation's brand.

Benefit 5. The servicescape, when effectively leveraged using the corporate brand, provides more cues regarding the sport organization's ability to deliver high service quality and customer satisfaction to the potential consumer than firms that do not actively utilize the servicescape to leverage the corporate brand for the consumer. It should also be noted here that even though service quality and customer satisfaction are closely related, the specific environmental circumstance may alter which of the two is given primary attention by the organization. Focusing on the wrong variable may reduce efficiency of effort and overall firm profitability.

Benefit 6. Sport organizations that leverage the corporate brand with the servicescape at the overall, dimension, and sub-dimension levels are more profitable than organizations that do not make this distinction.

Benefit 7. The corporate sport brand is maximized when the organization's servicescape is consistent with and conveys the sports firm's intended overall message to the consumer (i.e., mission, vision, and values statements).

Benefit 8. Sport organizations that focus on leveraging the servicescape tend to be more market oriented than those firms that do not seek to leverage their brand through in-park experience.

Benefit 9. Sport organizations that leverage corporate brands with the servicescape can develop a sustainable competitive advantage in the marketplace that differentiates the firm from its competitors. According to Brian Shallcross, Bowie Baysox General Manager, . ."whether it's the little slice of Camden Yards feel that Aberdeen's Ripken Stadium offers or relaxing in the lawn seating area beyond the Blue Crabs' outfield wall, each team's management strives to make its stadium a one-stop shop for fun and entertainment."[24]

Conclusions

The recent economic downturn (i.e., 2009–2012) both domestically and abroad has made consumers more conscientious with respect to how they spend their disposable income. Fierce competition in the marketplace places an ever-increasing demand on businesses to increase "value" for the consumer. So, how does a 21st-century sport organization create a sustainable competitive advantage that will add value to the triple bottom line?

Sport marketers must find ways to continue to enhance the experience fans have at sporting events if they are to continue to enjoy the level of growth that has been documented over the past few years. From a managerial perspective, this chapter highlights the importance of the servicescape as it relates to the quality of the sport experience, positive affect, and the organization's ability to leverage its brand. New innovations are needed, similar to the ones the Atlanta Braves introduced at Turner Field in 2012, that strengthen brands by providing a more attractive servicescape. These types of innovations not only increase the perceived quality, satisfaction, and brand awareness of fans, but also help enhance the new fan's experience, thus potentially turning them into a more loyal fan.

There is a suggestion in the branding literature calling for companies to focus on citizenship and performance as a way to help differentiate the organization from its competitors. In the 21st century this corporate citizenship and performance can be obtained by utilizing the ballpark to message a green marketing corporate mission/objective to the public and potential fans that may be seeking environmentally sensitive organizations to support. As stated earlier in the chapter, the intent here is to provide the reader with the ability to create a sustainable competitive advantage in the marketplace. Also, this sustainable competitive advantage will contribute directly to the sport organization's triple bottom line value, and that triple bottom line includes financial, social, and environmental aspects of the business.

Some firms account for the fact that a consumer does not always buy the highest quality service or the lowest cost service. Therefore, it appears that service organizations with limited resources may need to focus on areas other than typical ones (i.e., low cost provider, physical product components, etc.) for developing, maintaining, and expanding a sustainable competitive advantage in their industry. Fierce competition in the sport industry (e.g., network media rights for sport teams) means decisions some owners and front office personnel make may threaten long-term viability and place the organization at risk. A growing amount of research focuses domestically and internationally on the green LEED servicescape. Environmental stewardship and green in-park practices are becoming much more important that they were in the past.

Indeed, some potential consumers may be less knowledgeable about the sporting event itself, but more attracted by peripheral aspects of the product such as its "green LEED stadium environment."

The sport organization can leverage the servicescape and its brand to create a sustainable competitive advantage that will significantly contribute to the entity's triple bottom line. This is possible as depicted in Figure 9.2, because the physical environment (i.e., the servicescape) plays a similar role to a physical good's package in that it communicates a distinct image of what is included to the market segment for which the service is intended (i.e., the 2012 Atlanta Braves updates to Turner Field). Some sport organizations are using the servicescape and the emotional responses generated from it to influence fan behavior. Rhetorically, what would have happened to the Atlanta Braves' profitability (i.e., financially, socially, and environmentally) had they not made the 2012 Turner Field Updates?

Some forward thinking and profitable teams are finding answers to these and other strategic questions about leveraging a sport organization's brand with the servicescape. A good question to ask is whether you expanded your organization's overall business practices soundly by studying complex services marketing models similar to Figure 9.2, or whether you've simply been lucky so far with your previous decisions on major capital investments in facilities? Anecdotally speaking, it is said that with few exceptions sport organizations like most businesses attempt to build/acquire/obtain facilities for the least expensive price per square foot. Unfortunately for them, few are aware of the following small point of information: the building price, creation cost, or purchase/lease price is only roughly 15% of the total cost to acquire and operate that space over a normal useful life period. In other words, a large number of organizations in general are focused on the smallest price or cost when making decisions on acquiring facilities. Few focus on or are even aware of the 85% dollar amount (i.e., price, costs, etc.) that it takes in addition to the building/lease/rental/purchase/etc. price to operate the space over its useful life. This chapter strongly suggests developing an increased understanding of the built environment to leverage your organization's brand. This uses the servicescape as a strategic tool for keeping your organization effectively positioned to weather the fierce competition of the 21st century.

References

1. Bitner, M. J. (2000). The Servicescape. In T. Swartz & D. Iacobucci (Eds.), *Handbook of services marketing & management*. Thousand Oaks, CA: Sage Publications, Inc.
2. Bitner M. J. (1992, April). Servicescapes: The impact of physical surroundings on customers and employees. *Journal of Marketing, 56*, 57–71.
3. Hightower, R., Jr. (2010). Commentary on conceptualizing the servicescape construct in 'A Study of the Service Encounter in Eight Countries'. *Marketing Management Journal, 20*(1), 76–86; and Hightower, R., Jr., & Shariat, M. (2009). Servicescape's hierarchical factor structure model. *Global Review of Business and Economic Research Journal, 5*(2), 375–398; and Bitner, M. J. (1992, April). Servicescapes: The impact of physical surroundings on customers and employees. *Journal of Marketing, 56*, 57–71; and Baker, J. (1986). The role of the environment in marketing services: The consumer perspective. In J. A. Cecil (Ed.), *The services challenge: Integrating for competitive advantage (pp. 79–84)*. American Marketing Association, Chicago, IL; and Sommer, R. (1966). Man's proximate environment *Journal of Social Issues, 22*(4), 59–70.

4. Bitner M. J. (1992, April). Servicescapes: The impact of physical surroundings on customers and employees. *Journal of Marketing, 56*, 57–71.
5. Kotler, P. (1973). Atmospherics as a marketing tool. *Journal of Retailing, 49* (Winter), 48–64.
6. Baker, J. (1986). The role of the environment in marketing services: The consumer perspective. In J. A. Cecil (Ed.), *The Services Challenge: Integrating for Competitive Advantage* (pp. 79–84). American Marketing Association, Chicago, IL; and Baker, J., Grewal, D., Levy, M. (1992). An experimental approach to making retail store environment decisions. *Journal of Retailing, 68* (Winter), 445–460; and Baker, J., Grewal, D., Parasuraman, A. (1994). The influence of store environment on quality inferences and store image. *Journal of the Academy of Marketing Science, 22* (Fall), 328–339.
7. Sommer, R. (1966) Man's proximate environment. *Journal of Social Issues, 22*(4), 59–70.
8. Hall, E. T. (1963). Proxemics. In New York Academies of Medicine (Ed.) *Man's image in medicine and anthropology.* New York: International Universities Press; and Sommer, R. (1966). Man's proximate environment. *Journal of Social Issues, 22*(4), 59–70; and Mehrabian A., Russell, J. A. (1974). *An approach to environmental psychology.* Cambridge, MA: Massachusetts Institute of Technology.
9. Kronheim, D. (n.d.). Minor League Baseball 2011 attendance analysis. Retrieved from www.numbertamer.com
10. Anonymous. (2012, March 21). The business of baseball 2012. *Forbes Magazine*
11. Bitner M. J. (1992, April). Servicescapes: The impact of physical surroundings on customers and employees. *Journal of Marketing, 56*, 57–71.
12. Anonymous.(2010). Direct quote from Pat O'Conner public statements at Business of Baseball presentation 2010 Winter Baseball Meetings, Orlando, FL.
13. Hightower, R., Jr., & Mohammad, S. (2009). Servicescape's hierarchical factor structure model. *Global Review of Business and Economic Research Journal, 5*(2), 375–398; and Hightower, R., Jr., Brady, M. K., & Baker, T. (2002). Investigating the role of the physical environment in hedonic service consumption: An exploratory study of sporting events. *Journal of Business Research, 55*(9), 697–707.
14. Ibid.
15. Wakefield, K. L., Blodgett, J. G., & Sloan, H. J. (1996, January). Measurement and management of sportscape. *Journal of Sport Management, 10*, 15–31.
16. Bitner M. J. (1992, April). Servicescapes: The impact of physical surroundings on customers and employees. *Journal of Marketing, 56*, 57–71.
17. Wakefield, K. L., Blodgett, J. G., & Sloan, H. J. (1996, January). Measurement and management of sportscape. *Journal of Sport Management, 10*, 15–31.
18. Anonymous. (2012, April 12). MiLB written communication on Project Brand announcement 2012 Baseball Winter Meetings, Nashville, Tennessee
19. Ibid.
20. Ibid.
21. Anonymous. (2012, April 12). Plenty of new things at Turner Field will greet fans in 2012. Atlanta Braves Press Release.
22. Donovan, R. J., Rossiter, J. R. (1982) Store atmosphere: An environmental psychology approach. *Journal of Retailing, 58* (Spring), 34–57.
23. Farmer, L. (2008, August 15). At Maryland's six minor league baseball stadiums, the game is only a small part of the experience. *Baltimore Daily Record.*
24. Ibid.

10

Brand-Event Fit in Sport Sponsorship

Kevin Gwinner
Kansas State University

Abstract: Sport sponsorship is an important and increasingly popular method for firms to build awareness for their brand as well as position their brand in the mind of their targeted consumer. Some evidence has emerged in the academic literature suggesting that when sponsoring brands "fit" with the event being sponsored they are more effective (e.g., brand recall, event attitude, and stock price). In the marketing and sport sponsorship literature, the fit or congruence construct has been defined in numerous ways (e.g., functional based, image based, historical relationship based, etc.). Additionally, a variety of theoretical perspectives (e.g., schema theory, attribution theory, etc.) by which fit/congruence is proposed to influence sponsorship effectiveness have been offered. In this chapter, brand fit with a sponsored event is discussed in terms of what fit means, the benefits of fit in sport sponsorship, and if fit can be created when not naturally present.

Keywords: brand, congruence, event, fit, sponsorship, sport

Introduction

A long-term relationship approach to business partnerships reflects the current best practice and thinking among leading companies in the world. Rather than focusing on the "one time" sale, those firms opting for competitive advantage are concerned with customer satisfaction, repeat sales, and upgraded sales over time as the business relationship between the customer and selling firm matures and deepens. Sport sponsorship arrangements should be viewed with this same long-term, relational approach in order to reap the maximum benefit for both the sponsor and the sport organization.[1] Most sports and event marketing managers will be able to list a variety of benefits that accrue to the sports team or event when they are able to keep their current sponsors happy and returning year after year. Benefits for the sport organization in this setting include year after year renewal of the sponsorship, increasing levels of sponsorship, and positive associations with the sponsoring brand. However, what is it that the sponsoring brand receives from the sponsor arrangement that will keep them coming back year after year?

Because a sponsor's repeat patronage depends on their satisfaction, one can look to how well their goals are being met in the sponsorship arrangement to understand the likelihood of their continuing sponsorship investment. Sponsoring brands will have a variety of goals related to their decision to sponsor a sporting event (or any event, for that matter). Although support of socially responsible causes (e.g., breast cancer awareness events, Special Olympics) may be pursued for purely altruistic motives, more and more sponsoring organizations are seeking to understand how their support not only helps the

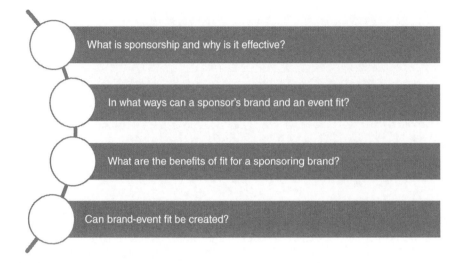

Figure 10.1 An Overview of Chapter 10

charitable organization being sponsored, but also serves as a promotional opportunity for the brand.[2] This is even more the case with the sponsorship of sporting events (e.g., The Rose Bowl presented by Vizio) and stadiums (e.g., Sports Authority Field at Mile High Stadium) where no charitable cause is evident. Common promotional goals include hospitality opportunities for the sponsor's clients, increasing consumer awareness among the sponsor's target markets, and creating image associations through the sponsorship. Prior research in sponsorship has found that several of the goals most important to sponsors, most notably awareness and image goals, are influenced by the perceived fit between the sponsoring brand and the organization/event being sponsored. As such, for a sport organization looking to attract sponsors, understanding the issue of fit as it relates to current and potential sponsors can help in selecting sponsors, selling to sponsors, retaining sponsors, and upgrading sponsors. For companies looking to sponsor sporting events, understanding the role of fit can help in selecting from among the many events vying for their sponsorship dollar. This chapter takes a detailed look at sponsor fit so that sport organizations can take informed steps to better maintain long-term relationships with their sponsoring partners.

First, as outlined in Figure 10.2, we review sponsorship in general, including what it can do for a brand, how prevalent sponsorship is, and how results can be measured. Then, we explore the issue of fit in depth. The concepts of types of fit, the benefits of fit, and creating fit are addressed in that discussion. We conclude with a discussion of competitive advantage through sponsorship.

Sponsorship

Although sponsorship has some similarities to advertising and philanthropy, Speed and Thompson[3] suggest that sponsorship differs from advertising and altruism due to the presence of a third party and a commercial motivation. The definition by

Figure 10.2 Key Questions in Sport Sponsorship

Meenaghan[4] is frequently used in the academic literature to define sponsorship. His definition states that sponsorship is "the provision of assistance either financial or in-kind to an activity or commercial organization for the purpose of achieving commercial objectives" (p. 9). Thus, this definition places an emphasis on the exchange aspect of sponsorship, with the objective of meeting business goals. Another definition of sponsorship focuses on "sponsorship-linked marketing",[5] which is described as the "orchestration and implementation of marketing activities for the purpose of building and communicating an association to a sponsorship" (p. 15). This definition places emphasis on the notion that the association benefits of sponsorship are not automatic, but instead must be developed through the brand's promotional activities. Taking these two definitions together, sponsorship can be thought of as a commercial exchange to achieve business goals for both sponsor and sponsee through association. The benefits to the sponsee are typically in the form of a financial fee, while the sponsor often seeks heightened brand awareness, or a more favorable image or attitude toward their product.

The association with the event is largely what the financial or in-kind assistance (from Meenaghan's definition) is paying for, but success in creating these associations is only effective when activation, or leveraging, is a key component of the sponsorship investment. Fullerton[6] defines activation as "the set of strategic efforts that are designed to support and enhance the sponsorship" (p. 209). This can require a significant investment by the sponsor above and beyond the cost of the sponsorship. Estimates for effective activation often range from one to three times the cost of the sponsorship fees, and include activities such as advertising the sponsorship, incorporating the event logo into the brand's packaging, distributing free products or premiums at the event, and implementing a consumer sales overlay to distribute discounted tickets with each product purchase. In truth, the range of possible activation activities is only limited by the imagination and budget of the sponsoring brand. The key goal of activation is to associate the sponsor and the property in the mind of the consumer. In doing so, the affinity felt for the team, sport, or event becomes associated with the sponsoring brand.

Activation is the mechanism for taking the rights fees that have been purchased and turning them into a meaningful and positive association. Southwest Airlines provides a recent example of sponsorship activation using multiple approaches. Southwest Airlines renewed its home game sponsorship of the NBA's Denver Nuggets. To properly make the association between the Nuggets and Southwest Airlines, the sponsorship activation includes in-arena signage, promotions, and contests. As a way to celebrate the continued relationship, and as another way to activate it, Southwest Airlines hosted a "Bags Fly Free" event on opening night outside of the Pepsi Center where the Nuggets play. The first 40 fans to arrive at the tent and say "Bags Fly Free only on Southwest Airlines" were entered into a drawing for a chance to win tickets to the Nuggets' games and roundtrip tickets on Southwest Airlines. As such, because of the location of the contest and the prizes involved, a link is made between Southwest Airlines and the Denver Nuggets.

Support has been found for the idea that the image of the sporting event is transferred to the sponsoring brand (the sponsor) from the event (the sponsee) through the associations that are built through sponsorship.[7] This image transfer process is based on an "associative memory" view of brand image[8], which holds that a brand's image is composed of all of the associations that consumers link with the brand (e.g., high quality, durable, fashionable). These associations come from a variety of sources such as price information, personal experiences with the brand or product category, packaging, advertising, etc. For example, if consumers view plastic packaging as durable (perhaps compared to cardboard packages), then the durable aspect of the package will become associated in memory with the product inside the package. Likewise, in a sport sponsorship context, an event perceived as prestigious may have that association transferred to the brands that sponsor that event. This process is consistent with the manner in which celebrity endorsement has been proposed to work.[9] Specifically, the image of the celebrity endorser (e.g., Tiger Woods) is transferred to the endorsed brand (e.g., Buick) when the two are paired in an advertisement.

A good example of this is the endorsement of Transamerica by golfer Zach Johnson. To capitalize on the tremendous success that Zach Johnson has had on the golf course in the PGA, Transamerica has developed and executed a number of print advertisements, website pages, and television commercials. Their primary focus is to link qualities that Transamerica feels are embodied in Mr. Johnson and can be transferred to their financial services firm. Chief among these attributes are power, strategy, and performance, all of which are prominently mentioned in the advertisements. In sport sponsorship it is generally thought that the image of the event (e.g., the Masters Golf Tournament) is transferred to, or becomes affiliated with, the image of the sponsor (e.g., IBM). However, it is interesting to consider when the transfer direction might go the other way, from brand to event. Such a circumstance might occur if the brand's image was strongly entrenched in consumers' minds and the event's image is less developed, as perhaps in the case of a new event. In this case, the brand has an image, but the event does not, and therefore the association direction is in the direction of the event.

Sponsorship's Effectiveness

One reason that company spending on sponsorship activities is so high is that it appears to work. Sponsorship research has linked sponsorship to positive outcomes such as higher brand recall and awareness, positive attitude toward the sponsors, and stronger purchase intentions.[10,11] Generally, sponsorship recall has been shown to work as expected, in that prominent sponsors that have a strong association with the event are more easily recalled than those that do not.[12] Although one study found that accurate recall in a field test was relatively modest, it also found recall increased with the number of games the fan attended.[13] That study provides support for the proposition that fans may use a sponsor's relatedness with the event (i.e., fit) in their attempt to verify vague recollections of which firms were the sponsor.

In a study of managers' perceptions of the value of sponsorship, it was found that among those responsible for making sponsorship arrangements, most felt that participation in sponsorship activities contributed to the ability of their brand to differentiate itself from competitors and added financial value to the sponsoring brand.[14] Indeed, research has found that the impact of a firm announcing "official product" status with many professional sports leagues has led to increases in shareholder wealth as measured by movement in stock prices following such announcements.[15] Similar stock price increases were found with regard to announcements of stadium naming rights, another form of sponsorship.[16]

Another indication of the perceived effectiveness of sponsorship is its continued growth. The IEG Sponsorship Report shows sponsorship expenditures across all categories (e.g., sports, causes, arts, etc.) by North American countries grew by 3.9% to $17.2 billion in 2010 (globally sponsorship spending topped $46.3 billion).[17] Although sponsorship is possible for a variety of events, sport sponsorships dominate, generating the most sponsorship dollars and visibility of any type of sponsorship, with sports accounting for 68 cents out of every dollar spent on sponsorship.[17] Even in the economically uncertain year of 2011, sponsorship growth showed no signs of stopping, with the four major U.S. professional sports leagues increasing sponsorship revenue by 7.9% that year.[18] As such, from a magnitude perspective, there is a reason to focus on sport sponsorship. However, in addition to the size of sport sponsorship, the inherent excitement generated by sports competition and the fierce levels of loyalty many spectators have for teams and events are key reasons that sport sponsorship in particular can be valuable to brands.

Three areas of sponsorship may represent unique challenges to companies hoping to use this medium to promote their brands. First, unlike more traditional forms of advertising, the message is not central for the viewers.[19] That is, the message is processed peripherally rather than centrally due to the audience's main focus being on the sporting event itself.[20] Unlike a television advertisement or a direct mail piece where an engaged viewer is listening to or reading the advertiser's message, in sponsorship there are less explicit forms of promotion linking the event and the brand. Common techniques include perimeter signage at arenas, mentions by broadcasters during the event, and onscreen exposure through television coverage of the scoreboard where the sponsor's logo appears. This less direct form of promotion (presence rather than preaching) is one reason that activation plays such an important role in making the association between the event and the sponsoring brand.

A second challenge for sponsorship is in the number of sponsors competing for attention at many events. The term sponsorship "clutter" is used to describe instances of overwhelming numbers of corporate sponsorships. In such a crowded field it is more difficult for any one sponsor to stand out from the crowd and be recognized by the audience. There is no better example of sponsorship clutter than at a NASCAR race, where it is common to see a racecar adorned with more than 15 sponsor logos of varying size and location prominence. Obviously, for the viewers watching these cars zoom by at 200 miles an hour, identifying sponsors can be difficult. Clearly the more sponsors, the less likely it is that a strong association will be made with the sport property.

Finally, a third challenge for sponsors comes from non-sponsoring brands attempting to associate themselves with a sport property without paying rights fees. Referred to as "ambush marketing," this occurs when a non-sponsoring brand engages in a promotional strategy attempting to capitalize on the popularity/prestige of a property by giving the false impression that it is a sponsor. Despite the recent efforts of some sport entities (e.g., FIFA and the Olympics) to enact rules and policies designed to stamp out ambushing, the fact remains that in most forms (and in most countries) it is not an illegal activity. The popularity of ambushing has grown due to the desire of many companies to avoid paying high rights fees, a lack of concern by the public, and accepting attitudes among companies toward engaging in ambush tactics. Ambushing can take many forms, including (a) sponsoring media broadcasts of the event, (b) using themed advertising, such as Nike using soccer-themed ads during the World Cup, (c) sponsoring individual players, (d) giving away merchandise (especially visible merchandise such as hats and shirts) that fans may choose to wear into the event, and (e) running contests that have prizes related to the sport (e.g., equipment or tickets). Regardless of the specific form that is taken by the ambush, it represents a challenge for actual sponsors because it creates confusion and additional clutter around the event, making it more difficult to establish the desired association between the legitimate sponsoring brand and the event.

Return on Investment

In the early days of sponsorship, a company sponsorship decision was often considered a form of philanthropy. This is not the case anymore. Sponsorship decisions are weighed carefully by most sophisticated companies and the money spent on sponsoring the event is considered an investment where appropriate returns are expected.[21] Despite large amounts of spending on sponsorship, sophisticated measures of sponsorship effectiveness are not common.[22] Most often sponsorship effects are discussed in terms of exposure; for example, how many minutes corporate signage at an event was broadcast over media, how many column inches are written about the sponsorship, or how many individuals were exposed to the corporate name at the event.[2] These measurements are then converted to a dollar amount representing the cost of purchasing an equivalent amount of advertising exposure. Several authors have criticized media exposure as a valid measure of sponsorship effectiveness, or at least have suggested that this form of measurement is guilty of overestimating sponsorship's impact.[21] Though media exposure measure may be a proxy for evaluating awareness objectives, it does little to show the effectiveness of image transfer.[22] Indeed, as Crompton notes, "as pressure on companies increases to demonstrate the return on sponsorship investments, many of them are likely to look to sport managers for the expertise to undertake evaluation studies. Increasingly, companies are requiring proposal packages seeking their support to include evaluation measures" (p. 280).[21] Instead of media equivalent types of measures, other goals can be assessed by directly surveying customers. These would include awareness levels, changes in image, and purchase intentions.

Brand-Event Fit

In the context of celebrity endorsers, much time, thought, and effort goes into considering who will be the "right" endorser for a particular brand. Attractiveness, expertise, and likability have long been characteristics sought in endorsers of products. However, having an endorser "fit" with the brand he or she is endorsing is also a consideration. Till and Busler[23] examined fit of an endorser with respect to how much expertise they have about the product category, with high fit being associated with endorsers who knew a lot about the product category (e.g., professional golfer Phil Mickelson and golf clubs). Thus, the more effective endorsements will come when there is a fit between the endorser and the product. In a similar way, sponsors act as endorsers of the event, in that they are offering their financial support to the sporting event. As the sponsor and sponsee become associated with each other, spectators, viewers, and participants will make judgments as to how well the two fit together. One might argue that Marlboro cigarettes do not fit well with the Ironman Triathlon, but perhaps Gatorade does. In a conceptual article with the aim of providing a framework for the various theoretical perspectives in sponsorship research, Cornwell, Weeks, and Roy[24] discuss congruence between the sponsor and event as the most frequently investigated concept in sponsorship research. The popularity of fit research in the sport sponsorship domain is due to both its innate appeal of matching similar things together and the strong research support found across many studies.

The term "elephant test" is sometimes used to describe situations in which an idea or object is hard to describe, but instantly recognizable when viewed. Fit between sponsor and sponsored event could be considered an idea where the elephant test might hold. Individuals (in the case of sports often taking the form of spectators, attendees, viewers, or participants) often will have a feel for whether a sponsor and the event fit together, even if they have difficulty in defining what makes it fit. Indeed, part of the confusion is the wide range of definitions, many of them rather vague, that are used to define fit in the literature. Fleck and Quester[19] have documented 16 different articles that define fit (called congruence in their article) in the sponsorship literature. Naturally, many of these definitions tend to evolve from the more general marketing literature, which often focused on fit between existing brands and new product extensions (e.g., Arm and Hammer Baking Soda introducing Arm and Hammer toothpaste).

Sometimes fit definitions are fairly general in nature, specifying a "link" between sponsor and event,[25] or a "logical connection" between sponsor and event (3).

Other researchers have attempted to more specifically categorize the type of fit. For example, McDonald[26] describes fit as occurring when the sponsor's product is used in the event (e.g., Pennzoil sponsoring a NASCAR race) or when some aspect of the sponsor is related to the event. He calls the first type "direct relevancy" and the second type "indirect relevancy." Gwinner[7] and Gwinner and Eaton[27] also use this approach, calling it "functional based" similarity when the brand is used during the event and "image based" similarity when the image of the brand is consistent with the image of the event (e.g., both brand and event are viewed as prestigious). The terms "logical link" and "strategic link" have been used to describe fit that occurs when the product is used in conjunction with the event (e.g., adidas shoes worn by players) and when the event audience and brand's target market match, respectively.[28] Others suggest the focus of fit should be shared attributes of the event and brand.[29] Recent work has used a broad approach to fit that argues consumers make judgments about fit on a number of dimensions. This describes high fit occurring when consumers perceive congruity between the brand and the sponsored event in areas of "mission, products, markets, technologies, attributes, brand concepts, or any other key association" (p. 155).[30]

Building on the idea that fit can be defined in many ways, Olson and Thjømøe[31] have put forth what they purport to be underlying dimensions of overall fit between a sponsor and an event. Their study identifies seven dimensions of fit: (i) use; (ii) size similarity; (iii) audience similarity; (iv) geographic similarity; (v) attitude similarity; (vi) image similarity; and (vii) time duration. One might think of these dimensions as different types of fit. Usage fit is achieved when sports participants or audience members are likely to use the sponsoring brand. Size similarity fit is when event and brand are either both large and prominent or both small and not prominent (i.e., there is a match in size). Audience similarity fit happens when the brand and the event share the same target audience. If both the brand and the event are national in scope or both are regional/local in scope, there is geographic similarity fit. Attitude similarity fit occurs when there is equal liking of both the brand and event. Image similarity fit occurs when both brand and event have the equivalent meaning or image. Finally, time duration fit is present when the brand and the event have a long history of association, regardless of their match on other fit types. That is, a brand may not fit in any other way, but because the brand has such a long history of supporting the event, the two are thought of as going together in the consumers' minds. Table 10.1 provides examples of the different fit types.

This notion of different fit dimensions or different types of fit begs the question of which is the best. That is, if a brand is seeking to engage in sport sponsorship, should it seek out an event that would result in a particular type of fit with the brand? Further, are multiple fits with a given event better than seeking an event with a single fit (i.e., is more better when it comes to fit)? Of course, this is a seemingly simple question with a complex answer, because the "best" fit depends on many factors. For example, the interplay between the fit type and the product category may influence which type is the best. Further, how "the best" is defined is a perplexing question that needs to be addressed. In some instances "best" might be measured by the pairing that results in the highest level of recall. But, of course, there are many other measures of "best" depending on the goals of the sponsoring brand. These could include changes in brand

Table 10.1 Fit Type Examples

Fit Type	Definition	Example*
Usage Similarity	When products made by the sponsoring brand are used during the event by spectators or participants.	Nike uniforms are used by players in the NFL.
Size Similarity	When sponsor and property are both small or both large in stature.	A local community bank and a local triathlon event are both small, local events.
Audience Similarity	When the target audience of the sponsoring brand is similar to the target audience of the event.	Axe deodorant and the Summer X-Games are both trying to appeal to an edgy, youth market.
Geographic Similarity	When both the sponsoring brand and the event operate in the same geographical region.	Jack Daniels and the Kentucky Derby both operate and are associated with the State of Kentucky.
Attitude Similarity	When both the sponsoring brand and event are equally liked by consumers.	Apple computer and the Olympics are both well regarded.
Image Similarity	When the image of the sponsoring brand and the image of the event are similar.	Lexus and the U.S. Open Tennis Tournament are both viewed as prestigious.
Time Duration	When the sponsoring brand has a long history of supporting the event.	Fed Ex has sponsored the Orange Bowl since 1991.

*Sponsor – Some brand-event pairings in the table are fictional, but illustrative of the pairing

attitude, purchase intentions, word-of-mouth propensity, and image change. Thus, what is deemed to be the best is dependent on what goals the firm is seeking to achieve through sponsorship.

Benefits of Fit

High levels of fit between the event and the sponsoring brand have been found to have many benefits for the brand. In a cause-related marketing context (e.g., we will donate $5 to charity X for every paid admission), donations to a high-fit charity can result in donation values 5 to 10 times greater than donations to low-fit charities.[32] Improving the attitude toward the sponsorship and/or the event has been a consistent finding in studies of fit. Roy and Cornwell[33] found that compared to low-fit brand-event pairings, sponsoring brands that were congruent with the sponsored event were viewed more positively by consumers. Presumably a more positive attitude toward the sponsor would ultimately result in higher purchase intentions. Likewise, Becker-Olsen and Simmons[34] found that a good fit between the event and brand resulted in higher attitudes toward the sponsor and the sponsorship. This same phenomenon, fit leading to positive attitudes, has been found in studies comparing websites with congruent and non-congruent sponsors.[10, 35] Indeed, fit's positive affect on attitudes toward sponsors is recounted by numerous studies.[30, 36, 37] In short, similarity breeds positive brand attitudes.

In addition to improved attitudes toward the brand, several other sponsorship outcomes are found to be enhanced through a good brand-event fit. Higher recall of the sponsoring brand has been found when the brand is related to the event.[38, 39, 35] Olson and Thjømøe[2] found that better fitting event-brand parings resulted in higher levels of attention to the sponsor, more favorable attitudes toward the sponsor, and a greater willingness to consider the sponsor's products. The impact of fit was magnified if the individual also had a strong affinity for the event. Cornwell, Pruitt, and Clark's[15] study was mentioned earlier in reference to the positive impact that public announcements of a brand becoming an official sponsor of a major sports league have on stock prices. With regard to fit, they find that when the brand is viewed as being congruent with the sponsored sports, the value of the share prices increased by an additional 11%. The generation of positive emotions about an event is also linked to fit. Martensen, Grønholdt, Bendtsen, and Jensen[40] found that fit is associated with positive emotions and negatively associated with negative emotions about an event. Research on the sponsorship of nonprofit organizations (e.g., Lowe's Home Improvement sponsoring Habitat for Humanity) finds that the nonprofit sponsee receives several benefits from being sponsored by a high-fit brand.[41] They find that "high-fit sponsorships help nonprofits build their brand identity via reinforcement of strong broad brand associations, strengthen specific brand associations related to integrity and nurturance that enhance brand meaning, and develop positive responses related to trust and sincerity of brands" (p. 78).

Creating Fit

What should a firm do if they decide to sponsor an event where there does not seem to be a readily apparent fit between their company's products and the event? Several reasons for doing so have been brought forth, including "(1) a desire to radically change an existing brand attitude or image, (2) a wish to continue with a sponsorship that was started before knowledge of poor fit was known, or (3) a sincere desire to use sponsoring as a way to support a worthy (but poor fitting) cause" (p. 64).[31] Another study suggested that the type of property selected for sponsorship is related to a corporation's identity as reflected in their mission statement.[42] This selection would seem to be without regard to the fit dimensions discussed earlier and instead more attuned to the type of corporate identity that is sought to be communicated. It turns out that even if sponsoring brand-event pairings are low in fit, explanations for why the brand is sponsoring the event can increase fit judgments. Research indicates that there is some value in "explaining" (called "articulation" in the sponsorship literature) to consumers why the firm is sponsoring a particular event, especially if a fit argument can be made. Weeks, Cornwell, and Drennan[36] examine sponsorship activation using online communications and find that that if a "sponsor-sponsee relationship has low congruence, then activational leveraging may help to enhance attitudes, but only when a non-commercially oriented explanation is used" (p. 651). That is, fit levels are raised when an argument not focusing on the business benefits of the sponsorship is put forward. Indeed, one study found that good articulation of the brand-event relationship resulted in a 30% increase in fit perceptions over bad articulation of the relationship.[31]

Fit might also be created through educational oriented communications that explain the basis for the match.[34] Research has shown in a social cause context that sponsorships have a more favorable effect when the communication about the sponsorship originates from the sponsored cause rather than from the sponsoring firm.[34, 30] Thus, the source of the message may have an impact when trying to convince an audience of fit. This gets to the idea of the consumer ascribing motivations to the sponsorship. Cornwell, Humphreys, Maguire, Weeks, and Tellegen[38] describe the concept of articulation as the brand's purposeful attempts to explain why it makes sense that they sponsor a particular event (i.e., to explain the fit between the two). Their study shows that low fit pairings can be strengthened through articulation. Roy and Cornwell[28] find that those spectators who are very knowledgeable of the event are better able than those with little knowledge to identify fit between events and brands of low brand equity (unfamiliar brands with few associations in memory). Further analysis showed that some experts were skeptical that low-equity sponsors should be associated with high-profile events. Thus, sponsors of high-equity brands may be better able than sponsors of low-equity brands to create congruence perceptions among those knowledgeable about the sporting event.

Incongruity in Event-Brand Pairings

An interesting counterargument to the notion that fit is a positive trait to be sought after in sponsorship has to do with some empirical findings and theoretical reasoning that suggest a slight lack of fit might be a good thing. Jarge, Watson, and Watson[43] postulate, based on congruity theory, that companies who sponsor events that are *inconsistent* with audience expectations (low fit) will have significantly higher recall rates than companies that sponsor events that are more consistent with audience expectations. Prior research has shown that information that is incongruent with prior expectations will result in individuals engaging in more effortful or elaborative processing, resulting in superior recall.[44]

Relatedly, Speed and Thompson[3] found, contrary to their hypothesis, that a high level of fit with a high-status event resulted in a negative impact on interest in the sponsor, attitude toward the sponsor, and willingness to buy the sponsor's products. In retrospectively trying to explain the unexpected finding, they suggest that sponsoring a high-status event may have been viewed as insincere by the respondents. Because the sponsor was viewed as commercially motivated instead of altruistically motivated, the effect on the interest, attitude, and purchase were diminished. They then argue that a degree of incongruence between event and sponsoring brand may be viewed as philanthropically motivated rather than commercially motivated.

From a theoretical perspective, some conceptualizations of schema theory suggest that a certain amount of incongruence makes one's brain work harder to understand why the two items are paired together, and may result in higher recall.[45] This results in greater elaboration and higher levels of awareness and recall. However, in a sponsorship context, low fit induced elaboration has been shown to be negatively biased and leads to unfavorable attitudes toward the sponsorship.[30] In addition to recall, schema theory can be used to predict affect for congruent versus incongruent pairs. Roy and Cornwell[33] found support consistent with schema theory that congruent sponsor-event pairings results in more positive affect.

Conclusion

What is the relevance of sponsorship in creating competitive advantage? The best competitive advantages are those that cannot be easily replicated by the competition. One mechanism that sponsorship uses in this regard is exclusivity arrangements. For example, an automobile manufacturer can lock in being the official "automotive" sponsor of a particular event, thus denying that opportunity to their competitors. Category exclusivity is rated as the most important benefit of sponsorship opportunities among sponsors.[46] Sponsorship works differently from advertising as a tool in the brand's promotional toolkit. Advertising's primary advantage over sponsorship is its ability to deliver a persuasive message. As discussed, sponsorship is more passive in that it is relying on the viewer/spectator to make the connection between the event and the sponsoring brand (presence rather than preaching). However, this image association is a powerful weapon for forming brand identity and is another aspect that is difficult for competitors to easily copy. As has been noted, there are tremendous advantages to having a good fit between the sponsor and the event. Companies should seek out sponsorship arrangements with strong fit to take advantage of these benefits. A still-open question is which type of fit will be best for matching companies and events. At this point in time there is little empirical evidence to guide those decisions. However, where poor fit exists there is an opportunity to create fit through activation efforts to inform the market as to why they should perceive some sort of fit, even if only loosely connected. Still, created fit may not be as effective as fit occurring naturally from one of the established types (i.e., use, size similarity, audience similarity, geographic similarity, attitude similarity, image similarity, or time duration).

Note

1. For simplicity, this chapter uses the term "event" to indicate the entity being sponsored by a company or a brand. It should be recognized that in most cases this entity could also be a specific team or facility (e.g., stadium orarena).

References

1. Farrelly, F. J., & Quester, P. G. (2005). Examining important relationship quality constructs of the focal sponsorship exchange. *Industrial Marketing Management, 34*, 211–219.
2. Olson, E. L., & Thjømøe, H. M. (2009). Sponsorship effect metric: assessing the financial value of sponsoring by comparisons to television advertising. *Journal of the Academy of Marketing Science, 37*, 504–515.
3. Speed, R., & Thompson, P. (2000). Determinants of sports sponsorship response. *Journal of the Academy of Marketing Science*, (2), 226–238.

4. Meenaghan, J. A. (1983). Commercial sponsorship. *European Journal of Marketing, 17* (7), 5–73.
5. Cornwell, T. B. (1995). Sponsorship-linked marketing development. *Sport Marketing Quarterly, 4*(4), 13–24.
6. Fullerton, S. (2010). *Sports marketing.* New York: McGraw-Hill/Irwin.
7. Gwinner, K. P. (1997). A model of image creation and image transfer in event sponsorship. *International Marketing Review, 14*(3), 145–158.
8. Keller, K. L. (1993). Conceptualizing, measuring, and managing customer-based brand equity. *Journal of Marketing, 57*(1), 1–22.
9. McCracken, G. (1989). Who is the celebrity endorser? Cultural foundations of the endorsement process. *Journal of Consumer Research, 16*(3), 310–321.
10. Rifon, N. J., Choi, S. M., Trimble, C. S., & Li, H. (2004). Congruence effects in sponsorship: The mediating role of sponsor credibility. *Journal of Advertising, 33*(1), 29–42.
11. Sneath, J. Z., Finney, R. Z., & Close, A. G. (2005). An IMC approach to event marketing: The effects of sponsorship and experience on customer attitudes. *Journal of Advertising Research, 45,* 373–381.
12. Wakefield, K. L., Becker-Olsen, K., & Cornwell, T. B. (2007). I spy a sponsor: The effects of sponsorship level, prominence, relatedness, and cueing on recall accuracy. *Journal of Advertising, 36* (4), 61–74.
13. Johar, G. V., Pham, M. T., & Wakefield, K. L. (2006, June). How event sponsors are really identified: A (baseball) field analysis. *Journal of Advertising Research, 46,* 183–198.
14. Cornwell, T. B., Roy, D. P., & Steinard, E. A. (2001). Exploring managers' perceptions of the impact of sponsorship on brand equity. *Journal of Advertising, 30*(2), 41–51.
15. Cornwell, T. B., Pruitt, S. W., & Clark, J. M. (2005). The relationship between major league sports' official sponsorship announcements and the stock prices of sponsoring firms. *Journal of the Academy of Marketing Science, 33,* 401–412.
16. Clark, J. M., Cornwell, T. B., & Pruitt, S. W. (2002). Corporate stadium sponsorships, signaling theory, agency conflicts, and shareholder wealth, *Journal of Advertising Research, 42,* 16–32.
17. IEG (2012a). IEG Sponsorship Report. Retrieved from https://www.sponsorship.com
18. IEG (2012b). Major Pro Sports Sponsorships to Total $2.46 Billion in 2011. Retrieved from https://www.sponsorship.com
19. Fleck N., & Quester P. (2007). Birds of a feather flock together . . . Definition, role and measure of congruence: An application to sponsorship. *Psychology & Marketing 24*(11), 975–1000.
20. Petty, R. E., & Cacioppo, J. T. (1983). Central and peripheral routes to persuasion: application to advertising. In L. Percy & A. Woodside (Eds.), *Advertising and consumer psychology* (pp. 3–23). Lexington, MA: D.C. Heath.
21. Crompton, J. L. (2004). Conceptualization and alternative operationalizations of the measurement of sponsorship effectiveness in sport. *Leisure Studies, 23,* 267–281.
22. Thjømøe, H. M., Olson, E. L., & Brønn, P. (2002). Decision making processes surrounding sponsorship activities. *Journal of Advertising Research, 42,* 6–15.
23. Till, B. D., & Busler, M. (2000). The match-up hypothesis: physical attractiveness, expertise, and the role of fit on brand attitude, purchase intent and brand beliefs. *Journal of Advertising, 29*(3), 1–13.
24. Cornwell, T. B., Weeks, C. S., & Roy, D. P. (2005). Sponsorship linked marketing: opening the black box. *Journal of Advertising, 34,* 21–42.
25. D'Astous, A., & Blitz, P. (1995). Consumer evaluations of sponsorship programmes. *European Journal of Marketing, 29*(12), 6–22.
26. McDonald, C. (1991). Sponsorship and the image of the sponsor. *European Journal of Marketing, 25*(11), 31–8.
27. Gwinner, K. P., & Eaton, J. (1999). Building brand image through event sponsorship: the role of image transfer. *Journal of Advertising, 28*(Winter), 47–57.
28. Roy, D. P., & Cornwell, T. B. (2004). The effects of consumer knowledge on responses to event sponsorships. *Psychology & Marketing, 21*(3), 185–207.
29. McDaniel, S. R. (1999). An investigation of match-up effects in sport sponsorship advertising: The implications of consumer advertising schemas. *Psychology & Marketing, 16*(2), 163–184.
30. Simmons, C. J., & Becker-Olsen, K. L. (2006). Achieving marketing objectives through social sponsorships. *Journal of Marketing, 70,* 154–169.
31. Olson, E. L., & Thjømøe, H. M. (2011). Explaining and articulating the fit construct in sponsorship. *Journal of Advertising, 40* (Spring), 57–70.
32. Pracejus, J. W., & Olsen, G. D. (2004). The role of brand/cause fit in the effectiveness of cause-related marketing campaigns. *Journal of Business Research, 57,* 635–640.
33. Roy, D. P., & Cornwell, T. B. (2003). Brand equity's influence on responses to event sponsorships. *Journal of Product & Brand Management, 12*(6), 377–393.
34. Becker-Olsen, K., & Simmons, C. J. (2002). When do social sponsorships enhance or dilute equity? Fit, message source, and the persistence of effects, *Advances in Consumer Research, 29,* 287–289.
35. Rodgers, S. (2003). The effects of sponsor relevance on consumer reactions to internet sponsorships. *Journal of Advertising, 32*(4), 66–76.

36. Weeks, C. S., Cornwell T. B., & Drennan J. C. (2008). Leveraging sponsorships on the Internet: Activation, congruence, and articulation. *Psychology and Marketing, 25*(7), 637–654.

37. Olson, E. L. (2010). Does sponsorship work in the same way in different sponsorship contexts? *European Journal of Marketing, 44*(1/2), 180–199.

38. Cornwell, T. B., Humphreys, M. S., Maguire, A.M., Weeks, C. S., & Tellegen, C. L. (2006). Sponsorship-linked marketing: The role of articulation in memory. *Journal of Consumer Research, 33*(3), 312–321.

39. Johar, G. V., & Pham, M. T. (1999, August). Relatedness, prominence, and constructive sponsor identification. *Journal of Marketing Research, 36*, 299–312.

40. Martensen, A., Grønholdt, L., Bendtsen, L., & Jensen, M. (2007). Application of a model for the effectiveness of event marketing. *Journal of Advertising Research, 47*, 283–301.

41. Becker-Olsen, K. L., & Hill, R. P. (2006). The impact of sponsor fit on brand equity: the case of nonprofit service providers. *Journal of Service Research, 9*(1), 73–83.

42. Cunningham, S., Cornwell, B., Coote, L., (2009). Expressing identity and shaping image: The relationship between corporate mission and corporate sponsorship. *Journal of Sport Management, 23*, 65–86.

43. Jagre, E., Watson, J. J., & Watson, J. G. (2001). Sponsorship and congruity theory: a theoretical framework for explaining consumer attitude and recall of event sponsorship. *Advances in Consumer Research, 28*, 439–445.

44. Heckler, S. E., & Childers, T. L. (1992, March). The role of expectancy and relevancy in memory for verbal and visual information: what is incongruency? *Journal of Consumer Research, 18*, 475–491.

45. Hastie, R. (1980). Memory for behavioral information that confirms or contradicts a personality impression. In R. Hastie, T. M. Ostrom, E. B. Ebbesen, R. S. Wyer, Jr., D. L. Hamilton, & D. E. Cariston (Eds.), *Person memory. The cognitive basis of social perceptions* (pp. 155–177). Hillsdale, NJ: Erlbaum.

46. IEG. (2012). Decision-maker survey: Sponsors report activation budgets have never been higher. Retrieved from http://www.sponsorship.com/Extra/IEG-Performance-Research-Study-Highlights-What-Spo.aspx

Part III

Topical Extensions

11

Recovery Marketing Strategies
A Continual Need in the Sport Industry*

Rick Burton
Syracuse University

Dennis Howard
University of Oregon

Abstract: The multi-billion-dollar global sport industry is frequently rocked with news of scandal, illegal maneuvering, or criminal activity. The consistency with which these events occur suggests future sport marketers should develop a heightened sensitivity to the likelihood that their brand (be it a league, team, player, owner, coach, consumer product or service) will suddenly come under intense scrutiny and receive significant negative attention. This can be debilitating and, if mismanaged, can hurt the future productivity and revenue-generating capacity of the entity. This chapter looks at meaningful ways in which sport marketers can better prepare to utilize recovery marketing strategies.

Keywords: brand image, media, negative PR, recovery strategy, scandal

Introduction

As most avid sports fans know, the thought that a sports league would lock out its players and potentially cancel regular season games is not a new one. The National Football League (NFL) and National Basketball Association (NBA) proved that convincingly in 2011 during protracted labor negotiations with their respective players' associations. And although the NFL settled with its players and didn't lose any regular season games, the NBA's lockout cost the league half a season and produced a great deal of negative media coverage and lost gate revenue.

Further, in what almost seems like a regular occurrence, the National Hockey League (NHL) shut down its league for the third time in 18 years on September 15, 2012. For many business operators (large or small), the concept of refusing to sell their product is unimaginable. But on September 16, NHL team owners prevented their players from practicing inside team-controlled facilities and from playing in league games.

*A variation of this work originally appeared as "Recovery Strategies for Sports Marketers" in the Spring 2000 issue of *Marketing Management*. It is presented here, in a revised form, with permission granted by the American Marketing Association.

**The authors would like to thank Syracuse University graduate sport management student Katie Rudy for her research support in making this chapter possible.

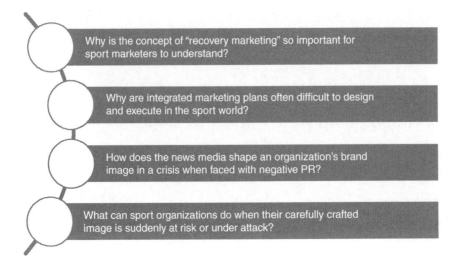

Figure 11.1 Overview of Chapter 11

By November, the League had cancelled its annual Outdoor Classic, a game traditionally played on New Year's Day in an open-air setting at a non-traditional hockey facility such as a football field or baseball stadium.

In the above situations, a business, due to labor disagreements, was unwilling to operate. Another image that unfortunately has become all too familiar in sports is that of an institution that suddenly must deal with horrific, damaging media coverage but still continue to function . . . and do so while the local, national, and international media are descending on that organization's main administrative office or corporate headquarters.

First to come to mind during the period of 2010–2012 was the image of intercollegiate athletic department administrators having to deal with matters ranging from philandering head coaches (Arkansas) to the urgent and significantly troubling matter of assistant coaches accused of criminal sexual behavior (Penn State, Syracuse). But that's not all. Universities were also accused of offering "phantom" courses to their NCAA stars (North Carolina) or illegally recruiting players for their football or basketball teams.

In the professional ranks, star athletes were accused of various criminal and ethical breaches, the most common tied to the issue of using performance-enhancing drugs. Here, the list of athletes implicated is simply too long to use parenthetical examples (and many, while not believed, have proclaimed their innocence). The most notable, however, would include Lance Armstrong, Roger Clemens, and Barry Bonds. Even the seemingly mundane reality of losing a star player for an entire season (think Peyton Manning of the Indianapolis Colts and the team's subsequent 0–13 start to the 2011 NFL campaign) is more commonplace than a student reader might imagine. What should the team do with printed marketing materials built around that star player? Adding to that, how should a professional franchise react when an owner cuts or trades that same legendary player and sends him into the free agency market?

Why Is a Recovery Strategy Necessary in Sport?

Does any of the above sound familiar? It should. That's because in the high-visibility, high-scrutiny world of sports marketing, the full script is rarely known and the outcomes are frequently unpredictable. It's why "recovery marketing" should be viewed as a fundamental and mandatory concept for most senior executives in the sport business community to master.

For many professionals, the concept of "recovery marketing" may be limited to their knowledge of the hotel or restaurant industry where a hurricane destroys an island or geographic region (think Hurricane Katrina in 2005 hitting New Orleans or 2012's Hurricane Sandy devastating parts of New York City and New Jersey). Some may think about a fatal airline crash or a cruise boat like the Costa Concordia sinking off the Italian coast in 2012.

For others, recovery marketing may invoke memories of an unseen consumer action such as the Tylenol product-tampering situation during the 1990s or the financial meltdown of the U.S. banking industry during the period of 2008–2011. It can even be created by a company's own marketing department. Such was the case when Coca-Cola decided to modify the taste of its then 99-year-old product in order to update the brand. The result: New Coke was rejected widely and Coca-Cola was forced to re-establish "traditional" Coke as its mainstay.

About the same time as the New Coke debacle, Swedish automaker Volvo decided to shoot a television commercial touting their safety features but got caught rigging their demonstration car with a special support system during the advertising's production. Readers can imagine the headaches of a safety-conscious company getting caught at what appeared to be "cheating" in the midst of promoting "safety" as a feature. The commonality in these situations is that the event's outcome or the media and public reaction was undesired, unexpected or, as it happened, unpredictable. Said another way, the history of the product's marketing had generally been unblemished (or managed for optimal brand attractiveness) and therefore had been reliable and un-remarked upon by the general community at large. That is, until the marketers lost control of their brand and short-term destiny.

Unfortunately, such loss of control is not unusual in the sports world. In fact, as sport marketers entered the second decade of the new millennium, they were increasingly realizing that it was only a matter of time before an unexpected "bombshell" was dropped on their laps. Want examples? There are too many to list, but a selection of 2011 or 2012 headlines might provide context:

1. "[Penn State's] Sandusky Indicted"[1]
2. "North Carolina's under-the-radar academic scandal continues to grow"[2]
3. "Badminton scandal rocks sport; 8 players expelled from Olympics"[3]
4. "New Orleans Saints defense had 'bounty' program, NFL says"[4]
5. "Doping scandal costs Lance Armstrong sponsors, charity role"[5]
6. "NBA lockout cancels the first two weeks of 2011–2012 NBA season"[6]

In the last headline shown above, the situation involved the National Basketball Association's 2011 decision to lock out their players and suspend play until an acceptable agreement could be reached with the League's Players' Association (NBPA).

It was the second time in less than six years that a major professional sports league had decided it was better to figuratively "take its product off the shelf" and not sell any product than to play games. The first situation involved the 2004–2005 NHL strike that cancelled an entire season, including the playing of the league's championship for the vaunted Stanley Cup. This was not the first time a league did not play for its season-ending title.

In 1994, Major League Baseball (MLB) effectively ended a particularly exciting base-ball season so completely that the game's World Series was not held for the first time in a season in which regular games were played. For some fans, the lingering and residual side effects of that strike lasted for years, as attendance and perceived avidity dropped.

Rick Welts, who was formerly an executive vice president and chief marketing officer of the NBA, was quoted after one NBA work stoppage in the 1990s as saying it was the most difficult year the league had ever been through. "We had a real resolve," said Welts, "that if we got it right, we would have an extended period of growth [for the NBA]. If we got it wrong, it would take a long time to get back." Although the NBA was ultimately able to secure a hard salary cap plus a rookie salary scale, and resume their games, albeit three months late, league officials like Welts were deeply concerned about how fans would react to a squabble among extremely wealthy players and even wealthier owners. "There was a lot of residual damage," said Welts. "It's like any other consumer product business—it can take years and years to come back. [For our part] we tried to learn from other sports about how to recover."

In some ways, the same situation existed in Salt Lake City prior to the 2002 Winter Olympics. Stung by global allegations (and convictions) that a bribing scandal had taken place, the once-pure Olympic movement was tarnished by fallout that seemed to be less about athlete greed or illegal substance abuse and more about influence, power, and benefits for International Olympic Committee (IOC) members. For Dick Schultz, then the executive director of the United States Olympic Committee (USOC), the Salt Lake City bid scandal created a firestorm of opinions by official Games' sponsors. Unfortunately, the scandal emerged just at the point when the Salt Lake Olympic Committee (SLOC) and USOC needed to conclude their fundraising in order to underwrite the competition. "Hopefully, [these convictions] won't refuel it," said Schultz at the time. "This is kind of a new twist on old news. You don't want to do something [wrong] that stirs people up again."[7]

In the case of sports, doing something wrong is why sport marketers who are dealing with professional sport franchises wring their hands and wipe their brows whenever they talk about building an integrated marketing plan. How can you confidently integrate marketing strategies when you can't control the most visible tactical elements (e.g., the team's performance, the star players, the coaches, or the owner)? Clearly, there are numerous uncontrollable variables and many of them, once exposed, are highly volatile when presented on the evening news.

Still, sport marketers must create compelling exchange daily and must be up to the task of addressing and recovering from acts of God (e.g., hurricanes, tornadoes, etc.), acts of Congress, and acts of criminal behavior. They must market their team or league after learning a star player spent the afternoon practice trying to strangle the head coach or after an ego-focused owner told a reporter he would move his storied franchise to another state if the city (and its taxpayers) didn't build him a new stadium.

Those team (or league) marketers may not control the product, pricing, or packaging but they still must observe the laws of disciplined thinking, strategic positioning, fiscal responsibility, and bottom-line accountability. On top of that, they must be willing, sometimes at significant cost, to protect the long-standing equity of the team, league, or organization. That's particularly hard if you know certain individuals have compromised the brand's position.

In the case of Coca-Cola, risk was less on the cola giant's mind, after the disastrous introduction of New Coke, than the "scientific approach" that allowed Coke executives "to look at data dispassionately" and "get on with trying the next experiment." According to Sergio Zyman,[8] Coke's former senior vice president of marketing, "Being able to stand up and say, 'That was a mistake and I want to correct it' is more important and powerful than saying 'I was right the first time and now I'm going to justify it.'"

Zyman wrote in his 1999 book, *The End of Marketing as We Know It*, "that under the old rules, we would have been so committed to proving we were right [about New Coke] that we would not have been able to admit even the possibility that we had a real problem—or opportunity—on our hands." Naturally, in hindsight, it is possible to bravely assert that the big cola machine, because of its market leadership position, was able to create new rules. What is more interesting, though, is the admission that a problem existed. Whereas a marketer at Coke, General Motors, or McDonald's is intimately familiar with the product and may be brought up through a rigid system of "conservative" marketing dictums, the touchstone remains that the organization controls the product.

Not so in sports marketing. Here, the players or participants control the action and frequently go in strange, unplanned directions on a moment's notice. As was seen during the 2012 NASCAR season, a race can end with drivers throwing racing helmets at moving cars (Tony Stewart) or pit crews brawling following a purposeful crash by a driver (Jeff Gordon). Or, even worse, as was witnessed in the final race of the 2011 Indy Car series, a Go Daddy promotional tactic to incent a driver to win $2.5 million (if they won the race after starting in last place) turned into a race-ending fatality when two-time Indy 500 champion Dan Wheldon was killed during the race at Las Vegas.

A baseball example could involve the unusual decision by the Washington Nationals to bench their star pitcher, Stephen Strasburg, before the 2012 season ended in order to protect his throwing arm. This decision was made due to frequent surgeries the right-hander had previously endured, but when the Nationals lost Game 5 of the National League Division Series at home to the St. Louis Cardinals, Nationals fans were understandably disappointed.

Mullin, Hardy, and Sutton[9] defined sport marketing as "consist[ing] of all activities designed to meet the needs and wants of sport consumers through exchange processes. Sport marketing has developed two major thrusts: the marketing of sport products and services directly to the consumers of sport, and marketing of other consumer and industrial products or services through the use of sports promotions" or sport imagery. They then added to their definition by noting that the term "sports consumers" covers a variety of involvement forms including "playing, officiating, watching, listening, reading and collecting." By some accounts, sports marketing might be viewed as being no different than toy marketing or consumer services marketing in general. Those individuals would suggest "marketing is marketing" regardless of specific category or industry. What makes sports marketing notable is perhaps its size, variability, and the passions it engenders among its targets, practitioners, and the executives or experts that evaluate marketing.

Sports Business Journal once ran advertising that suggested the size of the U.S. sports industry exceeded $194.64 billion.[10] By that tabulation, it would make activities involving sports (or sport imagery) one of the largest industries in America and a significant driver in the $15.17 trillion U.S. economy.[11] Naturally, it is difficult for experts to agree on what exactly constitutes "sports" but according to the SBJ article, the categories covered included sport product manufacturing, travel to sporting events, sponsorship, spectator spending, the staging of sports events, and licensing of sport product. Ultimately, we know sport are consistently present in the United States and many organizations are committed to reaching target consumers by selling them sport products or by employing sport imagery to sell more of their product.

One of the reasons professional sports is so popular is that when it is staged as a form of entertainment, it produces winners and losers and, in many cases, heroes and villains. When it is viewed as an individual exercise (i.e., running, hiking, climbing, fishing), it produces intense personal emotions/performances that are often hard to generate in most other pursuits. Thus, the marketing of sports involves unscripted moments, delivered by uncontrollable individuals, thinking highly personal thoughts. And sometimes, the outcomes of the participants are negative. This explains why sport marketers sometimes wake up in the morning and realize they have a fire burning. Maybe a player or coach got arrested or acted rashly under a harsh spotlight of media scrutiny. Maybe an advertisement inflamed or aggravated a demographic segment. Maybe the league's players just went out on strike or the league's owners locked the players out.

What Can Be Done?

Like many forms of marketing, a simple checklist can be constructed to ensure that sport marketers or senior executives involved with sport imagery think logically, functionally and proactively. Because time becomes critical in a negative situation, crisis leadership is significantly important and marketers must fully acknowledge the crucial role to be played by public relations specialists or executives.

Here are a few questions that can help shape any situation that suddenly (and unpredictably) unfolds that threatens to damage a brand's recognition or assessment:

1. What is the essence of the problem?
2. How are our core consumer and fringe consumer likely to react?
3. What contingency planning steps have been previously designed for this type of issue?
4. Does our contingency planning address this "hot" issue? If not, what is different from what we expected and what is now needed?
5. Has our public relations staff/agency/counsel been notified and briefed on the need to produce an initial statement?

6. Which senior executives should be involved with the creation of solutions? Have we pre-determined who is "allowed" to speak to the media on behalf of the company or brand?

7. Are we over-reacting? Meaning: Is it bad or really bad? On the other hand, are we under-estimating the potential damage this situation could create? Also, is it possible anyone in our organization is already covering up key facts we need to know? How comprehensive is our knowledge of the situation?

8. Do we anticipate a long-term or short-term negative media reaction?

9. Are we prepared to be honest and truthful (which is almost always the best practice to embrace) or do we need time to better understand how we want to influence the way the story is shaped?

10. Are our frontline executives comfortable with negative attention and prepared for roles they may not enjoy?

On the surface, this approach seems to accentuate the negative and in some ways it not only does, it must. But this approach is realistic because of the unique pedestal sports occupy. Many sport entities are high-profile organizations dealing with sophisticated consumer and media "critics." And, in an age of social networks, Facebook, Twitter, blogs, and phone texts can spread messages like wild fire. Most average fans know approximately how much money a player or coach makes. They know 'won-loss' records, shooting percentages, batting averages, and championship trophies delivered. They may have a vague (and often false) sense, from advertisements or game broadcast interviews, of what a player or coach is like. They may believe, in many ways, they have seen this situation before and therefore will be able to accurately predict the crime and, in their mind, the logical punishment.

Likewise, the media is fully aware that a negative situation is news and will sell papers, bring unique visitors to a website, or generate valuable ratings. As such, unforeseen negative activity frequently whips journalists into a veritable frenzy, with talk radio hosts or nightly newscasters seeking unique ways to forecast further doom. In these situations, news directors will often assign extra reporters or photographers to chronicle the mounting wave of public discussion and presumed organizational obligation.

Unlike traditional consumer products, which may only be covered in trade publications with any regularity, sports leagues, teams, and players are covered daily in most traditional and new media (e.g., newspapers, magazines, radio, television, internet, blogs, Google, Facebook, and Twitter). This means, in many cases, that editors or beat reporters, already familiar with the sport property and players, will be able to ask detailed and comprehensive questions immediately. In short, the media as well as socially networked fans won't need a "brush-up" to cover or comment on a negative story. Despite this attention, sport marketers can survive (and sometimes thrive) if they know what to do.

Is It Possible to Make Lemonade Out of Lemons?

Research shows that a large portion of dissatisfied clients can be retained if the right actions are taken. In fact, the service marketing literature indicates that effective recovery efforts can actually result in higher levels of customer satisfaction.[12,13] According to Zemke,[14] "Service recovery is about keeping customers coming back after the worst, or at least something very annoying, has happened" (p. 279). The intent is to save "at risk" customers. Recovery—returning a disaffected customer to a state of satisfaction after a service breakdown—has important economic implications for almost all businesses. However, for professional sport franchises, most working on modest profit margins of just 3%, the economics of customer retention take on an even more critical monetary significance. Continuing to put humans into stadium seats is an absolute necessity for those sport properties most dependent on game revenues.

The NHL, for example, was once thought to receive 60% of its total league revenues from ticket sales. When average income generated from concessions, parking, and other ancillary attendance-related activities are added in, the average NHL team depends on live attendance for almost three-fourths of its gross revenues. Although other leagues such as the NFL may not be as dependent on gate-related income as pro hockey, live attendance revenue streams are still crucial to the NBA, MLB, NFL, NAS-CAR, MLS, UFC, and WWF.

The crucial economics of recovery marketing to sport franchises become even more evident when the prominence of repeat attendance is taken into account. Bernard Mullin and his associates at The Aspire Group have frequently demonstrated the potency of the "80–20 principle" to sports teams. In an individual analysis of season attendance at Pittsburgh Pirates games, they found that indeed 80% of the increase in ticket sales from one season to another was produced by 20% of the existing attendees buying more tickets. The results indicate that teams must rely heavily on core customers, season ticket holders, to provide the lion's share of critically important gate receipts. Even the defection of just 10% of these key customers could have a devastating effect on a team's all-important bottom line.

For an NBA team with 10,000 full season ticket holders, for example, the failure of 1,000 of the current fan base to renew could conceivably result in 41,000 fewer seats sold over the 41-game home schedule. With league-wide averages of approximately $50 per ticket (circa 2012) and per capita expenditures exceeding $20 for food concessions, merchandise, and parking, 10% fewer ticket renewals could potentially cost an NBA team nearly $3 million in lost revenues. For many big city teams, the 'average' ticket and per capita spend is much higher than $70 and often exceeds $150.

Recovery Marketing Action Plan for Sport Organizations

Fortunately, over the past 20 years or so a considerable amount has been learned about how to best retain customers in the wake of a service failure or brand image implosion. Below is listed a four-step marketing recovery program with simple, straightforward recovery procedures that experience suggests should make a huge difference in overcoming fan disaffection.

1. Apologize to the consumers experiencing the service failure or dealing with disappointment from a brand they have traditionally valued. Make it personal, sincere, and evident.
2. Offer a value-added solution to the problem. At its core, the fan that underwrites the sport organization's bottom line did not cause the issue. But the same fan will be needed when the dust settles and the smoke clears.

3. Atone for any inconvenience by offering risk-reducing incentives (e.g., satisfaction guarantees) and/or rewards for repurchase (e.g., attractive branded gifts, reduced pricing for standard purchases, etc.).
4. Follow up with those consumers consistently, professionally, and frequently.

[Adapted from Ron Zemke's (1999) 6-step process for handling disappointed customers found in his book, *Service Recovery: Turning Oops! Into Opportunity.*]

As an informal case study, it is instructive to see how the National Basketball Association applied the above steps to effectively recover from their potentially devastating season shortening lockout in 1999 and again in 2011. Rick Welts, the former President of NBA Properties, then the marketing arm of the league, provided a detailed account of how the NBA attempted to win back fan support in 1999.

In Welt's opinion, the league orchestrated a systematic campaign to overcome widespread fan disaffection and, for many, disgust. Key elements of the campaign included the crucial role players assumed in reaching out to fans through a much publicized Valentine's Day card promotion. Players autographed tens of thousands of cards that were mailed directly to NBA season ticket holders inviting them to return. This outreach initiative accented the personal touch so important to successful recovery marketing. The league's proactive approach to recovering fan loyalty appeared to have some positive impact.

Contrary to doomsayers' predictions of an attendance drop of as much as 20%, by the end of the shortened season the decline was a mere 2.2%. According to the *Sports Business Journal*, almost 88% of all available seats were sold at NBA arenas that season. Many of the NBA teams supplemented the leagues' recovery efforts locally. The Portland Trail Blazers, for example, mounted their own personal contact campaign in which 300 staff members from ticket clerks to head coach Mike Dunleavy began calling each of the team's 16,500 season ticket holders the day the lockout ended. The three-day calling campaign relayed a simple message to their core customers: "We're Back in Business and We Need You!"

Season ticket holders were personally extended the NBA's offer of free admission to a team scrimmage or preseason game. Both options sold out immediately. Dave Cohen, then Director of Ticket Sales for the Portland team, stated that their personal contact campaign and the gift incentives "contributed significantly to achieving season ticket renewals that far exceeded our expectations." At the season's end, the Trail Blazers had managed to sell 97.4% of their ticket inventory, placing them well above the league-wide average of 87.9%.

Value-Added and Risk-Reducing Incentives Work

Research by Alice Kendrick[15] found that offering value-added gifts significantly enhanced customer retention and loyalty. Although her research did not focus specifically on service failures, Kendrick's work suggests that gift promotions may be particularly relevant in recovery situations because they serve as tangible atonement for the service breakdown. Kendrick discovered that the provision of unsolicited gifts engendered substantial goodwill among existing customers resulting in greater purchase activity. Her findings may provide a partial explanation, at least, for why the Portland Trail Blazers' season ticket renewal goals were realized so quickly. In their telemarketing campaign, in addition to conveying the League's offer of free admission to games and scrimmages, the Trail Blazers extended free food and beverage coupons to each of their fans. Though the "treats are on us" gesture was modest in nature, according to the Trail Blazers' Cohen, "it obviously meant a lot to our season ticket holders."

Service Guarantees: We Don't Play, You Don't Pay!

Another potentially effective service recovery tactic is the use of service guarantees such as "Your Satisfaction Guaranteed or Your Money Refunded." An appropriately designed unconditional guarantee has proven to be highly effective in a number of service contexts. Interestingly, there is only limited evidence of their use by professional sports teams. The New Jersey Nets (now Brooklyn Nets) provided an example of one team that successfully initiated a satisfaction guarantee program. The Nets extended the guarantee offer to new corporate season ticket buyers, promising that if the season tickets didn't help ticket holders increase their companies' sales the Nets would refund the cost of the tickets ($8,500) plus interest. According to Jim Leahy, Nets VP for Ticket Operations, "Everybody we issued that money-back guarantee to . . . renewed and the program helped the team generate $250,000 in new season ticket business."

Work by McDougall and his associates[16] suggested that a promise of complete satisfaction or full refund would be most effective in attempting to win back consumer confidence. From a recovery standpoint, the extension of a guarantee not only appeases the client for the existing service breach but, at the same time, offers protection against any potential future service failure. In fact, research indicates that an appropriately designed and executed guarantee program should convey several messages crucial to effective recovery: (a) a genuine willingness on the part of the company to redress the consumer's problem, (b) the service provider's commitment to quality and customer service, and (c) the virtual elimination of any (re)purchase risk by consumers.

In the informal case discussion above involving the NBA, the Portland Trail Blazers and New Jersey Nets, readers were given some simple concepts without the luxury of detailed commentary of how "recovery marketing" is considered. At the time this work was originally created, the authors interviewed the NBA's Rick Welts and enjoyed the luxury of asking a series of detailed questions about a topic like a league work stoppage. That interview, quite revealing at the time, is presented here in its original form.[17]

The NBA's Recovery Marketing Program: An Interview with the League's President of NBA Properties, Rick Welts

Q. 1:   *The NBA knew as the lockout proceeded that fans were being pushed away from the game. While that must have hurt people like yourself and David Stern, who had worked so hard to build the professional game, how did you start to plan the inevitable recovery process via marketing?*

Welts: Shortly into the lockout and before the beginning of the regular season, we began meeting to discuss what assets the NBA could bring to re-launching a season. Much of the attitude fans would have toward the NBA was going to be determined by when the season actually started and the atmosphere surrounding the completion of a new collective bargaining agreement. Because we had no way of knowing that, specific messages were not discussed, but rather we tried to collect and understand the tools which could be utilized by the league, teams, and players. Every department of the league had an opportunity to contribute.

Once it was clear that a significant portion of the season would be lost, we assembled a representative group of team executives—coaches, general managers, presidents, marketing and public relations people—and presented our best thinking about re-launching the NBA, if a collective bargaining agreement was reached. That group critiqued and improved our plan and added new elements, which strengthened it. The members of the group then became important leaders among their peers at the teams in making sure that everyone knew what had to be accomplished.

We all agreed that there was not a "marketing solution" to address the apathy, disappointment, or anger that fans had toward the NBA and its players for shutting down the league. We knew we had to take responsibility for the way fans felt about the work stoppage, and then invite fans back to the game in every way possible. The message had to be sincere and direct. Fans would view a "slick marketing campaign" as a sign that the league and the players just didn't understand the situation.

Q. 2: *You have talked before about how close the League came to losing the whole season. Were there two or more recovery marketing plans depending on outcomes? Talk a little about them and explain your comfort level with having to fix the worst case scenario.*

Welts: As the lockout continued, we had to face the increasing likelihood that the entire NBA season might be lost. So, while we had one group trying to plan a shortened NBA season, we also began discussing the issues that we would be facing if we lost an entire season. We got perilously close to that point within a few days. Ownership was prepared to cancel the season if an economic system could not be agreed upon that would give well-managed teams the opportunity to earn some fair return on investment.

Our conclusion was that we had no brilliant ideas about how to miss a full season of NBA basketball and emerge in terrific shape. If anything, the more that scenario was contemplated, the more important a deal that would salvage the season became. The expected impact on both the league and its players of losing an entire year was a major motivation to get a deal done. The worst case scenario was a very bad outcome for everyone involved.

Q. 3: *Once the lockout was resolved, the League instituted some tactical efforts such as free pre-season games, open scrimmages, and reduced ticket prices. To some people that might sound too simple (given the way the League roared back). Put some strategic context into those actions and the others the League employed. What role did marketing play in helping the NBA start the recovery process?*

Welts: Every effort that was undertaken was meant to directly connect fans to the players and to the game. The sooner people could focus on the game the quicker people would find triple-doubles more important than "Larry Bird exceptions." Most of the efforts were very simple and very straightforward. That contributed to their effectiveness.

The players had the most important role. Had the players not been as interested in reaching out to fans as the teams and league were, nothing would have been successful. The day the collective bargaining agreement was reached the players told us that they understood and accepted their responsibility in inviting fans back to the NBA. They were true to their word. We changed the NBA's successful "I Love this Game" campaign to "'I Still Love this Game" to acknowledge that we had stretched the bonds that connect fans to the game during the lockout, but that the game was still alive and exciting.

Our Valentine's Day television campaign showed players sending mountains of Valentine's Day cards to fans. That, combined with the actual mailing of tens of thousands of actually autographed Valentine's Day cards, along with an e-mail Valentine card to NBA fans around the world demonstrated an important sense of humor in asking fans back to the game.

We used NBA.com to instantly deliver the NBA schedule to fans and handed every fan in every NBA arena on opening night a CD that included the music, video highlights, the NBA schedule, NBA screen savers, and a new video game sampler.

Q. 4: *What role do the media play when a league, team, or organization must recover from a scandal or stoppage of play?*

Welts: Certainly, the media plays an important role in fans' perception and level of understanding of any issue. The electronic media is key to delivering information immediately. That information can also be delivered directly through video clips and sound bites from the people actually involved in the story. You can talk directly to a great number of fans. The print media can't be as timely but plays a vital role in analysis and commentary. The internet allows the most immediate and direct communication channel and will become increasingly important to all those delivering news. Organizations that understand the strengths and weaknesses of all media will do a better job getting their message across to fans.

Relationships are still very important in dealing with the media. Organizations can develop strong relationships with key media gatekeepers. This happens over time as a result of being responsive, being straightforward and direct. You also need to understand how the media works (deadlines, scheduled programming, tools that make stories more interesting like artwork or audio/video clips), which allows you to increase the ease and efficiency of the media's coverage of your story.

Q. 5: *Slight change here. While the Latrell Sprewell situation in Oakland was team specific, was there any feeling the League had to recover from that episode also? Does local marketing differ from national marketing in issues like lockouts, strikes, etc.?*

Welts: While incidents like the one you described are biggest in the local market, there is no such thing as strictly "local" in sports any longer. Fans, sponsors, and the media all have access to everything that is happening in sports. A league's ongoing role is to improve the performance of every team operation, as a poorly managed team will devalue the collective perception of all teams.

From a communications standpoint, the NBA's handling of the communications process during the lockout demonstrated the value of speaking with a single voice. All communication came from those directly involved in the process as directed by the Commissioner. Teams and owners deferred to designated spokespersons to deliver news and information about the bargaining process. This avoids mixed messages and misinformation, which make it more difficult to conduct meaningful negotiations.

Q. 6: *What are your opinions on sport brand equities and the constant damage/chipping away that seems to keep reaching the public? By that we mean player holdouts, free agency, injuries, sudden retirements (Barry Sanders), big retirements (Michael Jor-*

dan), franchise bankruptcy (Pittsburgh Penguins), etc. What does it all mean for sports marketers and what have they had to learn about managing the brand's equity?·

Welts: It means our jobs get harder. But you need to put sports in a societal context here. Individuals and industries that benefit from being objects of public interest also face a more challenging media environment than ever before. The media appetite for stories about teams and players has grown exponentially in the past decade.

When I worked as a public relations director for an NBA team in the late '70s, our postgame news conference was attended by four beat writers, a couple of visiting writers, and maybe one local television news crew. No more. No one had heard of ESPN or Access Hollywood and Fox was a movie company.

Public figures in all walks of life are scrutinized today in ways that athletes (and politicians and entertainers) could never have imagined 20 years ago. The private lives of public figures are the currency that many media outlets use to attract their readers and viewers. Is it any wonder that our sports figures or politicians seem a bit more tarnished today?

That same media appetite can create opportunity for creating exposure and positive stories as well.

References

1. Ganim, S. (2011, November 5). Sandusky indicted. *Patriot-News*, A1.
2. Solomon, J. (2012). North Carolina's under-the-radar academic scandal continues to grow. *The Birmingham News*. Retrieved from http://www.al.com/sports/index.ssf/2012/07/north_carolinas_under-the-rada.html
3. Dillman, L. (2012). London Olympics: Badminton scandal rocks sport; 8 players expelled. *Los Angeles Times*. Retrieved from http://articles.latimes.com/2012/aug/01/sports/la-sp-on-badminton-scandal-20120801
4. Varney, J. (2012). New Orleans Saints severely penalized by NFL for 'bounty' program. *The Times-Picayune*. Retrieved from http://www.nola.com/saints/index.ssf/2012/03/new_orleans_saints_are_penaliz.html
5. Pearson, M. (2012). Doping scandal costs Lance Armstrong sponsors, charity role. *CNN*. Retrieved from: http://www.cnn.com/2012/10/17/us/lance-armstrong-doping/index.html
6. Shipley, A. (2011). Lengthy NBA lockout looms, with owners and players deeply divided. *The Washington Post*. Retrieved from http://www.washingtonpost.com/sports/wizards/nba-lockout-looms-with-owners-and-players-deeply-divided/2011/06/29/AGKmz3qH_story.html
7. Burton, R., & Howard, D. (1999). Professional sports leagues: Marketing mix mayhem. *Marketing Management*, 8 (Spring).
8. Zyman, S. (1999). *The end of marketing as we know it*. New York: HarperCollins.
9. Mullin, B. J., Hardy, S., & Sutton, W. A. (1993). *Sports marketing*. Champaign, IL: Human Kinetics.
10. Anonymous. (2002). How $194.64 billion is spent in sports. *Sports Business Journal*. Retrieved from www.sportsbusinessdaily.com/images/random/SportsIndustry.pdf
11. Wolf, R. (2012). U.S. debt is now equal to economy. *USA Today*, A1.
12. Sarel, D. & Marmostein, H. (1999). The role of service recovery in HMO satisfaction. *Marketing Health Services*, 19 (Spring), 7–15.
13. Hart, C., Heskett, J. & Sasser, E. (1990). The profitable art of service recovery. *Harvard Business Review*, 68(4), 148–156.
14. Zemke, R. (1999). Service recovery: Turning oops! into opportunity. In R. Zemke, & J. Woods (Eds.), *Best practices in customer service*. Amherst, MA: HRD Press.
15. Kendrick, A. (1998). Promotional products vs. price promotion in fostering customer loyalty: A report of two controlled field experiments. *The Journal of Services Marketing*, 12(4) 312–326.
16. McDougall, G., Levesque, T., & Vander Plaat, P. (1998). Designing the service guarantee: Unconditional or specific. *The Journal of Services Marketing*, 12(4), 278–293.
17. Burton, R., & Howard, D. (1999). Professional sports leagues: Marketing mix mayhem. *Marketing Management*, 8 (Spring).

12

Leveraging Destinations through Sport Events

Mark P. Pritchard
Central Washington University

Abstract: Regardless of whether sport events are participant or spectator based, the scale of tourism-related business that results from these activities is unparalleled. Levels of public and private investment mean marketers need to be able to effectively coordinate and justify hosting events. The practice of leveraging benefits from large- and small-scale sport events, professional and amateur competitions, is not new. But ascertaining how to be successful and efficient with the venture stresses managing a full spectrum of event tasks and partners. A considerable body of work in sport tourism has been brought to bear in this chapter. Prior research and specific industry case studies offer the reader some strategic insights on how best to manage stakeholder benefits that can result from hosting events.

Keywords: destination marketing, sport events, strategic leveraging, tourism stakeholders

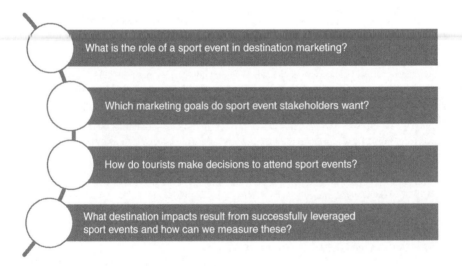

What is the role of a sport event in destination marketing?

Which marketing goals do sport event stakeholders want?

How do tourists make decisions to attend sport events?

What destination impacts result from successfully leveraged sport events and how can we measure these?

Figure 12.1 An Overview of Chapter 12

Introduction

In February and March 2010, Vancouver and Whistler hosted the international community and the world for the Olympic and Paralympic Games. Estimated at $1.76 billion CAD, the initial cost of producing the 2010 Winter Olympics games in Canada was substantial. Event planning and venue construction began in 2004,

Table 12.1 Vancouver Olympic Committee Budget Spending ($millions CAD)[1]

Category	Budgeted Amount	Spending thru July 2009	Balance thru 2009–10
Revenue, Marketing & Communication	$170.4	$72.2	$98.2
Sports & Game Operations	$247.0	$130.5	$116.5
Services & Game Operations	$616.0	$165.5	$450.5
Technology	$391.9	$219.9	$172.0
Workforce & Sustainability	$140.2	$81.5	$58.7
Finance	$126.6	$84.7	$41.9
Subtotal	$1,692.1	$754.3	$937.8
Contingency & Foreign Exchange Loss	$63.8		
Total	$1,755.9		

[1]Same as 1.

and 5 years later 45% of the operating budget had been spent. By March 2010, 6,689 contracts and purchase orders totaling $1.6 billion had been awarded. Of these, local provincial contracts in British Columbia accounted for 70% or approximately $1.1 billion of the work done. Table 12.1 details the magnitude of public monies invested in this particular sports event.[1] All told, hosting a mega-event is a very expensive undertaking but is it worth it? Why would governments and other public entities spend tremendous amounts in order to serve as the host destination for these mega-sports events?[2] Local or regional events still offer benefits, but mega-sports events operate on a much larger scale and usually attract significant media coverage that can deliver international markets.[3] Despite rising costs over the last 30 years for those hosting winter mega-sports events (e.g., Salt Lake City, $1.5 billion; Calgary, $1 billion; Lake Placid, $174 million),[4] host revenues from activities such as event broadcast fees have risen even more dramatically (e.g., Salt Lake City, $545 million; Calgary, $309 million; Lake Placid, $15.5 million). International broadcast rights for the Summer Games have also risen. Fees generated from Sydney alone covered 51% of the International Olympic Committee and 33% of Sydney's Organizing Committee's total budget.[5]

The scope of financial investment needed to host events stresses a need for scrutiny. This means management teams have to be able to determine if they are effective in getting the best return they can on the venture.[6] Understanding which advantages to leverage is necessary for practitioners.[7] Organizers cannot operate alone in this and hope things will come together at the last minute. The reality is destination marketing organizations (DMOs) have to run detailed planning sessions well in advance to build event synergies on the supply side (e.g., develop partnerships, share costs) and maximize returns on the demand side (e.g., spur effective activation, shape integrated marketing effort).[8] Table 12.1 notes the complex range of product and service connections Vancouver's Olympic Committee (VANOC) funded in order to host a mega-event.

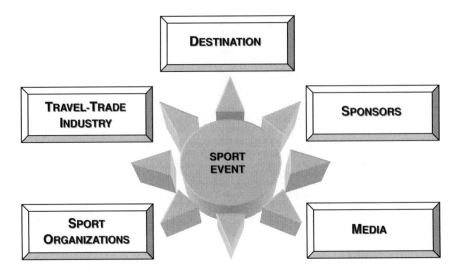

Figure 12.2 Sport Event Media Stakeholders *(Adapted from Getz & Fairley, 2004)*

Facilitating media coverage of the event is one of these expenses, and assisting related stakeholders here is essential to being able to effectively leverage exposure.[9] Figure 12.2 shows how managing an event's coverage entails (a) coordinating with media partners, (b) partnering with the region/country's DMO to meet their tourism goals, (c) involving sponsors (local/regional/national/international) and helping them activate their association, (d) working with the travel industry to maximize event access with packages and advertising that evoke the right mix of brand attributes (i.e., destination/event images that excite and attract), and (e) connecting with local sports groups to promote grass-roots buzz, word-of-mouth, and local volunteerism via community engagement.

The practice of leveraging benefits from small- or large-scale events is not new. But recent strategies employed at the 2000 Olympics in Sydney and the 2010 Winter Olympics in Vancouver took a slightly different approach, using publicly funded leveraging initiatives to target not only tourism development but longer-term business development for the region.[10] Faulkner and his colleagues discussed three tourism business goals behind DMOs successfully leveraging sport events.[11] These included:

- Building and augmenting competitive position, which entails branding and conveying favorable image impressions of the host destination or country.
- Boosting visitor spending at the destination (e.g., greater revenue via expanded retail offerings).
- Expanding the destination product offering and cultivating extended stay visitation patterns and pre/post-event tourism.

Along the same lines, Chalip used four core elements to recount slightly different destination strategies behind Australia's approach to leveraging tourism benefits from the Olympics:[12]

- Repositioning the country by capitalizing on media.
- Aggressively seeking convention business.

- Minimizing the diversion effect of the Games (i.e., visitors deterred by impressions of a crowded event/locale).
- Promoting pre- and post-Games touring.

Given the range of potential planning goals for sport events, for the 2010 Winter Games VANOC surveyed three previous North American hosts (2002, Salt Lake City; 1988, Calgary; 1980, Lake Placid). Their report expanded the list of benefits leveraged to include regional business and other social outcomes. For instance, export growth in previous host cities is quite remarkable (see Table 12.2).

Table 12.2 Export Growth in Previous Winter Games Host Cities[1]

Region (games)	*Average Nominal Export Growth (%)*		
	5 years Prior	*Games Year*	*5 years Post[a]*
Alberta (Calgary '88)	1	10	9
Utah (Salt Lake '02)	6	30	12
Piedmont (Torino '06)	1	9	4
Norway (Lillihammer '94)[b]	8	5	8
British Columbia (Vancouver '10)	4	n/a	n/a

[1]Same as 1.
[a]Post-Game data for Utah 3 years, Piedmont 2 years.
[b]Norwegian national exports used for contrast.

Gilbert Felli, Executive Director of the IOC, believes Canada and BC took "full advantage of learning from other Olympic and Paralympic Games to vigorously pursue (tourism) growth."[13] Many of the event goals VANOC identified went beyond the positive benefits such as enabling social interaction and civic celebration,[14] to suggest that host destination success could yield the following returns:[15]

- Increasing tourism to their regions.
- Reminding the world of the country's/region's attractions (brand attributes) during subsequent international competitions hosted there.
- Building sport participation.
- Serving as national hubs for recreational and competitive sport.
- Helping the country's top high-performance athletes achieve their full potential.
- Attracting major sport companies and businesses to locate there.
- Encouraging local children to excel in sports.

These points served as a guide for the DMO's strategic planning. The next section talks expressly about how destinations use sport events to impact tourism demand (i.e., lift awareness and appeal to potential visitors by reshaping impressions people have of the destination product).[16]

Figure 12.3 Strategic Considerations When Leveraging Events *(Adapted from Aaker, 2011)*

Using Sport Events to Market Destinations

David Aaker in his strategy text summarizes market-driven strategy nicely into two simple questions (see Figure 12.3): *how to compete* and *where to compete.*[17] These considerations readily shape the sort of marketing effort a DMO might undertake. When it comes to *where to compete*, sport events have the capacity to *access* and deliver unique markets (e.g., international and domestic visitors) that a host destination may not typically draw. For instance, take the flow of international visitors to Calgary, Alberta, pre- and post-Games as an example. Pre- versus post-Game visitation by international markets doubled over the course of a decade (from approximately 0.5 million to over a million tourists annually).[18] It is safe to say that hosting the event elevated Calgary as an attractive destination for the international market. Sport events can also drive tourism *demand* during a destination's shoulder or low season when the usual attractions are not drawing strongly.[19]

The unique value proposition and appeal of sport events are capable of elevating awareness in competitive markets typically saturated with leisure alternatives.[20] An industry acronym for achieving this in customers is TOMA, top-of-mind-awareness (i.e., that your brand is one of the first alternatives considered). Maintaining this type of mental presence in international and domestic markets is usually too expensive to contemplate for many destinations. Yet the level of media exposure that results from events, albeit for a limited season, often facilitates[21] keeping the destination at the top of places to visit in a potential visitor's evoked set.[22] Take for instance the media "afterglow" the 2010 Games in Vancouver enjoyed. Coverage included approximately 50,000+ hours of programming (47% greater than Torino), carried by some 300 TV stations and 100 online service providers, which resulted in 3.5 billion people watching on TV, the internet, or some other mobile device. NBC alone delivered 190 million U.S. viewers, whereas Yahoo's Olympic site garnered 32 million unique visitors.[23]

As shown in Figure 12.3, the other strategic element sport can address in destination marketing is *how to compete*? Events can become destination assets that shape how people perceive and value the product. Usually mega-events such as the Olympics or the World Cup only occur at a destination once.[24] However, some destinations reap the benefits of consistently hosting annual sport competitions (e.g., U.S. and French Open Tennis Tournaments at New York's Flushing Meadows and Paris' Roland Garros). One particular event began in 1935 and grew to be the best attended of all the Professional Golf Association (PGA) Tour's annual events, with an annual attendance of around 500,000 spectators. Arizona's Phoenix Open Golf Tournament was founded by the Phoenix Thunderbirds, a local civic group of mission-minded businessmen who helped co-ordinate the event for two main reasons: (a) to benefit local charities (e.g., Phoenix Children's Hospital) and (b) to help "promote the Valley of the Sun through sports."[25] According to some tourism experts, 50+ years of national media coverage in the desert each January has reframed (repositioned) how Americans and Canadians think of the desert now, as an attractive "snow-bird" get-away destination.[26]

Much like sport sponsorship,[27] the images of these destinations benefit from the qualities of the sport events they host. This has the potential to differentiate the city from other competing destinations and increase the attractiveness and uniqueness of the region's value proposition. Of course to be successful in this, DMOs must enable and leverage various partners in delivering the event. Although we tend to think first of spectator-based events, other public participant-based contests (like the New York City Marathon) or destination-based recreation specialties (e.g., sailing, skiing, golfing, or sport fishing) can embellish the image a destination product holds in the mind of potential visitors. For instance playing and watching golf has become a regular destination draw for Japanese sport tourists in Hawaii[28] and for Korean golf tourists in their Asia-Pacific holidays.[29] According to tourism researchers, sports and recreation features like this fall under the umbrella of the destination's service infrastructure in crafting the tourist's product experience.[30] One useful side to having a complex understanding of the destination product is that it allows us to see some of the creative event-destination synergies[31] or partnership strategies that could be developed (e.g., trip bundling or joint promotions). Adapting work by Murphy and colleagues, Figure 12.4 defines a range of attributes that help to shape the tourist experience and originate out of the destination environment.[32] This type of framework, which bundles destination attributes, serves as a basis for effectively delineating/evaluating which points-of-differentiation (PODs) make up or contribute the most to the tourist experience. Destinations typically rely more on attributes that are unique and hard to replicate (e.g., natural scenery). Sport events and activities do attract and figure in someone's appraisal of the destination, but the importance travellers ascribe to that element depends on the context for travel.[33]

Understanding that sport events are delivered relative to other destination features as part of a larger system is also important.[34] One implication is that we begin to appreciate how a marathon race (i.e., sport attraction service) delivered in New York can yield quite a different atmosphere for the destination visitor than one hosted in Boston.[35] Likewise, Major League Baseball rivalry games between the Giants and the Los Angeles Dodgers will offer quite a different service experience due to the local

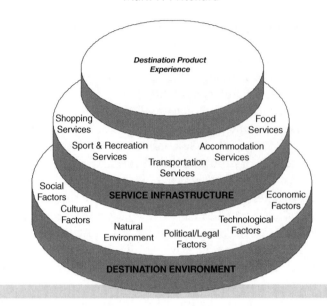

Figure 12.4 Sport Events and the Destination Experience *(Adapted from Murphy, Pritchard, & Smith, 2000)*[32]

Destination Attribute Definitions (Adapted from Pritchard & Havitz, 2006):[33]
Product features draw from two dimensions, *Infrastructure* and *Environment*.
Service Infrastructure

- **Food & Restaurants**—the perceptions of both the food and the service provided by restaurants.
- **Accommodation**—the perceptions of local accommodations, including hotels, motels, campgrounds, etc.
- **Transportation**—the perceptions of public transport facilities, roads, and signage.
- **Shopping**—the perceptions of local shopping facilities including service, merchandise, opening hours, etc.
- **Recreation**—the perceptions of destination sport and recreation services.
- **Tourist Information**—the perceptions of local information available, including access and accuracy, etc.

Destination Environment

- **Flora and Fauna**—perceptions of the local animal and plant life.
- **Natural Scenery**—perceptions of the local natural scenery and attractions.
- **Local People**—perceptions of the local people including friendliness, helpfulness, etc.
- **Historic Sites**—perceptions of local historic sites.
- **Local Amenities**—perceptions of the local amenities, not including accommodation or food services.
- **Cultural Activities**—perceptions of the local cultural sites and activities.

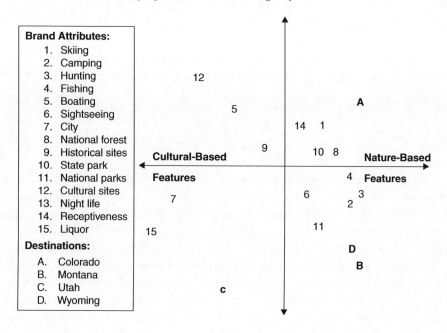

Figure 12.5 State Positioning Relative to Product Features (*Adapted from Gartner, 1989*)

environment that hosts them (San Francisco or Los Angeles).[36] The strategic point for sport marketers to leverage here is that a destination's locale should be used to craft unique value propositions. This was evident in NBC's coverage of the 2010 Winter Games, which was always introduced and framed by colorful images of the host environment, British Columbia. Points-of-differentiation (POD) along these lines are usually much more difficult for competitors to replicate/follow and help to develop a strong position or association in the mind of event visitors. Tourist survey responses and multidimensional scaling analysis give an example of how these mental associations translate into attribute-based differentiation. Figure 12.5's positioning grid shows how visitor perceptions of a sport can distinguish competitive alternatives.[37] Using a sample of U.S. travellers surveyed a decade earlier at the 2002 Winter Games in Salt Lake City, Figure 12.5 shows Colorado possessed a stronger connection (i.e., was closer in proximity) to the attributes of skiing (1) and national forests (8) than the other three U.S. states.

These image associations represent strong PODs a region's DMO could promote and position on. Conversely, tourist impressions of Utah, which has strong skiing facilities, appear weaker/more distant from this feature than they should be. This is a problem for the destination but could also become an unrealized POD that the destination has yet to establish/promote. One could argue that Utah's decision a decade later to host a mega-sports event (2002 Winter Olympics) rectified this perceptual brand deficiency. Media coverage of the Games in Salt Lake City effectively helped reposition the destination in the minds of domestic (U.S.) and international sport tourists. Reports from the Utah Office of Tourism observed that pre-Games skier visits numbered approximately 3 million annually. However, by 2008 skier visits to Utah had increased by almost 50% to approximately 4.5 million. In the same timeframe international tourism also substantially increased from pre-Games numbers of 600,000 to 750,000 visitors in 2008.[38] Building visitation and strengthening competitive position in domestic and international markets like this aligns with two key outcomes distinguishing successfully leveraged events (see previous lists of event goals).

Other examples of how destinations use sport as a positioning attribute and position can be found.[39] For instance, an adaptation of work by Kim and colleagues in Figure 12.6 shows the way a sample of Korean golfers perceived seven different international golf destinations. Again, sports-related attributes in each region's service infrastructure served as potential PODs for the destination. Specifically, these sport tourists felt Australia (A) and Hawaii (C) possessed fairly strong positions relative to two attributes, how well known a country's golf courses were (5) and the quality of their golf resort facilities (6). In contrast, perceptions of China (B) and Japan (D) place them further away from these two sport attributes. Both of these destinations were more closely associated with the features of (1) inexpensive travel costs and (9) night entertainment. As was the case with the previous positioning grid, placement can identify current strengths but it can also note a strategic direction we need to pursue for a stronger position with our customers. Thailand (G) gives some evidence of this, as it is closer to Australia and Hawaii on the destination-golf attributes than the other countries but still has some progress to make in order to reposition as a golf destination. Recent hosting of some big names in professional golf at a charity event in 2010 (e.g., Tiger Woods, Paul Casey, and Camilo Villegas) signals some intent by the country to strengthen its position along these lines and build a stronger association with the sport in its international target markets.[40]

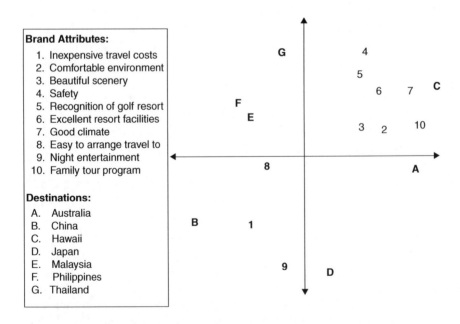

Figure 12.6 Korean Sport Tourists Perceptions of Overseas Golf Destinations (*Adapted from Kim, Chun, & Petrick, 2005*)

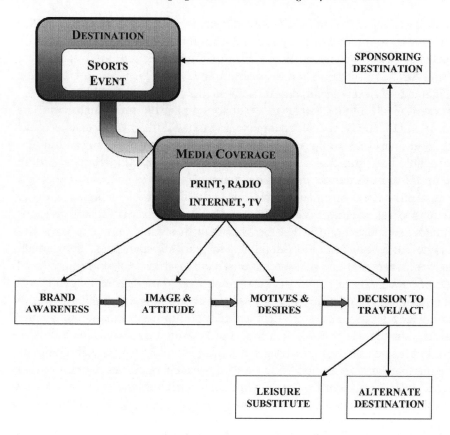

Figure 12.7 A Hierarchy of Media Effects on Consumer Response *(Adapted from Getz & Fairley, 2004; Siegel & Ziff-Levine, 1990)*

Understanding a Sport Tourist's Decision Making

Trying to understand why your customer acts is of seminal importance to the marketer. If we know the process we can look to influence the outcome. Figure 12.7's outline explains why a sport tourist might act and decide to attend an event. The sequence of psychological steps follows prior work that has been done on consumer responses to media exposure.[41] Earlier work reported either 6 steps (awareness→knowledge→liking→preference→conviction→purchase) or 4 stages (media exposure→information processing→communication effects→buyer action) that end in consumer action of one sort or another.[42] These sequences were later adapted to reflect a destination-visitor context.[43] As you can see in Figure 12.7, several of the event objectives mentioned earlier in the chapter are accounted for here.

The steps behind a sport tourist's decision to act and attend are placed in hierarchical order where the preceding stage is a necessary precondition for the next to occur (i.e., a sequential order of effects). Awareness of an event follows media exposure of one sort or another. Information from this exposure then alters the impression or image an observer holds about a destination. Image is the set of beliefs or perceptions that a person holds about an object. In the case of a destination, image can be thought of as a visual or mental impression of the place and what it would be like if you visited.[44] Perceptions of a destination usually involve a complex assortment of images and these play a crucial part in its selection and the decision to visit.[45] This is because favorable images heighten one's level of motivation and desire to visit. Chalip and Green examined sport event media and the impact of destination image on intention to visit. The study found that U.S. and New Zealand target markets had different impressions of the Australian Gold Coast that would explain the likelihood of them attending an Indy car race (U.S. visitors had images of a *safe environment, developed infrastructure, natural environment*: NZ visitor images were *novelty, convenience*).[46]

Once a customer's attention and interest is captured with favorable impressions, desire and action tend to follow. However, one of the interesting anomalies of leisure decisions such as attending a sports event is that the participant has quite a range of ways they can respond to this type of stimulus (i.e., fulfill their motivational desires). Some might attend the event whereas others will watch it on TV or a webcast.[47] People might travel to another related activity (e.g., play or practice golf instead of visiting the golf event) or engage in another type of leisure substitute (e.g., attend a movie, go hiking).[48] At this point we've already discussed how certain image perceptions of a destination might predispose some sport tourists to think of visiting a destination (e.g., ski in Colorado, golf in Hawaii). But how do these images trigger step 3, a person's motivation and desire to attend or participate in sport events? Understanding what energizes behavior often leads market researchers to consider the "why" behind consumption and the psychological motives driving purchase behavior.[49] Motives originate from internal factors that arouse and prompt goal-directed behavior. In general, motives to consume reflect a desire to satisfy internal needs through acquisition or action.[50] In the context of sport events, motives behind event consumption are said to reflect desires for certain experiential benefits.[51] For example, Kahle and colleagues describe the impact motivational processes like a desire for camaraderie (group affinity) or self-expression have on fan attendance.[52] Further efforts cite positive links between a desire for eustress (a positive form of stress or excitement derived from uncertainty), group affiliation, entertainment, self-esteem enhancement, and identification on spectator patronage.[53] Shoham et al. highlight the role identity construction and camaraderie play in motivating participation,[54] whereas others report desires such as vicarious achievement, fantasy and fun, excitement, aesthetics, and nostalgia prompting spectator behavior.[55]

Motivation research in travel and tourism also has a lengthy history. The ability of media to stimulate demand is well established, however, effective tourism marketing also rests soundly on an understanding of what motivates visitation.[56] Using the process of disequilibrium to explain why people feel out of balance or in need, Crompton describes two types of motives behind pleasure travel, those that *push* and those that *pull* (see Figure 12.8).[57] Push factors for visiting a destination event originate internally as socio-psychological drives, whereas pull factors are produced externally by various points of attraction in the destination product itself. Push factors are deemed useful for describing the desire to go on vacation, and pull motives reflect the influence of the destination in arousing those sentiments. Thus, effective media promotion or event coverage has the ability to communicate *hot buttons* that convey a felt need or desire that pushes or pulls a consumer to act/attend.[58]

Consumer research has also identified two types of motivational benefits or needs (experiential or functional) that consumers seek from products. Experiential benefits have been defined as desires that provide sensory pleasure. In this sense, motives such as exploration, excitement or relaxation describe experiential desires the potential tourist wants from visiting. The second set of functional needs are also active in the decision. These are product-based pragmatic benefits that shape searchs for a particular brand alternative that meets certain consumption-related needs. For example, questions like "is it affordable or convenient" or "does the trip accommodate children" may be important functional needs in the decision to travel to a destination. Although these motives may not be prime movers, they do shape whether or not people will choose a particular type of holiday.[59] Attending to your consumer's functional needs facilitates or enables the behavior you want to occur. However, failure to satisfy these factors will inhibit or prevent the traveler from choosing the brand/destination or the type of holiday you are suggesting in promotion (i.e., would be fun but just doesn't meet our needs).[60] When a consumer is motivated to attend/participate in a sport event yet has constraints[61] at work inhibiting that behavior, they tend to substitute and choose a surrogate (e.g., follow the event on tv, play the sport at home).[62] These behavioral choices could be passive or active modes of leisure consumption that satisfy the initial motivational prompt that aroused the person's sense of disequilibrium. Figure 12.8 depicts how after initial motivation, a consumptive appraisal process incorporates consideration of brand-specific facilitators or inhibitors. These factors shape choice in the evoked set and behavioral response in potential travelers to the event.[63]

Work on golf tourist motivations to visit has produced different mixes of motives prompting visitation (i.e., motivation-based segmentation).[64] These included a range of push and pull factors such as business opportunities, convenience or cost benefits, learning and challenge of courses, escape-relaxation, as well as social interaction. Research on what motivates or constrains decisions to attend sport events has also been done with U.S. travelers to the FIFA World Cup.[65] Support of the national team, socialization, eustress, vicarious achievement, and escape were all significant motives behind interest in the event. However, other than event interest, visitor desires to learn about the host country (Korea) had the largest direct effect on whether they attended.[66] Surprisingly, financial constraints did not play as large a role as one would think in preventing World Cup soccer travel. In fact the American sample's primary barrier to visitation resulted from perceptions of risk and concerns over safety about traveling to Korea.[67]

Evaluating the Impact of Destination Event Media

Research that evaluates the effectiveness of communication at sport events has been done. However, much of this work focuses on a much tighter range of research objectives than what has been done in the context of tourism events. For example, an assessment of media effects on spectators at a professional tennis tournament in Houston, Texas (ATP tour event) concentrated on four main questions:[68]

1.   What was the most effective media for making event attendees aware of the tennis tournament?

2. What was the preferred media outlet of event attendees for obtaining information about the tennis tournament?
3. Did the tennis tournament advertisement broadcast during the Super Bowl create awareness of the professional tennis tournament?
4. Did the tennis tournament advertisement broadcast during the Super Bowl influence respondents to attend the event?

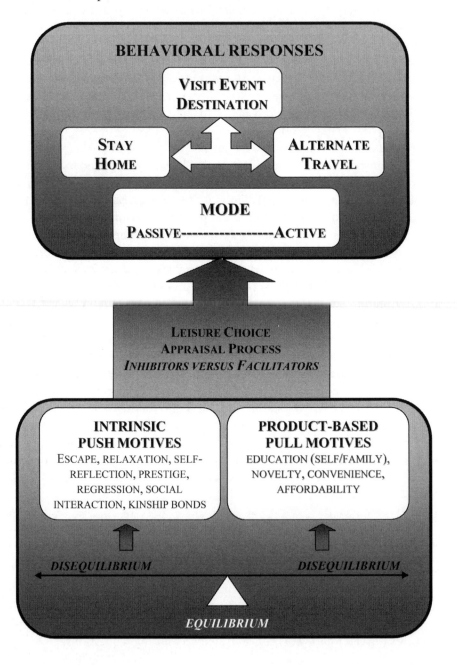

Figure 12.8 Motivational Processes of Destination Sport Visitation

Understanding the impact of a destination sport event and its media coverage tends to be a more complex matter. Work on this is a necessary requirement if practitioners want to justify economic expenditures, tweak any subsequent event planning, and inform follow-up campaigns.[69] Figure 12.7 gives the reader a basis for understanding the four main outcomes (awareness>>image>> desire/motivation behavior) that researchers focus on when determining the effectiveness of media exposure in stimulating traveler response.[70] The first point of assessment that most marketers go to is the behavioral outcome, how many people visited as a result of the event. Most of the time we look simply at the raw numbers and the visitation rate during a stated time frame. However, sometimes researchers want a clearer picture of what the actual sales effect was. This usually calls for benchmark comparisons between post-event numbers and visitation rates from previous years. Rather than assessing all travelers together, analysis along these lines tends to be done on a segment by segment basis (e.g., international markets, domestic or out of/in-state markets).[71] Some researchers have used field experiments to quantify visitation, as this can provide a more controlled examination of the numbers and isolates as best it can the effect of media exposure from pre-existing travel patterns to the destination. Travel researchers did this in Hawaii, looking at inbound tourism and visitation rates from different U.S. states following exposure to promotion.[72] The control group used for comparison included tracking visitation numbers from those cities, which although similar in size (e.g., standard metropolitan area with a population of 50,000+)[73], had not been exposed to the advertising campaign (as was the case with the treatment group).

Other researchers concentrate on whether or not event coverage changed awareness[74] or image[75] of the destination in key target markets. This approach questions whether potential visitors became more aware of or familiar with the destination as a result of the coverage.[76] Some destinations host mega-events in order to spark initial large-scale awareness and positive image. Much like price promotion, significant media coverage can elevate the destination in the mind of the consumer (i.e., they think of it more readily and retrieve it more quickly from memory).[77] If destination awareness and a favorable impression are established, product trial or visitation may result. One difficulty behind accurately determining impacts, and the effects of sport media at events, resides in defining the time frame.[78] If we want to calculate the impact of an event on subsequent visitation, what time frame would be appropriate, the number of visitors the following year, the next five years? In most cases consistently tracking the number of visitors five years after the event and comparing segment numbers should give the practitioner a solid basis for comparison and contrast. Some consideration can also be given to comparing quantitative "bumps" in visitation numbers with similar destinations and events.

Sampling is also a challenge: Who should we ask and how should we intercept people or obtain representative samples of attendees. Just sampling visitors at the stadium/event itself may not accurately capture or reflect the visitor population at the destination. Most studies on traveler impacts at destination events have more complex sampling frames and methods they employ to get an accurate view (multi-site, multi-methods, multiple times). For instance, visitor research at the Vancouver 2010 Olympics used (a) multiple tracking studies (ticket holder pre/post-Games surveys, U.S. and overseas pre/post-Games awareness surveys, post-Games survey of destination travel intentions to BC and Canada), (b) methods (e.g., intercept interviews, follow-up surveys), and (c) data collection points (e.g., 26+ destination intercept locations in one study alone) to assess six specific objectives:[79]

- Profile trip characteristics (origin, length of stay, activities, trip planning, & travel party makeup).
- Determine satisfaction with the Games experience, hospitality, and visitor servicing.
- Understand perceptions of Vancouver, Whistler, Richmond, and BC as a tourism destination.
- Assess intentions to return to BC tourism destinations.
- Explore WOM methods used to relay the 2010 Olympics experience (storytelling, blogs, Twitter).
- Determine ideal future communication and marketing methods to maximize the probability of a return visit to BC destinations.

In addition to the economic impact studies they commissioned,[80] this approach by Tourism British Columbia and its partners gives us a snapshot of the visitor aspect of what can be tracked and researched at sport events. Getz provides an even fuller framework that depicts five areas for potential research.[81] These range from studying stakeholder benefits, traveler characteristics, experiences and travel patterns, to various social, economic, or environmental impacts that might result.

Conclusion

This chapter has covered a lot of ground about how and why destinations host sport events. The review started by noting the complex array of stakeholders and detailed planning that is necessary for events to be successfully leveraged. Strategic considerations of how and why destinations use sport events to compete in the tourism industry followed. This first covered some discussion over how to think about events as part of the destination product. Remember that in order to manage and market something well you have to be able to define it. The implications of this for destination positioning and repositioning were then tackled with specific examples of destinations that used different sport attributes as PODs. Understanding the sport event consumer was the next major component of the discussion. This looked at how sport tourists make decisions and are motivated to attend an event. The material also covered how consumers are potentially affected by exposure to media coverage. This sought to provide answers as to how practitioners evaluate events and their impact. Follow-up estimations are a critical part of destination event management, and this section described some of the challenges behind conducting research on communication effectiveness and visitor tracking. To sum up, successful event management underscores the handling of a full spectrum of event tasks and partners. The complexity of these ventures is daunting. However, the discussion provided in this review offers some remedy to this, as it highlights a strategic path to event leveraging for those who host destination sports.

References

1. Pricewaterhouse Coopers. (2010). *The Games Effect: Preliminary Economic Impact of the 2010 Olympic & Paralympic Winter Games on British Columbia and Canada to March 31, 2010.* A report prepared for the Governments of British Columbia & Canada, the BC & Canadian Olympic Secretariats.
2. Whitelegg, D. (2000). Going for gold: Atlanta's bid for fame. *Journal of Urban and Regional Research, 24,* 801–817.
3. Ritchie, J. B., & Smith, B. (1991). The impact of a mega-event on host region awareness: A longitudinal study. *Journal of Travel Research, 30*(1), 3–10.
4. Delaney, J. (2006, May 17). Vancouver Olympics already stirring controversy. *The Epoch Times.* Retrieved from http://www.theepochtimes.com/news/6–3-17/39416.html
5. Burton, R. (2003). Olympic games host city marketing: An exploration of expectations and outcomes. *Sport Marketing Quarterly, 12*(1), 37–47.
6. Bennett, G., Cunningham, G., & Dees, W. (2006). Measuring the marketing communication activations of a professional tennis tournament. *Sport Marketing Quarterly, 15*(2), 91–101.
7. Chalip, L. (2006). Towards social leverage of sport events. *Journal of Sport & Tourism, 11*(2), 109–127; and Chalip, L., & Leyns, A. (2002). Local business leveraging of a sport event: Managing an event for economic benefit. *Journal of Sport Management, 16,* 132–158.
8. Getz, D. (1998). Trends, strategies, and issues in sport-event tourism. *Sport Marketing Quarterly, 7*(2), 8–13.
9. Getz, D., & Fairley, S. (2004). Media management at sport events for destination promotion: Case studies and concepts. *Event Management, 8,* 127–139.
10. O'Brien, D. (2005). Event business leveraging: The Sydney 2000 Olympic Games. *Annals of Tourism Research, 33,* 240–261.
11. Faulkner, B., Chalip, L., Brown, G., Jago, L., Marsh, R., & Woodside, A. (2000). Monitoring the tourism impacts of the Sydney 2000 Olympics. *Event Management, 6*(4), 231–246.
12. Chalip, L. (2002). Using the Olympics to optimize tourism benefits. University lecture given in Barcelona's Centre d'Estudis Olimpics. Retrieved from http://olympicstudies.uab.es/lectures/web/pdf/chalip.pdf
13. McKay, A. (2010). *Results of the 2010 Olympic Legacy Project.* Presentation given on behalf of Tourism BC at the Travel & Tourism Research Association's 2010 Canada Chapter Conference, Quebec City.
14. Getz, D. (1998). Trends, strategies, and issues in sport-event tourism. *Sport Marketing Quarterly, 7*(2), 8–13.
15. Kaplanidou, K., & Karadakis, K. (2010). Understanding the legacies of a host Olympic city: The case of the 2010 Vancouver Olympic Games. *Sport Marketing Quarterly, 19*(2), 110–117.
16. Chalip, L., & Green, C. (2003). Effects of sport event media on destination image and intention to visit. *Journal of Sport Management, 17,* 214–234.
17. Aaker, D. (2011) *Strategic market management* (9th ed.). New York: Wiley.
18. Getz, D. (1998). Trends, strategies, and issues in sport-event tourism. *Sport Marketing Quarterly, 7*(2), 8–13.
19. Murphy, P., & Pritchard, M. P. (1997). Destination price-value perceptions: An examination of origin and seasonal influences. *Journal of Travel Research, 35*(3), 16–23.
20. Ritchie, J. B., & Smith, B. (1991). The impact of a mega-event on host region awareness: A longitudinal study. *Journal of Travel Research, 30*(1), 3–10.
21. Um, S., & Crompton, J. (1992). The roles of perceived inhibitors and facilitators in pleasure travel destination decisions. *Journal of Travel Research, 30*(3), 18–25.
22. Woodside, A., & Sherrell, D. (1977). Traveler evoked, inept, and inert sets of vacation destinations. *Journal of Travel Research, 16*(1), 14–18.
23. Getz, D. (1998). Trends, strategies, and issues in sport-event tourism. *Sport Marketing Quarterly, 7*(2), 8–13.
24. Kim, N., & Chalip, L. (2004). Why travel to the FIFA World Cup? Effects of motives, background, interest, and constraints. *Tourism Management, 25,* 695–707.
25. WM Phoenix Open website. Retrieved from wmphoenixopen.com/thunderbirds/history-of-the-thunderbirds/
26. Coates, K., Healy, R., & Morrison, W. (2002). Tracking the Snowbirds: Seasonal migration from Canada to the U.S.A. and Mexico. *American Review of Canadian Studies, 32*(3), 433–450.
27. Gwinner, K. (1997). A model of image creation and image transfer in event sponsorship. *International Marketing Review, 14,* 145–158.
28. Cha, S., McCleary, K., & Uysal, M. (1995). Travel motivations of Japanese overseas travelers: A factor-cluster segmentation approach. *Journal of Travel Research, 34,* 33–39.
29. Kim, S., Chun, H., & Petrick, J. (2005). Positioning analysis of overseas golf tour destinations by Korean golf tourists. *Tourism Management, 26,* 905–917; and Jorge, J., & Monteiro, C. (2011). Competitive choice dimensions of golf destinations: A multivariate perceptual mapping analysis. *European Journal of Tourism, Hospitality & Recreation, 2*(3), 29–54.
30. Murphy, P., Pritchard, M. P., & Smith, B. (2000). The destination product and its impact on traveler perceptions. *Tourism Management, 21,* 43–52.

31. Harrison-Hill, T., & Chalip, L. (2005). Marketing sport tourism: Creating synergy between sport and destination. *Sport in Society, 8*, 302–320.

32. Pritchard, M. P., & Havitz, M., (2005). Ratios of tourist experience: It was the best of times it was the worst of times. *Tourism Analysis, 10*(3), 291–297

33. Pritchard, M. P., & Havitz, M., (2006). Destination appraisal: An analysis of critical incidents. *Annals of Tourism Research, 33*(1), 25–46.

34. Smith, S. (1994). The tourism product. *Annals of Tourism Research, 21*(3), 582–595.

35. Donovan, R., & Rossiter, J. (1982). Store atmosphere: An environmental psychology approach. *Journal of Retailing, 58* (Spring), 34–57; and Kotler, P. (1973). Atmospherics as a marketing tool. *Journal of Retailing, 49*(Winter), 48–64.

36. Hightower, R., Brady, M., & Baker, T. (2002). Investigating the role of the physical environment in hedonic service consumption: An exploratory study of sporting events. *Journal of Business Research, 55*(9), 697–707.

37. Gartner, W. (1989). Tourism image: Attribute measurement of State tourism products using multidimensional scaling techniques. *Journal of Travel Research, 28*(2), 16–20.

38. Pricewaterhouse Coopers. (2010). *The Games Effect: Preliminary Economic Impact of the 2010 Olympic & Paralympic Winter Games on British Columbia and Canada to March 31, 2010.* A report prepared for the Governments of British Columbia & Canada, the BC & Canadian Olympic Secretariats.

39. Kim, S., Chun, H., & Petrick, J. (2005). Positioning analysis of overseas golf tour destinations by Korean golf tourists. *Tourism Management, 26*, 905–917.

40. Associated Press. (2010, November 8). Tiger Woods gets VIP treatment in Thailand. *The Jakarta Post.* Retrieved from www.thejakartapost.com/news/2010/11/08/tiger-woods-gets-vip-treatment-thailand.html

41. Pritchard, M. P. (1998). Responses to destination advertising: Differences between inquirers and purchasers of a short vacation package. *Journal of Travel & Tourism Marketing, 8*(2), 31–52.

42. Lavidge, R., & Steiner, G. (1961, October). A model for predictive measurements of advertising effectiveness. *Journal of Marketing, 25*, 59–62; and Rossiter, J., & Percy, L. (1987). *Advertising and promotion management.* New York. McGraw-Hill.

43. Siegel, W., & Ziff-Levine, W. (1990). Evaluating tourism advertising campaigns: Conversion vs. advertising tracking studies. *Journal of Travel Research, 28*(3), 51–55; and Getz, D., & Fairley, S. (2004). Media management at sport events for destination promotion: Case studies and concepts. *Event Management, 8*, 127–139.

44. Echtner, C., & Ritchie, J. (1993). The measurement of destination image: An empirical assessment. *Journal of Travel Research, 32*(4), 3–13.

45. Gartner, W. (1993). Image formation process. *Journal of Travel & Tourism Marketing, 2*(2/3), 191–215.

46. Getz, D. (1998). Trends, strategies, and issues in sport-event tourism. *Sport Marketing Quarterly, 7*(2), 8–13.

47. Pritchard, M. P., & Funk, D. (2003). Consumptive frequency in spectator sports: A typology of event-media usage. In B. Crow (Ed.), *Sport Marketing Quarterly Abstracts* (p. 19). Sports Marketing Conference. Gainsville, FL.

48. Pritchard, M. P., & Funk, D. (2006). Symbiosis and substitution in spectator sport. *Journal of Sport Management, 20*(3), 297–320.

49. Kahle, L., Kambara, K., & Rose, G. (1996). A functional model of fan attendance motivations for college football. *Sport Marketing Quarterly, 5*(4), 51–60.

50. Assael, H. (1995). *Consumer behavior and marketing action,* (5th ed.). Cincinnati, OH: South-Western College Publishing.

51. James, J., & Ross, S. (2004). Comparing sport consumer motivations across multiple sports. *Sport Marketing Quarterly, 13*(1), 17–25.

52. Kahle, L., Kambara, K., & Rose, G. (1996). A functional model of fan attendance motivations for college football. *Sport Marketing Quarterly, 5*(4), 51–60.

53. Swanson, S., Gwinner, K., & Larson, B. (2001). Take me out to the ballgame: What motivates fan game attendance and word-of-mouth behavior? *American Marketing Association Conference Proceedings, 12*, 176–177.

54. Shoham, A., Rose, G., & Kahle, L. (2000). Practitioners of risky sports: A quantitative analysis. *Journal of Business Research, 47*(3), 237–251.

55. Madrigal, R. (2006). Measuring the multidimensional nature of sporting event consumption. *Journal of Leisure Research, 38*(3), 267–292; and Funk, D., Ridinger, L., & Moorman, A. (2004). Exploring the origins of involvement: Understanding the relationship between consumer motives and involvement with professional sport teams. *Leisure Sciences, 26*(2), 35–61.

56. Crouch, G. (1994). Promotion and demand in international tourism. *Journal of Travel & Tourism Marketing, 3*(3), 109–125; and Getz, D. (1998). Trends, strategies, and issues in sport-event tourism. *Sport Marketing Quarterly, 7*(2), 8–13.

57. Crompton, J. (1979). Motivations for pleasure vacation. *Annals of Tourism Research, 6*(4), 408–424.

58. Zhang, J., & Smith, D. (1997). The impact of broadcasting on the attendance of professional basketball games. *Sport Marketing Quarterly, 6*(1), 23–29.

59. Alexandris, K., Funk, D., & Pritchard, M. P. (2011). The impact of constraints on motivation, activity attachment and skier intentions to continue. *Journal of Leisure Research, 43*(1), 56–79; and Associated Press. (2010, November 8). Tiger Woods gets VIP treatment in Thailand. *The Jakarta Post.* Retrieved from www.thejakartapost.com/news/2010/11/08/tiger-woods-gets-vip-treatment-thailand.html

60. Getz, D. (1998). Trends, strategies, and issues in sport-event tourism. *Sport Marketing Quarterly, 7*(2), 8–13.

61. Pritchard, M. P., Funk, D., & Alexandris, K. (2009). Barriers to repeat patronage: The impact of spectator constraints. *European Journal of Marketing, 43*(1/2), 169–187; and Williams, P., & Fidgeon, P. (2000). Addressing participation constraints: A case study of potential skiers. *Tourism Management, 21*, 379–393.

62. Pritchard, M. P., & Funk, D. C. (2006). Symbiosis and substitution in spectator sport. *Journal of Sport Management, 20*, 297–320.

63. Getz, D. (1998). Trends, strategies, and issues in sport-event tourism. *Sport Marketing Quarterly, 7*(2), 8–13.

64. Kim, J., & Ritchie, J. (2012). Motivation-based typology: An empirical study of golf tourists. *Journal of Hospitality & Tourism Research, 36*(2), 251–280.

65. Getz, D. (1998). Trends, strategies, and issues in sport-event tourism. *Sport Marketing Quarterly, 7*(2), 8–13.

66. Green, B. (2001). Leveraging subculture & identity to promote sport events. *Sport Management Review, 4*, 1–19.

67. Sonmez, S., & Graef, A. (1998). Determining future travel behavior from past experience and perceptions of risk and safety. *Journal of Travel Research, 37*, 171–177.

68. Chalip, L. (2006). Towards social leverage of sport events. *Journal of Sport & Tourism, 11*(2), 109–127; and Chalip, L., & Leyns, A. (2002). Local business leveraging of a sport event: Managing an event for economic benefit. *Journal of Sport Management, 16*, 132–158.

69. Pricewaterhouse Coopers. (2010). *The Games Effect: Preliminary Economic Impact of the 2010 Olympic & Paralympic Winter Games on British Columbia and Canada to March 31, 2010.* A report prepared for the Governments of British Columbia & Canada, the BC & Canadian Olympic Secretariats; and Chalip, L. (2002). Using the Olympics to optimize tourism benefits. University lecture given in Barcelona's Centre d'Estudis Olimpics. Retrieved from http://olympicstudies.uab.es/lectures/web/pdf/chalip.pdf

70. Gartner, W. (1993). Image formation process. *Journal of Travel & Tourism Marketing, 2*(2/3), 191–215.

71. Kozak, M. (2002). Comparative analysis of tourist motivations by nationality and destination. *Tourism Management, 23*, 221–232.

72. Mok, H. (1990). A quasi-experimental measure of the effectiveness of destination advertising: Some evidence from Hawaii. *Journal of Travel Research, 29*(1), 30–34.

73. U.S. Census Bureau website definition. (n.d.). Retrieved from www.census.gov/population/metro/

74. Ritchie, J. B., & Smith, B. (1991). The impact of a mega-event on host region awareness: A longitudinal study. *Journal of Travel Research, 30*(1), 3–10.

75. Mossberg, L., & Hallberg, A. (1999). The presence of a mega-event: Effects on destination image and product-country images. *Pacific Tourism Review, 3*, 213–225 and Getz, D. (1998). Trends, strategies, and issues in sport-event tourism. *Sport Marketing Quarterly, 7*(2), 8–13.

76. Milman, A., & Pizam, A. (1995). The role of awareness and familiarity with a destination: The central Florida case. *Journal of Travel Research, 33*(3), 21–27.

77. Funk, D., & Pritchard, M. P. (2006). Sport publicity: Commitment's moderation of message effects. *Journal of Business Research, 59*(5), 613–621.

78. Ritchie, J. (1984). Assessing the impact of hallmark events: Conceptual and research issues. *Journal of Travel Research, 23*(1), 2–11; and Ritchie, J. B., & Smith, B. (1991). The impact of a mega-event on host region awareness: A longitudinal study. *Journal of Travel Research, 30*(1), 3–10.

79. Kaplanidou, K., & Karadakis, K. (2010). Understanding the legacies of a host Olympic city: The case of the 2010 Vancouver Olympic Games. *Sport Marketing Quarterly, 19*(2), 110–117.

80. Pricewaterhouse Coopers. (2010). *The Games Effect: Preliminary Economic Impact of the 2010 Olympic & Paralympic Winter Games on British Columbia and Canada to March 31, 2010.* A report prepared for the Governments of British Columbia & Canada, the BC & Canadian Olympic Secretariats.

81. Getz, D. (2008). Event tourism: Definition, evolution, and research. *Tourism Management, 29*, 403–428.

13

Leveraging eStrategies and the Online Environment

Kevin Filo
Griffith University

Daniel C. Funk
Temple University

Abstract: The new media technologies that comprise the online environment allow sport organizations to connect consumers from all over the globe. This connection occurs through an array of mechanisms, instantaneously, allowing individuals and the organization to interact, while each mechanism can be closely linked to another. These distinguishing characteristics of new media present a vast array of opportunities to organizations. The following chapter introduces four functions by which sport organizations can embrace new media technologies: monitor, respond, amplify, and lead. Upon introducing these four functions, four specific platforms are discussed, providing insight into how the four functions can be implemented through each respective technology: Facebook, Twitter, video (YouTube and viral video), and mobile technology. To illustrate leveraging strategies while providing insight into the opportunities afforded, a number of examples of successful employment of each technology are detailed.

Keywords: fan engagement, new media, social media

Introduction

Sport organizations have demonstrated recognition of the opportunity afforded by new media technologies, as well as a willingness to employ these technologies. This is evidenced by the array of sports teams that have embraced creating Facebook pages and Twitter feeds, while also developing YouTube channels and corporate blogs. Nonetheless, organizations are confronted by a variety of challenges in harnessing the power afforded through new media technologies. This chapter discusses such challenges along with examples of best practice that address the questions listed in Figure 13.1.

Five characteristics distinguish new media technologies from the traditional methods by which sport organizations could promote and market themselves. First, new media technologies transcend geographic boundaries in that a sport consumer can follow a team, player, league, or event from any part of the world. Second, the volume of communication inherent to new media refers to the vast array of technological platforms available to organizations and consumers, including Facebook, Twitter, blogs, and YouTube, as mentioned above. The number of different mechanisms available to consumers introduces the large number of customer engagement behaviors that organizations must effectively manage through identifying, evaluating, and acting

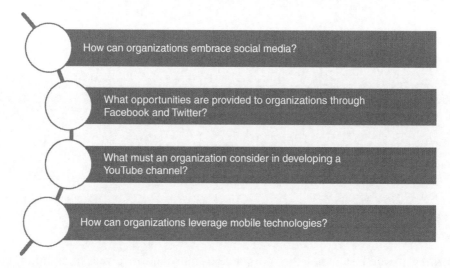

How can organizations embrace social media?

What opportunities are provided to organizations through Facebook and Twitter?

What must an organization consider in developing a YouTube channel?

How can organizations leverage mobile technologies?

Figure 13.1 An Overview to Leveraging Strategies and the Online Environment

upon them.[1] Third, the speed of communication afforded by new media technologies allows sport consumers to obtain information about teams, players, and events in real time. Fourth, new media technologies are highly interactive and allow for sport organizations to learn about consumers at the same time that sport consumers are learning about the organization. Finally, the interconnection and overlap within new media technologies represents the variety of ways that these technologies are linked and connected.[2] To illustrate, a sport consumer can "Like" an athlete on Facebook. The branded Facebook page for that athlete could have a link to the athlete's Twitter feed. This Twitter feed could include a link to the athlete's blog. And the blog could be linked to the athlete's team's official website, which features the team's YouTube channel.

These characteristics form the basis for this chapter. New media technologies connect individuals from all over the globe, through an array of mechanisms, in real time, allowing individuals and organizations to interact, while each platform can be closely connected to another. With this in mind, sport organizations must determine the best means to leverage new media technologies and ensure that each technology is bringing value to the organization. As depicted in Figure 13-2, this chapter introduces four different functions toward embracing new media: monitor, respond, amplify, and lead. From there, four different new media technologies—Facebook, Twitter, video, and mobile technology—are introduced to demonstrate how each can be used to serve these functions.

Embracing New Media

Sport organizations must embrace new media and learn to effectively leverage the technologies. This is not only due to the market penetration of new media technologies and relevance to the current sports marketing landscape, but also because the dialogue about sports teams, athletes, and events are occurring across new media technologies

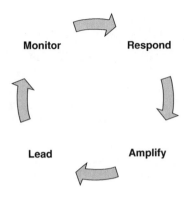

Figure 13.2 Embracing Social Media

regardless of whether or not the sport organizations are involved. In addition, new media technologies present a number of benefits to sport organizations, including creating publicity, providing an opportunity to learn about consumers, and offering an opportunity to target specific consumer segments. Through the activation of these benefits, organizations can use new media technologies to build community and participation among fans, develop programs integrating sponsors, and direct traffic to the official website and/or sponsor websites.

Accordingly, sport organizations must develop an approach for embracing new media technologies. Divol, Edelman, and Sarrazin[3] advance four primary functions to guide organizations in embracing new media technologies (see Table 13.1): to monitor, to respond, to amplify, and to lead consumer behavior. This approach is similar to the steps of find, listen, engage, and lead that have been advocated by others.[4]

Function: Monitoring

Monitoring involves continuously locating, listening to, and understanding the conversations that are taking place about your organization online. The resources required to implement this function can be extensive. Organizations such as the Boston Red Sox deploy a large team of interns and full-time staff to glean insights from the vast array

Table 13.1 Primary Functions Guiding Organizational Adoption of New Media Technology

Function	Definition
Monitor	Continuously locating, listening to, and understanding the conversations that are taking place about your organization online.
Respond	Beyond simply locating, listening to, and understanding the online conversations taking place, a response can be delivered.
Amplify	Strategically integrating new media technologies into marketing activities to allow for additional engagement and sharing among consumers.
Lead	Using these resources to activate long-term changes in attitude and behavior.

of online conversations taking place about the team across the online environment. As an additional example, Gatorade has implemented a "social media war room," a command center for monitoring the brand in real time across social media. The insights derived from this expansive operation are used to influence product development and marketing strategy.[5] Meanwhile, an assortment of free tools can be used to monitor online conversations about a brand. These tools include RSS feeds such as Google Alerts, blog search engines such as Technorati, resources to monitor blog comments such as Yacktrack, Twitter Search, and Friendfeed, a mechanism that aggregates various social accounts.[6] Investing in the resources and technology required to monitor online conversations can provide an organization with massive amounts of data to analyze and inform practice.

Function: Responding

A sport organization must determine when and how to respond beyond simply locating, listening to, and understanding the online conversations taking place. To that end, new media technologies represent a highly effective customer service resource. Once negative comments have been identified within the monitoring function, a response can be delivered. If delivered in a timely and engaging manner, positive outcomes can follow. Many organizations are developing "listening centers," similar to the 'social media war room' used by Gatorade. Listening centers are not only designed to monitor conversations in the online environment, but also serve as a toolkit for the deployment of an efficient, detailed, and prepared response to issues that emerge.[7]

Similarly, a number of airlines have Twitter feeds devoted to customer service, and the Best Buy corporation received a great deal of attention for the development of the Twelp Force, a collection of Best Buy employed technology experts who shared their advice and support via Twitter. The footwear company, Zappos, has further advanced its distinguished customer service reputation through creating a direct message interface on Twitter devoted exclusively to service issues. And the Xbox gaming system introduced 'Elite Tweet Fleet,' which holds the Guinness World Record title of "most responsive brand on Twitter."

These examples illustrate the positive benefits that can be obtained when comprehensive monitoring leads to efficient and effective responding via new media technologies. In addition, responding via new media technologies can often involve crisis management. An example of effective crisis management through new media technologies is how Syracuse University handled child molestation accusations against a former assistant basketball coach. The social media team at the University used the University's Facebook and Twitter accounts to stay in front of the story and provide constant communication and transparency to the University community.

Function: Amplifying

Amplifying via new media technologies refers to strategically integrating new media technologies into marketing activities to allow for additional engagement and sharing among consumers. Through amplification, sport organizations can use new media technologies to share new content with consumers, solicit content from consumers, encourage sharing among consumers, and foster loyalty. Amplification involves using new media technologies to provide consumers with not only a product or a service, but an experience in which the consumer can engage with the product/service, brand, other consumers and enthusiasts. For this, sport consumers represent a ripe audience based on the passion, enthusiasm, and expertise inherent to sport fandom. Sport organizations have employed a variety of amplifying strategies via social media, including photo sharing, trivia contests, and soliciting stories of fanship among consumers.

For example, Nike purposefully distributed their highly successful 2010 FIFA World Cup "Write the Future" advertisement on Facebook two days prior to the television launch. This early distribution was implemented in hopes of generating attention and engagement for the campaign in the online environment in advance of the premiere through traditional channels. Nike was successful in achieving this objective as the video received thousands of "Likes," comments, and shares before it had been seen on television. Nike marketers also felt this was an opportunity to create synergy and facilitate discussion across generations who had viewed the ad through the two different outlets. Additional examples of amplification through new media will be provided in the discussion of the different technologies.

Function: Leading

Finally, leading via new media technologies relates to using these resources to activate long-term changes in attitude and behavior. This can include using the wide volume of new media technologies to raise and sustain awareness of products, services, and promotions, as well as delivering incentives for continued engagement. As an example, the New Jersey Nets utilize two initiatives: the Facebook Fan of the Game and the Twitter Fan of the Game whereby active social media users among the Nets' community of fans are rewarded for their engagement through being allowed to write one status update on the team's official Facebook Page and Twitter feed (respectively) during each half. In addition, select nights across the season are deemed "Social Media Nights." On these nights, which take place two or three times per season, social media users who like the team on Facebook or follow the team on Twitter are offered an exclusive package for a game.

The packages include access to discounts on tickets, a gift bag with Nets branded merchandise, and access to an exclusive Nets experience—previous experience-based items offered included private post-game autograph sessions, free-throw shooting on the Nets' court, and spots on the Nets' High Five line. Leading can also involve using new media tools to solicit feedback after purchase. Many sport organizations create community-based discussion forums to solicit ideas to improve the game-day experience.

Embracing new media through the four functions of monitoring, responding, amplifying, and leading can facilitate successful leveraging of the online environment. However, additional insight can be provided regarding specific tools to better understand how to implement these four functions across different mechanisms. The following sections provide insight and detail regarding four new media tools: Facebook, Twitter, video (YouTube and viral video), and mobile technologies. Illustrative examples of best practices in sport promotion and marketing are included.

Facebook

The continuously growing number of users of Facebook makes this new media tool an important resource for sport organizations. Facebook is expected to reach 1 billion users in 2012. Those users spend 700 billion minutes per month on Facebook and there are over 1 billion objects (pages, events, community pages) with which users can interact.[8] Despite these numbers, sport organizations struggle to develop effective promotional campaigns and complement existing promotion through Facebook.

Consumers interact with their favorite brands on Facebook more than any other social media site. Research conducted by the marketing firm Chadwick Martin Bailey provides a number of interesting insights regarding this interaction. First, consumers are selective in terms of the brands they Like on Facebook. Of users who Like a brand, 78% Like fewer than 10 brands total. These Likes reflect active customers, as 58% of users Like a brand because they are already a customer. The most common form of interaction with brands is reading updates and newsfeeds (77%), followed by sharing (17%) and posting (13%). In addition, Liking a brand on Facebook introduces the semblance of a committed relationship, as 76% of users have never Un-Liked a brand. Finally, over 50% of users indicated they are more likely to recommend a brand to a friend after Liking, and over half also indicated they are more likely to purchase a product after Liking the brand.[9] The implications to be drawn from these findings suggest that brands should focus on attracting Likes through the provision of compelling content that is relevant to a wide audience. Also, the compelling content should be focused on informing and/or entertaining the consumer rather than on revenue-driven marketing messages.

The New England Patriots provide an example of these implications in practice. The organization provides compelling content to a wide audience via hosting an online "tailgate" on their Facebook page. This initiative is referred to as the JetBlue Patriots Pre-Game Social and involves a live radio broadcast, online chat, and photo submission across the hours leading up to each game. The objective of this initiative is inclusivity to allow individuals who are unable to attend the game to feel a part of the experience. The initiative is complemented by photos from the game-day experience. In addition, the organization has adopted a weekly "Ask a Pat" program on Facebook, in which the promotion team solicits questions for team personnel each week. One question is selected and a video response from the athlete is posted the next day on the team's page. Each Ask a Pat entry garners hundreds of comments and Likes that are then re-posted across those individuals' newsfeeds. Each of these initiatives represents a sport organization providing compelling content with a focus on informing and entertaining, rather than revenue generation.

Although Facebook users indicate that reading content represents their most frequently employed method of interacting with brands, opportunity still exists for soliciting information and opinions from consumers. Facebook allows organizations to encourage fans to voice their opinions and this can then shape decisions for marketing strategy. Meanwhile, photos and videos have been revealed to be the types of posts that are ranked highest by EdgeRank (Facebook's newsfeed filtering algorithm), and also attract the most engagement among users.[10]

A strategy employed by Budweiser in advance of the 2010 Super Bowl provides an example of effective incorporation of both of these principles. In the weeks leading up to the game, Facebook users were invited to vote for which advertisement the beer brand would air during the Super Bowl. In order to cast a vote, the user had to first 'Like' the brand on Facebook. Invitations to 'Like' the brand were provided through targeted advertisements on Facebook. Once the user 'Liked' the brand, s/he could then view the three video advertisements in contention, and cast her/his vote. Once the vote was cast, the vote and the corresponding video were published on that user's newsfeed so that their friends could view the video, comment on the vote, or perhaps cast their own vote. Budweiser received tens of thousands of votes, and followed up with a similar initiative in 2011 that asked users to guess which ads would be shown during the Super Bowl.

An additional consideration for sport organizations leveraging Facebook is targeting messages and posts. Facebook allows brands to target updates based on region, country, or language. In the United States, posts can also be targeted by city and state. This targeting is particularly relevant to sport organizations with global appeal. Manchester United successfully employs targeting on Facebook through two fronts. First, the organization has created 'Welcome' videos from players from different countries, which are then delivered to fans from those same countries. When a new user 'Likes' Manchester United, they are greeted by the welcome video from a player from that user's country (if applicable) in the native language. Second, the club employs targeted advertising to promote its North American exhibition match tours. Users who 'Like' Manchester United receive targeted advertisement promoting exhibition matches and including ticket information if and when the team has an exhibition in that user's region. Due in part to these targeted advertisements, Manchester United has sold out tickets for most matches during tours.

Facebook is the most popular social networking site in the world, and sport organizations must strive to use the tools provided through the site to engage fans. Twitter represents another highly popular social networking platform that affords sport organizations with opportunity. Strategies to leverage Twitter are discussed next.

Twitter

Twitter is a microblogging service founded in 2006 with the mission to tell people what they care about as it is happening in the world. As of June 2012, 400 million tweets are sent per day, and in that same month the service surpassed 500 million active users. The highest percentage of Twitter users reside in the United States (107.7 million), Brazil (33.3 million) and Japan (29. 9 million).[11] As a marketing tool, Twitter is used by individuals and organizations to break news, build community, and deliver customer service.

Organizations are increasingly turning to Twitter to break news about recent activities and updates. The emphasis in breaking news through Twitter is on adding to the conversation. With the high volume of technologies available (i.e., blogs, podcasts, Facebook, etc.) to consumers to learn about an organization, it becomes imperative for a team to be strategic in how Twitter is utilized to share information. In select instances, an organization may choose to share information and links through Twitter that are not necessarily centered around the team. For example, a team may provide information about the community in which it resides or the sport in general, rather than a strict focus on the organization. This strategy requires an understanding of what is relevant and valued by the target audience.

In other instances, a team may provide exclusive content regarding the organization to their Twitter followers. A number of teams across the NFL and NBA have received a great deal of attention and praise for tipping their draft choices via Twitter in advance of the official announcement. This strategy is viewed as a means to reward followers with inside information that, again, adds to the conversations taking place via Twitter. Using Twitter to break news and share information requires attention to media relations in that organizations must foster relationships with media personnel, independent bloggers, and dedicated fans through their collection of followers as well as those the organization follows. This relationship can be bolstered by sharing and re-tweeting content from these individuals to develop rapport and understanding. This can involve using www.search.twitter.com to employ a keyword search to find bloggers and fans writing and talking about the team. Re-tweeting and sharing posts from these individuals will be appreciated and can encourage them to do the same. This will help toward ensuring that news and updates provided by the organization are communicated widely and clearly by followers.

Building community through Twitter also involves adding to the conversation. Twitter represents an easy and effective tool to start contests among followers (e.g., photo submission) or to post trivia questions as part of a promotion. In addition, Twitter can be used to host virtual focus groups among followers based on a series of open-ended questions posed by the organization. In addition, hashtags—words or phrases prefixed with the symbol # to tag the topic—can be created to prompt discussion and solicit feedback on various topics relevant to the organization and followers. In addition, a variety of athletes regularly host question and answer sessions with their followers via Twitter wherein followers are invited to ask questions of the athlete with the responses posted on the interface. A number of organizations have created "scavenger hunts" via Twitter. Through these community-building promotions an organization creates a hashtag highlighting the team and then sets rewards for reaching select milestones concerning number of tweets sent using that hashtag. For instance, a team may make free tickets available to an event and for every thousand tweets sent, additional clues are provided to fans to assist in locating the tickets.

Twitter also provides an opportunity for an organization to address customer service issues on an individual basis. As noted above, a number of organizations have Twitter accounts dedicated exclusively to customer service. This can be adopted by sport organizations to improve the in-game service experience, and to better understand customer needs. In addition, Twitter has been used to enable customer service through the provision of exclusive deals and promotions to Twitter followers. Dell

Computers and Amazon.com represent two of the most successful companies in terms of sharing customer-service–based promotions through Twitter, and this strategy has been used by a variety of sport organizations in delivering discounts on merchandise and tickets to Twitter followers. Similarly, a number of teams and athletes have used strategies wherein a quick announcement is made through a Twitter feed indicating team personnel will be appearing at a specific public area with free tickets and the first Twitter follower to find them receives the tickets.

Two additional strategies that have been employed by sport organizations to leverage Twitter are Tweetups and in-game tweeting. These strategies add value to the conversation, and develop community. A Tweetup is an event where people who actively use Twitter are invited to meet in person. The NHL held the first ever sport-based Tweetup across a number of cities in advance of the 2009 playoffs, and received a great deal of positive feedback. The Essendon Football Club held the first Tweetup in Australia during the 2010 AFL season. Tweetups are now commonplace across the sport landscape. Tweetups are generally hosted at bars or restaurants near the stadium or venue, and present an excellent opportunity to integrate sponsors. After inviting Twitter followers to gather at a specific event, the sport organization must ensure that activities are organized to attract attendees beyond simply the opportunity to interact with individuals with similar interests. Accordingly, Tweetups generally include content such as speakers, panel discussions, increased access to team personnel, or contests. The purpose of a Tweetup is for a sport organization to allow for the community of fans to be strengthened.

Showcasing in-game tweeting is a practice that has been adopted by a number of sport organizations. Here, organizations feature live tweets from fans during games on the scoreboard within the stadium. This involves using a hashtag for the game, and requires an individual from the sport organization to filter the tweets received prior to posting. The Gold Coast Suns of the AFL have enjoyed success through this strategy. In-game tweeting can also incorporate sponsors, and can be developed into a contest with prizes for the best tweets.

Facebook and Twitter boast high usage and global penetration, but neither tool can boast the expansive library of rich content available through online video. YouTube represents the most popular site for video, and the site allows sport organizations to create and organize content through official channels. Strategies for leveraging YouTube as well as viral video are detailed next.

YouTube

YouTube has emerged as the clear leader in the online video space. YouTube attracts over 800 million unique visitors each month and over 4 billion hours of video are viewed each month. Beyond the reach of YouTube and the breadth of videos available, YouTube is distinguished by the platform's social component. Over 700 YouTube videos are shared each minute on Twitter and over 50% of all videos on YouTube have been rated or include comments from the viewing community. YouTube videos are rated by viewers who can choose to either Like or Dislike a video. Interestingly, for every dislike received on YouTube, the site receives 10 likes. The implication is that the YouTube community actively tells others what they enjoy.[12] Accordingly, YouTube represents a technology that sport organizations must use to create a presence and leverage effectively.

The first means by which sport organizations can utilize YouTube is through the creation of specific YouTube channels for their brand. A YouTube channel allows a sport organization to engage with consumers via video when and where consumers want it. A YouTube channel can feature both short- and long-form content. In developing a YouTube channel strategically, a sport organization must consider the following. First, as with Twitter and Facebook, an organization must ensure that the content shared via the YouTube channel is adding value to the community. The content must be relevant to the audience and viewers need to be given a reason to view and share the videos uploaded to the channel. It is important to remember that the YouTube channel may not provide direct revenue, thus the focus should be on engaging viewers and adding to the conversation.

To this end, sport organizations should strive toward a strategic creative format to the videos on offer within their channel. This can often involve the development of different themes. As an example, the Gold Coast Suns (http://www.youtube.com/user/goldcoastfc) feature a number of series available to viewers such as how to and strategy-based videos (Talkin' Tactics), videos highlighting the organization's community relations initiatives (Suns in the Community), and behind-the-scenes videos (Suns Raw). The content of the YouTube channel can also be focused on promoting the product of the organization. For instance, GoPro, a company that manufactures wearable HD cameras for sports, provides hundreds of videos showcasing their products in action through their official YouTube channel (http://www.youtube.com/user/goprocamera). Similarly, a number of sport organizations focus on highlight videos through their YouTube channels.

A YouTube channel also provides an opportunity for experimentation and innovation. Because of the user-friendly interface, the user control afforded, and the bandwidth available in terms of the sheer number of videos that can be uploaded, sport organizations can continually try new products/services and content on their YouTube channel. In addition, the viewer response that can be gleaned via YouTube videos (i.e., shares, likes) provides organizations with regular feedback for the different initiatives. This experimentation can serve to determine what content adds value to the conversation. In comparison to traditional marketing materials for an organization, the look and feel of a YouTube channel can be altered in an effort to optimize without a large investment in terms of time, money, or resources. Two organizations that represent effective experimentation across the YouTube channel are the surf brands Quiksilver (http://www.youtube.com/user/quiksilver) and Roxy (http://www.youtube.com/user/roxy). Each brand regularly updates and varies the content shared within their respective channels. This includes providing videos such as webisodes and mini-documentaries featuring behind-the-scenes access to sponsored athletes, instruction-based videos for new equipment, profiles of musicians popular with each brand's audience, and athlete vlogs (video logs). Both brands benefit from featuring products and services that translate well to video, but each leverages their YouTube channel through constant effort and experimentation to engage their audience.

An additional consideration for an organization's YouTube channel is search engine optimization (SEO). SEO involves maximizing a piece of content's ability to be recognized through search. With the extensive array of videos available via the platform, SEO is critical within YouTube. To address this, sport organizations must optimize their content by creating smart and logical titles for each video. In addition, descriptions that not only encompass what each video is about, but also align with likely search terms entered by consumers are imperative. Furthermore, videos within a YouTube channel can be tagged by keywords that, again, are logical and consistent with terms that would guide a consumer search for the content. SEO is made simpler for websites as search engines can read the words that comprise the content of the site. However, a search engine cannot view a video to determine the content (and words relevant to that content). Hence, YouTube channel managers must ensure that titles, keywords, and tags accurately reflect the content of each video.

The Ultimate Fighting Championship (UFC) provides an example of an organization that utilized SEO via the YouTube channel effectively (http://www.youtube.com/user/UFC). Most of the more important UFC fights are available to viewers on a pay-per-view basis. As a result, the organization must ensure that past fights are made available to viewers who were unable to watch the live pay-per-view offering, or for those individuals wanting to re-watch a fight. The UFC YouTube channel is the outlet used for this, and the past fights are archived in an extensive and organized fashion, allowing fans to easily search for and locate specific fights. The detailed level of organization provided has contributed to UFC having the second most viewed sport-based YouTube channel in North America.

A final consideration for a sport organization in creating and managing an official YouTube channel is fully understanding that YouTube is distinct from television (the traditional means by which video is relayed to consumers). A viewer on YouTube is not simply watching a video; rather that viewer is Liking (or disliking) a video, commenting on the video, or sharing the video via Twitter, Facebook, or blogs. Consequently, organizations can promote this type of interactivity through specific calls to action within their videos. In addition, YouTube Annotations allows YouTube channel managers to provide background information with videos, links within a video, and to create sequencing across multiple videos. Employing these tools can work toward ensuring that videos featured on the channel can be viewed by a larger audience. Additionally, YouTube allows users to subscribe to channels. Organizations employing a YouTube channel can ask viewers to subscribe to the channel, which can facilitate repeat viewing and foster an audience for future videos. Collectively, acknowledging and leveraging these distinctions from television can allow YouTube channel managers to turn viewers into marketers on behalf of the organization, championing their content.

The YouTube channels developed by Nike portray an organization that understands and activates the distinctions from traditional television (http://www.youtube.com/user/nike). Nike's YouTube channels are highly interactive and feature an urban focus. The videos often use non-traditional production equipment such as security cameras, webcams, and mobile phones. In addition, Nike creates different channels for different audiences, such as NikeFootball Portugal and NikeFootball UK. Furthermore, channels are developed for different brand categories including running, women's sports, football, etc. Across each of these channels, Nike includes various calls to action to engage consumers in commenting and sharing, as well as viewing additional videos. As a result, videos featured on Nike YouTube channels are some of the most frequently shared sport videos across social networks.

In select instances, YouTube has proactively sought sports-based partners to showcase their content. In 2010, YouTube partnered with Indian Premier League (IPL) cricket to broadcast matches. Through the partnership, YouTube was given exclusive rights to stream IPL matches online with the IPL and YouTube splitting the revenue from sponsorship and advertising. This marked the first cricket tournament ever broadcast on YouTube and the partnership remains in place in 2012. YouTube has also partnered with the Scottish Premier League (SPL) to provide match highlights and exclusive content for three soccer seasons starting in 2012–2013. SPL pursued the partnership in an effort to secure a larger global audience. It seems likely that similar partnerships will emerge between YouTube and sport entities striving toward attracting a global audience.

YouTube can also bolster the connection between fan and athlete. This can be achieved through videos created and uploaded by athletes for fans, and vice versa. In 2011, Kevin Love of the Minnesota Timberwolves created a series of videos promoting a fake cologne, while also soliciting votes for the NBA All-Star Game. A similar YouTube-based pitch for fan recognition was made in 2008 by NBA player Chris Bosh. Also, a fan may post a video to YouTube in an effort to interact with an athlete, or an athlete may view a video and then attempt to contact fans. For instance, Tyreke Evans of the Sacramento Kings called on a group of trick shot artists who went by the name of 'Dude Perfect' and had made a name for themselves via a collection of YouTube videos, to assist with the creation of viral videos to promote his campaign for the 2009–2010 NBA Rookie of the Year Award. In 2009, Shaquille O'Neal viewed a YouTube video of trick shots from Bruce Manley, a YouTube sensation referred to as the king of H.O.R.S.E, and promptly contacted him to challenge him to a game of H.O.R.S.E for $1,000.

Viral Video

Viral video has emerged as an important component of the online environment within sport promotion. Video has become an accessible and common form of content, with tools such as Facebook and Twitter representing mechanisms facilitating the sharing of this content. Viral video refers to a video that gains popularity due to sharing via the Internet, and viral video marketing is frequently employed by sport organizations. Within viral video marketing, sport organizations must emphasize concept over content, while focusing on entertaining consumers rather than selling to consumers (as with traditional marketing). The most effective viral videos are short in duration (less than five minutes in length) and do not reflect an outright advertisement. The most shared viral videos are those that are the most subtle in terms of promotion.

Viral videos are referred to as a "Lean Forward Experience," as watching a video represents time and attention the viewer has given to a brand rather than time and attention a brand has to pay for within traditional advertising. To facilitate the lean forward experience, viral videos must be easily shareable, and often include a call to action through an exposed URL or an invitation to share. Viral videos can provide a number of benefits to sport organizations, including exponential views through the spread and reach afforded by social media tools such as Facebook, Twitter, and YouTube. In addition, organizations employing viral video may be viewed as forward thinking and innovative. Furthermore, viral video reflects a cost-effective form of promotion as the sharing inherent to viral video offsets distribution costs. Sport organizations can employ a number of tactics to distribute viral videos. Representatives from organizations can share the video through online discussion forums or social media. Additionally, organizations can work with independent bloggers and media personalities who have a similar or desirable audience to ask or encourage the blogger to share the video.

A number of sport organizations have enjoyed success employing viral video. Equipment manufacturers such as Nike and Puma have created videos that have not only reached a wide audience, but also garnered a vast array of media attention. For example, the Puma Hard Chorus, a viral video produced in advance of an English football match conflicting with Valentine's Day in 2011, was shared over 65,000 times in advance of the holiday and the video has been viewed over 15 million times in total. Meanwhile, the video received coverage from each of the major newspapers in the UK and an assortment of football outlets. Most tellingly, the viral video garnered hundreds of "response videos" created by other clubs, teams, and fans. A number of other brands have used sports in the creation of viral videos. Gillette has seen incredible success with a collection of viral videos using athletes such as Roger Federer and Evan Longoria. The videos included subtle messaging for the brand and entertained audiences were left wondering whether the footage was real or fake. Once again, each video has reached a global audience evident through the large number of views and shares, while the unique approach taken through the concept has garnered a vast array of media mentions. Viral video is an opportune mechanism for sport organizations to leverage and, in doing so, engage consumers.

Each of the technologies outlined above provides consumers with information, engagement, and content on demand. However, each technology requires a mechanism by which that information, engagement, and content can be accessed. Consumers are increasingly comfortable obtaining content and engaging through mobile devices. Strategies for leveraging mobile technology are provided next.

Mobile Technology

Mobile devices represent the device by which sport organizations can deliver content to consumers using Facebook, Twitter, and YouTube where, when, and how the consumer wants the content delivered. The importance of leveraging mobile technology is demonstrated through the pervasiveness of the smartphone. Over 500 million smartphones were sold in 2011.[13] In addition, desirable global markets such as China, India, and Brazil reflect some of the top regions in terms of mobile phone use. Sport organizations have leveraged mobile technology through the development of mobile marketing applications, the employment of QR codes, and mobile ticketing.

Mobile marketing applications employed by sport organizations include real-time scores and updates, streams of audio and video feeds, broadcast information and exclusive video content, and promotional content such as sponsor-based contests. Examples of successful mobile marketing application in sports include MLB At Bat and IPL Cricket. MLB At Bat allows fans to order live games to stream, while also offering a free game of the day. The application also provides subscribers with video highlights, condensed game offerings, and home and away audio feeds of games. MLB At Bat is the number one sports-based mobile application of all time and was inducted into the Hall of Fame for iPhone, iPad, and MacWorld. The IPL Cricket mobile application includes push notifications that subscribers can set to alert users of updates and news before, during, and after matches. These push notifications are customizable by subscriber.

Real Madrid exemplifies the importance of mobile marketing as the organization employs a full-time department exclusively dedicated to mobile platforms and mobile marketing. This department strives toward two objectives: generating revenue through the distribution of mobile content and services, along with creating a mobile community.[14] Real Madrid focuses its mobile initiatives around providing subscribers with news, updates, and information, complemented by interactivity and access to team personnel. Real Madrid has developed an interactive game that allows users to compete against other users in a simulated penalty kick. In addition, the organization uses the mobile platform to connect subscribers with the team in a personalized manner. For instance, when the club wins a league trophy a video call is sent out to all Real Madrid mobile subscribers. Once the subscriber responds to the call they will see a video of one of the team's players saying, "Madridista we have won La Liga thanks very much for your support!" Furthermore, Real Madrid has used mobile technology to activate and leverage sponsorship for the club. The mobile application allows users to opt-in for marketing communication from team sponsors. This allows for the creation and distribution of a vast database that can be used by sponsors to engage with fans. This engagement can involve the creation of sponsor-based contests for fans. One contest administered by team sponsor Audi received over 150,000 entries.

QR codes are a second avenue for sport organizations to leverage mobile technology. QR codes allow organizations to link the physical world to the online world. QR code stands for quick response code, and the two-dimensional codes can be created at a low cost or no cost at all. A number of websites, including Google, allow for the creation of QR codes. The QR code can be scanned through a smartphone using an application that smartphone users can download for free. QR codes may appear in magazines, on signs, on buses, on business cards, or on almost any object by which consumers may obtain information. Once a user has scanned the code, their phone links to a website, video, or additional content complementing the source of the code.

The Detroit Red Wings provide an example of successful employment of QR codes to engage fans. The club embedded a QR code in printed game programs fans purchased for games. The QR code came with an explicit call to action urging fans to scan the code using their smartphone. Once scanned, the code linked to an exclusive video that complemented the player profiles printed within the program. In an effort to minimize confusion concerning the code and scanning process, the Red Wings introduced an instructional video that aired on the scoreboard during games. The promotion was highly successful and the organization plans to continue using QR codes to enhance fan access to the team, as well as to activate sponsorship opportunities.

Table 13.2 New Media Tools and Sport Marketing Examples

Technology	Opportunities	Example
Facebook	• Provide compelling content through branded page • Solicit information and opinions from consumers • Target messages	JetBlue Patriots Pre-Game Social on Facebook involves a live radio broadcast, online chat, and photo submission across the hours leading up to each game.
Twitter	• News and updates • Provide exclusive content • Build community • Customer service • Tweetups • Showcase in-game tweeting	The Essendon Football Club held the first Tweetup in Australia during the 2010 AFL season. Tweetups are generally hosted at bars or restaurants near the stadium or venue, and present an excellent opportunity to integrate sponsors.
Video	• Brand-specific YouTube channels • Exclusive content partnerships • Bolster the connection between fan and athlete • Facilitate viral marketing	Nike's YouTube channels are highly interactive and feature an urban focus. In addition, Nike creates different channels for different audiences.
Mobile	• Mobile marketing applications • QR codes • Mobile ticketing • Location-based marketing	Real Madrid employs a full-time department exclusively dedicated to mobile platforms and mobile marketing. This department strives toward two objectives: generating revenue through the distribution of mobile content and services, along with creating a mobile community.

An additional means by which sport organizations can leverage mobile technologies to improve the fan experience is through mobile ticketing. Mobile ticketing involves a game ticket delivered to fans' mobile phones through text or message. A unique bar-code is generated and delivered to the customer's mobile phone via SMS. The customer then receives their mobile ticket immediately, and the mobile ticket can be scanned at the venue upon arrival. Information is automatically transmitted to a database for organizers to track attendance in real time. Beyond real-time attendance tracking, the advantages of mobile ticketing include immediate ticket delivery, reduced distribution and operational costs associated with printing tickets, and customer convenience.

Mobile ticketing has been embraced across industries such as airlines, the arts, cinema, and music. A number of sport organizations have begun to employ the technology. Major League Baseball has been an early adopter, with teams such as the Oakland Athletics and San Francisco Giants introducing the service first. As of 2012, over half of the teams in the league offer mobile ticketing, and the Giants have partnered with the ticketing agency Stubhub to make mobile tickets available through third-party sales. In addition, the Dutch Premier League has used mobile ticketing and the PGA Tour has offered mobile tickets for select events. Across each of these examples consumer feedback has been positive.

Engaging with consumers via mobile technologies will only increase in importance for sport organizations (see examples in Table 13-2). In developing applications to leverage mobile platforms, sport organizations must create applications and content that complement consumer experiences rather than distract consumers from the experiences on offer. In addition, advancements in, and acceptance of, tablets and iPads provides further evidence of the importance of mobile application development. The Australian Open has received a great deal of praise for the development of an iPad application that serves to enhance the fan experience through the richness afforded by the medium. Meanwhile, the emergence of location-based social networking services connected to mobile devices such as FourSquare provide another avenue for leveraging mobile technology. FourSquare allows users to 'check in' to venues using a mobile website, text message, or application. The Washington Redskins have introduced an array of FourSquare-based promotions such as merchandise and concession discounts to incentivize checking in at the stadium. Collectively, each of these resources underscores the importance and opportunity that can be leveraged by organizations that seek to engage consumers via mobile technologies.

Conclusion

This chapter outlined a number of strategies for sport organizations to leverage within the online environment. Specifically this chapter introduced the factors that distinguish new media technologies as a means to introduce the opportunities new media presents to organizations. From there, four primary functions toward embracing new media were introduced: monitor, respond, amplify, and lead. After introducing each of these functions, four specific technologies within the online environment were discussed: Facebook, Twitter, YouTube and viral video, as well as mobile technologies. In discussing these technologies, examples were provided to illustrate how each technology can be used by sport organizations to implement each of the four functions.

The online environment will only continue to grow in importance for organizations. This presents opportunity for sport management researchers and practitioners alike. Accordingly, organizations will deploy more resources to this area in order to gain competitive advantage. These resources can be used to continuously navigate through the various technologies, while experimenting across the different platforms. In addition, lessons can be learned through organizations outside of the sport context on how to optimize the online environment. It is hoped that the ideas and examples introduced in this chapter provide a basis for further leveraging and innovation within the online environment.

References

1. van Doorn, J., Lemon, K. N., Mittal, V., Nass, S., Pick, D., Pirner, P., & Verhoef, P. C. (2010). Customer engagement behaviour: Theoretical foundations and research directions. *Journal of Service Research, 13,* 253–266.
2. Croteau, D., & Hoynes, W. (2003). Media society: Industries, images, and audiences (3rd ed.). Thousand Oaks, CA: Sage Publications.
3. Divol, R., Edelman, D., & Sarrazin, H. (2012). Demystifying social media. *McKinsey Quarterly,* Retrieved from http://www.mckinseyquarterly.com/Demystifying_social_media_2958
4. Hessert, K. (2009). Five secrets of unlocking the power of Twitter for college sports. Retrieved from http://www.cosida.com/news/2009/2/5/0205095609_2254.aspx

5. Contagious Magazine. (2010). Gatorade social media war room. Retrieved from http://www.contagiousmagazine.com/2010/06/gatorade_7.php
6. Schwabel, D. (2008). Top 10 free tools for monitoring your brand's reputation. Retrieved from http://mashable.com/2008/12/24/free-brand-monitoring-tools/
7. French, T., LaBerge, L., & Magill, P. (2012). Five 'no regrets' moves for superior customer engagement. *McKinsey Quarterly*. Retrieved from http://www.mckinseyquarterly.com/Five_no_regrets_moves_for_superior_customer_enagement_2999
8. Facebook Statistics (2012). Retrieved from http://www.facebook.com/note.php?note_id=141377535935074
9. Swallow, E. (2011). How consumers interact with brands on Facebook. Retrieved from http://mashable.com/2011/09/12/consumers-interact-facebook/
10. Ling, M. (2012). How to boost your Facebook Edgerank—9 key tips. Retrieved from http://www.affilorama.com/blog/boost-facebook-edgerank
11. Macmillan, G. (2012). Brazil now second biggest country on Twitter, UK fourth. Retrieved from http://wallblog.co.uk/2012/02/01/brazil-now-second-biggest-country-on-twitter-uk-fourth/
12. YouTube Statistics. (2012). Retrieved from http://www.youtube.com/t/press_statistics
13. Mobithinking. (2012). Retrieved from http://mobithinking.com/mobile-marketing-tools/latest-mobile-stats
14. McLaren, D. (2010). *Real Madrid and mobile marketing*. Retrieved from http://www.theuksportsnetwork.com/real-madrid-and-mobile-marketing

14

Leveraging Sport for Social Marketing and Corporate Social Responsibility (CSR)

Jeffrey L. Stinson
Central Washington University

Mark P. Pritchard
Central Washington University

Abstract: Sports play a crucial role in promoting pro-social behaviors by fans, participants, athletes, teams, and leagues. The prominent role of sports in modern society provides the industry with a unique platform for addressing social issues, and seeking benefits, for consumers, organizations, and the larger society. This chapter defines both social marketing and corporate social responsibility in the context of sports. Examples of team and organizational activities in each of these areas are explored and analyzed to underscore the social contribution sport can make to the greater good.

Keywords: corporate social responsibility, philanthropy, social marketing

Introduction

Sports and sport brands have been effectively leveraged to foster pro-social behaviors in a number of contexts. As in other areas of marketing, it is important to consider the role sport brands play in society. Compared to other areas of marketing inquiry in sports, the ability of sport brands to foster pro-social behaviors has been given little attention. Nevertheless, any cursory examination of sports teams and brands will reveal elements of socially responsible marketing, whether through encouraging donations to a charity organization, incenting kids to stay in school, or providing a foundation for community building. From the promotion of peace and truce agreements between warring factions in the ancient Olympic Games, to the current efforts of the NFL to support and raise funds for the United Way, sports have been and will continue to be a powerful social influence. This chapter will consider sports' social influence in two broad categories. First, we will examine sports in social marketing activities designed to influence the socially responsible behaviors of fans and other members of the general public. Second, we will review CSR strategies in sports, focusing on the creation of benefits for the company, the social cause, and society. Examples of team activities in each of these areas will be highlighted.

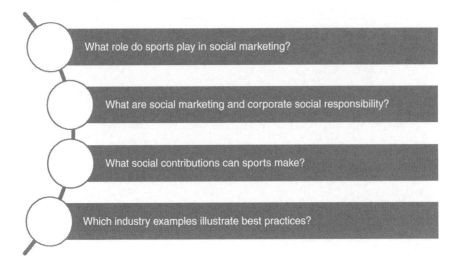

Figure 14.1 Overview of Chapter 14

Sport in Social Marketing

Noted social marketing researcher, Alan Andreasen, has defined social marketing as "the adaptation of commercial marketing technologies to programs designed to influence the voluntary behavior of target audiences to improve their personal welfare and that of the society of which they are a part."[1] Social marketing activities, then, are not necessarily designed to improve the welfare of the sport brand or business, but rather to improve the well-being of fans, the general public, and society as a whole. Sport brands may contribute directly or indirectly to various marketing mix strategies designed to encourage consumers' voluntary behaviors. In some cases, the sports team or brand is the focal element, such as the NFL's partnership with the United Way that encourages fans to support their local United Way organizations with contributions and volunteer activity. In other cases, the sport brand may be a more indirect influence, such as when Nike sponsors Team in Training. In either case, the sport brand is able to leverage its brand equity to encourage the pro-social voluntary behavior.

As you will remember from the discussion of consumer behavior in Chapter 2, sports are unique in the relationship the fan/participant has with the sport brand. The involvement and identification an individual has with a team, sport, or player creates a strong foundation for influencing the voluntary behaviors of that consumer. In effect, a highly involved fan will view the pro-social behavior as a pro-team behavior, and therefore, as a pro-individual behavior. Sports have the unique ability to leverage the involvement and identification of fans and participants to enhance and extend the voluntary, pro-social behaviors of the fan-base. We will focus specifically on social marketing strategies involving sport brands designed to encourage philanthropic activity (either through giving or volunteering), the social and educational development of youth, and the fostering of positive health-related behaviors.

Leveraging Sports to Encourage Philanthropic Behavior

Sports and sport brands are commonly leveraged to generate philanthropic activity. This section will examine the use of sports to generate donations for the sponsoring organization and the leveraging of sport brands to generate support for external organizations or causes. Non-profit organizations have long used sport events to raise money for their respective causes. You can probably quickly think of numerous sport-related activities (e.g., runs, golf tournaments, bike tours, etc.) that nonprofit organizations in your area use to raise money and awareness for their cause. In 2011, charities collected over $1.69 billion through the top 30 sport-related fundraising events alone, growth of 2.46% from 2010. The top events in the United States were the American Cancer Society Relay for Life ($415 million), the Susan G. Komen Race for the Cure ($131.3 million), the March of Dimes March for Babies ($105 million), the American Heart Association Heart Walk ($99.1 million), and the Leukemia and Lymphoma Society's Team in Training ($87.5 million).[2] In each of these cases, the nonprofit organization manages its own sport events in order to generate donations. The sports activity itself plays an integral role in the marketing mix of these events, essentially fulfilling the role of product (experience).

In other cases, charities may choose to align themselves with an already established sport event, team, or brand to raise money and awareness for the cause. For example, the U.S. Track and Field Association (USATF) estimates that runners and walkers in established events raise over $700 million per year for various charities.[3] In 2012, the charity program affiliated with the Boston Marathon raised $16 million for Boston and Massachusetts nonprofit organizations.[4] The Nike Women's Marathon held annually in San Francisco has raised over $60 million since 2004 for the Leukemia and Lymphoma Society,[5] and the Chicago Marathon reported raising over $10 million for charity every year since 2008.[6] The New York City Marathon has over 70 local, national, and international charity partners that use the event to raise money for their respective causes.[7]

Whether administering their own sporting events, or leveraging already established sport events and brands to raise money, charities must be aware of the motivations consumers have for participating in such events. A long-standing debate has centered on whether the cause or the event is the more important determinant of participation and fundraising. A 2007 study of charity-event participants in the UK found that involvement with the charity or cause was the most important determinant of an individual's decision to participate in a charity's sport fundraising event. Other important motivations for consumers to choose to participate in these fundraising events were the desire to pursue a healthy lifestyle, involvement with the sport, and the desire to mix socially with other event participants.[8] A U.S.-based study identified the three Cs of participation in charity sport events: Camaraderie, Cause, and Competency.[9] Camaraderie refers to the social motivations for participation reflected in participants feeling "part of something bigger than themselves" and their ability to collectively seek solutions for important problems (e.g., cure for cancer). Similar to the UK study, Cause reflects the participant's desire to raise money and awareness for the affiliated nonprofit cause. Finally, Competency reflects motives associated with the sports activity itself, including health and fitness benefits. Though the research with respect to cause vs. event is still in its early stages, both of these studies seem to suggest that both cause and event are important determinants of participation in charity sport events. Clearly, if an event is successful in addressing each of these motives, it will have the potential to benefit consumers and society, the two most important targets of a social marketing campaign.

Teams and sport brands have also chosen to align themselves with nonprofit organizations to influence the voluntary behavior of fans and local publics. Such partnerships are typically determined in one of two ways: either partner organizations are chosen based on geography, or partner organizations may be chosen based on relevance to the team/sport. For example, during the 2008–2009 fundraising campaign, the Seattle Seahawks served as the United Way campaign chair for King County, Washington. The campaign was the number one United Way fundraising campaign in the country, raising more than $100 million. The CEO of the United Way of King County noted the unprecedented awareness and participation the Seahawks were able to bring to the campaign, noting, "never before have we been able to reach so many people in the community."[10] This statement is all the more remarkable in that it comes from an organization that has had past campaign chairs from such notable organizations as Microsoft and Boeing.

Community support is not limited to leveraging the sport brand for increased financial support. Organizations such as the Chicago White Sox have expanded their efforts to include promoting community volunteer support. The White Sox Volunteer Corps brings players, front office staff, and fans together to serve nonprofit organizations near the team's home field on the south side of Chicago.[11] Other teams have chosen to align with causes more directly linked to their respective sports. For example, the Seahawks sister organization, the Seattle Sounders FC of Major League Soccer (MLS), has chosen to affiliate with the Washington Youth Soccer Association and Save the Children, a nonprofit organization using soccer as a platform for teaching healthy lifestyles to African youth.[12] As with other forms of partnership (i.e., sponsorship), the fit between charity and sport brand/team is critical to the success of the partnership. (See Chapter 10 for a discussion of sponsorship fit.) Choosing nonprofit partners that are relevant and important to the fan base and align with the competencies of the sport organization will lead to the most positive results. Philanthropic support for the partner organizations may be generated through direct request to fans, special events/promotions at games or events, or through other fundraising mechanisms such as auctions of sport-related products with proceeds benefitting the partnering organizations.

Unlike professional sport organizations, most colleges and universities attempt to leverage their intercollegiate athletic programs to generate additional support for the college or university itself. According to a Chronicle of Higher Education report, the University of North Carolina Chapel Hill raised $230 million for its athletic department in the five years ending in 2006, leading all U.S. colleges and universities.[13] Virginia, Ohio State, Florida, and Georgia rounded out the top five athletic fundraising institutions. Most of this charitable giving is the result of preferred seating programs, whereby donors make a contribution to secure ticket privileges and other desired benefits (e.g., parking privileges, club membership, etc.). At Florida, the school pursued activities designed to leverage its national championships in football and men's basketball. Paul Robell, the university's Vice President for Development, was quoted as saying "People are proud and feel good and kind of open their pockets a little more to keep that kind of record going."[14] Again, the involvement and identification fans have with the sport brand, in this case the University of Florida Gators, creates the potential to generate philanthropic activity. Research has indicated that the fan's desire to be affiliated with (or help build) a successful athletics program is a primary motive for this type of philanthropic behavior.[15].

Finally, sports have been leveraged in times of disaster or crisis to raise money and volunteer resources necessary for recovery. Although many of those efforts remain local in nature and never receive popular press attention, sport has played an important role in generating support for national and international disaster relief, including efforts following 9/11, the Asian tsunami, and Hurricane Katrina. In response to the tsunami, 24 of the world's best cricket players gathered in Melbourne, Australia, only 12 days after the disaster to raise nearly $10 billion in a match seen by a billion people in 122 countries.[16] Sports teams from high schools, colleges, and the professional ranks played a significant role in the $409 million raised by the American Red Cross in the days immediately following Hurricane Katrina.[17] Sports were not alone in responding to these disasters. Yet, the unique ability of sports to help galvanize an effort to generate volunteer, pro-social behavior is again illustrated.

Youth Socialization, Education, and Health

Sports, especially at the youth level, have long been recognized as a socialization agent. Participation in youth sports has been positively linked to moral development, values formation, and participation in cooperative behavior, among other benefits. Sports participation has also been tied to academic achievement and social adjustment.[18] Yet, these benefits are not automatic. As one author wrote "Although youth sport programs are not inherently good, they do have the potential to contribute to positive youth development."[19] Whether sports are a positive or negative socialization agent depends on the administration and organization of the sports event. In the end, it is the experience an individual has with the sport that determines the valence of the socialization. Thus, it is imperative that sport managers and marketers seek to implement strategies that will positively socialize youth and others involved with the sport.

Numerous calls have been made to reform youth sports with more focus on socialization and development rather than competition. Positive socialization also requires positive reinforcement and exposure to quality role models. Sport brands can play a role in this change (Interestingly enough, many authors assert a change in focus will also increase participation rates, perhaps offering a business benefit to the sport brand as well.)[20] One strategy sports teams and leagues can pursue in this regard is to provide "recreational" or "developmental" opportunities to their respective target markets. It is common in Europe, for example, for a professional sport club to offer participation opportunities at all levels of competition, from introductory youth leagues to top-level professional competition.[21] Thus a club, such as Barcelona FC, may have the opportunity to influence youth socialization throughout the child's development. While many of these activities, as noted with the Seattle Sounders FC examples above, focus on youth socialization and development, they are not limited to youth sports. Real Madrid operates "integration academies" in Spanish prisons designed to achieve many of the same positive socialization outcomes often associated with youth sports. The program aims to improve inmates' self-esteem, improve social skills, and teach "life" skills that will be valuable to inmates upon their release.[22]

Up to this point, the discussion has focused primarily on youth participation in sport. But, sports may also serve as a positive socialization agent through "passive sport participation." Passive sport participation includes watching sports on television, viewing a game or event in person, or following a favorite team through the internet. All offer the opportunity, particularly through language and modeling, to teach positive social values.[23] For example, teams may use their most prominent athletes as role models or spokespersons demonstrating positive behavior (e.g., modeling of good sportsmanship, modeling healthy habits). Or, sport brands may offer incentives to positively reward desired behaviors. For example, many NBA teams reward kids with strong school attendance records with tickets to the Martin Luther King, Jr. holiday games. The reward of the passive participation, in this case game tickets, reinforces the desired positive social behavior, in this case school attendance. Common themes in these social marketing campaigns include education and health-related behaviors. The NBA runs its Read to Achieve campaign with a focus on getting children and adults to read together to foster a life-long love of reading. The program involves coaches and players having "reading timeouts" in local schools and libraries, as well as book giveaways to program participants. The NBA estimates that it has reached 50 million children through the Read to Achieve Program.[24] Many teams have taken this one step further to seek positive role modeling from other spectators, creating an in-stadium environment that is conducive to positive socialization of children (and others.) Recognizing the critical need to attract young fans to games to ensure the long-term survival of many spectator sports, promoting positive experiences has become an important objective of many sport brand marketers. Family sections, playgrounds, language policies, etc. have all been instituted by professional teams to better control the passive participation of their fans.

Teams have also used this "passive" platform to encourage voluntary pro-social behavior on the part of all fans, especially in the encouragement of positive health-related behaviors. The "Got Milk" campaign has become famous for using athletes, among other celebrities, to encourage children and adults alike to consume recommended daily amounts of dairy products. The NFL has partnered with the American Urological Association Foundation to encourage men to participate in appropriate prostate screening check-ups.[25] Similarly the WNBA, through its WNBA Cares program, supports breast cancer awareness and the American Heart Association. Further, through the WNBA Fit program, teams design and participate in programs focused on the health, fitness, nutrition, and self-esteem of women of all ages.[26]

Social marketing efforts are not limited to sports teams and athletes. Sport brands are also able to leverage themselves to encourage pro-social behavior. Nike used its brand strength in South Africa to develop a multimedia campaign designed to increase HIV testing and promote safe sex behaviors. The program included mobile HIV testing units at sporting events and joined forces with a popular soccer team to have the team's players wear "Life is not a game; Wear a condom" t-shirts in pre-game warm-ups.[27] ESPN has used its ubiquitous presence in the average American household to partner with the National Responsible Fatherhood Clearinghouse to promote positive father engagement and involvement with children. The "Take time to be a Dad today" campaign is designed to "promote responsible, caring, and effective parenting; encourage and support healthy marriages and married fatherhood; and reduce the adverse effects of father absence."[28]

Like the ability of sports to foster philanthropic behavior, the ability of sports to function as a positive socializing agent is largely rooted in the involvement and identification individuals have with sports. Ensuring the use of sports as a positive socialization agent is critical. One study found participation in sports activities lagged only school-related activities for families with children between the ages of 8 and 10. Of families' time on activities outside of school, 24% was related to sports activities.[29] The pervasive influence of sports within the family structure further amplifies the need for sport to be used positively in socialization.

Sports in Community Development

Not only do sports have the capacity to be positive socialization agents, sports can contribute positively to community development. Three opportunities to leverage sports for community development are economic development, place marketing, and social welfare.[30] Economic development has primarily focused on the job opportunities made available by the sport, on contributions to the local tax base, and on redevelopment of areas surrounding new sport facilities. Numerous anecdotal cases support the ability of sports to contribute to the redevelopment of inner-city areas in Baltimore, Indianapolis, and San Diego, among others. Additionally, sports can contribute to the brand equity of the community itself. Researchers have attempted to link the presence of professional sports organizations with the ability of the community to attract business, residents, and visitors. Finally, research has documented increases in prosocial behavior within the community due to the increased sense of attachment fans feel toward the community as a result of their fandom.[31] Such behavior can address community-related social problems. Like youth socialization, however, these community development benefits are not inherent in the sport product or brand. Whether sports contribute positively or negatively to community development is not a function of sport themselves, but a function of the implementation and management of sports in the community. Sport brands must seek to effectively leverage themselves to positively influence community development. Many sport organizations have made clear attempts to do just that.

Organizations seeking to support economic development require integration and planning with the area's overall development strategy. Simply put, "Build it and they will come" is not often a successful community development strategy. The success of the Baltimore Oriole's ballpark in rejuvenating the Inner Harbor section of the city has largely been credited to the specific planning incorporating the stadium as one asset, albeit a major asset, in the area's redevelopment. Cities around the world continue to bid for the Olympic Games and other notable athletic competitions so that they might be known as an "Olympic city" or as a "Super Bowl host." Such events add to the brand equity associated with the city. Again, the most successful of these efforts require significant coordination between the sport organization and the city.[32]

Effective leveraging of the sport brand for social welfare involves partnering with relevant partners to address social problems affecting the community and creating opportunities for interaction and community building among fans. As noted earlier, organizations like the Chicago White Sox have effectively leveraged the team brand to bring together players, front office staff, and fans to volunteer in the community immediately surrounding U.S. Cellular Field, to build community and solve community problems. Other sport organizations have taken more unique approaches to bringing diverse members of the community together. The Real Madrid Foundation recently held their Marathon for Social Integration designed to bring together children with and without disabilities with immigrant children to foster social awareness and understanding.[33] The common bond of sports, soccer in this case, can be leveraged to create unique opportunities for interaction among groups that under normal circumstances may not have much contact with one another.

The pervasiveness of sports at the local, national, and international levels provides a platform for sports to contribute positively to consumers and society through social marketing programs. Sport marketers must be conscious of actively and positively leveraging the sport brand to achieve these benefits. Simply providing the sport product alone will not result in the achievement of these pro-social outcomes.

Corporate Social Responsibility

Corporate social responsibility (CSR) has been defined as a firm's "status and activities with respect to its perceived societal, or at least stakeholder obligations."[34] With more than 80% of Fortune 500 companies actively engaged in programs to address CSR issues through such activities as cause-related marketing, environmentally and socially sustainable manufacturing, and corporate philanthropy, some authors argue that CSR has become a critical success factor for any business. sport organizations and brands are not immune from these pressures. At the corporate, team, and athlete level, ample evidence exists that pressure to participate in CSR fosters pro-social behavior on the part of the teams and athletes themselves.

A good corporate social responsibility strategy should provide, if not maximize, benefits to the company/brand, benefits to the consumer, and benefits to the focal social issue or cause.[35] Company or brand benefits may center on increased awareness, more positive consumer attitudes, and stronger levels of consumer attachment to the company or brand. In the sport context, CSR activities may strengthen consumers' involvement and identification with the team or sport brand. Hoeffler and Keller identified six potential ways CSR activities can contribute toward building brands in the mind of the consumer: (a) maintaining brand awareness, (b) enhancing brand image, (c) establishing brand credibility, (d) evoking brand feelings, (e) creating a sense of brand community, and (f) eliciting brand engagement.[36] In addition to these positives, companies may also hope to achieve higher market share, obtain price premiums, and develop a more loyal customer base as a result of CSR activities. Research on CSR activities suggest effects on market outcomes like these are more difficult to achieve or document than is the case with internal (psychological) responses to CSR, such as consumer attitude toward the brand.[37]

Consumers should also benefit from effective CSR campaigns. Research has suggested that the mere presence of a CSR campaign can increase a consumer's perception of his or her own well-being. Additionally, as many of the examples outlined in the socialization section above illustrate, effective CSR campaigns can benefit consumers by shaping or modifying behaviors. Whether the CSR activity benefits the consumer through healthier eating behaviors, participating in regular exercise, or completing their education, an effective CSR campaign should offer significant benefit to the consumer. Finally, successful CSR campaigns should benefit the issue or social cause that is the target of the campaign. Most CSR campaigns achieve these objectives by bringing awareness and positive attitudes to the cause or the nonprofit partner. These efforts may subsequently result in increased contributions, volunteers, and other support of the cause. It is critical that a CSR campaign be evaluated on all three areas of benefit. Failure to benefit one of the three areas is an indication of a sub-optimal CSR campaign.

Recent discussions on CSR observed that some companies use several strategic pillars to support their CSR platforms. For example, believing their CSR efforts could serve "as a catalyst for growth and innovation." Nike focused on developing four strategic pillars for its CSR: (a) to improve conditions in factories for workers, (b) to design for a better world, (c) to achieve climate neutrality, and (d) to unleash personal potential through sport.[38] Another case of multiple pillars can be seen in the efforts of a sports outfitter, REI (Recreation Equipment Inc.). Founded in 1938 by a group of Pacific Northwest mountaineers, this major retail co-op is passionate about inspiring, educating, and outfitting its members and the community for outdoor adventure. Like Nike, REI also formed four strategic areas to support their CSR. This platform focused their efforts on (a) promoting environmental stewardship, (b) increasing access to outdoor recreation through education, (c) leading by example with outdoor volunteerism, and (d) providing philanthropic contributions and gear donations.[39]

A content analysis of 818 newsletters from 29 different U.S. professional sports teams (Major League Baseball = 9, National Football League = 7, National Hockey League = 7, National Basketball Association = 6) identified the range and frequency of CSR activities some franchises undertake. The results identified six main categories teams use to build their CSR platforms. Category descriptions and their frequency of use are noted below:[40]

- Monetary charitable events—auctions, raffles, and golf tournaments, etc. (40.3%).
- Nonmonetary charitable events—food, clothing, toy, and back-to-school drive, etc. (14.3%).
- Volunteerism and community outreach—sports camp, visiting schools/hospitals, etc. (12.6%).
- Social awareness promotions—breast cancer, heritage days, children, health and environmental awareness, etc. (11.3%).
- Community appreciation events—armed services or serve & protect appreciation day (10.8%).
- Events honoring "meritable" work in the community—coach/player of the week, scholar athletes, etc. (9.1%).

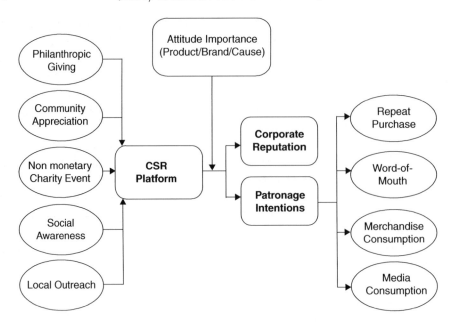

Figure 14.2 A Model of a CSR Platform's Antecedents and Outcomes (Adapted from Walker & Kent, 2009)[43]

Adapting prior work, a model of how a CSR platform is developed and can impact on consumers is shown in Figure 14.2. This depiction provides an illustration of consumer-related outcomes, but does not lay out some of the benefits other stakeholders might enjoy from strong CSR. For instance, both sponsors and employees may benefit from CSR building a strong corporate reputation in the marketplace. What the model does show, however, are a range of behavioral responses such as repeat purchase, media consumption, or positive word-of-mouth that might develop in consumers as a direct result of the psychological capital CSR can generate (i.e., brand-building through awareness, image, positive feelings).[41] The antecedents shown on the left of the model differ slightly from Walker and Kent's original diagram. Here, instead of the six types of CSR activities classified earlier, five are shown. This is because *meritorious recognition* can be subsumed as a communication element in an organization's *community outreach & volunteerism* efforts. Another adaptation in the model is the moderating effect of Attitude Importance. The original intent behind Walker and Kent showing this connection lay in the notion that strong team identification had the capacity to dramatically enhance the effectiveness of CSR. This is consistent with previous research on the effects of publicity, which describes how one's commitment can alter the way consumers process positive and negative information. For instance, committed and identified fans recall and retain more facts from exposure to publicity but filter out or screen negative elements though a process of selective perception.[42]

Figure 14.2 enlarges the role of this concept by going beyond attitudes of (a brand's) importance common to committed and identified fans[44], to consider how importance of the sport product[45] (i.e., a fan of the sport itself) or significance of a charitable cause[46] (e.g., women's health, poverty) can alter both the perception and effectiveness of a company's CSR efforts. Case in point, research into women's professional soccer has linked how particular causes a team adopts (i.e., support of women's opportunities) can resonate with and heighten spectator attitudes of importance.[47] These sentiments in turn would moderate and strengthen patron intentions relative to the brand and positively reinforce the company's reputation among its patrons.

Although sport organizations can choose from quite a range of options, activities, and tactics to employ, one of the more significant elements in the development of any CSR campaign is the choice of cause or social issue the team/brand identifies with. Like much of the discussion around successful sponsorship in Chapter 10, the concept of fit is critical in the selection of a cause or issue with which a company, team, or player wishes to align CSR activities. Causes or issues should be chosen that are consistent with the capability of the organization to address or improve the cause or issue, and with the organization's target market's needs and wants.[48] The better the fit and alignment between cause, customer, and organization, the stronger the likelihood that the CSR campaign will be effective at bringing added benefit to all three groups.

Social issues and causes can be divided into three categories.[49] Generic social issues are those issues that are important to society but are not closely aligned with an organization's core competencies and not likely to affect the competitiveness of the company. As a result, generic social issues are usually not ideal choices for a particular CSR campaign. (Note: The classification of social issues is organization dependent. One firm's core competencies may be more closely aligned than another firm's core competencies to address any particular social issue. Thus, for one company, an issue may be a generic social issue, while for another organization the issue may have better fit.) Value chain social issues are those issues that may be affected significantly by a company's activities within the course of normal business. Nike deciding to donate shoes to orphans would be an example of a value chain social issue CSR campaign. Value chain social issues are a better fit than generic social issues for the firm, but may not maximize benefit to company, customers, and cause. Social dimensions of competitive context are those social issues, in the organization's external environment, that affect the underlying competitive factors for the firm. These issues not only allow for substantial benefit to customers and cause, but also allow an opportunity for a company (or industry) to develop competitive advantage. Major League Baseball's CSR activities designed to re-introduce baseball into inner-city urban cores might be classified as a social dimension of competitive context. Not only are youth the foundation for future players in the industry, but they are also the industry's lifeblood as future fans. Thus MLB can undertake CSR activities that improve the well-being of the youth themselves, providing safe, clean places to play; address and improve social issues such as drug use and gang membership in inner cities; and, at the same time, contribute to the long-term business benefit of Major League Baseball itself. Ideally, then, organizations should choose social issues for their CSR activities that are at a minimum value chain social issues, and better yet, are social dimensions of competitive context.

Sports, given their unique nature as has been developed and addressed throughout the majority of this textbook, also are unique in their ability to address social issues through CSR. Aaron Smith and Hans Westerbeek identified seven unique features of sport as they affect CSR:[50]

1. Sports' mass media and distribution power.
2. Sports' youth appeal.
3. The positive health impacts of sport participation.
4. Sports' pervasiveness as a form of social interaction.
5. Sports' ability to generate sustainability awareness.
6. The cultural understanding and integration opportunities addressed through sport.
7. Sports' ability to offer immediate gratification benefits.

Each of these elements can be seen in the socially responsible activities that illustrate this chapter. With the unique ability to participate in CSR, sport organizations also have additional responsibility to manage their brands in a socially responsible manner. A look at several examples of successful CSR programs follows.

Environmental management and sustainability is one area of CSR that has drawn significant attention in sports. Whether increased in-stadium recycling, or research and development in materials and manufacturing processes, for many sport organizations, environmental sustainability is a value chain social issue or a social dimension of competitive context worthy of CSR attention. Many sport apparel manufacturers now have explicit, public policies on environmental practice. Nike has chosen to address many environmental and manufacturing issues through its "Considered Design" program. "Nike is combining sustainability principles and innovative design to produce performance products for athletes. At its core, it's about reducing or eliminating toxics and waste, increasing the use of environmentally preferred materials and using Nike's innovation to create a future with more sustainable products."[51] Nike expects all of its footwear to meet its Considered Design standards of being produced with the minimum amount of material necessary, and designed for easy disassembly, recycling, and safe disposal. All Nike apparel is expected to meet the standard in 2015, and all Nike equipment is targeted for the standards by 2020. In addition, Nike has adopted pro-environmental policies in areas such as leather sourcing from Brazil and its potential impacts on the Amazon rain forest. Nike has also joined Levi Strauss & Co., Starbucks, Sun Microsystems, and The Timberland Company to form the Business for Innovative Climate and Energy Project in conjunction with Ceres. The group is promoting strong environmental legislation and policy from the U.S. government.[52]

Another manufacturer that has focused a significant amount of attention on environmental practice is Brooks. Brooks, a Seattle-based running shoe and apparel manufacturer, developed the first biodegradable midsole for running shoes. Traditional running shoe midsoles can last over 1,000 years in a landfill. Brooks' biodegradable technology has cut that time to 20 years and ensures that the product biodegrades into usable by-products.[53] In 2010, Brooks launched its "Green Silence" shoe, manufactured with 75% post-consumer recycled material. Brooks has also redesigned its shoe boxes (100% post-consumer recycled materials) to be fully biodegradable, and developed environmental practices and policies throughout the company that have allowed it to win multiple environmental awards, including the *Footwear News* 2008 Green Award, the *Runner's World* 2008 International Green Award, and the first-ever Great Green Business Award from Plant a Tree USA in 2008. Interestingly, however, Brooks has chosen to make available all of the innovation and technology that has led to these environmental sustainability

improvements. Treating their technology as "open source," Brooks has made its proprietary development of biodegradable running shoe materials available to other manufacturers. According to Jim Weber, Brooks CEO, environmental sustainable practices are
not sources of long-term competitive advantage for the firm. Rather, good environmental policy is now an industry key success factor, where customers simply expect firms to
be environmentally (and socially) responsible.[54] Weber, and Brooks, feel that the socially
responsible action is to share positive developments in design and innovation that will
improve manufacturing and delivery processes for all manufacturers. Brooks has gone
so far as to provide resources on their website for customers to learn how to reduce their
own carbon footprints and environmental impacts. Further, Brooks plans to move into
its new "ultra-green, living building" headquarters being built in Seattle by late 2013.[55]

Manufacturing companies are not alone in their efforts to address environmental and sustainability issues. Major League Baseball, in association with the Natural
Resources Defense Council, has developed the Team Greening Program.[56] Efforts have
included stepped-up recycling programs, the adoption of energy-efficient and low-
flow appliances to conserve energy and water, and the adoption of alternative, clean
energy sources. The Philadelphia Phillies were the first MLB team to join the Environmental Protection Agency's Green Power Partnership. The Phillies have, among other
actions, chosen to meet 100% of their energy needs from wind power, provided credits
to players and team employees to use clean energy sources at home, and recycled cook-
ing oil used in the stadium's concessions as bio-diesel fuel. In 2007, the Washington
Nationals opened the first major sports stadium facility to be LEED Silver certified.
The Minnesota Twins followed, opening a LEED certified stadium, Target Field, in
2010. And, the NHL's Pittsburg Penguins achieved LEED gold certification in their
new hockey arena. Each of the major U.S.-based professional sports leagues has developed environmental programs, and 75% of professional sports teams are engaged in
formal activities designed to increase environmental sustainability.

Colleges and universities, while lagging behind the efforts of their professional
counterparts, continue to address environmental issues as well. Although a 2009 study
found that only 44% of athletic departments stated that environmental practices were
a high priority in their units, several schools have adopted environmentally friendly
policies.[57] The University of Colorado, for example, is targeting a 90% recycling and
compost rate of waste from its football stadium. Other schools, like the University of
Wisconsin, have hosted carbon-neutral football games, off-setting the environmental
footprint of the activity by planting trees or purchasing carbon offsets.

Many participant-based sporting events are also pursuing environmentally responsible strategies. The Council for Responsible Sport has developed a certification system
for participant based sporting events based on activities in six categories: waste, climate,
equipment and materials, community and outreach, health promotion, and innovation.[58] Among certified events are the Los Angeles Marathon, the Austin Marathon, and
the Marin County Triathlon, which has achieved the highest certification, Evergreen. In
2009, the ING Hartford Marathon was carbon neutral for the first time. The marathon
will continue adopting environmentally sustainable activities and purchase carbon offsets
for the remaining environmental impact of the event. It is quite clear that, whether at the
manufacturer, professional, or amateur sport level, sport brands and organizations are
tackling the CSR challenges surrounding environmental sustainability.

Another CSR program common among sports (and other organizations) is Cause Related Marketing (CRM). CRM has been defined as "a strategic positioning and marketing tool which links a company or brand to a relevant social cause or issue, for mutual benefit."[59] Multiple studies have indicated, both inside and outside the sports industry, the potential positive benefits associated with CRM programs. When effectively designed and implemented, CRM programs can positively influence attitudes toward teams and players, and may potentially influence purchase and consumption patterns.[60] However, one study has concluded that CRM's influence on sport consumption intentions is smaller than for other types of products and services.[61] Still, CRM programs offer the potential to be successful CSR activities, benefitting the company, cause, and society.

Successful CRM programs have several requirements that should be met.[62] First, as mentioned previously, there should be good fit between the organization and the partner cause. The cause should be important, relevant, and in alignment with the values and beliefs of a sport organization's target markets. Second, the organization must be committed to the CRM program. Significant internal involvement with the cause may lessen potential consumer skepticism toward the CRM program. Third, there must be tangible exchange, financial or otherwise, between the sport organization and the partner cause. Simply pairing organization and cause logos is not sufficient. Tangible exchange of financial, human, or other resources is another sign of the sport organization's commitment to the CRM program. Finally, successful CRM programs must be promoted. If consumers are not aware of the organization's CRM efforts, those efforts are unlikely to influence consumers. This reduces the potential positive company benefits (i.e., no attitude change, no change in purchase intentions) as well as potential positive cause benefits (increased donations and volunteers).

Nearly every sports team and organization through their CSR efforts participates in some level of CRM. Perhaps one of the most successful CRM campaigns in recent memory aligned a brand, athlete, and cause to tremendous effect. Since 2004, Nike has partnered with Lance Armstrong and the Lance Armstrong Foundation.[63] The program has met all of the requirements of successful CSR and CRM programs. From a CRM perspective, the cause is relevant and important to Nike's target market. One in three Americans will be diagnosed with some form of cancer in their lifetimes.[64] The widespread effect of cancer clearly includes Nike's target market. Nike also has demonstrated significant organizational commitment to the cause. Internally, the company continues to innovate in efforts to bring awareness to the Lance Armstrong Foundation. For example, Nike developed a "Chalkbot" that was able to chalk thousands of consumer messages in support of Lance Armstrong and cancer survivors on the roads of France during the 2009 Tour de France.[65] From the start of the relationship, Nike has contributed tangibly to LAF, through financial, marketing, and other resources. Nike funded the first five million yellow "Live Strong" wristbands sold in addition to making an initial $1,000,000 gift to LAF. Finally, Nike continues to promote its relationship with LAF, including maintaining a website specifically devoted to Lance Armstrong and the LAF (www.wearyellow.com).

---

*This chapter was written prior to Lance Armstrong's admissions to using performance enhancing substances and techniques, and the dissolution of the Nike/LAF partnership.

The end result of this successful CRM design is an effective CSR campaign that benefits the company, the cause, and society. Nike initially benefitted by distributing the "Live Strong" wristbands in Niketown stores and other Nike retailers, driving additional traffic to the store and brand. Nike continues to benefit through the sales of "Wear Yellow" products and the positive associations consumers make with the CRM effort. LAF benefits not only from the substantial financial support provided by Nike, but from the significant awareness brought to the cause, resulting in increased participation in LAF events, increased fundraising, and increased numbers of volunteers. The CSR campaign also significantly benefits society, addressing cancer research and survivor support. Although not every successful CRM or CSR campaign need be of this magnitude, the Nike-LAF partnership clearly demonstrates the potential positive benefits of these cause-related marketing efforts.

A third CSR activity undertaken by sports companies, teams, and athletes is corporate philanthropy, often through the formation of a foundation. The foundations often serve as the charitable arms of the organizations. The hallmark of corporate philanthropy is that there is no expectation of business benefit (at least financially) from the corporate support of chosen causes. In fact, many corporate foundations do not heavily publicize their activities. True to the notion of philanthropy, these activities are undertaken primarily to benefit the cause and society. There may still be internal benefits to the business such as increased morale and camaraderie behind the effort to support a chosen cause, but as with individual philanthropy, corporate philanthropy is not pursued for self-benefit. Virtually every team and sport organization has a foundation. Typically, a certain percentage of profits is allocated to the foundation to manage and distribute to chosen causes and nonprofit organizations. Most organizations choose to select one or a few types of causes to support, guiding the foundation's activities. For example, the Seattle Seahawks Charitable Foundation directs all of its efforts to youth development through sport participation.[66] The Foundation supports, among others, Special Olympics of Washington, the Boys and Girls Clubs Washington State Association, and Big Brothers Big Sisters of Puget Sound.

Many players now also form their own foundations to manage and guide their own charitable activities. Dwayne Wade, for example, has established the Wade's World Foundation (www.wadesworldfoundation.org) to promote education, health, and social skills for at-risk children.[67] Efforts to date have been focused on organizations in Wade's hometown of Chicago, and in the south Florida area of his Miami Heat team.

Conclusion

It is impossible in one chapter to cover and illustrate the entire gamut of socially responsible activities a company, team, or athlete could pursue. What should be clear is that whether leveraging the brand to influence individual philanthropic behavior, socialization, and community development, or for Corporate Social Responsibility activities, sports are uniquely positioned to foster pro-social behaviors. In fact, it may be argued that the uniqueness of sport makes pursuing and encouraging socially responsible activities an imperative. As future sport managers, developing successful CSR activities will become increasingly important. Focusing on activities that will benefit the company, the cause or social issue, and society will help direct those efforts.

References

1. Andreasen A. R. (2007). Social marketing: Its definition and domain. In G. T. Gundlach, L. G. Block, & W. L. Wilkie (Eds.). *Explorations of marketing in society*, Mason, OH: Thompson.
2. Anonymous. (n.d.). Run Walk Ride 30 Study. Retrieved from http://runwalkride.com/research.asp
3. Geer, J. (2007). *USATF study reveals charity fundraising by runners, walkers surges to $714+ million.* Indianapolis, IN: USATF.
4. Anonymous. (n.d.). 2012 Boston Marathon weekend will mean $137.5M. Retrieved from http://www.bostonmarathon.org
5. Geer, J. (2007). *USATF study reveals charity fundraising by runners, walkers surges to $714+ million.* Indianapolis, IN: USATF.
6. Anonymous. (n.d.). Charity program. Retrieved from http://www.chicagomarathon.com
7. Anonymous. (n.d.). Participating charities. Retrieved from http://www.ingnycmarathon.org
8. Bennett, R., Mousley, W., Kitchin, P., & Ali-Choudhury, R. (2007). Motivations for participating in charity-affiliated sporting events. *Journal of Customer Behavior, 6*(2), 155–178.
9. Filo, K., Funk, D. C., & O'Brien, D. (2009). The meaning behind attachment: Exploring camaraderie, cause, and competency at a charity sport event. *Journal of Sport Management, 23*, 361–387.
10. Erlandson, J. (2009). *Tough economy doesn't discourage King County from giving back.* Seattle, WA: UWKC.
11. Merkin, S. (2009, May 10). *White sox launch volunteer corps.* MLB.com
12. Romero, J. (2009, August 17). Sounders FC to collect school supplies for local students. *The Seattle Times.*
13. Wolverton, B. (2007, October 5). Growth in sport gifts may mean fewer athletic donations. *The Chronicle of Higher Education.*
14. Garry, S. (2007, April 2). Athletic success a big win for school: University of Florida administrators are trying to make sure the school's sports success helps its reputation and fundraising. *The Miami Herald.*
15. Mahony, D. F., Gladden, J. M., & Funk, D. C. (2003). Examining athletic donors at NCAA division I institutions. *International Sports Journal, 7*, 9–27.
16. Conn, M. (2005, January 10). It's not just cricket-Tsunami disaster benefit match. *The Australian.*
17. Koch, W. (2005, September 7). Storm giving outpaces that of 9/11, tsunami. *USA Today.*
18. Kremer-Sadlik, T., & Kim, J. L. (2007). Lessons from sports: Children's socialization to values through family interaction during sports activities. *Discourse & Society, 18*(1), 35–52.
19. Wells, M. S., & Arthur-Banning, S. G. (2008). The logic of youth development: constructing a logic model of youth development through sport. *Journal of Park and Recreation Administration, 26*(2), 189–202.
20. Wells, M. S., & Arthur-Banning, S. G. (2008). The logic of youth development: constructing a logic model of youth development through sport. *Journal of Park and Recreation Administration, 26*(2), 189–202.
21. Anonymous. (n.d.). FC Barcelona information. Retrieved from http:www.fcbarcelona.com
22. Anonymous. (n.d.). Integration academies in prisons. Retrieved from http://www.realmadrid.com
23. Kremer-Sadlik, T., & Kim, J. L. (2007). Lessons from sports: Children's socialization to values through family interaction during sports activities. *Discourse & Society, 18*(1), 35–52.
24. Anonymous. (n.d.). Read to achieve. Retrieved from http://www.nba.com
25. Isett, W. (2009). NFL season kicks off with campaign to know your stats about prostate cancer. Retrieved from http://www.auanet.org
26. Anonymous. (n.d.). WNBA cares. Retrieved from http://www.wnba.com
27. Anonymous. (n.d.). Nike's campaign commended: Aids in South Africa addressed. Retrieved from http://www.nikebiz.com
28. Anonymous. (2009). Ad council and national responsible fatherhood clearinghouse join ESPN to encourage fathers to "Take time to be a dad today." Retrieved from http://www.fatherhood.gov
29. Kremer-Sadlik, T., & Kim, J. L. (2007). Lessons from sports: Children's socialization to values through family interaction during sports activities. *Discourse & Society, 18*(1), 35–52.
30. Sparvero, E., & Chalip, L. (2007). Professional teams as leverageable assets: strategic creation of community value. *Sport Management Review, 10*, 1–30.
31. Soto, J. J. L. (2009). Real Madrid foundation's VII marathon. Retrieved from http://www.realmadrid.com

32. Bhattacharya, C. B., & Sen. S. (2004). Doing better at doing good: When, why, and how consumers respond to corporate social initiatives. *California Management Review, 47*(1), 9–24.

33. Hoeffler, S., & Keller W. (2002). Building brand equity through corporate societal marketing. *Journal of Public Policy & Marketing, 21*(1), 78–89.

34. CSR Wire (2013). CSR profile of Nike Inc. Retrieved from http://www.csrwire.com/members/12858-Nike-Inc-

35. CSR Wire (2013). CSR profile of REI. Retrieved from http://www.csrwire.com/members/10977-Recreational-Equipment-Inc-REI-

36. Walker, M., Kent, A., & Vincent, J. (2010). Communicating socially responsible initiatives: An analysis of U.S. professional teams. *Sport Marketing Quarterly, 19*(4), 187–194.

37. Hoeffler, S., & Keller W. (2002). Building brand equity through corporate societal marketing. *Journal of Public Policy & Marketing, 21*(1), 78–89.

38. Funk, D., & Pritchard, M. P. (2006). Sport publicity: Commitment's moderation of message effects. *Journal of Business Research, 59*(5), 613–621.

39. Walker, M., & Kent, A. (2009). Do fans care? Assessing the influence of corporate social responsibility on consumer attitudes in the sport industry. *Journal of Sport Management, 29*, 743–769.

40. Lee, J., & Ferreira, M. (2011). Cause-related marketing: The role of team identification in consumer choice of team licensed products. *Sport Marketing Quarterly, 20*(3), 157–169.

41. Mason, D. (1999). What is the sports product and who buys it? The marketing of professional sports leagues. *European Journal of Marketing, 33*(3/4), 402–418.

42. Irwin, R., Lachowetz, T., Cornwell, B., & Clark, J. (2003). Cause-related sport sponsorship: An assessment of spectator beliefs, attitudes, and behavioral intentions. *Sport Marketing Quarterly, 12*(2), 131–139.

43. Pritchard, M. P., & Funk, D. (2010). The formation and effect of attitude importance in professional sport. *European Journal of Marketing. 44*(7/8), 1017–1036.

44. Porter, M. E., & Kramer, M. R. (2006, December). Strategy and society: The link between competitive advantage and corporate social responsibility. *Harvard Business Review*, 78–92.

45. Walker, M., & Kent, A. (2009). Do fans care? Assessing the influence of corporate social responsibility on consumer attitudes in the sport industry. *Journal of Sport Management, 29*, 743–769.

46. Smith, A., & Westerbeek, H. (2007). Sport as a vehicle for deploying corporate social responsibility. *Journal of Corporate Citizenship, 25*, 43–54.

47. Koontz, K. (n.d.). For a sustainable future: Event revealed considered collection. Retrieved from http://www.nikebiz.com

48. Anonymous. (n.d.) Nike and Bicep partner to work on climate change and energy issues. Retrieved from www.Nikebiz.com

49. Anonymous. (n.d.). BIOMOGO: The world's first biodegradable midsole. Retrieved from http://www.brooksrunning.com

50. Weber, J. (2009, February 19). The Brooks story: Being real trumps being big. CWU College of Business Business-to-Business Speaker Series.

51. Pryne, E. (2012, October 19). Ultra-green Seattle office project draws corporate HQ, complaints. *Seattle Times*. Retrieved from http://www.seattletimes.com

52. Scarr, M. (2008, October 20). MLB encouraging teams to go green. MLB.com.

53. Moltz, D. (2009, July 30). Sports and sustainability. *Inside Higher Ed.*

54. Anonymous. (n.d.). ReSport certification standards 2.0. Retrieved from http://www.resport.org

55. Pringle, H., & Thompson, M. (1999). *Brand spirit: How cause related marketing builds brands.* Chichester, UK: Wiley & Sons.

56. Lachowetz, T., & Gladden, J. (2003, December/January). A framework for understanding cause-related sport marketing programs. *International Journal of Sports Marketing & Sponsorship*, 313–333.

57. Roy, D. P., & Graeff, T. R. (2003). Consumer attitudes toward cause-related marketing activities in professional sports. *Sport Marketing Quarterly, 12*(3), 163–172.

58. Moltz, D. (2009, July 30). Sports and sustainability. *Inside Higher Ed.*

59. McGlone, C., & Martin, N. (2006). Nike's corporate interest lives strong: A case of cause-related marketing and leveraging. *Sport Marketing Quarterly, 15*(3), 184–188.

60. Anonymous. (n.d.). Cancer statistics. Retrieved from http://www.livestrong.org

61. Anonymous. (n.d.). Chalkbot. Retrieved from http://www.nike.com

62. Anonymous. (n.d.). Seattle Seahawks charitable foundation. Retrieved from http://www.seahawks.com

63. Anonymous. (n.d.). Wade's World Foundation: Our mission. Retrieved from://www.wadesworldfoundation.org*This chapter was written prior to Lance Armstrong's admissions to using performance enhancing substances and techniques, and the dissolution of the Nike/LAF partnership.

Index